Kommunikation und Kybernetik in Einzeldarstellungen
Herausgegeben von H. Wolter und W. D. Keidel
3

Speech Analysis
Synthesis and Perception

Second Edition

By

James L. Flanagan

Head, Acoustics Research Department
Bell Laboratories
Murray Hill, New Jersey

With 258 Figures

Springer-Verlag · Berlin · Heidelberg · New York 1972

ISBN 3-540-05561-4 Springer-Verlag Berlin · Heidelberg · New York
ISBN 0-387-05561-4 Springer-Verlag New York · Heidelberg · Berlin

Typesetting, printing and binding: Universitätsdruckerei H.Stürtz AG, Würzburg

Preface to the Second Edition

The first edition of this book has enjoyed a gratifying existence. Issued in 1965, it found its intended place as a research reference and as a graduate-level text. Research laboratories and universities reported broad use. Published reviews—some twenty-five in number—were universally kind. Subsequently the book was translated and published in Russian (Svyaz; Moscow, 1968) and Spanish (Gredos, S.A.; Madrid, 1972).

Copies of the first edition have been exhausted for several years, but demand for the material continues. At the behest of the publisher, and with the encouragement of numerous colleagues, a second edition was begun in 1970. The aim was to retain the original format, but to expand the content, especially in the areas of digital communications and computer techniques for speech signal processing. As before, the intended audience is the graduate-level engineer and physicist, but the psychophysicist, phonetician, speech scientist and linguist should find material of interest.

Preparation of the second edition could not have advanced except for discussions, suggestions and advice from many colleagues. In particular, professors and scientists who have used the book in their university lectures, both here and abroad, provided valuable comment about organization and addition of new material. Also, research colleagues, especially my associates in the Acoustics Research Department at Bell Laboratories, provided critical assessment of technical data and views about emphasis. To list individually all who influenced these factors would require inordinate space. Rather, I commend to you their many scientific contributions described among the following pages. Naturally, any shortcomings in exposition or interpretation rest solely with me.

The task of examining page proofs was shared, with notable enthusiasm, among several associates. I owe special thanks to Doctors L. R. RABINER, R. W. SCHAFER, N. S. JAYANT, A. E. ROSENBERG, J. L. HALL, R. C. LUMMIS, J. M. KELLY and J. R. HASKEW for this assistance. Further, I am indebted to my company, Bell Laboratories, for supporting the work and making its facilities available for typing and drafting. My secretary, Mrs. B. MaSaitis, bore the brunt of this work and deserves special praise. As earlier, the efficient staff of Springer, through the organization of Dr. H. Mayer-Kaupp, shielded me from many details in actualizing the printed volume.

Finally, again, to my wife and sons I express warm thanks for their contribution of weekends which might have been spent otherwise.

Warren Township, New Jersey   James Flanagan
January 15, 1972

Preface to the First Edition

This book has its origin in a letter. In November of 1959, the late Prof. Dr. WERNER MEYER-EPPLER wrote to me, asking if I would contribute to a series he was planning on Communication. His book "Grundlagen und Anwendungen der Informationstheorie" was to serve as the initial volume of the series.

After protracted consideration, I agreed to undertake the job provided it could be done outside my regular duties at the Bell Telephone Laboratories. Shortly afterwards, I received additional responsibilities in my research organization, and felt that I could not conveniently pursue the manuscript. Consequently, except for the preparation of a detailed outline, the writing was delayed for about a year and a half. In the interim, Professor MEYER-EPPLER suffered a fatal illness, and Professors H. WOLTER and W. D. KEIDEL assumed the editorial responsibilities for the book series.

The main body of this material was therefore written as a leisure-time project in the years 1962 and 1963. The complete draft of the manuscript was duplicated and circulated to colleagues in three parts during 1963. Valuable comments and criticisms were obtained, revisions made, and the manuscript submitted to the publisher in March of 1964. The mechanics of printing have filled the remaining time.

If the reader finds merit in the work, it will be owing in great measure to the people with whom I have had the good fortune to be associated. In earlier days at the M.I.T. Acoustics Laboratory, my association with Professor K. N. STEVENS, Dr. A. S. HOUSE, and Dr. J. M. HEINZ was a great priviledge. During this same time, and on two separate occasions, Dr. G. FANT was a guest researcher at the M.I.T. laboratory. Later, during a summer, I had the priviledge of working as a guest in Dr. FANT's laboratory in Stockholm. On all occasions I profited from his views and opinion.

In more recent times, my associates at Bell Laboratories have been a constant stimulus and encouragement. Beginning with Dr. J. R.

PIERCE, under whose direction research in speech and hearing has taken on renewed vigor, Doctors E. E. DAVID, Jr., M. R. SCHROEDER, M. V. MATHEWS, J. L. KELLY, Jr., N. GUTTMAN, P. B. DENES, G. G. HARRIS, and many, many others have provided sage advice, valuable collaboration and a stimulating research atmosphere. I am certain that this collection of technical talent is duplicated at no other place in the world.

I am greatly in the debt of numerous colleagues for valuable criticism and comment of the draft material. Their appraisals have aided materially in the revisions. Besides several of those already named, Professor G. E. PETERSON and Dr. H. K. DUNN, and a number of their associates at the University of Michigan, provided a wealth of valuable suggestions. Professor OSAMU FUJIMURA of the University of Electro-Communications, Tokyo, supplied many penetrating remarks, particularly on points relating to vocal-tract acoustics. Dr. W. A. VAN BERGEIJK of Bell Laboratories reviewed Chapter IV in detail. Messrs. A. M. NOLL, J. L. SULLIVAN, and H. R. SILBIGER, also of the Laboratories, studied the entire manuscript and supplied numerous helpful comments.

It is with deep regret that I conclude this effort without the counsel of Professor MEYER-EPPLER. I sincerely hope that it fulfills his original concept of the volume. I wish to express my appreciation to Professor WOLTER and to Professor KEIDEL for their continued support during the preparation. Also, the many details could not have been surmounted without the help of Dr. H. MAYER-KAUPP of Springer.

Finally, to my wife and family I express my deep appreciation for their contribution of my time.

Warren Township, New Jersey   JAMES FLANAGAN
July 29, 1964

Contents

Speech Analysis
Synthesis and Perception

Second Edition
1972

I. Voice Communication

"Nature, as we often say, makes nothing in vain, and man is the only animal whom she has endowed with the gift of speech. And whereas mere voice is but an indication of pleasure or pain, and is therefore found in other animals, the power of speech is intended to set forth the expedient and inexpedient, and therefore likewise the just and the unjust. And it is a characteristic of man that he alone has any sense of good and evil, of just and unjust, and the like, and the association of living beings who have this sense makes a family and a state."

ARISTOTLE, *Politics*

Man's primary method of communication is speech. He is unique in his ability to transmit information with his voice. Of the myriad varieties of life sharing our world, only man has developed the vocal means for coding and conveying information beyond a rudimentary stage. It is more to his credit that he has developed the facility from apparatus designed to subserve other, more vital purposes.

Because man was constructed to live in an atmosphere, it is not unnatural that he should learn to communicate by causing air molecules to collide. In sustaining longitudinal vibrations, the atmosphere provides a medium. At the acoustic level, speech signals consist of rapid and significantly erratic fluctuations in air pressure. These sound pressures are generated and radiated by the vocal apparatus. At a different level of coding, the same speech information is contained in the neural signals which actuate the vocal muscles and manipulate the vocal tract. Speech sounds radiated into the air are detected by the ear and apprehended by the brain. The mechanical motions of the middle and inner ear, and the electrical pulses traversing the auditory nerve, may be thought of as still different codings of the speech information.

Acoustic transmission and reception of speech works fine, but only over very limited distances. The reasons are several. At the frequencies used by the vocal tract and ear, radiated acoustic energy spreads spatially and diminishes rapidly in intensity. Even if the source could produce great amounts of acoustic power, the medium can support only limited variations in pressure without distorting the signal. The sensitivity of the receiver—the ear—is limited by the acoustic noise of the environment and by the physiological noises of the body. The acoustic wave is not, therefore, a good means for distant transmission.

Through the ages men have striven to communicate at distances. They are, in fact, still striving. The ancient Greeks are known to have used intricate systems of signal fires which they placed on judiciously selected mountains for relaying messages between cities. One enterprising Greek, AENEAS TACITUS by name, is credited with a substantial improvement upon the discrete bonfire message. He placed water-filled earthen jars at the signal points. A rod, notched along its length and supported on a cork float, protruded from each jar. At the first signal light, water was started draining from the jar. At the second it was stopped. The notch on the rod at that level represented a previously agreed upon message. (In terms of present day information theory, the system must have had an annoyingly low channel capacity, and an irritatingly high equivocation and vulnerability to jamming!)

History records other efforts to overcome the disadvantages of acoustic transmission. In the sixth century B. C., Cyrus the Great of Persia is supposed to have established lines of signal towers on high hilltops, radiating in several directions from his capital. On these vantage points he stationed leather-lunged men who shouted messages along, one to the other. Similar "voice towers" reportedly were used by JULIUS CAESAR in Gaul. (Anyone who has played the party game of vocally transmitting a story from one person to another around a circle of guests cannot help but reflect upon the corruption which a message must have suffered in several miles of such transmission.)

Despite the desires and motivations to accomplish communication at distances, it was not until man learned to generate, control and convey electrical current that telephony could be brought within the realm of possibility. As history goes, this has been exceedingly recent. Less than a hundred years have passed since the first practical telephone was put into operation. Today it is estimated that more than 200 million telephones are in use.

1.1. The Advent of Telephony

Many early inventors and scientists labored on electrical telephones and laid foundations which facilitated the development of commercial telephony. Their biographies make interesting and humbling reading for today's communication engineer comfortably ensconced in his well-equipped laboratory. Among these men, ALEXANDER GRAHAM BELL is considered by many not only to have produced and demonstrated the first practicable telephone, but also have made its first commercial application. Some contend that ELISHA GRAY was at least concomitant with BELL in his developments. Others claim PHILIPP REIS anticipated both BELL and GRAY by several years. Depending upon the country, one can find factions in support of still other inventors. Regardless of when, and through whose efforts electrical telephony ceased to be a dream and yielded to practice, there is enough praise and admiration for all these early scientists.

Among the pioneers BELL was somewhat unique for his background in physiology and phonetics. His comprehension of the mechanisms of speech and hearing was undoubtedly valuable, if not crucial, in his electrical experimentation. Similar understanding is equally important with today's telephone researcher. It was perhaps his training that influenced BELL—according to his assistant WATSON—to summarize the telephony problem by saying "If I could make a current of electricity vary in intensity precisely as the air varies in density during the production of a speech sound, I should be able to transmit speech telegraphically." This is what he set out to do and is what he accomplished. BELL'S basic notion—namely, preservation of acoustic waveform—clearly proved to be an effective means for speech transmission. To the present day most telephone systems operate on this principle.

Although the waveform principle is exceedingly satisfactory and has endured for almost a century, it probably is not the most efficient means for voice transmission. Communication engineers have recognized for many years that a substantial mismatch exists between the information capacity of the human source-sink and the capacity of the "waveform" channel. Specifically, the channel is capable of transmitting information at rates much higher than those the human can assimilate.

Recent developments in communication theory have established techniques for quantifying the information in a signal and the rate at which information can be signalled over a given facility. These analytical tools have accentuated the desirability of matching the transmission channel to the information source. From their application, conventional telephony has become a much-used example of disparate source rate and channel capacity. This disparity—expressed in numbers—has provided much of the impetus toward investigating more efficient means for speech coding and for reducing the bandwidth and channel capacity used to transmit speech.

1.2. Efficient Transmission of Speech

The elementary relations of information theory define the information associated with the selection of a discrete message from a specified ensemble. If the messages of the set are x_i, are independent, and have probability of occurrence $P(x_i)$, the information associated with a selection is $I = -\log_2 P(x_i)$ bits. The average information associated with selections from the set is the ensemble average

$$H(X) = - \sum_i P(x_i) \log_2 P(x_i)$$

bits, or the source entropy.

Consider, in these terms, a phonemic transcription of speech; that is, the written equivalent of the meaningfully distinctive sounds of speech. Take English for example. Table 1.1 shows a list of 42 English phonemes including vowels, diphthongs and consonants, and their relative frequencies of occurrence in prose (DEWEY). If the phonemes are selected for utterance with equal probability [i.e., $P(x_i) = \frac{1}{42}$] the average information per phoneme would be approximately $H(X) =$ 5.4 bits. If the phonemes are selected independently, but with probabilities equal to the relative frequencies shown in Table 1.1, then $H(X)$ falls to 4.9 bits. The sequential contraints imposed upon the selection of speech sounds by a given language reduce this average information still further[1]. In conversational speech about 10 phonemes are uttered per second. The written equivalent of the information generated is therefore less than 50 bits/sec.

The conventional voice link is of course not a discrete channel but a continuous one. For a continuous channel, an existence proof can be given for the maximum error-free rate of information transmission (SHANNON and WEAVER). If the channel has bandwidth BW cps and signal and noise powers S and N, respectively, a method of coding exists such that information can be signalled, with arbitrarily small error, at a rate $C = BW \log_2 [1 + (S/N)]$ bits/sec. A conventional (waveform) voice channel has a bandwidth typically around 3000 cps, or more, and a signal-to-noise ratio of about 30 db. The formula therefore indicates that such a channel has the capacity to transmit information at rates on the order or 30000 bits/sec.

Similar bit rates are encountered in conventional digital transmission of speech waveforms (without further encoding). In PCM transmission for example, the signal is sampled at the Nyquist rate (2 BW) and, to

---

[1] Related data exist for the letters of printed English. Conditional constraints imposed by the language are likewise evident here. If the 26 English letters are considered equiprobable, the average information per letter is 4.7 bits. If the relative frequencies of the letters are used as estimates of $P(x_i)$, the average information per letter is 4.1 bits. If digram frequencies are considered, the information per letter, when the previous letter is known, is 3.6 bits. Taking account of trigram frequencies lowers this figure to 3.3 bits. By a limit-taking procedure, the long range statistical effects can be estimated. For sequences up to 100 letters in literary English the average information per letter is estimated to be on the order of one bit. This figure suggests a redundancy of about 75 per cent. If statistical effects extending over longer units such as paragraphs or chapters are considered, the redundancy may be still higher (SHANNON).

Table 1.1. *Relative frequencies of English speech sounds in standard prose.*
(After DEWEY)

Vowels and diphthongs			Consonants		
Pho-neme	relative frequency of occur-rence %	$-P(x_i) \log_2 P(x_i)$	Pho-neme	relative frequency of occur-rence %	$-P(x_i) \log_2 P(x_i)$
I	8.53	0.3029	n	7.24	0.2742
a	4.63	0.2052	t	7.13	0.2716
æ	3.95	0.1841	r	6.88	0.2657
ɛ	3.44	0.1672	s	4.55	0.2028
ɒ	2.81	0.1448	d	4.31	0.1955
ʌ	2.33	0.1264	l	3.74	0.1773
i	2.12	0.1179	ð	3.43	0.1669
e, eɪ	1.84	0.1061	z	2.97	0.1507
u	1.60	0.0955	m	2.78	0.1437
aɪ	1.59	0.0950	k	2.71	0.1411
ou	1.30	0.0815	v	2.28	0.1244
ɔ	1.26	0.795	w	2.08	0.1162
U	0.69	0.0495	p	2.04	0.1146
au	0.59	0.0437	f	1.84	0.1061
ɑ	0.49	0.0376	h	1.81	0.1048
o	0.33	0.0272	b	1.81	0.1048
ju	0.31	0.0258	ŋ	0.96	0.0644
ɔɪ	0.09	0.0091	ʃ	0.82	0.0568
			g	0.74	0.0524
			j	0.60	0.0443
			tʃ	0.52	0.0395
			dʒ	0.44	0.0344
			θ	0.37	0.0299
			ʒ	0.05	0.0055
Totals 38			62		

$H(X) = - \sum_i P(x_i) \log_2 P(x_i) = 4.9$ bits. If all phonemes were equiprobable, then $H(X) = \log_2 42 = 5.4$ bits.

maintain tolerable distortion, the amplitude is commonly quantized to an accuracy of one or two per cent. For a 64 level (6 bit) quantization, therefore, a typical bit rate is $2(3\,000) \log_2 64 = 36\,000$ bits/sec.

These capacities are on the order of six or seven hundred times greater than that apparently required for the written equivalent. The latter presumably should require a bandwidth of only about 5 cps for the 30 db S/N channel. Does this mean that the acoustic speech signal contains 600 times more information than its discretely transcribed equivalent? Or does it suggest that the acoustic time-waveform is an inefficient code for the speech information? Does it imply that the human is capable of processing information at 30000 bits/sec? Or does it mean that the receiver discards much of the transmitted information?

Intuitively it is clear that the acoustic signal contains more information than the written equivalent. How much more is not clear. Indeed it is not clear that such a measure can be made. The information rate of a continuous source can be defined only after a fidelity criterion is established for representing the signal in terms of a specific code. The criterion for defining the source entropy might be either subjective or objective. In speech communication the perceptual ability of the receiver usually dictates the necessary precision. Certain of these abilities can be established by psychoacoustic measurement. Different rates are ascribed to the source depending upon the coded form of the information and upon the perceptual criteria which apply. For example, if intelligibility and quality were the criteria, the source rate and channel capacity would be expected to be greater than if intelligibility alone were the criterion.

Although it may not be possible to answer the question "How much information is in the speech wave?", one can show from synthesis experiments that speech, closely equivalent perceptually to a specific waveform coding, can be transmitted over channels with capacities appreciably less than 30000 bits/sec. Present indications are that these capacities might eventually be made as low as one thousand to two thousand bits/sec. More will be said about such possibilities in a later chapter.

1.3. Capacity of the Human Channel

As just suggested, it is the fidelity criterion which establishes the information rate of a source. The criterion is determined by the ability of the receiver to discriminate differences in the received signal. Psychoacoustic experimentation with auditory limens often provides an upper bound to this ability. More basic, perhaps, but also more difficult to measure and apply in transmission system design, is the ability of man to assimilate and process information.

A number of experimental efforts have been made to assess man's informational capacity. The experiments necessarily concern specific, idealized perceptual tasks. They consequently yield information measures which are strictly interpretable only within the framework of the particular experiment. In most cases it is difficult to generalize or to extrapolate the results to more complex and applied communication tasks. Even so, the results do provide quantitative indications which might reasonably be taken as order-of-magnitude estimates for human communication in general.

In one response task, for example, subjects were required to echo verbally, as fast as possible, stimuli presented visually (LICKLIDER, STEVENS and HAYES). The stimuli consisted of random sequences of binary digits, decimal digits, letters and words. The maximal rates achieved in this processing of information were on the order of 30 bits/sec. When the response mode was changed to pointing to targets by hand, the rates fell to about 15 bits/sec.

The same study considered the possibility for increasing the rate by using more than a single response mode, namely, by permitting manual and vocal responses. For this two-channel processing, the total rate was found to be approximately the sum of the rates for the individual response modes, namely about 45 bits/sec. In the experience of the authors this was a record figure for the unambiguous transmission of information through a human channel.

Another experiment required subjects to read lists of common monosyllables aloud (PIERCE and KARLIN). Highest rates attained in these tests were 42 to 43 bits/sec. It was found that prose could be read faster than randomized lists of words. The limitation on the rate of reading was therefore concluded to be mental rather than muscular. When the task was changed to reading and tracking simultaneously, the rates decreased.

A different experiment measured the amount of information subjects could assimilate from audible tones coded in several stimulus dimensions (POLLACK and FICKS). The coding was in terms of tone frequency, loudness, interruption rate, spatial direction of source, total duration of presentation and ratio of on-off time. In this task subjects were found capable of processing 5.3 bits per stimulus presentation. Because presentation times varied, with some as great as 17 sec, it is not possible to deduce rates from these data.

A later experiment attempted to determine the rate at which binaural auditory information could be processed (WEBSTER, J. C.). Listeners were required to make binary discriminations in several dimensions: specifically, vowel sound; sex of speaker; ear in which heard; and, rising or falling inflection. In this task, the best subject could receive correctly just under 6 bits/sec. Group performance was a little less than this figure.

As indicated earlier, these measures are determined according to particular tasks and criteria of performance. They consequently have significance only within the scopes of the experiments. Whether the figures are representative of the rates at which humans can perceive and apprehend speech can only be conjectured. Probably they are. None of the experiments show the human to be capable of processing information at rates greater than the order of 50 bits/sec.

Assuming this figure does in fact represent a rough upper limit to man's ability to ingest information, he might allot his capacity in various ways. For example, if a speaker were rapidly uttering random equi-probable phonemes, a listener might require all of his processing ability to receive correctly the written equivalent of the distinctive speech sounds. Little capacity might remain for perceiving other features of the speech such as stress, inflection, nasality, timing and other attrib-utes of the particular voice. On the other hand, if the speech were idle social conversation, with far-reaching statistical constraints and high redundancy, the listener could direct more of his capacity to analyzing personal characteristics and articulatory peculiarities.

In protracted conversation the constraints of the language and the reasonably efficient human memory usually enable a listener to switch between a decoding of phonemic content and an observation of personal traits. Prosodic information can be assimilated along with phonemic features which relate directly to the written equivalent of the spoken information. The latter are customarily identified with speech intel-ligibility, while the former is loosely associated with speech quality. Intelligibility is conventionally quantified in terms of articulation scores and rates of receiving the written-equivalent information. Speech quality, as yet, has little basis for quantification. Until both intelligibil-ity and quality can be suitably defined, the fidelity criteria for estimating speech information rates will not be firmly established.

1.4. Analysis-Synthesis Telephony: An Approach to Improved Efficiency

Despite the equivocal aspects surrounding estimates of human channel capacity and speech information rates, it is clear that a mis-match exists between the capacity of the conventional voice channel and the information rate of the source feeding it. One approach toward improving the match is to incorporate into the transmission system as many as possible of the constraints characterizing the production and perception of speech. This information, built into the communication link, is information that need not be transmitted. Another way of viewing the situation is that the channel, so constrained, confines the message ensemble to the sounds of speech. In general, no other sounds will be transmitted with acceptable fidelity.

Having built into the system constraints appropriate to production and perception, communication is effected by signalling certain para-meters of the constraints. The nature of the incorporated constraints therefore influences the form of coding for the speech information. Assume, for example, that the limitations on the mechanical movements of the vocal tract are to be taken into account in the transmission system. One receiving device for realizing such restrictions might be a mechanical or electrical analog of the vocal mechanism. Speech information might then be coded and transmitted in terms of tract dimensions, deformations, and properties of vocal excitation.

Voice communication systems in which a conscious effort is made to improve efficiency by constraining the facility according to the characteristics of speech and hearing are customarily referred to as *analysis-synthesis systems*. The term is often taken as synonymous with speech-compression or band-saving systems. A main purpose of this monograph is to set forth the fundamental properties of speech and hearing which relate to communication systems of the analysis-synthesis type. A further purpose is to outline techniques for utilizing the properties of speech and hearing in practical transmission systems.

In attending to these objectives, the physiological and acoustical properties of the human vocal apparatus will be considered first. Next, the fundamental principles of the hearing mechanism will be examined. These basic expositions will then be followed by topics in speech analysis, speech synthesis, and speech perception. The final discussion will center on application of the preceding results to realizable speech-coding systems.

II. The Mechanism of Speech Production

2.1. Physiology of the Vocal Apparatus

Speech is the acoustic end product of voluntary, formalized motions of the respiratory and masticatory apparatus. It is a motor behavior which must be learned. It is developed, controlled and maintained by the acoustic feedback of the hearing mechanism and by the kinesthetic feedback of the speech musculature. Information from these senses is organized and coordinated by the central nervous system and used to direct the speech function. Impairment of either control mechanism usually degrades the performance of the vocal apparatus[1].

The speech apparatus also subserves the more fundamental processes of breathing and eating. It has been conjectured that speech evolved when ancient man discovered he could supplement his communicative hand signals with related "gestures" of his vocal tract. Sir RICHARD PAGET sums up this speculation quite neatly. "What drove man to the

---

[1] Most of us are aware of the difficulties that partially or totally deaf persons have in producing adequate speech. Even more familiar, perhaps, are the temporary difficulties in articulation experienced after the dentist desensitizes a large mouth area by an injection of anesthetic.

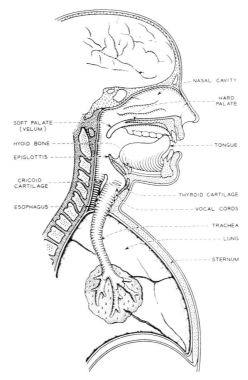

Fig. 2.1. Schematic diagram of the human vocal mechanism

invention of speech was, as I imagine, not so much the need of expressing his thoughts (for that might have been done quite satisfactorily
by bodily gesture) as the difficulty of 'talking with his hands full'. It
was the continual use of man's hands for craftsmanship, the chase,
and the beginnings of art and agriculture, that drove him to find other
methods of expressing his ideas—namely, by a specialized pantomime
of the tongue and lips."

The machinery involved in speech production is shown schematically
in Fig. 2.1. The diagram represents a mid-sagittal section through the
vocal tract of an adult. The primary function of inhalation is accomplished by expanding the rib cage, reducing the air pressure in the lungs,
and drawing air into the lungs via nostrils, nasal cavity, velum port and
trachea (windpipe). Air is normally expelled by the same route. In eating,
mastication takes place in the oral cavity. When food is swallowed
the structures at the entrance to the trachea are drawn up under the
epiglottis. The latter shields the opening at the vocal cords and prevents

food from going into the windpipe. The esophagus, which normally lies collapsed against the back wall of the throat, is at the same time drawn open to provide a passage to the stomach.

The vocal tract proper is an acoustical tube which is nonuniform in cross-sectional area. It is terminated by the lips at one end and by the vocal cord constriction at the top of the trachea at the other end. In an adult male the vocal tube is about 17 cm long and is deformed in cross-sectional area by movement of the articulators; namely, the lips, jaw, tongue and velum. The cross-sectional area in the forward portion of the tract can be varied from zero (i.e., complete closure) to upwards of 20 cm^2.

The nasal tract constitutes an ancillary path for sound transmission. It begins at the velum and terminates at the nostrils. In the adult male the cavity has a length of about 12 cm and a volume on the order of 60 cc. It is partitioned over part of its front-to-back extent by the nasal septum. Acoustic coupling between the nasal and vocal tracts is controlled by the size of the opening at the velum. In Fig. 2.1 the velum is shown widely open. In such a case, sound may be radiated from both the mouth and nostrils. In general, nasal coupling can substantially influence the character of sound radiated from the mouth. For the production of non-nasal sounds the velum is drawn tightly up and effectively seals off the entrance to the nasal cavity. In an adult male the area of the velar opening can range from zero to around 5 cm^2.

The source of energy for speech production lies in the thoracic and abdominal musculatures. Air is drawn into the lungs by enlarging the chest cavity and lowering the diaphragm. It is expelled by contracting the rib cage and increasing the lung pressure. Production of vowel sounds at the softest possible level requires a lung pressure of the order of 4 cm H$_2$O. For very loud, high-pitched sounds, on the other hand, pressures of about 20 cm H$_2$O or more are not uncommon. During speaking the lung pressure is maintained by a steady, slow contraction of the rib cage.

As air is forced from the lungs it passes through the trachea into the pharynx, or throat cavity. The top of the trachea is surmounted by a structure which is shown in additional detail in Fig. 2.2. This is the larynx. The cartilaginous frame houses two lips of ligament and muscle. These are the vocal cords and are denoted VC. The slit-like orifice between the cords is called the glottis. The knobby structures, protruding upward posterior to the cords, are the arytenoid cartilages, and are labelled AC. These cartilages support the fleshy cords and facilitate adjustment of tension. The principal outside cartilages of the larynx "box" are the anterior thyroid (labelled TC in Fig. 2.2) and the posterior cricoid. Both of these can be identified in Fig. 2.1.

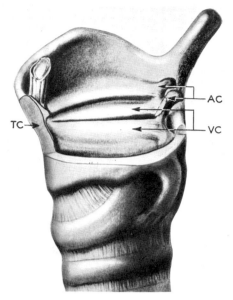

Fig. 2.2. Cut-away view of the human larynx. (After FARNSWORTH.) VC-vocal cords;
AC-arytenoid cartilages; TC-thyroid cartilage

The voiced sounds of speech are produced by vibratory action of the vocal cords. Production of sound in this manner is called phonation. Qualitatively, the action proceeds in the following manner. Imagine the relatively massive, tensed vocal cords to be initially together. The subglottal pressure is increased sufficiently to force them apart with a lateral acceleration. As the air flow builds up in the orifice, the local pressure is reduced according to the Bernoulli relation, and a force acts to return the cords to a proximate position. As the cords are again drawn together the flow is diminished, and the local pressure approaches the subglottal value. The relaxation cycle is then repeated[1]. The mass and compliance of the cords, and the subglottal pressure, essentially determine the period of the oscillation. This period is generally shorter than the natural period of the cords; that is, the cords are driven in a forced oscillation.

The variable area orifice produced by the vibrating cords permits quasi-periodic pulses of air to excite the acoustic system above the vocal cords. The mechanism is somewhat similar to blowing a tone on

---

[1] The vibratory cycle may be started with the cords initially apart. In this case, the Bernoulli pressure first causes the cords to be drawn together. The so-called "breathy attack" is apparently produced in this manner.

a brass instrument, where the vibrating lips permit quasiperiodic pulses of air to excite the resonances of the flared horn. Over the past years the vibratory action of the vocal cords has been studied in considerable detail. Direct observations can be made by positioning a 45-degree mirror toward the back of the mouth, near the naso-pharynx. Stroboscopic illumination at the proper frequency slows or "stops" the vibratory pattern and permits detailed scrutiny.

Still more revealing and more informative is the technique of high-speed photography, pioneered by FARNSWORTH, in which moving pictures are taken at a rate of 4000 frames/sec, or higher. The technique

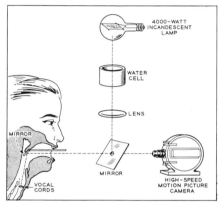

Fig. 2.3. Technique for high-speed motion picture photography of the vocal cords.
(After FARNSWORTH)

is illustrated in Fig. 2.3. The cords are illuminated by an intense light source via the arrangement of lenses and mirrors shown in the diagram. Photographs are taken through an aperture in the large front mirror to avoid obstructing the illumination. The result of such photography is illustrated in Fig. 2.4. The figure shows six selected frames in one cycle of vibration of the cords of an adult male. In this case the fundamental frequency of vibration, or voice "pitch", is 125 cps.

The volume flow of air through the glottis as a function of time is similar to (though not exactly proportional to) the area of the glottal opening. For a normal voice effort and pitch, the waveform can be roughly triangular in shape and exhibit duty factors (i.e., ratios of open time to total period) commonly of the order of 0.3 to 0.7. The glottal volume current therefore has a frequency spectrum relatively rich in overtones or harmonics. Because of the approximately triangular waveform, the higher frequency components diminish in amplitude at about 12 db/octave.

The waveform of the glottal volume flow for a given individual can vary widely. In particular, it depends upon sound pitch and intensity. For low-intensity, low-pitched sounds, the subglottal pressure is low, the vocal cord duty factor high, and the amplitude of volume flow low. For high-intensity, high-pitched sounds, the subglottal pressure is large, the duty factor small and the amplitude of volume flow great. The amplitude of lateral displacement of the vocal cords, and hence the maximum glottal area, is correlated with voice intensity to a surprisingly small extent (FLETCHER). For an adult male, common peak values of glottal area are of the order of 15 mm^2.

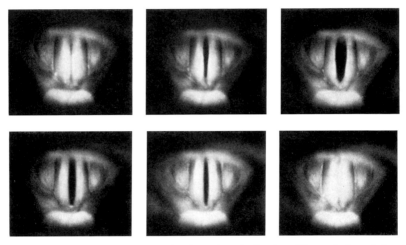

Fig. 2.4. Successive phases in one cycle of vocal cord vibration. The total elapsed time is approximately 8 msec

Because of its relatively small opening, the acoustic impedance of the glottal source is generally large compared to the acoustic impedance looking into the vocal tract, at least when the tract is not tightly constricted. Under these conditions changes in tract configuration have relatively small (but not negligible) influence upon the glottal volume flow. For tight constriction of the tract, the acoustic interaction between the tract and the vocal-cord oscillator can be pronounced.

Another source of vocal excitation is produced by a turbulent flow of air created at some point of stricture in the tract. An acoustic noise is thereby generated and provides an incoherent excitation for the vocal system. The unvoiced continuant sounds are formed from this source. Indirect measurements and theory suggest that the spectrum of the noise, at its point or region of generation, is relatively broad and uniform. The vocal cavities forward of the constriction usually are the most influential in spectrally shaping the sound.

A third source of excitation is created by a pressure buildup at some point of closure. An abrupt release of the pressure provides a transient excitation of the vocal tract. To a crude approximation the aperiodic excitation is a step function of pressure, and might be considered to have a spectrum which falls inversely with frequency. The closure can be effected at various positions toward the front of the tract; for example, at labial, dental, and palatal positions. The transient excitation can be used with or without vocal cord vibration to produce voiced or unvoiced plosive sounds.

Whispered speech is produced by substituting a noise source for the normally vibrating vocal cords. The source may by produced by turbulent flow at the partially closed glottis, or at some other constricted place in the tract.

2.2. The Sounds of Speech

To be a practicable medium for the transmission of information, a language must consist of a finite number of distinguishable, mutually-exclusive sounds. That is, the language must be constructed of basic linguistic units which have the property that if one replaces another in an utterance, the meaning is changed. The acoustic manifestations of a basic unit may vary widely. All such variations, however – when heard by a listener skilled in the language – signify the same linguistic element. This basic linguistic element is called a *phoneme* (BLOCH and TRAGER). Its manifold acoustic variations are called *allophones*.

The phonemes might therefore be looked upon as a code uniquely related to the articulatory gestures of a given language. The allophones of a given phoneme might be considered representative of the acoustic freedom permissible in specifying a code symbol. This freedom is not only dependent upon the phoneme, but also upon its position in an utterance.

The set of code symbols used in speech, and their statistical properties, depend upon the language and dialect of the communicators. When a linguist initially studies an unknown language, his first step is to make a phonetic transcription in which every perceptually-distinct sound is given a symbol. He then attempts to relate this transcription to behavior, and to determine which acoustically-distinguishable sounds belong to the same phoneme. That is, he groups together those sounds which are not distinct from each other in meaning. The sounds of each group differ in pronounciation, but this difference is not important to meaning. Their difference is merely a convention of the spoken language.

Features of speech which may be phonemically distinct in one language may not be phonemic in another. For example, in certain Chinese dialects pitch inflections are crucial in signifying distinctive speech sounds. In Western languages this generally is not the case. Another striking example is the agglutinative language of the South African Hottentots in which vocal clicks, completely foreign to Western languages, are phonemic.

The preceding implications are that speech is, in some sense, discrete. Yet an oscillographic representation of the sound pressure wave emanating from a speaker producing connected speech shows surprisingly few gaps or pause intervals. Connected speech is coupled with a near continuous motion of the vocal apparatus from sound to sound. This motion involves changes in the configuration of the vocal tract as well as in its modes of excitation. In continuous articulation the vocal tract dwells only momentarily in a state appropriate to a given phoneme.

The statistical constraints of the language greatly influence the precision with which a phoneme needs to be articulated. In some cases it is merely sufficient to make a vocal gesture in the direction of the normal configuration to signal the phoneme. Too, the relations between speech sounds and vocal motions are far from unique, although normal speakers operate with gross similarity. Notable examples of the "many-valuedness" of speech production are the compensatory articulation of ventriloquists and the mimicry of parrots and myna birds.

Despite the mutability of the vocal apparatus in connected speech, and the continuous nature of the speech wave, humans can subjectively segment speech into phonemes. Phoneticians are able to make written transcriptions of connected speech events, and phonetic alphabets have been devised for the purpose. (One of the earliest dates from the Hindus around 300 BC.) The often-accepted standard in modern times is the alphabet of the International Phonetic Association (IPA). This alphabet provides symbols for representing the speech sounds of most of the major languages of the world.

A phonetic symbol used for a phonetic transcription is conventionally enclosed in brackets []. When used to indicate a phoneme, it is usually enclosed in virgules // (FAIRBANKS). In the remainder of this book the former would often be appropriate, particularly with reference to the characteristics of specific utterances. Generally, however, the broad phonetic properties of an utterance and the phoneme group to which it belongs will be of more importance. The latter notation will therefore be used exclusively to enclose all phonetic symbols.

Classification of speech sounds is customarily accomplished according to their manner and place of production. Phoneticans have found this method convenient to indicate the gross characteristics of sounds.

For example, the articulation of vowel sounds is generally described by the position of the tongue hump along the vocal tract (which is often, but not always, the place of greatest constriction) and the degree of the constriction. This classification method will be employed in the following discussion of speech sounds. The examples extend to the sounds of English speech of General American (GA) dialect.

2.21. Vowels

The vowel sounds of GA speech are normally produced exclusively by vocal cord (or voiced) excitation of the tract. In normal articulation, the tract is maintained in a relatively stable configuration during most of the sound. The vowels are further characterized by negligible (if any) nasal coupling, and by radiation only from the mouth (excepting that which passes through the cavity walls).

If the nasal tract is effectively coupled to the vocal tract during the production of a vowel, the vowel becomes nasalized. When the 12 vowels of GA speech are classified according to the tongue-hump-position/ degree-of-constriction scheme, they may be arranged as shown in Table 2.1. Along with each vowel is shown a key word containing the vowel.

Table 2.1. *Vowels*

Degree of constriction	Tongue hump position		
	front	central	back
High	/i/ eve	/ɝ/ bird	/u/ boot
	/I/ it	/ɚ/ over (unstressed)	/ʊ/ foot
Medium	/e/ hate *	/ʌ/ up	/o/ obey *
	/ɛ/ met	/ə/ ado (unstressed)	/ɔ/ all
Low	/æ/ at		/ɑ/ father

* These two sounds usually exist as diphthongs in GA dialect. They are included in the vowel table because they form the nuclei of related diphthongs. See Section 2.27 for further discussion. (See also PETERSON and LEHISTE.)

The approximate articulatory configurations for the production of these sounds (exclusive of the two unstressed vowels) are shown qualitatively by the vocal tract profiles in Fig. 2.5 (POTTER, KOPP and GREEN). The physiological basis for the front-back/high-low classification is particularly well illustrated if the profiles for the vowels /i, æ, a, u/ are compared[1].

[1] These profiles, and the ones shown subsequently in this chapter, mainly illustrate the oral cavity. The important pharynx cavity and the lower vocal tract are not drawn. Their shapes may be deduced from x-rays (see Figs. 5.29 through 5.31, for example).

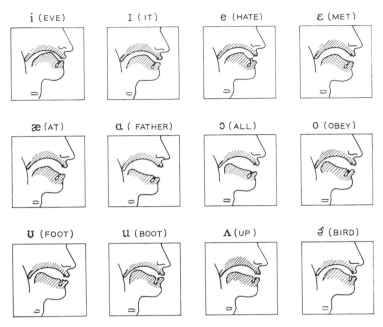

Fig. 2.5. Schematic vocal tract profiles for the production of English vowels.
(Adapted from POTTER, KOPP and GREEN)

2.22. Consonants

The consonants constitute those sounds which are not exclusively voiced and mouth-radiated from a relatively stable vocal configuration. They generally are characterized by greater tract constrictions than the vowels. They may be excited or radiated differently, or both. The short-time dynamic motions of the vocal apparatus are crucial to the production of an important class of consonants. Those consonants for which vocal motion is not requisite may be uttered as sustained sounds (as vowels may be) and hence are termed *continuants*.

2.221. Fricative Consonants. Fricatives are produced from an incoherent noise excitation of the vocal tract. The noise is generated by turbulent air flow at some point of constriction. Common constrictions for producing fricative consonants are those formed by the tongue behind the teeth (dental), the upper teeth on the lower lip (labio-dental), the tongue to the gum ridge (alveolar), the tongue against the hard or soft palate (palatal or velar, respectively), and the vocal cords constricted and fixed (glottal). Radiation of fricatives normally occurs from the mouth. If the vocal cord source operates in conjunction with the noise source, the fricative is a voiced fricative. If only the noise source is used, the fricative is unvoiced.

Both voiced and unvoiced fricatives are continuant sounds. Because a given fricative articulatory configuration can be excited either with or without voicing, the voiced and voiceless fricatives form complementary pairs called *cognates*. The fricative consonants of the GA dialect are listed in Table 2.2, along with typical "places" of articulation and key words for pronunciation.

Vocal tract profiles for these sounds are shown in Fig. 2.6. Those diagrams in which the vocal cords are indicated by two small lines are the voiced fricatives. The vocal cords are shown dashed for the glottal fricative (h).

Table 2.2. *Fricative consonants*

Place of articulation	Voiced	Voiceless
Labio-dental	/v/ vote	/f/ for
Dental	/ð/ then	/θ/ thin
Alveolar	/z/ zoo	/s/ see
Palatal	/ʒ/ azure	/ʃ/ she
Glottal		/h/ he

2.222. Stop Consonants. Among those consonants which depend upon vocal tract dynamics for their creation are the stop consonants. To produce these sounds a complete closure is formed at some point in the vocal tract. The lungs build up pressure behind this occlusion, and the pressure is suddenly released by an abrupt motion of the articulators. The explosion and aspiration of air help to characterize the stops. The closure can be labial, alveolar, palatal or velar. The stop can be produced with or without simultaneous voicing. In fact, a voiced consonant may employ voiced excitation to build up the requisite pressure, in which case voicing starts before the pressure release. The cognate pairs of stops, with typical places of articulation, are shown in Table 2.3.

Table 2.3. *Stop consonants*

Place of articulation	Voiced	Voiceless
Labial	/b/ be	/p/ pay
Alveolar	/d/ day	/t/ to
Palatal/velar	/g/ go	/k/ key

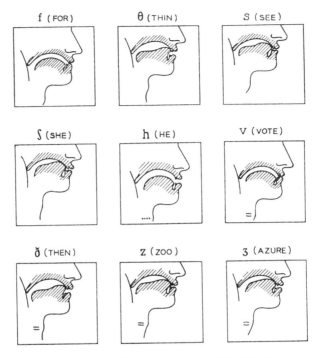

Fig. 2.6. Vocal tract profiles for the fricative consonants of English. The short pairs of lines drawn on the throat represent vocal cord operation. (Adapted from POTTER, KOPP and GREEN)

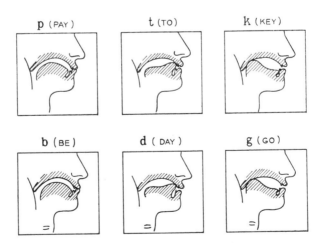

Fig. 2.7. Articulatory profiles for the English stop consonants. (After POTTER, KOPP and GREEN)

Articulatory profiles for these sounds are shown in Fig. 2.7. Each position is that just prior to the pressure release.

2.223. Nasal Consonants. The nasal consonants, or nasals, are normally excited by the vocal cords and hence are voiced. A complete closure is made toward the front of the vocal tract, either by the lips, by the tongue at the gum ridge, or by the tongue at the hard or soft palate. The velum is opened wide and the nasal tract provides the main sound transmission channel. Most of the sound radiation takes place at the nostrils. The closed oral cavity functions as a side branch resonator coupled to the main path, and it can substantially influence the sound radiated. Because the nasals can be sustained, they are classed as continuants. The GA nasal consonants are listed in Table 2.4, and their vocal profiles are illustrated in Fig. 2.8.

Table 2.4. *Nasals*

Place	
Labial	/m/ me
Alveolar	/n/ no
Palatal/velar	/ŋ/ sing
	(no initial form)

m (ME)   n (NO)   ŋ (SING)

Fig. 2.8. Vocal profiles for the nasal consonants. (After POTTER, KOPP and GREEN)

2.224. Glides and Semivowels. Two small groups of consonants contain sounds that greatly resemble vowels. These are the glides /w, j/ and the semivowels /r, l/ (FAIRBANKS). Both are characterized by voiced excitation of the tract, no effective nasal coupling, and sound radiation from the mouth. The glides are dynamic sounds, invariably precede a vowel, and exhibit movement toward the vowel. The semivowels are continuants in which the oral channel is more constricted than in most vowels, and the tongue tip is not down. These sounds for the GA dialect are listed, according to place of articulation, in Table 2.5. Their profiles, for the beginning positions, are given in Fig. 2.9.

Table 2.5. *Glides and semi-vowels*

Place		
Palatal	/j/	you
Labial	/w/	we
		(no final form)
Palatal	/r/	read
Alveolar	/l/	let

W (WE)   j (YOU)   r (READ)   l (LET)

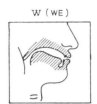 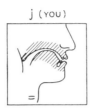 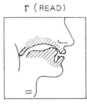 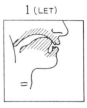

Fig. 2.9. Vocal tract configurations for the beginning positions of the glides and semivowels. (After POTTER, KOPP and GREEN)

2.225. Combination Sounds: Diphthongs and Affricates. Some of the preceding vowel or consonant elements can be combined to form basic sounds whose phonetic values depend upon vocal tract motion. An appropriate pair of vowels, so combined, form a diphthong. The diphthong is vowel-like in nature, but is characterized by change from one vowel position to another. For example, if the vocal tract is changed from the /e/ position to the /ɪ/ position, the diphthong /eɪ/ as in *say* is formed. Other GA diphthongs are /ɪu/ as in *new*, /ɔɪ/ as in *boy*; /aυ/ as in *out*, /aɪ/ as in *I*, and /oυ/ as in *go*.

As vowel combinations form the diphthongs, stop-fricative combinations likewise create the two GA affricates. These are the /tʃ/ as in *chew* and the /dʒ/ as in *jar*.

2.3. Quantitative Description of Speech

The preceding discussion has described the production of speech in a completely qualitative way. It has outlined the mechanism of the voice and the means for producing an audible code which, within a given language, consists of distinctive sounds. However, for any transmission system to benefit from prior knowledge of the information source, this knowledge must be cast into a tractable analytical form that can be employed in the design of signal processing operations. Detailed inquiry into the physical principles underlying the speech-producing mechanism is therefore indicated.

The following chapter will consider the characteristics of the vocal system in a quantitative fashion. It will treat the physics of the vocal and nasal tracts in some depth and will set forth certain acoustical properties of the vocal excitations. The primary objective — as stated earlier — is to describe the acoustic speech signal in terms of the physical parameters of the system that produced it. Because of physiological and linguistic constraints, such a description carries important implications for analysis-synthesis telephony.

III. Acoustical Properties of the Vocal System

The collection of olfactory, respiratory and digestive apparatus which man uses for speaking is a relatively complex sound-producing system. Its operation has been described qualitatively in the preceding chapter. In this chapter we would like to consider in more detail the acoustical principles underlying speech production. The treatment is not intended to be exhaustive. Rather it is intended to circumscribe the problems of vocal tract analysis and to set forth certain fundamental relations for speech production. In addition, it aims to outline techniques and method for acoustic analysis of the vocal mechanism and to indicate their practical applications. Specialized treatments of a number of these points can be found elsewhere[1].

3.1. The Vocal Tract as an Acoustic System

The operations described qualitatively in the previous chapter can be crudely represented as in Fig. 3.1. The lungs and associated respiratory muscles are the vocal power supply. For voiced sounds, the expelled air causes the vocal cords to vibrate as a relaxation oscillator, and the air stream is modulated into discrete puffs or pulses. Unvoiced sounds are generated either by passing the air stream through a constriction in the tract, or by making a complete closure, building up pressure behind the closure and abruptly releasing it. In the first case, turbulent flow and incoherent sound are produced. In the second, a brief transient excitation occurs. The physical configuration of the vocal tract is highly variable and is dictated by the positions of the articulators; that is, the jaw, tongue, lips and velum. The latter controls the degree of coupling to the nasal tract.

---

[1] For this purpose G. FANT, *Acoustic Theory of Speech Production*, is highly recommended. Besides presenting the acoustical bases for vocal analysis, this volume contains a wealth of data on vocal configurations and their calculated frequency responses. An earlier but still relevant treatise is T. CHIBA and M. KAJIYAMA, *The Vowel; Its Nature and Structure*. Another excellent and more recent analysis of vowel articulation is G. UNGEHEUER, *Elemente einer akustischen Theorie der Vokalartikulation*.

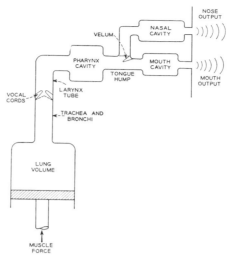

Fig. 3.1. Schematic diagram of functional components of the vocal tract

In general, several major regions figure prominently in speech production. They are: (a) the relatively long cavity formed at the lower back of the throat in the pharynx region; (b) the narrow passage at the place where the tongue is humped; (c) the variable constriction of the velum and the nasal cavity; (d) the relatively large, forward oral cavity; (e) the radiating ports formed by the mouth and nostrils.

Voiced sounds are always excited at the same point in the tract, namely at the vocal cords. Radiation of voiced sounds can take place either from the mouth or nose, or from both. Unvoiced excitation is applied to the acoustic system at the point where turbulent flow or pressure release occurs. This point may range from an anterior position [such as the labio-dental excitation for /f/] to a posterior position [such as the palatal excitation for /k/]. Unvoiced sounds are normally radiated from the mouth. All sounds generated by the vocal apparatus are characterized by properties of the source of excitation and the acoustic transmission system. To examine these properties, let us first establish some elementary relations for the transmission system, then consider the sound sources, and finally treat the combined operation of sources and system.

The length of the vocal tract (about 17 cm in man) is fully comparable to the wavelength of sound in air at audible frequencies. It is therefore not possible to obtain a precise analysis of the tract operation from a lumped-constant approximation of the major acoustic components. Wave motion in the system must be considered for frequencies above several hundred cps. The vocal and nasal tracts constitute lossy tubes of non-uniform cross-sectional area. Wave motion in such tubes is difficult to describe, even for lossless propagation. In fact, exact solutions to the wave equation are available only for two nonuniform geometries, namely for conical and hyperbolic area variations (MORSE). And then only the conical geometry leads to a one-parameter wave.

So long as the greatest cross dimension of the tract is appreciably less than a wavelength (this is usually so for frequencies below about 4000 cps), and so long as the tube does not flare too rapidly (producing internal wave reflections), the acoustic system can be approximated by a one-dimensional wave equation. Such an equation assumes cophasic wave fronts across the cross-section and is sometimes called the Webster equation (WEBSTER). Its form is

$$\frac{1}{A(x)} \frac{\partial}{\partial x} \left[A(x) \frac{\partial p}{\partial x} \right] = \frac{1}{c^2} \frac{\partial^2 p}{\partial t^2}, \tag{3.1}$$

where $A(x)$ is the cross-sectional area normal to the longitudinal dimension, p is the sound pressure (a function of t and x) and c is the sound velocity. In general this equation can only be integrated numerically, and it does not include loss. At least three investigations, however, have made use of this formulation for studying vowel production (CHIBA and KAJIYAMA; UNGEHEUER; HEINZ, 1962a, b).

A more tractable approach to the analysis problem (both computationally and conceptually) is to impose a further degree of approximation upon the nonuniform tube. The pipe may be represented in terms of incremental contiguous sections of right circular geometry. The approximation may, for example, be in terms of cylinders, cones, exponential or hyperbolic horns. Although quantizing the area function introduces error, its effect can be made small if the lengths of the approximating sections are kept short compared to a wavelength at the highest frequency of interest. The uniform cylindrical section is particularly easy to treat and will be the one used for the present discussion.

3.2. Equivalent Circuit for the Lossy Cylindrical Pipe

Consider the length dx of lossy cylindrical pipe of area A shown in Fig. 3.2a. Assume plane wave transmission so that the sound pressure and volume velocity are spatially dependent only upon x. Because of its mass, the air in the pipe exhibits an inertance which opposes acceleration. Because of its compressibility the volume of air exhibits a compliance. Assuming that the tube is smooth and hard-walled, energy losses can occur at the wall through viscous friction and heat conduction. Viscous losses are proportional to the square of the particle velocity, and heat conduction losses are proportional to the square of the sound pressure.

The characteristics of sound propagation in such a tube are easily described by drawing upon elementary electrical theory and some well-known results for one-dimensional waves on transmission lines. Consider sound pressure analogous to the voltage and volume velocity analogous to the current in an electrical line. Sound pressure and volume velocity for plane wave propagation in the uniform tube satisfy the same wave equation as do voltage and current on a uniform transmission line. A dx length of lossy electrical line is illustrated in Fig. 3.2b. To develop the analogy let us write the relations for the electrical line. The per-unit-length inductance, capacitance, series resistance and shunt conductance are L, C, R, and G respectively. Assuming sinusoidal time dependence

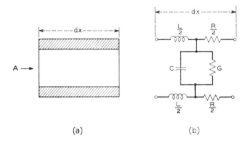

(a)   (b)

Fig. 3.2a and b. Incremental length of lossy cylindrical pipe. (a) acoustic representation; (b) electrical equivalent for a one-dimensional wave

for voltage and current, ($Ie^{j\omega t}$ and $E\,e^{j\omega t}$), the differential current loss and voltage drop across the dx length of line are

$$dI = -Ey\,dx \quad \text{and} \quad dE = -Iz\,dx, \tag{3.2}$$

where $y=(G+j\omega C)$ and $z=(R+j\omega L)$.

The voltage and current therefore satisfy

$$\frac{d^2 E}{dx^2} - zyE = 0 \quad \text{and} \quad \frac{d^2 I}{dx^2} - zyI = 0, \tag{3.3}$$

the solutions for which are

$$E = A_1 e^{\gamma x} + B_1 e^{-\gamma x}$$
$$I = A_2 e^{\gamma x} + B_2 e^{-\gamma x}, \tag{3.4}$$

where $\gamma = \sqrt{zy} = (\alpha+j\beta)$ is the propagation constant, and the A's and B's are integration constants determined by terminal conditions.

For a piece of line l in length, with sending-end voltage and current E_1 and I_1, the receiving-end voltage and current E_2 and I_2 are given by

$$E_2 = E_1 \cosh \gamma l - I_1 Z_0 \sinh \gamma l$$
$$I_2 = I_1 \cosh \gamma l - E_1 Y_0 \sinh \gamma l, \tag{3.5}$$

where $Z_0 = \sqrt{z/y}$ and $Y_0 = \sqrt{y/z}$ are the characteristic impedance and admittance of the line. Eq. (3.5) can be rearranged to make evident the impedance parameters for the equivalent four-pole network

$$E_1 = Z_0 I_1 \coth \gamma l - Z_0 I_2 \operatorname{csch} \gamma l$$
$$E_2 = Z_0 I_1 \operatorname{csch} \gamma l - Z_0 I_2 \coth \gamma l. \tag{3.6}$$

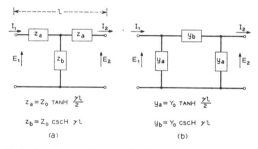

Fig. 3.3 a and b. Equivalent four-pole networks for a length l of uniform transmission line. (a) T-section; (b) π-section

The equivalent T-network for the l length of line is therefore as shown in Fig. 3.3a. Similarly, a different arrangement makes salient the admittance parameters for the four-pole network.

$$I_1 = Y_0 E_1 \coth \gamma l - Y_0 E_2 \operatorname{csch} \gamma l$$
$$I_2 = Y_0 E_1 \operatorname{csch} \gamma l - Y_0 E_2 \coth \gamma l. \tag{3.7}$$

The equivalent π-network is shown in Fig. 3.3b.

One recalls also from conventional circuit theory the lossless case corresponds to $\gamma = \sqrt{zy} = j\beta = j\omega\sqrt{LC}$, and $Z_0 = \sqrt{L/C}$. The hyperbolic functions then reduce to circular functions which are purely reactive. Notice, too, for *small loss* conditions, (that is, $R \ll \omega L$ and $G \ll \omega C$) the attenuation and phase constants are approximately

$$\alpha \cong \frac{R}{2}\sqrt{C/L} + \frac{G}{2}\sqrt{L/C} \tag{3.8}$$

$$\beta \cong \omega\sqrt{LC}.$$

Having recalled the relations for the uniform, lossy electrical line, we want to interpret plane wave propagation in a uniform, lossy pipe in analogous terms. If sound pressure, p, is considered analogous to voltage and acoustic volume velocity, U, analogous to current, the lossy, one-dimensional, sinusoidal sound propagation is described by the same equations as given in (3.3). The propagation constant is complex (that is, the velocity of propagation is in effect complex) and the wave attenuates as it travels. In a smooth hard-walled tube the viscous and heat conduction losses can be represented, in effect, by an I^2R loss and an E^2G loss, respectively. The inertance of the air mass is analogous to the electrical inductance, and the compliance of the air volume is analogous to the electrical capacity. We can draw these parallels quantitatively[1].

3.21. The Acoustic "L"

The mass of air contained in the dx length of pipe in Fig. 3.2a is $\rho A\, dx$, where ρ is the air density. The differential pressure drop in accelerating this mass is by NEWTON's law:

$$dp = \rho\, dx\, \frac{du}{dt} = \rho\, \frac{dx}{A} \cdot \frac{dU(x,t)}{dt},$$

where u is particle velocity and U is volume velocity.

For $U(x,t) = U(x)\, e^{j\omega t}$

$$dp = j\omega \rho\, \frac{dx}{A}\, U$$

and

$$\frac{dp}{dx} = j\omega L_a U,$$

(3.9)

where $L_a = \rho/A$ is the acoustic inertance *per unit length*.

3.22. The Acoustic "R"

The acoustic R represents a power loss proportional to U^2 and is the power dissipated in viscous friction at the tube wall (INGÅRD). The easiest way to put in evidence this equivalent surface resistance is to consider the situation shown in Fig. 3.4. Imagine that the tube wall is a plane surface, large in extent, and moving sinusoidally in the x-direction with velocity $u(t) = u_m e^{j\omega t}$. The air particles proximate to the wall experience a force owing to the viscosity, μ, of the medium. The power expended per unit area in dragging the air with the plate is the loss to be determined.

---

[1] The reader who is not interested in these details may omit the following four sections and find the results summarized in Eq. (3.33) of Section 3.25.

Consider a layer of air dy thick and of unit area normal to the y axis. The net force on the layer is

$$\mu \left[\left(\frac{\partial u}{\partial y} \right)_{y+dy} - \left(\frac{\partial u}{\partial y} \right)_{y} \right] = \rho \, dy \, \frac{\partial u}{\partial t},$$

where u is the particle velocity in the x-direction. The diffusion equation specifying the air particle velocity as a function of the distance above the wall is then

$$\frac{\partial^2 u}{\partial y^2} = \frac{\rho}{\mu} \frac{\partial u}{\partial t}. \tag{3.10}$$

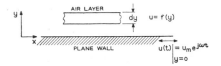

Fig. 3.4. Relations illustrating viscous loss at the wall of a smooth tube

For harmonic time dependence this gives

$$\frac{d^2 u}{dy^2} = j \frac{\omega \rho}{\mu} u = k_v^2 u, \tag{3.11}$$

where $k_v = (1+j) \sqrt{\omega \rho / 2\mu}$, and the velocity distribution is

$$u = u_m e^{-k_v y} = u_m e^{-\sqrt{\omega \rho / 2\mu} \, y} e^{-j \sqrt{\omega \rho / 2\mu} \, y}. \tag{3.12}$$

The distance required for the particle velocity to diminish to $1/e$ of its value at the driven wall is often called the boundary-layer thickness and is $\delta_v = \sqrt{2\mu/\omega\rho}$. In air at a frequency of 100 cps, for example, $\delta_v \cong 0.2\,\text{mm}$.

The viscous drag, per unit area, on the plane wall is

$$F = -\mu \left(\frac{\partial u}{\partial y} \right)_{y=0} = \mu k_v u_m,$$

or

$$F = u_m (1+j) \sqrt{\omega \mu \rho / 2}. \tag{3.13}$$

Notice that this force has a real part and a positive reactive part. The latter acts to increase the apparent acoustic L. The average power dissipated per unit surface area in this drag is

$$\bar{P} = \tfrac{1}{2} |F| u_m \cos \vartheta = \tfrac{1}{2} u_m^2 R_s, \tag{3.14}$$

where $R_s = \sqrt{\omega \rho \mu / 2}$ is the per-unit-area surface resistance and ϑ is the phase angle between F and u, namely, $45°$. For a length l of the acoustic tube, the inner surface area is $S \cdot l$, where S is the circumference. Therefore, the average power dissipated *per unit length* of the tube is $\bar{P} \cdot S = \frac{1}{2} u_m^2 \cdot S \cdot R_s$, or in terms of the acoustic volume velocity

$$\bar{P} \cdot S = \frac{1}{2} U_m^2 R_a ,$$

where   (3.15)

$$R_a = \frac{S}{A^2} \sqrt{\omega \rho \mu / 2} ,$$

and A is the cross-sectional area of the tube. R_a is then the per-unit-length acoustic resistance for the analogy shown in Fig. 3.2.

As previously mentioned, the reactive part of the viscous drag contributes to the acoustic inductance per unit length. In fact, for the same area and surface relations applied above, the acoustic inductance obtained in the foregoing section should be increased by the factor $\frac{A^2}{S} \sqrt{\mu \rho / 2 \omega}$, or

$$L_a = \frac{\rho}{A} \left(1 + \frac{S}{A} \sqrt{\frac{\mu}{2 \rho \omega}} \right) .$$ (3.16)

Thus, the viscous boundary layer increases the apparent acoustic inductance by effectively diminishing the cross-sectional area. For vocal tract analysis, however, the viscous boundary layer is usually so thin that the second term in (3.16) is negligible. For example, for a circular cross-section of 9 cm², the second term at a frequency of 500 cps is about $(0.006) \rho / A$.

3.23. The Acoustic "C"

The analogous acoustic capacitance, or compliance, arises from the compressibility of the volume of air contained in the dx length of tube shown in Fig. 3.2a. Most of the elemental air volume $A\,dx$ experiences compressions and expansions which follow the adiabatic gas law

$$P V^\eta = \text{constant},$$

where P and V are the total pressure and volume of the gas, and η is the adiabatic constant[1]. Differentiating with respect to time gives

$$\frac{1}{P} \frac{dP}{dt} = -\frac{\eta}{V} \frac{dV}{dt} .$$

---

[1] η is the ratio of specific heat at constant pressure to that at constant volume. For air at normal conditions, $\eta = c_p / c_v = 1.4$.

The diminution of the original air volume, owing to compression caused by an increase in pressure, must equal the volume current into the compliance; that is,

$$U = -\frac{dV}{dt},$$

and

$$\frac{1}{P}\frac{dP}{dt} = \frac{\eta U}{V}.$$

For sinusoidal time dependence $P = P_0 + p e^{j\omega t}$, where P_0 is the quiescent pressure and is large compared with p. The volume flow into the compliance of the $A\,dx$ volume is therefore approximately

$$U = j\omega \frac{V}{P_0 \eta} \cdot p = j\omega \frac{A\,dx}{P_0 \eta} \cdot p. \tag{3.17}$$

From wave considerations $P_0\eta$ can be shown to equal ρc^2. The volume velocity into the per-unit-length compliance can therefore be written as

$$U = j\omega \cdot C_a \cdot p,$$

where

$$C_a = \frac{A}{P_0 \eta} = \frac{A}{\rho c^2} \tag{3.18}$$

is the per-unit-length acoustic compliance.

3.24. The Acoustic "G"

The analogous shunt conductance provides a power loss proportional to the square of the local sound pressure. Such a loss arises from heat conduction at the walls of the tube. The per-unit-length conductance can be deduced in a manner similar to that for the viscous loss. As before, it is easier to treat a simpler situation and extend the result to the vocal tube.

Consider a highly conductive plane wall of large extent, such as shown in Fig. 3.5. The air above the boundary is essentially at constant pressure and has a coefficient of heat conduction λ and a specific heat c_p. Suppose the wall is given an oscillating temperature $T|_{y=0} = T_m e^{j\omega t}$. The vertical temperature distribution produced in the air is described by the diffusion equation (HILDEBRAND)

$$\frac{\partial^2 T}{\partial y^2} = \frac{c_p \rho}{\lambda}\frac{\partial T}{\partial t},$$

or

$$\frac{\partial^2 T}{\partial y^2} = j\omega \frac{c_p \rho}{\lambda} T. \tag{3.19}$$

The solution is $T = T_m e^{-k_h y}$, where

$$k_h = (1+j) \sqrt{\frac{\omega c_p \rho}{2\lambda}}, \qquad (3.20)$$

which is the same form as the velocity distribution due to viscosity. In a similar fashion, the boundary layer depth for temperature is $\delta_h = \sqrt{2\lambda/\omega c_p \rho}$, and $k_h = (1+j)/\delta_h$.

Now consider more nearly the situation for the sound wave. Imagine an acoustic pressure wave moving parallel to the conducting boundary,

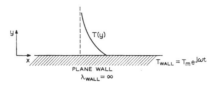

Fig. 3.5. Relations illustrating heat conduction at the wall of a tube

that is, in the x-direction. We wish to determine the temperature distribution above the wall produced by the sound wave. The conducting wall is assumed to be maintained at some quiescent temperature and permitted no variation, that is, $\lambda_{\text{wall}} = \infty$. If the sound wavelength is long compared to the boundary extent under consideration, the harmonic pressure variation above the wall may be considered as $P = P_0 + p$, where P_0 is the quiescent atmospheric pressure and $p = p_m e^{j\omega t}$ is the pressure variation. (That is, the spatial variation of p with x is assumed small.) The gas laws prescribe

$$PV^\eta = \text{constant} \quad \text{and} \quad PV = RT \quad \text{(for unit mass)}.$$

Taking differentials gives

$$\frac{dV}{V} = -\frac{1}{\eta} \frac{dP}{P} \quad \text{and} \quad \frac{dP}{P} + \frac{dV}{V} = \frac{dT}{T}. \qquad (3.21)$$

Combining the equations yields

$$\frac{dP}{P} \left(1 - \frac{1}{\eta}\right) = \frac{dT}{T}, \qquad (3.22)$$

where

$$dP = p = p_m e^{j\omega t}$$

$$dT = \tau = \tau_m e^{j\omega t},$$

so from (3.22)

$$\tau_m = \frac{T_0}{P_0} \left(\frac{\eta-1}{\eta} \right) p_m.$$ (3.23)

At the wall, $y=0$ and $\tau(0)=0$ (because $\lambda_{wall}=\infty$). Far from the wall (i.e., for y large), $|\tau(y)|=\tau_m$ as given in (3.23). Using the result of (3.20), the temperature distribution can be constructed as

$$\tau(y, t) = [1 - e^{-k_h y}] \tau_m e^{j\omega t},$$

or

$$\tau(y, t) = \frac{P_0}{T_0} \left(\frac{\eta-1}{\eta} \right) [1 - e^{-k_h y}] p_m e^{j\omega t}.$$ (3.24)

Now consider the power dissipation at the wall corresponding to this situation. A long wavelength sound has been assumed so that the acoustic pressure variations above the boundary can be considered $p = p_m e^{j\omega t}$, and the spatial dependence of pressure neglected. Because of the temperature distribution above the boundary, however, the particle velocity will be nonuniform, and will have a component in the y-direction. The average power flow per unit surface area into the boundary is $\overline{p u_{y_0}^t}$, where u_{y_0} is the velocity component in the y direction at the boundary. To examine this quantity, u_y is needed.

Conservation of mass in the y-direction requires

$$\rho \frac{\partial u_y}{\partial y} = -\frac{\partial \rho}{\partial t}.$$ (3.25)

Also, for a constant mass of gas $d\rho/\rho = -dV/V$ which with the second equation in (3.21) requires

$$\frac{dP}{P} - \frac{d\rho}{\rho} = \frac{dT}{T}.$$ (3.26)

Therefore,

$$\frac{\partial u_y}{\partial y} = \left(\frac{1}{T_0} \frac{\partial \tau}{\partial t} - \frac{1}{P_0} \frac{\partial p}{\partial t} \right),$$ (3.27)

and

$$u_y = \int \frac{\partial u_y}{\partial y} \cdot dy$$

$$u_y = \frac{j\omega p}{P_0} \left\{ \frac{\eta-1}{\eta} \left(y + \frac{e^{-k_y y}}{ky} \right) - y \right\}.$$ (3.28)

And,

$$u_{yo} = p \, \frac{\omega}{c} \, \frac{\eta-1}{\rho c} \, \frac{j}{1+j} \, \delta_h \, . \tag{3.29}$$

The equivalent energy flow into the wall is therefore

$$W_h = \overline{p u_{yo}{}'} = \frac{\omega}{c} \, \frac{\eta-1}{\rho c} \, \delta_h \, \frac{1}{\sqrt{2}} \, \frac{1}{T} \int_0^T P_m^2 \cos\left(\omega t + \frac{\pi}{4}\right) \cos \omega t \cdot dt$$

$$W_h = \frac{1}{4} \, \frac{\omega}{c} \, \frac{\eta-1}{\rho c} \, \delta_h \, p_m^2 = \frac{1}{2} \, G_\alpha \, p_m^2 \,, \tag{3.30}$$

where G_α is an equivalent conductance per unit wall area and is equal

$$G_\alpha = \frac{1}{2} \, \frac{\omega}{c} \, \frac{\eta-1}{\rho c} \, \sqrt{\frac{2\lambda}{\omega c_p \rho}} \, . \tag{3.31}$$

The equivalent conductance per unit length of tube owing to heat conduction is therefore

$$G_\alpha = S \, \frac{\eta-1}{\rho c^2} \, \sqrt{\frac{\lambda \omega}{2 c_p \rho}} \,, \tag{3.32}$$

where S is the tube circumference.

To reiterate, both the heat conduction loss G_a and the viscous loss R_a are applicable to a smooth, rigid tube. The vocal tract is neither, so that in practice these losses might be expected to be somewhat higher. In addition, the mechanical impedance of the yielding wall includes a mass reactance and a conductance which contribute to the shunt element of the equivalent circuit. The effect of the wall reactance upon the tuning of the vocal resonances is generally small, particularly for open articulations. The contribution of wall conductance to tract damping is more important. Both of these effects are estimated in a later section.

3.25. Summary of the Analogous Acoustic Elements

The per-unit-length analogous constants of the uniform pipe can be summarized.

$$L_a = \frac{\rho}{A} \,, \qquad\qquad C_a = \frac{A}{\rho c^2} \,,$$

$$R_a = \frac{S}{A^2} \, \sqrt{\frac{\omega \rho \mu}{2}} \,, \qquad G_a = S \, \frac{\eta-1}{\rho c^2} \, \sqrt{\frac{\lambda \omega}{2 c_p \rho}} \,, \tag{3.33}$$

where A is tube area, S is tube circumference, ρ is air density, c is sound velocity, μ is viscosity coefficient, λ is coefficient of heat conduction,

η is the adiabatic constant, and c_p is the specific heat of air at constant pressure[1].

Having set down these quantities, it is possible to approximate the nonuniform vocal tract with as many right circular tube sections as desired. The transmission characteristics can be determined either from calculations on equivalent network sections such as shown in Fig. 3.3, or from electrical circuit simulations of the elements. When the approximation involves more than three or four network loops, manual computation becomes prohibitive. Computer techniques can then be used to good advantage.

A further level of approximation can be made for the equivalent networks in Fig. 3.3. For a given length of tube, the hyperbolic elements may be approximated by the first terms of their series expansions, namely,

$$\tanh x = x - \frac{x^3}{3} + \frac{2x^5}{15} \cdots,$$

and

$$\sinh x = x + \frac{x^3}{3!} + \frac{x^5}{5!} \cdots,$$

so that

$$z_a = Z_0 \tanh \frac{\gamma l}{2} \cong \tfrac{1}{2}(R_a + j\omega L_a)l$$

and

$$\frac{1}{z_b} = \frac{1}{Z_0}\sinh \gamma l \cong (G_a + j\omega C_a)l. \tag{3.34}$$

The error incurred in making this approximation is a function of the elemental length l and the frequency, and is

$$\left(1 - \frac{x}{\tanh x}\right) \text{ and } \left(1 - \frac{x}{\sinh x}\right),$$

respectively. In constructing electrical analogs of the vocal tract it has been customary to use this approximation while keeping l sufficiently small. We shall return to this point later in the chapter.

We will presently apply the results of this section to some simplified analyses of the vocal tract. Before doing so, however, it is desirable to establish several fundamental relations for sound radiation from the mouth and for certain characteristics of the sources of vocal excitation.

---

[1] $\rho = 1.14 \times 10^{-3}$ gm/cm³ (moist air at body temperature, 37° C).
$c = 3.5 \times 10^4$ cm/sec (moist air at body temperature, 37° C).
$\mu = 1.86 \times 10^{-4}$ dyne-sec/cm² (20° C, 0.76 m. Hg).
$\lambda = 0.055 \times 10^{-3}$ cal/cm-sec-deg (0° C).
$c_p = 0.24$ cal/gm-degree (0° C, 1 atmos.).
$\eta = 1.4$.

3.3. The Radiation Load at the Mouth and Nostrils

At frequencies where the transverse dimensions of the tract are small compared with a wavelength, the radiating area of the mouth or nose can be assumed to have a velocity distribution that is approximately uniform and cophasic. It can therefore be considered a vibrating surface, all parts of which move in phase. The radiating element is set in a baffle that is the head. To a rough approximation, the baffle is spherical and about 9 cm in radius for a man.

MORSE has derived the radiation load on a vibrating piston set in a spherical baffle and shows it to be a function of frequency and the relative sizes of the piston and sphere. The analytical expression for the load is involved and cannot be expressed in closed form. A limiting condition, however, is the case where the radius of the piston becomes small compared with that of the sphere. The radiation load then approaches that of a piston in an infinite, plane baffle. The latter is well known and can be expressed in closed form. In terms of the normalized acoustic impedance

$$z = Z_A \cdot \frac{A}{\rho c} = \frac{p}{U} \cdot \frac{A}{\rho c}$$

(that is, per-unit-free-space impedance), it is

$$z_p = \left[1 - \frac{J_1(2ka)}{ka}\right] + j\left[\frac{K_1(2ka)}{2(ka)^2}\right], \tag{3.35}$$

where $k = \omega/c$, a is the piston radius, A the piston area, $J_1(x)$ the first order Bessel function, and $K_1(x)$ a related Bessel function given by the series

$$K_1(x) = \frac{2}{\pi}\left[\frac{x^3}{3} - \frac{x^5}{3^2 \cdot 5} + \frac{x^7}{3^2 \cdot 5^2 \cdot 7}\cdots\right].$$

For small values of ka, the first terms of the Bessel functions are the most significant, and the normalized radiation impedance is approximately

$$z_p \cong \frac{(ka)^2}{2} + j\frac{8(ka)}{3\pi}; \quad ka \ll 1. \tag{3.36}$$

This impedance is a resistance proportional to ω^2 in series with an inductance of normalized value $8a/3\pi c$. The parallel circuit equivalent is a resistance of $128/9\pi^2$ in parallel with an inductance of $8a/3\pi c$.

By way of comparison, the normalized acoustic load on a vibrating sphere is also well known and is

$$z_s = \frac{jka}{1 + jka}, \tag{3.37}$$

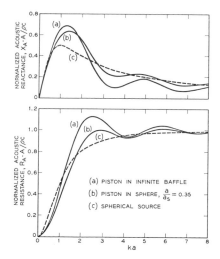

Fig. 3.6. Normalized acoustic radiation resistance and reactance for (a) circular piston in an infinite baffle; (b) circular piston in a spherical baffle whose radius is approximately three times that of the piston; (c) pulsating sphere. The radius of the radiator, whether circular or spherical, is a

where a is the radius of the sphere. Note that this is the parallel combination of a unit resistance and an a/c inductance. Again, for small ka,

$$z_s \cong (ka)^2 + j(ka); \quad ka \ll 1. \tag{3.38}$$

Using Morse's results for the spherical baffle, a comparison of the real and imaginary parts of the radiation impedances for the piston-in-sphere, piston-in-wall, and pulsating sphere is made in Fig. 3.6. For the former, a piston-to-sphere radius ratio of $a/a_s = 0.35$ is illustrated. The piston-in-wall curves correspond to $a/a_s = 0$. For $ka < 1$, one notices that the reactive loads are very nearly the same for all three radiators. The real part for the spherical source is about twice that for the pistons.

These relations can be interpreted in terms of mouth dimensions. Consider typical extreme values of mouth area (smallest and largest) for vowel production. A man articulating a rounded vowel such as /u/ produces a mouth opening on the order of 0.9 cm². For an open vowel such as /a/ an area of 5.0 cm² is representative. The radii of circular pistons with these areas are 0.5 cm and 1.3 cm, respectively. For frequencies less than about 5000 cps, these radii place ka less than unity. If the head is approximated as a sphere of 9 cm radius, the ratios of piston-to-sphere radii for the extreme areas are 0.06 and 0.1, respectively. For these dimensions and frequencies, therefore, the radiation load on the mouth is not badly approximated by considering it to be the load on a piston in an infinite wall. The approximation is even better for the nostrils whose radiating area is smaller. For higher frequencies and large mouth areas, the load is more precisely estimated from the piston-in-sphere relations. Notice, too, that approximating the normalized mouth-radiation load as that of a pulsating sphere leads to a radiation resistance that is about twice too high.

3.4. Spreading of Sound about the Head

In making acoustic analyses of the vocal tract one usually determines the volume current delivered to the radiation load at the mouth or nostrils. At these points the sound energy is radiated and spreads spatially. The sound is then received by the ear or by a microphone at some fixed point in space. It consequently is desirable to know the nature of the transmission from the mouth to the given point.

The preceding approximations for the radiation impedances do not necessarily imply how the sound spreads about the head. It is possible for changes in the baffling of a source to make large changes in the spatial distribution of sound and yet produce relatively small changes in the radiation load. For example, the piston-in-wall and piston-in-sphere were previously shown to be comparable assumptions for the radiation load. Sound radiated by the former is of course confined to the half-space, while that from the latter spreads spherically. The lobe structures are also spatially different.

One might expect that for frequencies where the wavelength is long compared with the head diameter, the head will not greatly influence the field. The spatial spreading of sound should be much like that produced by a simple spherical source of strength equal to the mouth volume velocity. At high frequencies, however, the diffraction about the head might be expected to influence the field.

A spherical source, pulsating sinusoidally, produces a particle velocity and sound pressure at r distance from its center equal respectively to

$$u(r) = \frac{a u_0}{r} \frac{jka}{1+jka} \frac{1+jkr}{jkr} e^{-jk(r-a)},$$

and

$$p(r) = \frac{\rho c a u_0}{r} \frac{jka}{1+jka} e^{-jk(r-a)}, \tag{3.39}$$

where a is the radius, u_0 is the velocity magnitude of the surface, and $k = \omega/c$. [Note the third factor in $u(r)$ accounts for the "bass-boost" that is obtained by talking close to a velocity microphone, a favorite artifice of nightclub singers.] If $ka \ll 1$, the source is a so-called simple (point) source, and the sound pressure is

$$p(r) = \frac{j\omega\rho U_0}{4\pi r} e^{-jkr},\qquad(3.40)$$

where $U_0 = 4\pi a^2 u_0$ is the source strength or volume velocity. The simple source therefore produces a sound pressure that has spherical symmetry and an amplitude that is proportional to $1/r$ and to ω.

MORSE has derived the pressure distribution in the far field of a small vibrating piston set in a spherical baffle. Assuming that the mouth and

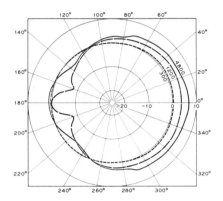

Fig. 3.7. Spatial distributions of sound pressure for a small piston in a sphere of 9 cm radius. Pressure is expressed in db relative to that produced by a simple spherical source of equal strength

head are approximately this configuration, with a 9 cm radius roughly appropriate for the sphere, the radiation pattern can be expressed relative to that which would be produced by a simple source of equal strength located at the same position. When this is done, the result is shown in Fig. 3.7. If the pressure field were identical to that of a simple spherical source, all the curves would fall on the zero db line of the polar plot. The patterns of Fig. 3.7 are symmetrical about the axis of the mouth (piston) which lies at zero degrees. One notices that on the mouth axis the high frequencies are emphasized slightly more than the $+6$ db/oct variation produced by the simple source (by about another $+2$ db/oct for frequencies greater than 300 cps). Also some lobing occurs, particularly at the rear of the "head".

The question can be raised as to how realistic is the spherical approximation of the real head. At least one series of measurements has been carried out to get a partial answer and to estimate spreading of sound about an average life-sized head (FLANAGAN, 1960a). A sound

Fig. 3.8. Life-size mannequin for measuring the relation between the mouth volume velocity and the sound pressure at an external point. The transducer is mounted in the mannequin's head

transducer was fitted into the head of the adult mannequin shown in Fig. 3.8. The transducer was calibrated to produce a known acoustic volume velocity at the lips of the dummy, and the amplitude and phase of the external pressure field were measured with a microphone. When the amplitudes are expressed relative to the levels which would be produced by a simple source of equal strength located at the mouth, the results for the horizontal and vertical planes through the mouth are shown in Fig. 3.9.

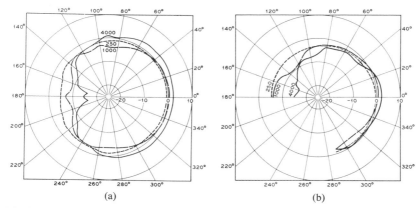

Fig. 3.9 a and b. Distribution of sound pressure about the head, relative to the distribution for a simple source; (a) horizontal distribution for the mannequin; (b) vertical distribution for the mannequin

One notices that for frequencies up to 4000 cps, the pressures within vertical and horizontal angles of about ± 60 degrees, centered on the mouth axis, differ from the simple source levels by no more than ± 3 db. Simultaneous phase measurements show that within this same solid angle, centered on the mouth axis, the phase is within approximately 30 degrees of that for the simple source. Within these limits, then, the function relating the volume velocity through the mouth to the sound pressure in front of the mouth can be approximated as the simple source function of Eq. (3.40). Notice that $p(r)/U_0 \sim \omega$, and the relation has a spectral zero at zero frequency.

3.5. The Source for Voiced Sounds

3.51. Glottal Excitation

The nature of the vocal tract excitation for voiced sounds has been indicated qualitatively in Figs. 2.1 through 2.4. It is possible to be more quantitative about this mechanism and to estimate some of the acoustical properties of the glottal sound source. (The glottis, as pointed out earlier, is the orifice between the vocal cords.) Such estimates are based mainly upon a knowledge of the subglottal pressure, the glottal dimensions, and the time function of glottal area.

The principal physiological components of concern are illustrated schematically in Fig. 3.10. The diagram represents a front view of the subglottal system. The dimensions are roughly appropriate for an adult male (JUDSON and WEAVER). In terms of an electrical network, this system might be thought analogous to the circuit shown in Fig. 3.11.

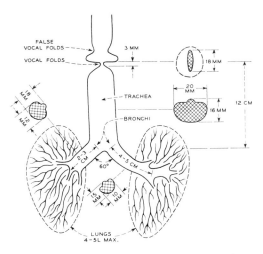

Fig. 3.10. Schematic diagram of the human subglottal system

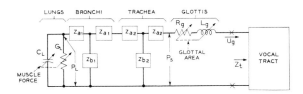

Fig. 3.11. An equivalent circuit for the subglottal system

A charge of air is drawn into the lungs and stored in their acoustic capacity C_L. The lungs are spongy tissues and exhibit an acoustic loss represented by the conductance G_L. The loss is a function of the state of inflation. The muscles of the rib cage apply force to the lungs, raise the lung pressure P_L, and cause air to be expelled – via the bronchi and trachea – through the relatively small vocal cord orifice. (Recall Fig. 3.1.) Because of their mass and elastic characteristics, the cords are set vibrating by the local pressure variations in the glottis. The quasi-periodic opening and closing of the cords varies the series impedance $(R_g + j\omega L_g)$ and modulates the air stream. The air passing into the vocal tract is therefore in the form of discrete puffs or pulses. As air is expelled, the rib-cage muscles contract and tend to maintain a constant lung pressure for a constant vocal effort. The lung capacity is therefore reduced so that the ratio of air charge to capacity remains roughly constant.

The bronchial and tracheal tubes — shown as equivalent T-sections in Fig. 3.11 — are relatively large so that the pressure drop across them is small[1]. The subglottal pressure P_s and the lung pressure P_L are therefore nearly the same. The variable-area glottal orifice is the time-varying impedance across which most of the subglottic pressure is expended. The subglottal potential is effectively converted into kinetic energy in the form of the glottal volume velocity pulses, U_g.

For frequencies less than a couple of thousand cps, the main component of the glottal impedance is the resistive term. For many purposes in vocal tract analysis, it is convenient to have a small-signal (ac) equivalent circuit of the glottal resistance; that is, a Thevenin equivalent of the circuit to the left of the X's in Fig. 3.11. Toward deducing such an equivalent, let us consider the nature of the time-varying glottal impedance and some typical characteristics of glottal area and volume flow.

3.52. Glottal Impedance

To make an initial estimate of the glottal impedance, assume first that the ratio of the glottal inertance to resistance is small compared to the period of area variation (that is, the L_g/R_g time constant is small compared with the fundamental period, T). We will show presently the conditions under which this assumption is tenable. For such a case, the glottal volume flow may be considered as a series of consecutively established steady states, and relations for steady flow through an orifice can be used to estimate the glottal resistance.

Flow through the vocal cord orifice in Fig. 3.10 can be approximated as steady, incompressible flow through the circular orifice shown in Fig. 3.12. The subglottal and supraglottal pressures are P_1 and P_2, respectively. The particle velocity in the port is u, the orifice area is A and its depth (thickness) is d. If the cross-sectional areas of the adjacent tubes are much larger than A, variations in P_1 and P_2 caused by the flow

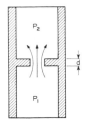

Fig. 3.12. Simple orifice approximation to the human glottis

---

[1] The branching bronchi are represented as a single tube having a cross-sectional area equal to the sum of the areas of the branches.

are small, and the pressures can be assumed sensibly constant. Also, if the dimensions of the orifice are small compared with the wavelength of an acoustic disturbance, and if the mean flow is much smaller than the speed of sound, an acoustic disturbance is known essentially instantaneously throughout the vicinity of the orifice, and incompressibility is a valid assumption. Further, let it be assumed that the velocity distribution over the port is uniform and that there is no viscous dissipation.

Under these conditions, the kinetic energy per-unit-volume possessed by the air in the orifice is developed by the pressure difference $(P_1 - P_2)$ and is

$$(P_1 - P_2) = \frac{\rho u^2}{2}. \tag{3.41}$$

The particle velocity is therefore

$$u = \left[\frac{2(P_1 - P_2)}{\rho} \right]^{\frac{1}{2}}. \tag{3.42}$$

We can define an orifice resistance, R_g^*, as the ratio of pressure drop to volume flow

$$R_g^* = \frac{\rho u}{2A} = \frac{\rho U}{2A^2}, \tag{3.43}$$

where $U = u \cdot A$ is the volume velocity. In practice, P_2 is essentially atmospheric pressure, so that $(P_1 - P_2) = P_s$, the excess subglottal pressure, and

$$R_g^* = \frac{(2\rho P_s)^{\frac{1}{2}}}{2A}. \tag{3.44}$$

In situations more nearly analogous to glottal operation, the assumptions of uniform velocity distribution across the orifice and negligible viscous losses are not good. The velocity profile is generally not uniform, and the streamlines are not straight and parallel. There is a contraction of the jet a short distance downstream where the distribution is uniform and the streamlines become parallel (vena contracta). The effect is to reduce the effective area of the orifice and to increase R_g^*. Also, the pressure-to-kinetic energy conversion is never accomplished without viscous loss, and the particle velocity is actually somewhat less than that given in (3.42). In fact, if the area and flow velocity are sufficiently small, the discharge is actually governed by viscous laws. This can certainly obtain in the glottis where the area of opening can go to zero. Therefore, an expression for orifice resistance — valid also for small velocities and areas — might, as a first approximation, be a linear combination of kinetic and viscous terms

$$R_g = R_v + k \left(\frac{\rho U}{2A^2} \right), \tag{3.45}$$

where R_v is a viscous resistance and k is a real constant. For steady laminar flow, R_v is proportional to the coefficient of viscosity and the length of the conducting passage, and is inversely proportional to a function of area.

To find approximations of the form (3.45), WEGEL and VAN DEN BERG et al. have made steady-flow measurements on models of the human larynx. Both investigations give empirical formulas which agree in order of magnitude. VAN DEN BERG'S data are somewhat more extensive and were made on plaster casts of a normal larynx. The glottis was idealized as a rectangular slit as shown in Fig. 3.13. The length, l, of the slit was maintained constant at 18 mm, and its depth, d, was

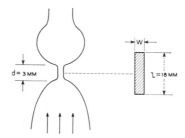

Fig. 3.13. Model of the human glottis. (After VAN DEN BERG et al.)

maintained at 3 mm. Changes in area were made by changing the width, w. Measurements on the model show the resistance to be approximately

$$R_g = \frac{P_s}{U} = \frac{12\mu d}{lw^3} + 0.875 \frac{\rho U}{2(lw)^2}, \qquad (3.46)$$

where μ is the coefficient of viscosity. According to VAN DEN BERG, (3.46) holds within ten per cent for $0.1 \leq w \leq 2.0$ mm, for $P_s \leq 64$ cm H_2O at small w, and for $U \leq 2000$ cc/sec at large w. As (3.46) implies, values of P_s and A specify the volume flow, U.

The glottal area is $A = lw$ so that the viscous (first) term of (3.46) is proportional to A^{-3}. The kinetic (second) term is proportional to uA^{-1} or, to the extent that u can be estimated from (3.42), it is approximately proportional to $P_s^{\frac{1}{2}} A^{-1}$. Whether the viscous or kinetic term predominates depends upon both A and P_s. They become approximately equal when $(\rho P_s)^{\frac{1}{2}} A^2 = 19.3 \ \mu d l^2$. For typical values of vocal P_s, this equality occurs for glottal areas which generally are just a fraction (usually less than $\frac{1}{5}$) of the maximum area. In other words, over most of the open cycle of the vocal cords the glottal resistance is determined by the second term in (3.46).

As pointed out previously, (3.46) is strictly valid only for steady flow conditions. A relevant question is to what extent might (3.46) be applied in computing the glottal flow as a function of time when $A(t)$ and P_s are known. The question is equivalent to inquiring into the influence of the inertance of the glottal air plug. Because the pressure drop across the bronchi and trachea is small, and because P_s is maintained sensibly constant over the duration of several pitch periods by the low-impedance lung reservoir[1], the circuit of Fig. 3.11 can, for the present purpose, be simplified to that shown in Fig. 3.14. Furthermore, it is possible to show that at most frequencies the driving point impedance of the vocal

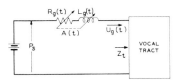

Fig. 3.14. Simplified circuit for the glottal source

tract, Z_t, is small compared with the glottal impedance. If the idealization $Z_t=0$ is made, then $U_g(t)$ satisfies

$$U_g(t) R_g(t) + \frac{d}{dt} [L_g(t) U_g(t)] = P_s, \qquad (3.47)$$

where Eq. (3.46) can be taken as the approximation to $R_g(t)$ and, neglecting end corrections, $L_g(t) = \rho d/A(t)$.

Because R_g is a flow-dependent quantity, Eq. (3.47) is a nonlinear, first-order differential equation with nonconstant coefficients. For an arbitrary $A(t)$, it is not easily integrated. However, a simplification in the area function provides some insight into the glottal flow. Consider that $A(t)$ is a step function so that

$$A(t) = A_0; \quad t \geq 0$$

$$= 0; \quad t < 0, \quad \text{and} \quad U_g(0) = 0.$$

Then dL_g/dt is zero for $t > 0$, and the circuit acts as a flow-dependent resistance in series with a constant inductance. A step of voltage (P_s) is applied at $t = 0$. The behavior of the circuit is therefore described by

$$\frac{dU_g}{dt} = \frac{1}{L_g} (P_s - R_g U_g). \qquad (3.48)$$

[1] VAN DEN BERG et al. estimate the variation to be less than five per cent of the mean subglottal pressure. P_s was measured by catheters inserted in the trachea and esophagus.

At $t=0$, $U_g(0)=0$ and

$$\frac{dU_g}{dt}\bigg|_{t=0}=\frac{P_s}{L_g},$$

so that initially

$$U_g(t)\cong\frac{P_s}{L_g}t \qquad \text{(for positive } t \text{ near zero)}.$$

Similarly, at $t=\infty$, $dU_g/dt=0$ and $U_g(\infty)=P_s/R_g$. The value of $U_g(\infty)$ is the steady-flow value which is conditioned solely by R_g. In this case U_g is the solution of $P_s-U_g R_g=0$, and is the positive root of a second-degree polynominal in U_g.

A time constant of a sort can be estimated from these asymptotic values of the flow build-up. Assume that the build-up continues at the initial rate, P_s/L_g, until the steady-state value $U_g(\infty)$ is achieved. The time, T, necessary to achieve the build-up is then

$$U_g(t)=\frac{P_s}{L_g}\,T=U_g(\infty)=\frac{P_s}{R_g},$$

or

$$T=\frac{L_g}{R_g}. \tag{3.49}$$

Since R_g is a sum of viscous and kinetic terms R_v and R_k, respectively, the time constant $L_g/(R_v+R_k)$ is smaller than the smaller of L_g/R_v and L_g/R_k. If the step function of area were small, R_v would dominate and the L_g/R_v time constant, which is proportional to A^2, would be more nearly appropriate. If the area step were large, the L_g/R_k constant would apply. In this case, and to the extent that R_v might be neglected [i.e., to the extent that R_g might be approximated as $R_k=0.875(2\rho P_s)^{\frac{1}{2}}/2A$], the L_g/R_k constant is proportional to $P_s^{-\frac{1}{2}}$ and is independent of A.

On the basis of these assumptions, a plot of the factors L_g/R_v and L_g/R_k is given in Fig. 3.15. Two values of P_s are shown for L_g/R_k, namely 4 cm H_2O and 16 cm H_2O. The first is about the minimum (liminal) intensity at which an adult male can utter a vowel. The latter corresponds to a fairly loud, usually high-pitched utterance. The value of L_g/R_g is therefore less than the solid curves of Fig. 3.15.

The curves of Fig. 3.15 show the greatest value of the time constant (i.e., for liminal subglottic pressure) to be of the order of a quarter millisecond. This time might be considered negligible compared with a fundamental vocal cord period an order of magnitude greater, that is, 2.5 msec. The latter corresponds to a fundamental vocal frequency of 400 cps which is above the average pitch range for a man's voice. To a first order approximation, therefore, the waveform of glottal volume velocity can be estimated from P_s and $A(t)$ simply by applying (3.46).

Notice also from the preceding results that for $L_g/R_g \cong 0.25$ msec (i.e., $P_s \cong 4$ cm H_2O) the inductive reactance becomes comparable to the resistance for frequencies between 600 and 700 cps. For $P_s = 16$ cm H_2O, the critical frequency is about doubled, to around 1 300 cps. This suggests that for frequencies generally greater than about 1 000 to 2 000 cps, the glottal impedance may exhibit a significant frequency-proportional term, and the spectrum of the glottal volume flow may reflect the influence of this factor.

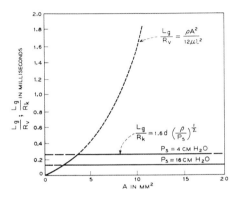

Fig. 3.15. Ratios of glottal inertance (L_g) to viscous and kinetic resistance (R_v, R_k) as a function of glottal area (A)

If the effects of inertance are neglected, a rough estimate of the glottal volume velocity can be made from the resistance expression (3.46). Assuming constant subglottal pressure, the corresponding volume velocity is seen to be proportional to A^3 at small glottal areas and to A at larger areas. Typical volume velocity waves deduced in this manner for a man are shown in Fig. 3.16 (FLANAGAN, 1958). The area waves are measured from high speed motion pictures of the glottis (see Fig. 2.3 in Chapter 2), and the subglottal pressure is estimated from the sound intensity and direct tracheal pressure measurements. The first condition is for the vowel /æ/ uttered at the lowest intensity and pitch possible. The second is for the same sound at a louder intensity and the same pitch. In the first case the glottis never completely closes. This is characteristic of weak, voiced utterances. Note that the viscous term in R_g operates to sharpen the leading and trailing edges of the velocity wave. This effect acts to increase the amplitude of the high-frequency components in the glottal spectrum.

The spectrum of the glottal volume flow is generally irregular and is characterized by numerous minima, or spectral zeros. For example,

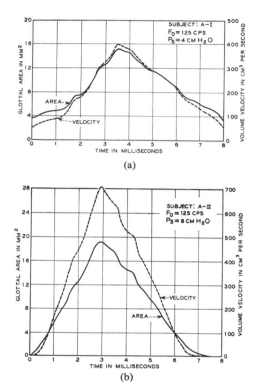

(a)

(b)

Fig. 3.16a and b. Glottal area and computed volume velocity waves for single vocal periods. F_0 is the fundamental frequency: P_s is the subglottal pressure. The subject is an adult male phonating /æ/. (After FLANAGAN, 1958)

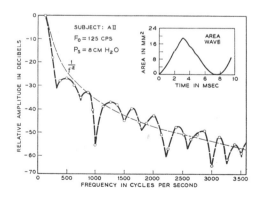

Fig. 3.17. Calculated amplitude spectrum for the glottal area wave AII shown in Fig. 3.16. (After FLANAGAN, 1961b)

if the wave in Fig. 3.16b were idealized as a symmetrical triangle, its spectrum would be of the form $(\sin x/x)^2$ with double-order spectral zeros occurring for $\omega = 4n\,\pi/\tau_0$, where n is an integer and τ_0 is the open time of the glottis. If the actual area wave of Fig. 3.16b is treated as periodic with period $1/125$ sec, and its Fourier spectrum computed (most conveniently on a digital computer), the result is shown in Fig. 3.17 (FLANAGAN, 1961b). The slight asymmetry of the area wave causes the spectral zeros to lie at complex frequencies, so that the spectral minima are neither equally spaced nor as pronounced as for the symmetrical triangle.

3.53. Small-Signal Equivalent Source for the Glottis

Considering only the resistance R_g, given in Eq. (3.46), it is possible to approximate an ac or small-signal equivalent source for the glottal source. Such a specification essentially permits the source impedance to be represented by a time-invariant quantity and is useful in performing vocal tract calculations. The Thevenin (or Norton) equivalent generator for the glottis can be obtained in the same manner that the ac equivalent circuit for an electronic amplifier is derived. According to (3.46)

$$U_g(t) = f(P_s, A).$$

The glottal volume velocity, area and subglottic pressure are unipolar time functions. Each has a varying component superposed upon a mean value. That is,

$$U_g(t) = U_{g0} + U'(t)$$

$$A(t) = A_0 + A'(t)$$

$$P_s(t) = P_{s0} + P'_s(t).$$

Expanding $U_g(t)$ as a Taylor series about (P_{s0}, A_0) and taking first terms gives

$$U_g(P_s, A) = U_g(P_{s0}, A_0) + \frac{\partial U_g}{\partial P_s}\bigg|_{P_{s0}, A_0}(P_s - P_{s0}) + \frac{\partial U_g}{\partial A}\bigg|_{P_{s0}, A_0}(A - A_0) + \cdots,$$

$$= U_{g0} + U'_g(t),$$

and

$$U'_g(t) = \frac{\partial U_g}{\partial P_s}\bigg|_{P_{s0}, A_0} P'_s + \frac{\partial U_g}{\partial A}\bigg|_{P_{s0}, A_0} A'(t). \tag{3.50}$$

One can interpret (3.50) as an ac volume velocity (current) source of value $\partial U_g/\partial A|_{P_{s0}, A_0} A'(t)$ with an inherent conductance $\partial U_g/\partial P_s|_{P_{s0}, A_0}$. The source delivers the ac volume current $U'_g(t)$ to its terminals. The source configuration is illustrated in Fig. 3.18. The instantaneous polarity of $P'_s(t)$ is reckoned as the pressure beneath the glottis relative to that above.

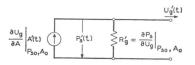

Fig. 3.18. Small-signal equivalent circuit for the glottal source. (After FLANAGAN, 1958)

The partials in (3.50) can be evaluated from (3.46). Let

$$R'_g = \frac{\partial P_s}{\partial U_g}\bigg|_{P_{s0}, A_0}.$$

Then

$$\frac{\partial P_s}{\partial U_g} = R_g + U_g \frac{\partial R_g}{\partial U_g},$$

and

$$R'_g = (R_v + 2R_k)_{P_{s0}, A_0}. \tag{3.51}$$

The magnitude of the equivalent velocity source is simply

$$\frac{\partial U_g}{\partial A}\bigg|_{P_{s0}, A_0} A'(t) = \left[u + A\frac{\partial u}{\partial A}\right]_{P_{s0}, A_0} A'(t).$$

Neglecting the viscous component of the resistance, Eq. (3.42) may be used to approximate u, in which case $\partial u/\partial A = 0$ and

$$\frac{\partial U_g}{\partial A}\bigg|_{P_{s0}, A_0} \cong \left(\frac{2P_{s0}}{\rho}\right)^{\frac{1}{2}} A'(t). \tag{3.52}$$

The approximations (3.51) and (3.52) therefore suggest that the ac resistance of the glottal source is equal the viscous (first) term of (3.46) plus twice the kinetic (second) term, and that the ac volume current source has a waveform similar to the time-varying component of $A(t)$. To consider a typical value of R'_g, take $P_{s0} = 10$ cm H_2O and $A_0 = 5$ mm^2. For these commonly encountered values R'_g is computed to be approximately 100 cgs acoustic ohms. This source impedance can be compared with typical values of the acoustic impedance looking into the vocal tract (i.e., the tract driving point impedance). Such a comparison affords an insight into whether the glottal source acts more nearly as a constant current (velocity) generator or a voltage (pressure) source.

The driving point impedance of the tract is highly dependent upon vocal configuration, but it can be easily estimated for the unconstricted shape. Consider the tract as a uniform pipe, 17 cm long and open at the far end. Assuming no nasal coupling, the tract is terminated only by the mouth radiation impedance. The situation is illustrated in Fig. 3.19.

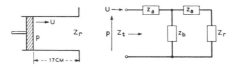

Fig. 3.19. Simplified representation of the impedance looking into the vocal tract at the glottis

Using the transmission line relations developed earlier in the chapter, the impedance Z_t looking into the straight pipe is

$$Z_t = Z_0 \frac{Z_r \cosh \gamma l + Z_0 \sinh \gamma l}{Z_0 \cosh \gamma l + Z_r \sinh \gamma l}, \qquad (3.53)$$

where $l = 17$ cm, and the other quantities have been previously defined. If for a rough estimate the pipe is considered lossless, $\gamma = j\beta$ and (3.53) can be written in circular functions

$$Z_t = Z_0 \frac{Z_r \cos \beta l + j Z_0 \sin \beta l}{Z_0 \cos \beta l + j Z_r \sin \beta l}, \qquad (3.54)$$

where $Z_0 = \rho c / A$, $\beta = \omega/c$. The maxima of Z_t will occur at frequencies where $l = (2n+1)\lambda/4$, so that $\beta l = (2n+1)\pi/2$ and $\cos \beta l = 0$. The maxima of Z_t for the lossless pipe are therefore

$$Z_{t_{\max}} = Z_0^2 / Z_r, \qquad (3.55)$$

and the pipe acts as a quarter-wave transformer. The minima, on the other hand, are $Z_{t_{\min}} = Z_r$ and the pipe acts as a half-wave transformer.

To estimate $Z_{t_{\max}}$, we can use the radiation impedance for the piston in the infinite baffle, developed earlier in the chapter [see Eq. (3.36)].

$$Z_r = z_p \frac{\rho c}{A} = \frac{\rho c}{A} \left[\frac{(ka)^2}{2} + j \frac{8}{3\pi} (ka) \right], \qquad (3.56)$$

where

$$a = \sqrt{A/\pi}, \quad \text{and} \quad ka \ll 1.$$

As a reasonable area for the unconstricted tract, take $A = 5$ cm^2. The first quarter-wave resonance for the 17 cm long pipe occurs at a frequency of about 500 cps. At this frequency

$$Z_r |_{500 \text{ cps}} = (0.18 + j0.81), \quad \text{and} \quad Z_{t_{\max}} |_{500 \text{ cps}} = \frac{(\rho c/A)^2}{Z_r} = 86 \underline{/-77^\circ}$$

cgs acoustic ohms. This driving point impedance is comparable in size to the ac equivalent resistance of the glottal source just determined.

As frequency increases, the magnitude of Z_r increases, and the load reflected to the glottis at the quarter-wave resonances becomes smaller.

At the second resonance, for example, $Z_r|_{1500\ cps} = (1.63 + j\,2.44)$ and $Z_{t_{max}}|_{1500\ cps} = 24\underline{/-56°}$ cgs acoustic ohms. The reflected impedance continues to diminish with frequency until at very high frequencies $Z_t = Z_0 = 8.4$ cgs acoustic ohms. Note, too, that at the half-wave resonances of the tract, i.e., $l = n\lambda/2$, the sine terms in (3.54) are zero and $Z_t = Z_r$.

The input impedance of the tract is greatest therefore at the frequency of the first quarter-wave resonance (which corresponds to the first formant). At and in the vicinity of this frequency, the driving point impedance (neglecting all losses except radiation) is comparable to the ac resistance of the glottal source. At all other frequencies it is less. For the unconstricted pipe the reflected impedance maxima are capacitive because the radiation load is inductive. To a first approximation, then, the glottal source appears as a constant volume velocity (current) source except at frequencies proximate to the first formant. As previously discussed, the equivalent vocal cord source sends an ac current equal to $u \cdot A'(t)$ into Z_t in parallel with R_g'. So long as constrictions do not become small, changes in the tract configuration generally do not greatly influence the operation of the vocal cords. At and near the frequency of the first formant, however, some interaction of source and tract might be expected, and in fact does occur. Pitch-synchronous variations in the tuning and the damping of the first formant — owing to significant tract-source interaction — can be observed experimentally[1].

3.6. The Source for Noise and Transient Excitation of the Tract

Our present knowledge of the mechanism and properties of noise and transient excitation of the vocal tract is considerably less than our understanding of voiced excitation. Not least among the reasons are the difficulties connected with direct measurement of the tract configuration, the size of constrictions, the spectral properties and inherent impedance of the source, and its spatial distribution. Noise excitation is generated by the air stream at a constriction. The resulting rotational flow and eddies produce a sound pressure which is largely random. The sound /ʃ/, for example, is produced by forcing air through the narrow constriction between the tongue and the roof of the mouth. Turbulent flow can also be generated by directing an air jet across an obstacle or sharp edge. The upper teeth serve this purpose in the production of

---

[1] The acoustic mechanism of vocal-cord vibration and the interactions between source and system are discussed in more detail later. An acoustic oscillator model of the cords is derived in Chapter VI and a computer simulation of the model is described.

dental fricatives such as /f/. One fricative consonant, /h/, is produced by turbulent flow generated at the glottis. The excitation mechanism is similar to that for the front-excited fricatives except the nonvibrating vocal cords create the constriction.

Stop consonants are produced by making a complete closure at an appropriate point (labial, dental or palatal), building up a pressure behind the occlusion, and sharply releasing the pressure by an abrupt opening of the constriction. This excitation is therefore similar to exciting an electrical network with a step function of voltage. The stop explosion is frequently followed by a fricative excitation. This latter element of the stop is similar to a brief fricative continuant of the same articulation.

Because it is spatially distributed, the location of the noise source in the tract is difficult to fix precisely. Generally it can be located at the constriction for a short closure, and just anterior to a longer constriction. In terms of a network representation, the noise source and its inherent impedance can be represented as the series elements in Fig. 3.20. P_s is the sound pressure generated by the turbulent flow and Z_s is the inherent impedance of the source. The series connection of the source can be qualitatively justified by noting that a shunt connection of a low-impedance pressure source would alter the mode structure of the vocal network. Furthermore, experimentally measured mode patterns for consonants appear to correspond to the series connection of the exciting source (FANT, 1960).

Although the spectral characteristics and inherent impedance of the noise source are not well known, estimates of these quantities can be made from a knowledge of the sound output and the tract configuration, and from measurements on tube models (HEINZ, 1958). Data obtained in this manner suggest that the spectrum is relatively flat in the mid-audio frequency range and that the source impedance is largely resistive. In fact, the relations for orifice resistance developed in the previous section appear to give reasonable estimates for the inherent impedance.

Voiced fricative sounds, such as /v/, are produced by simultaneous operation of the glottal and turbulent sources. Because the vibrating vocal cords cause a pulsive flow of air, the turbulent sound generated at the constriction is modulated by the glottal puffs. The turbulent sound is therefore generated as pitch-synchronous bursts of noise.

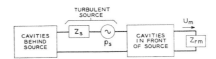

Fig. 3.20. Equivalent circuit for noise excitation of the vocal tract

It is possible to be a little more quantitative about several aspects of fricative and stop excitation. For example, MEYER-EPPLER (1953) has carried out measurements on fricative generation in constricted plastic tube models of the vocal tract. He has related these measurements to human production of the fricative consonants /f, s, ʃ/. For these vocal geometries a critical Reynold's number, R_{ec}, apparently exists below which negligible turbulent sound is produced. MEYER-EPPLER found that the magnitude of the noise sound pressure P_r — measured at a distance r from the mouth of either the model or the human — is approximately described by

$$P_r = K(R_e^2 - R_{ec}^2), \tag{3.57}$$

where K is a constant, R_e is the dimensionless Reynold's number $R_e = uw\rho/\mu$ and, as before, u is the particle velocity, ρ the air density, μ the coefficient of viscosity and w the effective width of the passage.

We recall from the earlier discussion [Eq. (3.41)] that for turbulent flow at a constriction the pressure drop across the orifice is approximately $P_d = \rho u^2/2 = \rho U^2/2A^2$. Therefore, $R_e^2 = 2\rho(w/\mu)^2 P_d$ and (3.57) can be written

$$P_r = (K_1 w^2 P_d - K_2); \quad P_r \geqq 0, \tag{3.58}$$

where K_1 and K_2 are constants. This result indicates that, above some threshold value, the fricative sound pressure in front of the mouth is proportional to the pressure drop at the constriction (essentially the excess pressure behind the occlusion) and to the square of the effective width of the passage.

By way of illustrating typical flow velocities associated with consonant production, a constriction area of 0.2 cm^2 and an excess pressure of 10 cm H$_2$O are not unusual for a fricative like /s/. The particle velocity corresponding to this pressure is $u = (2P_d/\rho)^{\frac{1}{2}} \cong 4100$ cm/sec[1] and the volume flow is $U \cong 820$ cm^3/sec.

If the constricted vocal passage is progressively opened and the width increased, a constant excess pressure can be maintained behind the constriction only at the expense of increased air flow. The flow must be proportional to the constriction area. The power associated with the flow is essentially $P_d U$ and hence also increases. Since the driving power is derived from the expiratory muscles, their power capabilities determine the maximum flow that can be produced for a given P_d. At some value of constriction area, a further increase in area, and consequently in w, is offset by a diminution of the P_d that can be maintained. The product $w^2 P_d$ in (3.58) then begins to decrease and so does the intensity of the fricative sound.

---

[1] Note this velocity is in excess of 0.1 Mach!

Voiceless stop consonants contrast with fricatives in that they are more transient. For strongly articulated stops, the glottis is held open so that the subglottal system contributes to the already substantial volume behind the closure (V_B). The respiratory muscles apply a force sufficient to build up the pressure, but do not contract appreciably to force air out during the stop release. The air flow during the initial part of the stop release is mainly turbulent, with laminar streaming obtaining as the flow decays. In voiced stops in word-initial position (for example /d, g/), voicing usually commences following the release, but often (for example, in /b/) can be initiated before the release.

In very crude terms, stop production can be considered analogous to the circuit of Fig. 3.21. The capacitor C_B is the compliance ($V_B/\rho c^2$)

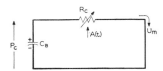

Fig. 3.21. Approximate vocal relations for stop consonant production

of the cavities back of the closure and is charged to the excess pressure P_c. The resistance R_c is that of the constriction and is, according to the previous discussion [Eq. (3.43)], approximately $R_c = \rho U_m/2A^2$. Suppose the constriction area is changed from zero as a step function, that is,

$$A(t)=0; \quad t<0$$
$$= A; \quad t\geq 0.$$

The mouth volume current then satisfies

$$U_m R_c + \frac{1}{C_B}\int_0^t U_m\,dt = P_c,$$

or

$$\frac{\rho U_m^2}{2A^2} + \frac{1}{C_B}\int_0^t U_m\,dt = P_c, \quad \text{for } U_m>0,$$

and the solution for positive values of U_m is

$$U_m(t) = \left(\frac{2P_c}{\rho}\right)^{\frac{1}{2}} A\left[1 - \frac{At}{C_B(\rho 2P_c)^{\frac{1}{2}}}\right]. \tag{3.59}$$

According to (3.59) the flow diminishes linearly with time during the initial phases of the stop release. At the indicated rate, the time to deplete the air charge would be

$$t_1 = \frac{C_B(\rho 2P_c)^{\frac{1}{2}}}{A}. \tag{3.60}$$

As the flow velocity becomes small, however, the tendency is toward laminar streaming, and the resistance becomes less velocity dependent [see first term in Eq. (3.46)]. The flow decay then becomes more nearly exponential[1].

---

[1] This can be seen exactly by letting R_c include a constant (viscous) term as well as a flow-dependent term. Although the differential equation is somewhat more complicated, the variables separate, and the solution can be written in terms of U_m and $\ln U_m$.

Let

$$R_c = r_v A^{-3}(t) + r_k A^{-2}(t)|U_m|,$$

where r_v and r_k are constants involving air density and viscosity [as described in Eq. (3.46)]. If the constriction area is changed stepwise from zero to A at time zero, the resulting flow will again be unipolar and now will satisfy

$$(r_k/A^2)\,U_m^2 + (r_v/A^3)\,U_m + 1/C_B \int_0^t U_m\,dt = P_C.$$

The variables in this equation are separable and the solution can be obtained by differentiating both sides with respect to time. This yields

$$\frac{r_v}{A^3}\left(\frac{dU_m}{dt}\right) + 2\frac{r_k}{A^2}U_m\frac{dU_m}{dt} + \frac{U_m}{C_B} = 0$$

and

$$\frac{r_v C_B}{A^3}\left(\frac{dU_m}{U_m}\right) + 2\frac{r_k C_B}{A^2}dU_m = -dt.$$

Integrating termwise gives

$$\frac{r_v C_B}{A^3}\ln U_m\Big]_0^t + 2\frac{r_k C_B}{A^2}U_m\Big]_0^t = -t.$$

At $t=0$, $U_m = U_0$, where U_0 is the positive real root of the quadratic

$$\left(\frac{r_k}{A^2}\right)U_0^2 + \frac{r_v}{A^3}U_0 - P_C = 0.$$

Then

$$\ln\left(\frac{U_m}{U_0}\right) + \frac{2r_k A}{r_v}(U_m - U_0) + \frac{tA^3}{r_v C_B} = 0.$$

Note

for A large: $U_m \approx \left[U_0 - \left(\frac{A^2}{2r_k C_B}\right)t\right]$

for A small: $U_m \approx U_0\,e^{-\left(\frac{A^3}{r_v C_B}\right)t}.$

It also follows that

$$\frac{dU_m}{dt} = \frac{-U_m}{\dfrac{r_v C_B}{A^3} + \dfrac{2r_k C_B}{A^2}U_m}$$

$$\approx \frac{-A^2}{2r_k C_B}, \text{ for large } A$$

$$\approx \frac{-U_m A^3}{r_v C_B}, \text{ for small } A.$$

To fix some typical values, consider the production of a voiceless stop such as /t/. According to FANT (1960), realistic parameters for articulation of this sound are $P_c = 6$ cm H_2O, $V_B = \rho c^2 C_B = 4$ liters (including lungs) and $A = 0.1$ cm^2. Assuming the area changes abruptly, substitution of these values into (3.59) and (3.60) gives $U_m(0) = 320$ cm^3/sec and $t_1 = 130$ msec. The particle velocity at the beginning of the linear decay is $u_m(0) = 3200$ cm/sec. After 50 msec it has fallen to the value 1300 cm/sec which is about the lower limit suggested by MEYER-EPPLER for noise generation. As FANT points out, the amount of air consumed during this time is quite small, on the order of 10 cm^3.

Both STEVENS (1956) and FANT (1960) emphasize the importance of the open glottis in the production of a strong stop consonant. A closed glottis reduces V_B to something less than 100 cm^3, and the excess pressure which can be produced behind the constriction is typically on the order of 3 cm H_2O. For such conditions is it difficult to produce flows sufficient for noise generation. The turbulent noise produced during the stop release is essentially a secondary effect of the excitation. The primary excitation is the impact of the suddenly applied pressure upon the vocal system. As mentioned earlier, this excitation for an abrupt area change is analogous to a step function of voltage applied to an electrical circuit. Such a source is characterized by a spectrum which is proportional to $1/\omega$, or diminishes in amplitude at -6 db/oct.

3.7. Some Characteristics of Vocal Tract Transmission

Some of the fundamental relations developed in the foregoing sections can now be used to put in evidence certain properties of vocal transmission. These characteristics are easiest demonstrated analytically by highly simplifying the tract geometry. Calculations on detailed approximations are more conveniently done with computers. Although our examples generally will be oversimplified, the extensions to more exact descriptions will in most cases be obvious.

As a first step, consider the transmission from glottis to mouth for nonnasal sounds. Further, as an ultimate simplification, consider that the tract is uniform in cross section over its whole length l, is terminated in a radiation load whose magnitude is negligible compared with the characteristic impedance of the tract, and is driven at the glottis from a volume-velocity source whose internal impedance is large compared to the tract input impedance. The simple diagram in Fig. 3.22 represents this situation. The transmission function relating the mouth and glottal volume currents is then

$$\frac{U_m}{U_g} = \frac{z_b}{z_b + z_a} = \frac{1}{\cosh \gamma l}. \tag{3.61}$$

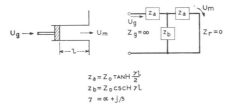

$$z_a = Z_0 \tanh \frac{\gamma l}{2}$$
$$z_b = Z_0 \operatorname{csch} \gamma l$$
$$\gamma = \alpha + j\beta$$

Fig. 3.22. Relation between glottal and mouth volume currents for the unconstricted tract. The glottal impedance is assumed infinite and the radiation impedance is zero

The normal modes (poles) of the transmission are the values of γl which make the denominator zero. These resonances produce spectral variations in the sound radiated from the mouth. They are

$$\cosh \gamma l = 0$$
$$\gamma l = \pm j(2n+1)\frac{\pi}{2}, \quad n = 0, 1, 2, \ldots. \tag{3.62}$$

The poles therefore occur at complex values of frequency. Letting $j\omega = \sigma + j\omega = s$, the complex frequency, and recalling from (3.8) that $\gamma = \alpha + j\beta$ and $\beta \cong \omega/c$ for small losses, the complex pole frequencies may be approximated as

$$s_n \cong -\alpha c \pm j \frac{(2n+1)\pi c}{2l}, \quad n = 0, 1, 2, \ldots [1]. \tag{3.63}$$

The transmission (3.61) can be represented in factored form in terms of the roots of the denominator, namely

$$II(s) = \frac{U_m(s)}{U_g(s)} = \prod_n \frac{s_n s_n^*}{(s - s_n)(s - s_n^*)}, \tag{3.64}$$

where s_n^* is the complex conjugate of s_n, and the numerator is set to satisfy the condition

$$\left. \frac{U_m(j\omega)}{U_g(j\omega)} \right|_{j\omega=0} = \frac{1}{\cosh \alpha l} \cong 1,$$

for small α. The transmission is therefore characterized by an infinite number of complex conjugate poles[2]. The manifestations of these normal modes as spectral peaks in the output sound are called *formants*. The

---

[1] Actually α is an implicit function of ω [see Eq. (3.33)]. However, since its frequency dependence is relatively small, and since usually $\sigma_n \ll \omega_n$, the approximation (3.63) is a convenient one.

[2] Rigorous justification of the form (3.64) has its basis in function theory (TITCHMARSH; AHLFORS). See Chapter VI, Sec. 6.22 for further discussion of this point.

transmission (3.64) exhibits no zeros at finite frequencies. Maxima occur in

$$|H(j\omega)| \quad \text{for } \omega = \pm(2n+1)\frac{\pi}{2}\frac{c}{l},$$

and the resonances have half-power cps bandwidths approximately equal to $\Delta f = \sigma/\pi = \alpha c/\pi$. For an adult male vocal tract, approximately 17 cm in length, the unconstricted resonant frequencies therefore fall at about $f_1 = 500$ cps, $f_2 = 1\,500$ cps, $f_3 = 2\,500$ cps, and continue in $c/2l$ increments.

In the present illustration the only losses taken into account are the classical heat conduction and viscous losses discussed earlier. A calculation of formant bandwidth on this basis alone will consequently be abnormally low. It is nevertheless instructive to note this contribution to the formant damping. Recall from Eq. (3.8) that for small losses

$$\alpha \cong \frac{R_a}{2}\sqrt{\frac{C_a}{L_a}} + \frac{G_a}{2}\sqrt{\frac{L_a}{C_a}},$$

where R_a, G_a, L_a and C_a have been given previously in Section (3.25). At the first-formant frequency for the unconstricted tract (i.e., 500 cps), and assuming a circular cross-section with typical area 5 cm², α is computed to be approximately 5.2×10^{-4}, giving a first-formant bandwidth $\Delta f_1 = 6$ cps. At the second formant frequency (i.e., 1\,500 cps) the same computation gives $\Delta f_2 = 10$ cps. The losses increase as $f^{\frac{1}{2}}$, and at the third formant (2\,500 cps) give $\Delta f_3 = 13$ cps.

It is also apparent from (3.64) that $H(s)$ is a minimum phase function (that is, it has all of its zeros, namely none, in the left half of the s-plane) so that its amplitude and phase responses are uniquely linked (that is, they are Hilbert transforms). Further, the function is completely specified by the s_n's, so that the frequency *and* amplitude of a formant peak in $|H(j\omega)|$ are uniquely described by the pole frequencies. In particular if the formant damping can be considered known and constant, then the amplitudes of the resonant peaks of $|H(j\omega)|$ are implicit in the imaginary parts of the formant frequencies $\omega_1, \omega_2, \ldots$, (FANT, 1956; FLANAGAN, 1957c). In fact, it follows from (3.61) that

$$|H(j\omega)|_{\omega=\omega_n} = \frac{1}{|\cosh(\alpha+j\beta)l|_{\omega=\omega_n}}$$

$$= \frac{1}{|j\sinh \alpha l|} \tag{3.65}$$

$$\cong \frac{1}{\alpha l},$$

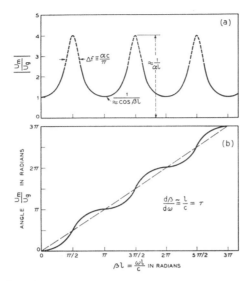

Fig. 3.23. Magnitude and phase of the glottis-to-mouth transmission for the vocal tract approximation shown in Fig. 3.22

where $\beta = \omega/c$ and $\omega_n = (2n+1)\,\pi c/2l$. Notice, too, that the phase angle of $H(j\omega)$ advances π radians in passing a formant frequency ω_n so the amplitude and phase response of $H(j\omega)$ appear as in Fig. 3.23. In the same connection, note that for the completely lossless case

$$H(j\omega) = \frac{1}{\cos\dfrac{\omega l}{c}}.$$

3.71. Effect of Radiation Load upon Mode Pattern

If the radiation load on the open end of the tube is taken into account, the equivalent circuit for the tube becomes that shown in Fig. 3.24. Here A_t is the cross-sectional area of the tract and A_m is the radiating area of the mouth with equivalent radius a_m. The thickness of the mouth constriction is assumed negligible, the glottal impedance is high, and

Fig. 3.24. Equivalent circuit for the unconstricted vocal tract taking into account the radiation load. The glottal impedance is assumed infinite

cross dimensions are small compared with a wavelength. The transmission from glottis to mouth is therefore

$$\frac{U_m}{U_g} = \frac{1}{\cosh \gamma l + \dfrac{Z_r}{Z_0} \sinh \gamma l},$$

or, more conveniently,

$$\frac{U_m}{U_g} = \frac{\cosh \gamma_r l}{\cosh(\gamma + \gamma_r)l}, \tag{3.66}$$

where $\gamma_r l = \tanh^{-1} Z_r/Z_0$. Note that for $Z_r \ll Z_0$, $\cosh \gamma_r l \cong 1$ and for low loss $Z_0 \cong \rho c/A_t$.

By the transformation (3.66), the radiation impedance is carried into the propagation constant, so that

$$(\gamma + \gamma_r) = \left[\alpha + j\beta + \frac{1}{l} \tan^{-1} \frac{Z_r}{Z_0} \right]$$

$$= (\alpha + j\beta + \alpha_r + j\beta_r) = (\alpha' + j\beta') = \gamma'.$$

If the radiation load is taken as that on a piston in a wall [see Eq. (3.36) in Sec. 3.3] then

$$Z_r \cong \frac{\rho c}{A_m} \left[\frac{(ka)^2}{2} + j\frac{8ka}{3\pi} \right], \qquad ka \ll 1, \tag{3.67}$$

where a equals the mouth radius a_m. Expanding $\tanh^{-1} Z_r/Z_0$ as a series and taking only the first term (i.e., assuming $Z_r \ll Z_0$) gives

$$\gamma_r \cong \frac{1}{l} \frac{A_t}{A_m} \left[\frac{(ka)^2}{2} + j\frac{8ka}{3\pi} \right] \tag{3.68}$$

$$= \alpha_r + j\beta_r.$$

For low loss $\beta \cong \omega/c = k$, so that

$$(\alpha' + j\beta') = \left[\alpha + \frac{A_t}{A_m} \frac{(\beta a)^2}{2l} \right] + j\beta \left[1 + \frac{A_t}{A_m} \frac{8a}{3\pi l} \right]. \tag{3.69}$$

Again the poles of (3.66) occur for

$$e^{2\gamma' l} + 1 = 0$$

or

$$\gamma' = \pm j\frac{(2n+1)\pi}{2l}, \qquad n = 0, 1, 2, \dots. \tag{3.70}$$

Letting $j\omega \to s = (\sigma + j\omega)$, and remembering that in general $\sigma_n \ll \omega_n$, the poles are approximately

$$s_{nr} \cong \frac{1}{1 + \dfrac{A_t 8a}{A_m 3\pi l}} \left[-\left(\alpha c + \frac{A_t \omega^2}{2\pi l c}\right) \pm j \frac{(2n+1)\pi c}{2l} \right], \tag{3.71}$$

$$n = 0, 1, 2, \ldots \qquad (Z_r \ll Z_0).$$

The general effect of the radiation, therefore, is to decrease the magnitude of the imaginary parts of the pole frequencies and to make their real parts more negative.

For the special case $A_m = A_t$, the modes are

$$s_{nr} \cong \left(\frac{3\pi l}{3\pi l + 8a}\right) \left[-\left(\alpha c + \frac{a^2 \omega^2}{2lc}\right) \pm j \frac{(2n+1)\pi c}{2l} \right]. \tag{3.72}$$

Using the values of the example in the previous section, $A_t = 5$ cm^2, $l = 17$ cm, the spectral resonances (formants) are lowered in frequency by the multiplying factor $3\pi l/(3\pi l + 8a) = 0.94$. The original 500 cps first formant is lowered to 470 cps, and the 1 500 cps second formant is lowered to 1 410 cps. The first formant bandwidth is increased to about $\Delta f_1 \cong 0.94(6+4) = 9$ cps, and the second formant bandwidth to about $\Delta f_2 \cong 0.94(10+32) = 40$ cps. The same computation for the third formant gives $\Delta f_3 \cong 100$ cps. The latter figures begin to be representative of formant bandwidths measured on real vocal tracts with the glottis closed (HOUSE and STEVENS, 1958; DUNN, 1961; VAN DEN BERG, 1955). The contributions of the radiation, viscous and heat losses to Δf_1 are seen to be relatively small. Glottal loss and cavity wall vibration generally are more important contributors to the first formant damping.

As (3.72) indicates, the contribution of the radiation resistance to the formant damping increases as the square of frequency, while the classical heat conduction and viscous loss cause α to grow as $\omega^{\frac{1}{2}}$. The radiation reactance is inertive and causes the formant frequencies to be lowered. For $A_m = A_t$, Eq. (3.71) shows that the radiation reactance has the same effect as lengthening the vocal tract by an amount $(8a/3\pi)$.

3.72. Effect of Glottal Impedance upon Mode Pattern

The effect of the equivalent glottal impedance can be considered in much the same manner as the radiation load. To keep the illustration simple, again assume the radiation load to be negligible compared with the characteristic impedance of the uniform tract, but take the glottal impedance as finite. This situation is depicted by Fig. 3.25. Similar to

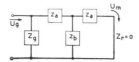

Fig. 3.25. Equivalent circuit for the unconstricted vocal tract assuming the glottal impedance to be finite and the radiation impedance to be zero

the previous instance, the volume velocity transmission function can be put in the form

$$\frac{U_m}{U_g} = \frac{1}{\dfrac{z_a}{Z_g}\left(\dfrac{Z_g}{z_b}+\dfrac{z_a}{z_b}+1\right)+1+\dfrac{z_a}{Z_g}}$$

$$= \frac{1}{\cosh \gamma\, l + \dfrac{Z_0}{Z_g}\sinh \gamma\, l} \qquad (3.73)$$

$$= \frac{\cosh \gamma_g\, l}{\cosh(\gamma+\gamma_g)\, l} ,$$

where $\gamma_g l = \tanh^{-1} Z_0/Z_g$, and the glottal impedance is transformed into the propagation constant. Again taking the first term of the series expansion for $\tanh^{-1} Z_0/Z_g$ (i.e., assuming $Z_g \gg Z_0$) gives

$$(\gamma+\gamma_g) \cong \left(\alpha+j\beta+\frac{1}{l}\,\frac{Z_0}{Z_g}\right).$$

The equivalent glottal impedance may be approximated as $Z_g = (R'_g+j\omega L_g)$, where R'_g is the ac equivalent resistance determined previously in Eq. (3.51), and L_g is the effective inductance of the glottal port. The zeros of the denominator of (3.73) are the poles of the transmission, and an argument similar to that used in the preceding section for low losses ($Z_0 \cong \rho c/A_t$, $\beta \cong \omega/c$) leads to

$$s_{ng} \cong \frac{1}{1-\left(\dfrac{L_g Z_0 c}{l\,|Z_g|^2}\right)}\left\{-\left(\alpha c+\frac{R'_g Z_0 c}{l\,|Z_g|^2}\right)\pm j\,\frac{(2n+1)\pi c}{2l}\right\}. \qquad (3.74)$$

According to (3.74), the effect of the finite glottal impedance is to increase the damping of the formant resonances (owing to the glottal loss R'_g) and to increase the formant frequencies by the factor multiplying the bracketed term (owing to the glottal inductance). A sample calculation of the effect can be made. As typical values, take a subglottic pressure (P_s) of 8 cm H_2O, a mean glottal area (A_0) of 5 mm², a glottal orifice thickness (d) of 3 mm, a vocal tract area (A_t) of 5 cm² and a tract length (l) of 17 cm. For these conditions the glottal resistance, computed according to Eq. (3.51), is $R'_g \cong 91$ cgs acoustic ohms. The glottal inductance is $L_g = \sigma d/A_0 = 6.8 \times 10^{-3}$ cgs units. At about the frequency of the first formant, that is, $\omega \cong \pi c/2l = 2\pi$ (500 cps), the multiplying factor has a value $1/(1-0.014)$, so that the first formant resonance is increased from its value for the infinite glottal impedance condition by about 1.4%. The effect of the glottal inductance upon formant tuning is greatest for the lowest formant because $|Z_g|$ increases with frequency. The same computation for the second formant (≈ 1500 cps) shows the multiplying factor to be $1/(1-0.010)$. One notices also that the effect of the multiplying term is to shorten the apparent length of the tract to

$$\left(1 - \frac{L_g Z_0 c}{|Z_g|^2}\right).$$

The resonant bandwidth for the first formant is computed to be

$$\Delta f_1 = \frac{1}{(1-0.014)} [6 \text{ cps} + 56 \text{ cps}] = 63 \text{ cps},$$

which is reasonably representative of first formant bandwidths measured in real speech. The contribution of the glottal loss R'_g to formant damping is greatest for the lowest formant. It diminishes with increasing frequency because $|Z_g|$ grows with frequency. At the second formant frequency, the same calculation gives $\Delta f_2 = (1/1-0.010)$ (10 cps + 40 cps) = 51 cps. One recalls, too, that the heat conduction and viscous losses (which specify α) increase as $\omega^{\frac{1}{2}}$, while the radiation loss increases as ω^2 (for $ka \ll 1$). The lower-formant damping is therefore influenced more by glottal loss, and the higher-formant damping is influenced more by radiation loss.

In this same connection, one is reminded that the glottal resistance and inductance (used here as equivalent constant quantities) are actually time varying. There is consequently a pitch-synchronous modulation of the pole frequencies s_{ng} given in (3.74). That is, as the vocal cords open, the damping and resonant frequency of a formant increase, so that with each glottal period the pole frequency traverses a small locus in the complex-frequency plane. This pitch-synchronous change in formant damping and tuning can often be observed experimentally, particularly in inverse filtering of formants. It is most pronounced for the first formant.

3.73. Effect of Cavity Wall Vibration

The previous discussion has assumed the walls of the vocal tract to be smooth and rigid. The dissipative elements of concern are then the radiation resistance, the glottal resistance, and the viscous and heat

conduction losses at the cavity walls. The human vocal tract is of course
not hard-walled, and its surface impedance is not infinite. The yielding
walls can consequently contribute to the energy loss in the tract and can
influence the mode tuning. We would like to estimate this effect.

The finite impedance of the tract wall constitutes an additional
shunt path in the equivalent "T" (or π) section for the pipe (see Fig. 3.3).
Because the flesh surrounding the tract is relatively massive and exhibits viscous loss, the additional shunt admittance for the frequency
range of interest (i.e., speech frequencies) can be approximated as a
per-unit-length reciprocal inductance or inertance ($\Gamma_w = 1/L_w$) and a
per-unit-length conductance ($G_w = 1/R_w$) in parallel[1]. The modified equivalent "T" section is shown in Fig. 3.26.

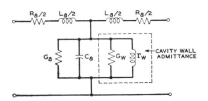

Fig. 3.26. Representation of wall impedance in the equivalent T-section for a length l of
uniform pipe

Let us note the effect of the additional shunt admittance upon the
propagation constant for the tube. As before, the basic assumption is
that a plane wave is propagating in the pipe and that the sound pressure
at any cross section is uniform and cophasic. Recall that

$$\gamma = \alpha + j\beta = \sqrt{yz},$$

where y and z are the per-unit-length shunt admittance and series impedance, respectively. The latter quantities are now

$$z = (R_a + j\omega L_a)$$

$$y = (G_a + G_w) + j\left(\omega C_a - \frac{\Gamma_w}{\omega}\right). \tag{3.75}$$

Again, most conditions of interest will be relatively small-loss situations
for which

$$R_a \ll \omega L_a$$

and

$$(G_a + G_w) \ll \left(\omega C_a - \frac{\Gamma_w}{\omega} \right).$$

Also, in general, the susceptance of the air volume will exceed that of the walls and $\omega C_a \gg \Gamma_w / \omega$. Following the earlier discussion [see Eq. (3.8)] the attenuation constant for this situation can be approximated by

$$\alpha \cong \frac{1}{2} R_a \sqrt{\frac{C_a}{L_a}} + \frac{1}{2} (G_a + G_w) \sqrt{\frac{L_a}{C_a}}. \tag{3.76}$$

In a like manner, the phase constant is given approximately by

$$\beta \cong \omega \sqrt{L_a \left(C_a - \frac{\Gamma_w}{\omega^2} \right)} = \frac{\omega}{c'}. \tag{3.77}$$

The effective sound velocity c' in a pipe with "massive" walls − that is, with negative susceptance − is therefore faster than for free space. The pipe appears shorter and the resonant frequencies are shifted upward. The effect is greatest for the lower frequencies. The same result can be obtained more elegantly in terms of specific wall admittance by writing the wave equation for the cylindrical pipe, noting the radial symmetry and fitting the boundary impedance conditions at the walls (MORSE). In addition to the plane-wave solution, the latter formulation also gives the higher cylindrical modes.

Results (3.76) and (3.77) therefore show that vibration of the cavity wall contributes an additive component to the attenuation constant, and when the wall is predominantly mass-reactive, its effect is to diminish the phase constant or increase the speed of sound propagation. Following the previous technique [see Eq. (3.63)], the natural modes for a uniform tube of this sort are given by

$$s_{nw} = \left[-\alpha c' \pm j \frac{(2n+1)\pi c'}{2l} \right] \tag{3.78}$$

$$= (\sigma_{nw} + j\omega_{nw}); \quad n = 0, 1, 2, \ldots.$$

To calculate the shunting effect of the walls in the real vocal tract, it is necessary to have some knowledge of the mechanical impedance of the cavity walls. Such measurements are obviously difficult and apparently have not been made. An order-of-magnitude estimate can be made, however, by using mechanical impedance values obtained for other surfaces of the body. At best, such measurements are variable, and the impedance can change appreciably with place. The data do, however, permit us to make some very rough calculations.

One set of measurements (FRANKE) has been made for chest, thigh and stomach tissues, and these have been applied previously to estimate the wall effect (HOUSE and STEVENS, 1958). For frequencies above about 100 cps, the fleshy areas exhibit resistive and mass reactive components. The specific impedances fall roughly in the range 4000–7000 dyne-sec/cm³. A typical measurement on the stomach surface gives a specific impedance that is approximately

$$z_s = (r_s + j x_s) = (r_s + j \omega l_s)$$

$$= (6500 + j \omega 0.4),$$

(3.79)

for $(2\pi \cdot 200) \leq \omega \leq (2\pi \cdot 1000)$.

This specific series impedance can be put in terms of equivalent parallel resistance and inductance by

$$r_p = \frac{r_s^2 + x_s^2}{r_s} \quad \text{and} \quad j x_p = j \frac{r_s^2 + x_s^2}{x_s}.$$

These specific values (per-unit-area) can be put in terms of per-unit-length of tube by dividing by S, the inner circumference, to give

$$R_w = \frac{r_s^2 + x_s^2}{r_s S} \quad \text{and} \quad j X_w = j \frac{r_s^2 + x_s^2}{x_s S}.$$

Therefore,

$$G_w = \frac{r_s S}{r_s^2 + x_s^2} \quad \text{and} \quad -j \frac{\Gamma_w}{\omega} = -j \frac{\omega l_s S}{r_s^2 + x_s^2},$$

where,

$$\Gamma_w = \frac{\omega^2 l_s S}{r_s^2 + x_s^2}.$$

(3.80)

Assuming the vocal tract to be unconstricted and to have a uniform cross-sectional area of 5 cm² (i.e., $S = 7.9$ cm), we can compute the effect of the wall admittance upon the propagation constant, the formant bandwidth and formant frequency. According to (3.76) and (3.77), the wall's contribution to α and β is

$$\alpha_w \cong \frac{G_w}{2} \sqrt{\frac{L_a}{C_a}},$$

and

$$\beta_w \cong \omega \sqrt{L_a \left(C_a - \frac{l_s S}{r_s^2 + x_s^2} \right)}$$

$$\cong \frac{\omega}{c} \left[1 - \frac{\rho c^2 l_s}{a (r_s^2 + x_s^2)} \right],$$

(3.81)

where the radius of the tube is $a = \sqrt{A/\pi}$, and the bracketed expression is the first two terms in the binomial expansion of the radical.

Substituting the measured values of r_s and l_s and computing α_w, β_w and formant bandwidths at approximately the first three formant frequencies gives[1]

Frequency	α_w	β_w	$\Delta f_w = \dfrac{\alpha_w c'}{\pi}$
500 cps	4.7×10^{-3}	$\dfrac{\omega}{c}(1 - 0.011)$	50 cps
1 500 cps	3.6×10^{-3}	$\dfrac{\omega}{c}(1 - 0.008)$	40 cps
2 500 cps	2.5×10^{-3}	$\dfrac{\omega}{c}(1 - 0.006)$	30 cps

[1] Using $c = 3.5 \times 10^4$ cm/sec and $\rho = 1.14 \times 10^{-3}$ gm/cm^3.

The contribution of wall loss to the formant bandwidth is therefore greatest at the lowest formant frequency and diminishes with increasing formant frequency. These computed values, however, when combined with the previous loss contributions actually seem somewhat large. They suggest that the walls of the vocal tract are more rigid than the stomach tissue from which the mechanical impedance estimates were made.

The increase in formant tuning, occasioned by the mass reactance of the cavity walls, is seen to be rather slight. It is of the order of one per cent for the lower formants and, like the damping, diminishes with increasing frequency.

3.74. Two-Tube Approximation of the Vocal Tract

The previous sections utilized a uniform-tube approximation of the vocal tract to put in evidence certain properties. The uniform tube, which displays modes equally spaced in frequency, comes close to a realistic vocal configuration only for the unconstricted schwa sound /ə/. Better insight into the interaction of vocal cavities can be gained by complicating the approximation one step further; namely, by approximating the tract as two uniform, cascaded tubes of different cross section. To keep the discussion tractable and focused mainly upon the transmission properties of the tubes, we again assume the glottal impedance to be high compared with the input impedance of the tract, and the radiation load to be negligible compared with the impedance level at the mouth. This situation is represented in Fig. 3.27.

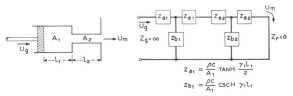

$$z_{a1} = \frac{\rho c}{A_1} \text{ TANH } \frac{\gamma_1 l_1}{2}$$

$$z_{b1} = \frac{\rho c}{A_1} \text{ CSCH } \gamma_1 l_1$$

Fig. 3.27. Two-tube approximation to the vocal tract. The glottal impedance is assumed infinite and the radiation impedance zero

For the circuit shown in Fig. 3.27, the mouth-to-glottis volume current ratio is

$$\frac{U_m}{U_g} = \frac{1}{\left(1 + \dfrac{z_{a2}}{z_{b2}}\right)\left(1 + \dfrac{z_{a1}}{z_{b1}} + \dfrac{z_{a2}}{z_{b1}}\right) + \dfrac{z_{a2}}{z_{b1}}},$$

which reduces to

$$\frac{U_m}{U_g} = \frac{1}{(\cosh \gamma_1 l_1)(\cosh \gamma_2 l_2)\left(1 + \dfrac{A_1}{A_2} \tanh \gamma_1 l_1 \tanh \gamma_2 l_2\right)} . \qquad (3.82)$$

The poles of (3.82) occur for

$$\frac{A_1}{A_2} \tanh \gamma_2 l_2 = -\coth \gamma_1 l_1 . \qquad (3.83)$$

If the tubes are lossless, the hyperbolic functions reduce to circular functions and all impedances are pure reactances. The normal modes then satisfy

$$\frac{A_1}{A_2} \tan \beta l_2 = \cot \beta l_1 . \qquad (3.84)$$

Because the vocal tract is relatively low loss, Eq. (3.84) provides a simple means for examining the mode pattern of the two-tube approximation. For example, consider the approximations shown in Fig. 3.28 to the articulatory configurations for four different vowels. The reactance functions of (3.84) are plotted for each case, and the pole frequencies are indicated.

One notices that the high front vowel /i/ exhibits the most disparate first and second formants, while the low back vowel /a/ gives rise to the most proximate first and second formants. The neutral vowel /ə/, corresponding to the unconstricted tract, yields formants uniformly spaced 1000 cps apart. The reactance plots also show that increasing the area ratio (A_1/A_2) of the back-to-front cavities results in a decrease of the first formant frequency. On the classical $F1$ vs $F2$ plot, the first two

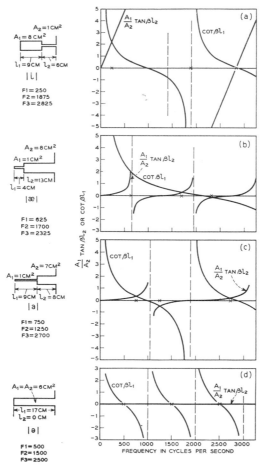

Fig. 3.28 a–d. Two-tube approximations to the vowels /i, æ, a, ə/ and their undamped mode (formant) patterns

modes for the four approximations fall as shown in Fig. 3.29. The unconstricted /ə/ sound occupies the central position. For comparison, formant data for four vowels — as spoken by adult males — are also plotted (PETERSON and BARNEY)[1]. The lower left corner of the classical

[1] Most of the vocal tract dimensions used to illustrate acoustic relations in this chapter are appropriate to adult males. Women and children have smaller vocal apparatus. Since the frequencies of the resonant modes are inversely related to the tract length, the vowel formants for women and children are higher than for the men. According to CHIBA and KAJIYAMA, the young adult female vocal tract is 0.87 as long as the young adult male. The female formants, therefore, should be about 15% higher than those of the male. This situation is also reflected in the measurements of PETERSON and BARNEY.

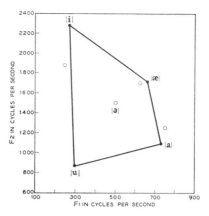

Fig. 3.29. First formant (F 1) versus second formant (F 2) for several vowels. Solid points are averages from PETERSON and BARNEY's data for real speech uttered by adult males. Circles are for the two-tube approximation to the vowels shown in Fig. 3.28

vowel plot, the area appropriate to the vowel /u/, has been indicated for completeness. Because of lip rounding, however, the vowel /u/ cannot be approximated in terms of only two tubes.

Eq. (3.84) also makes salient an aspect of compensatory articulation. The mode pattern for $l_1 = a$, $l_2 = b$, is exactly the same as for $l_1 = b$, $l_2 = a$. In other words, so long as the area ratio for the back and front cavities is maintained the same, their lengths may be interchanged without altering the formant frquencies. This is exactly true for the idealized lossless tubes, and is approximately so for practical values of loss. This interchangeability is one freedom available to the ventriloquist. It is also clear from (3.84) that if $l_1 = 2l_2$, the infinite values of cot βl_1 and tan βl_2 are coincident (at $\beta l_2 = \pi/2$) and indicate the second mode. The second formant frequency can therefore be maintained constant by keeping the tube lengths in the ratio of $2:1$. The same constancy applies to the third formant if the length ratio is maintained at $3:2$.

3.75. Excitation by Source Forward in Tract

As pointed out earlier, fricative sounds (except for /h/) are excited by a series pressure source applied at a point forward in the tract. It is pertinent to consider the mouth volume velocity which such an excitation produces.

A previous section showed that for glottal excitation the maxima of glottis-to-mouth transmission occurred at the natural (pole) frequencies of the vocal system, and the transmission exhibited no zeros. If excitation is applied at some other point in the system, without altering the network, the normal modes of the response remain the same. The transmission can, however, exhibit zeros. For the series excitation these zeros must occur at frequencies where the impedance looking back from the source (toward the glottis) is infinite.

By way of illustration let us retain the simple two-tube model used previously. Because the turbulent source for voiceless sound is spatially distributed, its exact point of application is difficult to fix. Generally it can be thought to be applied either at or just forward of the point of greatest constriction. The former seems to be more nearly the case for sounds like /ʃ, f, p, k/; the latter for /s, t/. Consider first the case where the source is forward of the constriction. The two-tube circuit is shown in Fig. 3.30. The back cavity is shown closed, and the impedance of the glottis and larynx tube is considered to be high (compared

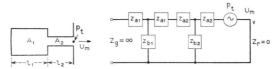

Fig. 3.30. Two-tube approximation to the vocal tract with excitation applied forward of the constriction

to the impedance level of the back cavity) even though the glottis may be open. The radiation impedance is again considered small compared with the impedance level at the mouth, and the inherent impedance of the source *per se* is considered small.

The complex frequency (LAPLACE) transform of the transmission (U_m/p_t) can be written in the form

$$\frac{U_m(s)}{p_t(s)} = H(s)\, G(s),\qquad (3.85)$$

where $H(s)$ is a given in (3.64) and contains all the poles of the system, and $G(s)$ is a function which includes all the zeros and constants appropriate to nonglottal excitation. In this particular case, U_m/p_t is simply the driving point admittance at the lips. It is

$$\frac{U_m}{p_t} = \frac{(z_{b2}+z_{b1}+z_{a1}+z_{a2})}{z_{a2}(z_{b2}+z_{b1}+z_{a1}+z_{a2})+z_{b2}(z_{b1}+z_{a1}+z_{a2})},$$

which can be put into the form

$$\frac{U_m}{p_t} = \frac{\dfrac{1}{Z_{01}}\sinh\gamma_1 l_1 \sinh\gamma_2 l_2 \left(\coth\gamma_2 l_2 + \dfrac{A_2}{A_1}\coth\gamma_1 l_1\right)}{\cosh\gamma_1 l_1 \cosh\gamma_2 l_2 \left[1 + \dfrac{A_1}{A_2}\tanh\gamma_1 l_1 \tanh\gamma_2 l_2\right]}.\qquad (3.86)$$

The zeros of transmission occur at frequencies which make the numerator zero, and therefore satisfy

$$\coth \gamma_2 \, l_2 = -\frac{A_2}{A_1} \coth \gamma_1 \, l_1$$

or

$$\tanh \gamma_1 \, l_1 = -\frac{A_2}{A_1} \tanh \gamma_2 \, l_2 ,$$

which for lossless conditions reduces to

$$\tan \beta \, l_1 = -\frac{A_2}{A_1} \tan \beta \, l_2 . \tag{3.87}$$

As an example, let us use (3.87) and (3.84) to determine the (lossless) zeros and poles of U_m/p_t for an articulatory shape crudely representative of /s/. Take

$$A_1 = 7 \, \text{cm}^2, \qquad A_2 = 0.2 \, \text{cm}^2$$

$$l_1 = 12.5 \, \text{cm}, \qquad l_2 = 2.5 \, \text{cm}.$$

The pertinent reactance functions are plotted in Fig. 3.31, and the poles and zeros so determined are listed.

The lower poles and zeros lie relatively close and essentially nullify one another. The first significant uncompensated zero lies in the vicinity of 3400 cps, with the first uncompensated pole in the neighborhood of

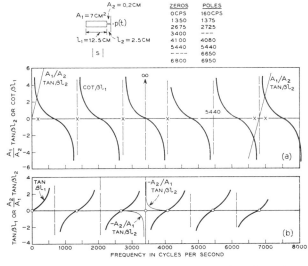

Fig. 3.31 a and b. Two-tube approximation to the fricative /s/. The undamped pole-zero locations are obtained from the reactance plots

6650 cps. These two features, as well as the near-cancelling pole-zero pairs, can often be seen in the spectra of real /s/ sounds. For example, Fig. 3.32 shows two measurements of the natural speech fricative /s/ (HUGHES and HALLE). For this speaker, the peak in the vicinity of 6000–7000 cps would appear to correspond with the uncompensated pole, the dip in the vicinity of 3000 cps with the zero. The peak and valley alternations at the lower frequencies reflect roughly the effect of

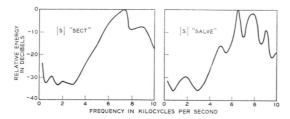

Fig. 3.32. Measured spectra for the fricative /s/ in real speech. (After HUGHES and HALLE)

pole-zero pairs such as indicated in the reactance diagrams. The measured spectra presumably include the transformation from mouth volume current to pressure at a fixed point in space, as described in Eq. (3.40). The spectra therefore include a zero at zero frequency owing to the radiation.

To further examine the influence of source position upon the transmission, suppose the turbulent source is applied more nearly at the junction between the two tubes rather than at the outlet. This situation is crudely representative of sounds like /f/, /k/ or possibly /ʃ/. In /f/, for example, the turbulent flow is produced at the constriction formed by the upper teeth and lower lip. The cavities behind the teeth are large, and the lips forward of the constriction form a short, small-area tube. The circuit for such an arrangement is shown in Fig. 3.33. The transmission from source to mouth is

$$\frac{U_m}{p_t} = \frac{z_{b2}}{z_{b2}(z_{a1}+z_{a2}+z_{b1})+z_{a2}(z_{b2}+z_{a1}+z_{a2}+z_{b1})}$$

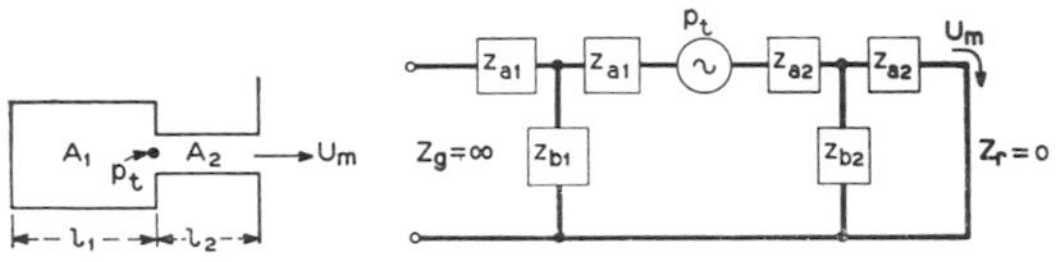

Fig. 3.33. Two-tube approximation to the vocal tract with the source of excitation applied at the tube junction

or

$$\frac{U_m}{p_t} = \frac{\dfrac{1}{Z_{01}} \sinh \gamma_1 l_1}{\cosh \gamma_1 l_1 \cosh \gamma_2 l_2 \left[1 + \dfrac{A_1}{A_2} \tanh \gamma_1 l_1 \tanh \gamma_2 l_2\right]} . \quad (3.88)$$

The system poles are the same as before, but the zeros now occur at

$$\frac{1}{Z_{01}} \sinh \gamma_1 l_1 = 0,$$

or

$$s_m = \left(-\alpha_1 c \pm j \frac{m \pi c}{l_1}\right); \quad m = 0, 1, 2, \dots . \quad (3.89)$$

Again for the lossless case, the zeros occur for $\sin \beta l_1 = 0$, or for frequencies

$$f_m = m \frac{c}{2 l_1} \text{ cps} \quad (m = 0, 1, 2, \dots),$$

where the length of the back cavity is an integral number of half wavelengths. The zeros therefore occur in complex-conjugate pairs except for $m = 0$. The real-axis zero arises from the impedance of the back cavity volume at zero frequency. Specifically, for the lossless situation at low frequencies, the numerator of (3.88) approaches

$$\lim_{\omega \to 0} \frac{1}{Z_{01}} \sin \beta l_1 \cong \frac{\omega l_1}{Z_{01} c} = \frac{A_1 l_1}{\rho c^2} \omega = \omega C_1, \quad \text{where } C_1 = \frac{V_1}{\rho c^2}$$

is the acoustic compliance of the back cavity.

The result (3.89) makes clear the reason that a labio-dental fricative such as /f/ exhibits a relatively uniform spectrum (devoid of large maxima and minima) over most of the audible frequency range. A crude approximation to the articulatory configuration for /f/ might be obtained if the parameters of Fig. 3.33 are taken as follows: $A_1 = 7$ cm^2, $A_2 = 0.1$ cm^2, $l_1 = 14$ cm, $l_2 = 1$ cm. As before the poles occur for $\cot \beta l_1 = A_1 / A_2 \tan \beta l_2$. Because of the large value of A_1 / A_2 and the small value of l_2, the poles occur very nearly at the frequencies which make $\cot \beta l_1$ infinite; namely

$$f_n \cong n \frac{c}{2 l_1}, \quad n = 0, 1, 2, \dots .$$

(The first infinite value of $\tan \beta l_2$ occurs at the frequency $c/4 l_2$, in the vicinity of 8500 cps.) The zeros, according to (3.89), occur precisely at the frequencies

$$f_m = m \frac{c}{2 l_1}, \quad m = 0, 1, 2, \dots,$$

so that each pole is very nearly cancelled by a zero. The transmission U_m/P_t is therefore relatively constant until frequencies are reached where the value of $A_1/A_2 \tan \beta l_2$ has its second zero. This relative flatness is generally exhibited in the measured spectra of real /f/ sounds such as shown in Fig. 3.34 (HUGHES and HALLE).

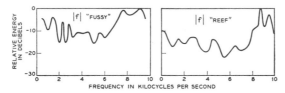

Fig. 3.34. Measured spectra for the fricative /f/ in real speech. (After HUGHES and HALLE)

3.76. Effects of the Nasal Tract

This highly simplified and approximate discussion of vocal transmission has so far neglected the properties of the nasal tract. The nasal tract is called into play for the production of nasal consonants and for nasalizing certain sounds primarily radiated from the mouth. Both of these classes of sounds are voiced. For the nasal consonants, an oral closure is made, the velum is opened and the sound is radiated chiefly from the nostrils. The blocked oral cavity acts as a side branch resonator. In producing a nasalized vowel, on the other hand, coupling to the nasal tract is introduced by opening the velum while the major radiation of sound continues from the mouth. Some radiation, usually lower in intensity, takes place from the nostrils.

The functioning of the combined vocal and nasal tracts is difficult to treat analytically. The coupled cavities represent a relatively complex system. Precise calculation of their interactions can best be done by analog or digital computer simulation. Nevertheless, it is possible to illustrate computationally certain gross features of the system by making simplifying approximations. More specifically, suppose the pharynx cavity, mouth cavity and nasal cavity are each approximated as uniform tubes. The equivalent network is shown in Fig. 3.35.

Notice that, in general, the parallel branching of the system at the velum causes zeros of nasal output at frequencies where the driving point impedance (Z_m) of the mouth cavity is zero, and vice versa. At such frequencies, one branch traps all the velar volume flow. In particular for nasal consonants, /m, n, ŋ/, $Z_{rm} = \infty$ and $U_m = 0$. Zeros then occur in the nasal output at frequencies for which $Z_m = 0$ for the closed oral cavity. Nasal consonants and nasalized vowels are generally characterized by resonances which appear somewhat broader, or more

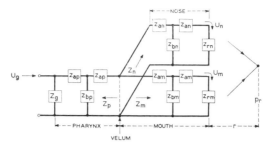

Fig. 3.35. An equivalent circuit for the combined vocal and nasal tracts. The pharynx, mouth and nasal cavities are assumed to be uniform tubes

highly damped, than those for vowels. Additional loss is contributed by the nasal tract which over a part of its length is partitioned longitudinally. Its inner surface is convoluted, and the cavity exhibits a relatively large ratio of surface area to cross-sectional area. Viscous and heat conduction losses are therefore commensurately larger.

Following the approach used earlier, and with the purpose of indicating the origin of the poles and zeros of a nasal consonant, let us make a crude, simple approximation to the vocal configuration for /m/. Such an approximation is illustrated in Fig. 3.36. The poles of the nasal output will be determined by the combined pharynx, mouth and nasal cavities, while the side-branch resonator—formed by the closed oral cavity—will introduce zeros wherever its input impedance is zero. Considering the system to be lossless, the radiation load to be negligible, and the glottal impedance to be high, the easiest way to estimate the pole frequencies is to find the frequencies where the velar admittance (at the point where the three cavities join) is zero. This requires

$$\sum_{k=p,\,m,\,n} Y_k = 0 = \frac{1}{Z_{0m}} \tan \beta l_m + \frac{1}{Z_{0p}} \tan \beta l_p - \frac{1}{Z_{0n}} \cot \beta l_n \qquad (3.90)$$

$$= A_m \tan \beta l_m + A_p \tan \beta l_p - A_n \cot \beta l_n \,.$$

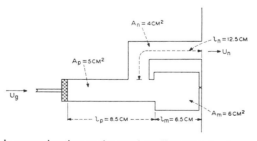

Fig. 3.36. A simple approximation to the vocal configuration for the nasal consonant /m/

The zeros of transmission occur for

$$Z_m = 0 = \frac{\rho c}{A_m} \cot \beta l_m$$

or

$$\beta l_m = (2n+1)\frac{\pi}{2}, \qquad n = 0, 1, 2, \ldots$$

or

$$f = (2n+1)\frac{c}{4 l_m}. \tag{3.91}$$

The mode pattern determined by relations (3.90) and (3.91) is shown in Fig. 3.37. One sees that the first pole of the coupled systems is fairly low, owing to the substantial length of the pharynx and nasal tract and the mouth volume. A pole and zero, additional to the poles of the pure vowel articulation, are introduced in the region of 1000 cps. This mode pattern is roughly representative of all the nasal consonants in that the pharynx and nasal tract have roughly the same shape for all. The first zero falls at approximately 1300 cps in the present example. For the consonants /n and ŋ/, the oral cavity is progressively shorter, and the zero would be expected to move somewhat higher in frquency. By way of comparison, the measured spectrum of a real /m/ is shown in Fig. 3.38 (FANT, 1960). In this measured spectrum, the nasal zero appears to be reflected by the relatively broad spectral minimum near 1200 cps. The larger damping and appreciable diminution of spectral amplitude at the higher frequencies is characteristic of the nasal consonants.

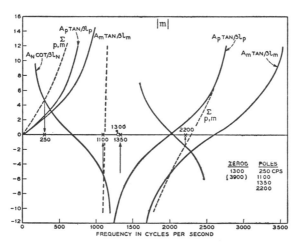

Fig. 3.37. Reactance functions and undamped mode pattern for the articulatory approximation to /m/ shown in Fig. 3.36

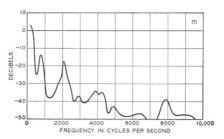

Fig. 3.38. Measured spectrum for the nasal consonant /m/ in real speech. (After Fant, 1960)

3.77. Four-Tube, Three-Parameter Approximation of Vowel Production

To illustrate fundamental relations, the preceding sections have dealt with very simple approximations to the vocal system. Clearly these crude representations are not adequate to describe the gamut of articulatory configurations employed in a language. The approximations can obviously be made better by quantizing the vocal system into more and shorter tube sections. For vowel production in particular, one generally can identify four main features in the tract geometry. These are the back pharynx cavity, the tongue hump constriction, the forward mouth cavity and the lip constriction (see Fig. 3.1). Approximation of these features by four abutting tubes gives a description of vocal transmission substantially more precise than the two-tube approximation. The first several normal modes of the four-tube model are reasonably good approximations to the lower formants of real vowels. Such a four-tube model is illustrated in Fig. 3.39a (adapted from Fant, 1960).

If the glottal impedance is taken as large and the radiation load small, the glottal-to-mouth transmission is

$$\frac{U_m}{U_g} = \frac{1}{\displaystyle\prod_{n=1}^{4} (\cosh \gamma_n l_n)(ab+cd)},$$

where

$$a = \left(1 + \frac{A_1}{A_2} \tanh \gamma_1 l_1 \tanh \gamma_2 l_2\right)$$

$$b = \left(1 + \frac{A_3}{A_4} \tanh \gamma_3 l_3 \tanh \gamma_4 l_4\right)$$

$$c = \frac{A_2}{A_3} \left(\tanh \gamma_3 l_3 + \frac{A_3}{A_4} \tanh \gamma_4 l_4\right)$$

$$d = \frac{A_1}{A_2} (\tanh \gamma_1 l_1 + \tanh \gamma_2 l_2).$$

(3.92)

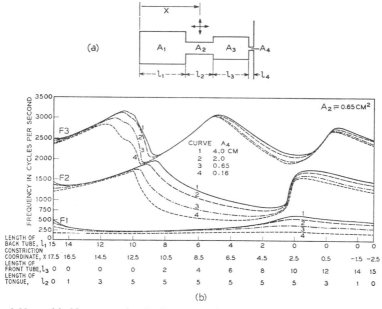

Fig. 3.39 a and b. Nomogram for the first three undamped modes ($F1$, $F2$, $F3$) of a four-tube approximation to the vocal tract. (Data adapted from FANT, 1960.) The parameter is the mouth area, A_4. Curves 1, 2, 3 and 4 represent mouth areas of 4, 2, 0.65 and 0.16 cm², respectively. Constant quantities are $A_1 = A_3 = 8$ cm², $l_4 = 1$ cm and $A_2 = 0.65$ cm². Abscissa lengths are in cm

One notices that if $l_3 = l_4 = 0$, Eq. (3.92) reduces to the two-tube relations given by Eq. (3.82).

To demonstrate how the first several normal modes of such a cavity arrangement depend upon configuration, FANT (1960) has worked out detailed nomograms for several combinations of A's and l's. One of these is particularly relevant and essentially depicts the scheme followed by DUNN (1950) in his development of an electrical vocal tract analog. It is reproduced in adapted form in Fig. 3.39b. The constraints are as follows: $l_2 + l_2 + l_3 = 15$ cm; $l_4 = 1$ cm; $A_1 = A_3 = 8$ cm²; $A_2 = 0.65$ cm²; and $l_2 = 5$ cm, provided tube 2 is terminated by cavities on both sides. The parameters are the distance from the glottis to the center of the tongue constriction, x, and the mouth area, A_4. For very large and very small values of x, l_3 and l_1 are zero, respectively, and the length l_2 is varied to satisfy the total length condition. The variation of the first three normal modes for a range of values of the parameters and for one value of the tongue constriction ($A_2 = 0.65$ cm²) are shown in Fig. 3.39b.

These data show that a shift of the tongue constriction from a back ($x \approx 3$ cm) to a front position ($x \approx 9$ cm) is generally associated with a transition from high $F1$-low $F2$ to low $F1$-high $F2$. (This general tendency was also evident in the two-tube models discussed in Section 3.74.) Increasing the lip rounding, that is decreasing A_4 (as well as increasing l_4), generally reduces the frequencies of all formants. Although not shown here, decreasing the tongue constriction reduces the frequency variations of the formants with place of constriction. In terms of absolute cps, the variations in $F1$ are generally smaller than those of the higher formants. Perceptually, however, the percentage change in formant frequency is more nearly the important quantity. This point will be discussed further in Chapter VII.

Owing to the substantial coupling between the connecting tubes, a particular formant cannot be strictly associated with a particular resonance of a particular vocal cavity. The normal mode pattern is a characteristic of the whole coupled system. Numerous efforts have been made in the literature to relate specific formants to specific vocal cavities, but this can be done exactly only when the constrictions are so small in size that the cavities are, in effect, uncoupled. In instances where the coupling is small, it is possible to loosely associate a given formant with a particular resonator. The treachery of the association, however, can be simply illustrated. If a forward motion of the tongue hump causes a resonant frequency to rise—for example, $F2$ for $3 < x < 9$ cm in Fig. 3.39—the suggestion is that the resonance is mainly influenced by a cavity of diminishing length, in this case the mouth cavity. On the other hand, the same resonance might be caused to rise in frequency by a tongue retraction and a consequent shortening of the pharynx cavity—for example, $F2$ for $16 > x > 13$ cm. It is therefore clear that a given formant may be principally dependent upon different cavities at different times. It can change its cavity-mode affiliation with changes in vocal configuration. In fact, its dependence upon the mode of vibration of a particular cavity may vary.

The four-tube approximation to vowel production implies that vowel articulation might be grossly described in terms of three parameters, namely, the distance from the glottis to the tongue-hump constriction, x; the size of the tongue constriction, A_2; and a measure of lip rounding such as the area-to-length ratio for the lip tube, A_4/l_4. This basis notion has long been used qualitatively by phoneticians to describe vowel production. It has been cast into quantitative frameworks by DUNN (1950), STEVENS and HOUSE (1955), FANT (1960) and COKER (1968), in connection with work on models of the vocal mechanism.

As pointed out earlier, DUNN has used the scheme much as represented in Fig. 3.39, that is, with constant-area tubes approximating the tract adjacent to the constriction. STEVENS and HOUSE and FANT have extended the scheme by specifying constraints on the taper of the vocal tract in the vicinity of the constriction. STEVENS and HOUSE use a parabolic function for the area variation, and FANT uses a section of a catenoidal horn (i.e., a hyperbolic area variation). Both use fixed dimensions for the larynx tube and the lower pharynx. In perceptual experiments with synthetic vowels, STEVENS and HOUSE find that a reasonably unique relation exists between the allowed values of x, A_2 and A_4/l_4 and the first three vowel formants. Although these three parameters provide an adequate description of most nonnasal, nonretroflex, vowel articulations, it is clear that they are not generally sufficient for describing consonant and nasal configurations.

Later work by COKER has aimed at a more detailed and physiologically meaningful description of the vocal area function. COKER'S articulatory model is specified by seven, relatively-orthogonal parameters: the $x-y$ position coordinates of the tongue body; the degree and the place of the tongue tip constriction; the mouth area; the lip protrusion; and the degree of velar (nasal) coupling. Each parameter has an associated time constant representative of its vocal feature. This articulatory model has been used as the synthesis element in an automatic system for converting printed text into synthetic speech (COKER, UMEDA and BROMAN)[1].

3.78. Multitube Approximations and Electrical Analogs of the Vocal Tract

As the number of elemental tubes used to approximate the vocal shape becomes large, the computational complexities increase. One generally resorts to analog or digital aids in solving the network when the number of approximating sections exceeds about four. In early work analog electrical circuitry has proven a useful tool for simulating both vocal and nasal tracts. It has been used extensively by DUNN (1950); STEVENS, FANT and KASOWSKI; FANT (1960); STEVENS and HOUSE (1955, 1956); and ROSEN. The idea is first to approximate the linear properties of the vocal mechanism by a sufficiently large number of tube sections and then to approximate, in terms of lumped-constant electrical elements, the hyperbolic impedances of the equivalent T or π networks shown in Fig. 3.3. At low frequencies the lumped-constant circuit behaves as a distributed transmission line and simulates the one-dimensional acoustic wave propagation in the vocal tract. The number of approximating tube sections used, the approximation of the hyperbolic elements, and the effect of cross modes in the actual vocal tract determine the highest frequency for which the electrical transmission line is an adequate analog.

---

[1] See further discussion of this system in Chapters V and VI.

As shown previously, the elements of the T-section equivalent of the cylindrical tube are

$$z_a = Z_0 \tanh \frac{\gamma l}{2} \quad \text{and} \quad z_b = Z_0 \operatorname{csch} \gamma l.$$

Taking first-order approximations to these quantities gives

$$z_a \cong Z_0 \left(\frac{\gamma l}{2} \right) \quad \text{and} \quad z_b \cong Z_0 \left(\frac{1}{\gamma l} \right)$$

(3.93)

$$z_a \cong Z_0 \tfrac{1}{2} (\alpha + j\beta) l \qquad z_b \cong Z_0 \frac{1}{(\alpha + j\beta) l}.$$

From the relations developed earlier, $Z_0 = [(R+j\omega L)/(G+j\omega C)]^{\frac{1}{2}}$ and $\gamma = [(R+j\omega L)(G+j\omega C)]^{\frac{1}{2}}$, where R, G, L and C have been given in terms of per-unit-length acoustical quantities in Eq. (3.33). The T-elements are therefore approximately

$$z_a = \tfrac{1}{2} (R+j\omega L) l \quad \text{and} \quad z_b = \frac{1}{(G+j\omega C) l}.$$

In general, the acoustical quantities R_a, L_a, G_a and C_a [in Eq. (3.33)] will not correspond to practical electrical values. It is usually convenient to scale the acoustical and electrical impedance levels so that

$$Z_{0e} = k Z_{0a}$$

or

$$\left[\frac{R_e + j\omega L_e}{G_e + j\omega C_e} \right]^{\frac{1}{2}} = \left[\frac{k R_a + j\omega k L_a}{\dfrac{G_a}{k} + \dfrac{j\omega C_a}{k}} \right]^{\frac{1}{2}}.$$

(3.94)

By way of indicating the size of a practical scale constant k, consider the low-loss situation where

$$Z_{0e} = \sqrt{\frac{L_e}{C_e}} = k Z_{0a} = k \sqrt{\frac{L_a}{C_a}} = k \left(\frac{\rho c}{A} \right),$$

(3.95)

where A is the cross-sectional area of the acoustic tube. A practical value for Z_{0e} is 600 electrical ohms, and a typical value of A is 8 cm². Therefore $k = 600/5.3 = 113$, and the mks impedances of the per-unit-length electrical elements are scaled up by 113 times the cgs impedances of the per-unit-length acoustic elements.

Note, too, that $\beta l \cong \omega l/c = \omega l_e \sqrt{L_e C_e} = \omega l_a \sqrt{L_a C_a}$. Since the velocity of sound and the air density in a given length of tube are constant, maintaining the $L_e C_e$ product constant in the electrical line is equivalent to maintaining constant velocity of sound propagation in the simulated pipe. Similarly, changes in the pipe area A are represented by proportional changes in the C_e/L_e ratio.

The electrical simulation is of course applicable to both vocal and nasal tracts. Choice of the elemental cylinder length l, the electrical scale constant k, and a knowledge of the cross-sectional area A along the tract are the only parameters needed to determine the lossless elements of the transmission line. An estimate of tract circumference along its length is needed to compute the viscous and heat conduction losses (R and G). The radiation loads at the mouth and nostrils are obtained by applying the electrical scale constant to the acoustic radiation impedances obtained earlier in the chapter. It is likewise possible to apply these techniques to the subglottal system and to incorporate it into the electrical simulation. At least four designs of electrical vocal tracts have been developed for studying vocal transmission and for synthesizing speech (DUNN, 1950; STEVENS, FANT and KASOWSKI; FANT, 1960; ROSEN). At least one design has been described for the subglottal system (VAN DEN BERG, 1960).

The digital computer is also an exceedingly effective tool for analyzing multi-tube approximations to the vocal tract. Its ability to carry out complex calculations at high speed makes the solution of 20 or 30-section approximations to the tract almost elementary. At least two computer programs for calculating transfer functions and normal modes for multitube approximations have been used (FANT, 1960; MATHEWS and WALKER).

Another approach has been to represent the cylindrical sections in terms of the reflection coefficients at their junctions (KELLY and LOCHBAUM; MERMELSTEIN; STRONG). This simulation also produces a response which, after digital-to-analog conversion, represents the speech waveform. It therefore can be used effectively as a synthesizer.

In another study of speech synthesis a computer program has been derived that is the difference equation equivalent of the multi-section, bilateral transmission line (FLANAGAN and LANDGRAF). This formulation allows computation of instantaneous pressure and velocity along the transmission line, including the sound pressure radiated from the mouth. When supplied a time-varying area function representative of realistic articulation, its calculated output represents samples of the synthesized speech waveform. Both analog and digital representations of the vocal system will be considered further in a later discussion on speech synthesis.

3.8. Fundamentals of Speech and Hearing in Analysis-Synthesis Telephony

The preceding sections have set forth certain basic acoustic principles for the vocal mechanism. Not only do these relations concisely describe the physical behavior of the source of speech signals, but they imply a good deal about efficient communication. They suggest possibilities for coding speech information in forms other than merely the transduced pressure wave. The normal mode and excitation relations, for example, indicate a schema on which an analysis-synthesis transmission system might be based. The same can be said for describing the vocal tract by articulatory parameters. Both results reflect constraints peculiar to the speech-producing mechanism.

As yet, however, the properties of hearing and the constraints exhibited by the ear have not entered the discussion. The next chapter proposes to establish certain fundamental properties of the mechanism of hearing — so far as they are known. The exposition will follow a pattern similar to that of the present chapter. The results of both fundamental discussions will then be useful in subsequent consideration of speech analysis and speech synthesis.

IV. The Ear and Hearing

The ultimate recipient of information in a speech communication link usually is man. His perceptual abilities dictate the precision with which speech data must be processed and transmitted. These abilities essentially prescribe fidelity criteria for reception and, in effect, determine the channel capacity necessary for the transmission of voice messages. It consequently is pertinent to inquire into the fundamental mechanism of hearing and to attempt to establish capabilities and limitations of human perception.

As suggested earlier, speech information — originating from a speaker, traversing a transmission medium and arriving at a listener — might be considered at a number of stages of coding. On the transmitter side, the stages might include the acoustic wave, the muscular forces manipulating the vocal mechanism, or the physical shape and excitation of the tract. On the receiver side, the information might be considered in terms of the acoustic-mechanical motions of the hearing transducer, or in terms of the electrical pulses transmitted to the brain over the auditory nerve. Characteristics of one or more of these codings might have application in practicable transmission systems.

The previous chapter set forth fundamental relations between the acoustics and the physiology of the vocal mechanism. We will subsequently have occasion to apply the results to analysis-synthesis telephony. In the present chapter we wish to establish similar relations for the ear. Later we will utilize these in discussions of auditory discrimination and speech perception.

4.1. Mechanism of the Ear

The acousto-mechanical operation of the peripheral ear has been put on a rather firm base. This knowledge is due primarily to the brilliant experiments carried out by G. VON BÉKÉSY, and for which he was awarded the Nobel Prize in 1961. In contrast, present knowledge is relatively incomplete about inner-ear processes for converting mechanical motion into neural activity. Still less is known about the transmission of neural information to the brain and the ultimate mechanism of perception.

Despite these difficulties, it is possible to quantify certain aspects of perception without knowing in detail what is going on inside the "black box". Subjective behavior, in response to prescribed auditory stimuli, can of course be observed and measured, and such data are useful guideposts in the design of speech communication systems. In some instances the correlations between perceptual behavior and the physiological operation of the peripheral ear can be placed in clear evidence. The present discussion aims to indicate current understanding of auditory physiology and psychoacoustic behavior, and to illustrate the extent to which the two can be brought into harmony.

The primary acoustic transducer of the human is shown schematically in Fig. 4.1. The acousto-mechanical components of the organ are conventionally divided according to three regions, namely, the outer ear, the middle ear, and the inner ear.

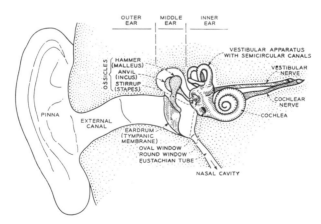

Fig. 4.1. Schematic diagram of the human ear showing outer, middle and inner regions. The drawing is not to scale. For illustrative purposes the inner and middle ear structures are shown enlarged

4.11. The Outer Ear

As commonly understood, the term *ear* usually applies to the salient, convoluted appendage on the side of the head. This structure is the pinna, and it surrounds the entrance to the external ear canal. Its main function in man is to protect the external canal – although its directional characteristics at high audible frequencies probably facilitate localization of sound sources. (In some animals, the directional acoustic properties of the pinna are utilized more fully.)

In man, the external ear canal, or meatus, is about 2.7 cm in length and about 0.7 cm in diameter. Its volume is on the order of 1 cm^3, and its cross-section is oval-to-circular in shape with an area 0.3 to 0.5 cm^2 (BÉKÉSY and ROSENBLITH; DAVIS, 1951). The meatus is terminated by a thin membrane which is the eardrum, or tympanic membrane. The membrane has the form of a relatively stiff, inwardly-directed cone with an included angle of about 135°. Its surface area is on the order of 0.8 cm^2. To a rough approximation, the meatus is a uniform pipe – open at one end and closed at the other. It has normal modes of vibration which occur at frequencies where the pipe length is an odd multiple of a quarter wavelength. The first mode therefore falls at $f \cong c/4(2.7) \cong$ 3 000 cps. This resonance might be expected to aid the ear's sensitivity in this frequency range. Measurements do in fact show that it provides a sound pressure increase at the ear drum of between 5 and 10 db over the value at the canal entrance (WIENER and ROSS).

4.12. The Middle Ear

Just interior to the eardrum is the air-filled, middle-ear cavity which contains the ossicular bones. The function of the ossicles is mainly one of impedance transformation from the air medium of the outer ear to the liquid medium of the inner ear[1]. The malleus, or hammer, is fixed to and rests on the eardrum. It makes contact with the incus, or anvil, which in turn connects via a small joint to the stapes, or stirrup. The footplate of the stirrup seats in a port, the oval window, and is retained there by an annular ligament. The oval window is the entrance to the inner ear.

A sound wave impinging on the outer ear is led down the external meatus and sets the eardrum into vibration. The vibration is transmitted via the three ossicular bones into the inner ear. The acousto-mechanical impedance of the inner ear is much greater than that of air, and for efficient transmission of sound energy an impedance transformation (a step up) is required. The ossicles provide such. First their lever action

---

[1] This impedance transformation is important to the basic role of the middle ear; that is, the conversion of an external sound pressure into a fluid volume displacement in the inner ear (see Sec. 4.13).

alone provides a force amplification of about 1.3 (BÉKÉSY, 1960). That is, a force applied to the hammer appears at the stirrup footplate multiplied by 1.3. Second, the effective area of the eardrum is much greater than that of the stirrup, so that the ratio of pressure applied at the stirrup to that applied at the eardrum is essentially 1.3 times the ratio of the effective areas of drum and stirrup. BÉKÉSY has measured this pressure transformation and finds it to be on the order of 15:1.

The middle ear structure serves another important purpose, namely, it provides protection against loud sounds which may damage the more delicate inner ear. The protective function is generally assumed to be served by two tympanic muscles — especially the tensor-tympani which connects the middle of the eardrum to the inner region of the head. Reflex contractions presumably attenuate the vibratory amplitude of the drum. BÉKÉSY points out, however, that voluntary contractions of the tensor and changes in the static pressure of the meatus only slightly reduce the vibrational amplitude of the drum. The contractions consequently can have only small effect in protecting against sound pressures that extend over a wide range of magnitudes. This fact can be established from measurements of the acoustic impedance at the drum.

In detailed studies on the mode of vibration of the ossicles, BÉKÉSY observed that at low and moderate sound intensities the stapes motion is principally a rotation about an axis through the open "hoop" of the stirrup. The movement is illustrated in Fig. 4.2a. At sound intensities near and above the threshold of feeling, the motion of the stapes changes more to a rotation about an axis running longitudinally through the "arch" of the stapes, as shown in Fig. 4.2b. In the latter mode, the effective volume displacement is small because the upper-half of the footplate advances by about as much as the lower half recedes.

Contraction of the middle ear muscles increases with sound intensity, so that the ossicles are prevented from bouncing out of contact and causing excessive distortion at the high levels. This control of distortion

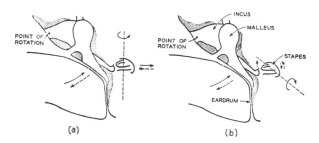

Fig. 4.2a and b. Vibration modes of the ossicles. (a) sound intensities below threshold of feeling (b) intensities above threshold of feeling. (After BÉKÉSY, 1960)

over the amplitude range from threshold-of-hearing to near threshold-of-feeling — while at the same time protecting the inner ear from harmful vibrational levels — apparently accounts for the elaborate middle-ear structure[1].

One of the important characteristics of the middle ear is its transmission as a function of frequency, that is, the volume displacement of the stapes footplate produced by a given sound pressure at the eardrum. A number of efforts have been made to measure or to deduce this characteristic (BÉKÉSY, 1960; Zwislocki, 1957, 1959; MØLLER, 1961, 1962). The results are somewhat disparate, suggesting that not only is the characteristic a function of intensity in the living human, but that it may vary substantially from individual to individual.

If the fluid of the inner ear is considered incompressible and the walls of the cochlea rigid, then the volume displacement of the round window must be the same as that of the stapes footplate. At low frequencies the combined elasticity of the drum, ossicles and round window membrane controls the stirrup motion. That is, the system acts like a spring, with the stapes displacement proportional to, and in phase with, the eardrum pressure. Somewhere between about 1000 and 3000 cps the mass reactance of the system becomes important, and the motion passes from a stiffness-controlled vibration to a viscous-controlled one and finally to a mass-controlled motion. For a given sound pressure at the drum, the stirrup displacement begins to diminish in amplitude and lag in phase as frequency increases.

BÉKÉSY (1960) has made a number of measurements of middle-ear transmission by directly observing the volume displacement of the round window. The transmission properties can also be deduced from a knowledge of the middle-ear topology, the input mechanical impedance to the inner ear, and the acoustic impedance at the eardrum. This approach has been used by ZWISLOCKI (1957, 1959) and by MØLLER (1961) to develop analog circuits of the middle ear. All these results agree in gross aspects but suggest that substantial variability can exist in the characteristic. By way of comparison, the transmission of the middle ear according to several determinations is shown in Fig. 4.3a–d.

For the data in Fig. 4.3b, BÉKÉSY obtains a critical "roll-off" frequency for middle-ear transmission of about 800 cps. For the data in Fig. 4.3a, it is clearly higher, possibly around 3000 cps. ZWISLOCKI's result in Fig. 4.3c places it somewhere in the vicinity of 1500 cps, and

---

[1] One can appreciate the difficulties posed in duplicating this mechanical linkage with prosthetic devices. For example, one middle-ear prosthesis involves replacing damaged or diseased ossicles by a plastic strut joining the drum and the stapes footplate. The protection against distortion and high-amplitude vibration, normally provided by the middle ear, are difficult to include in such a construction.

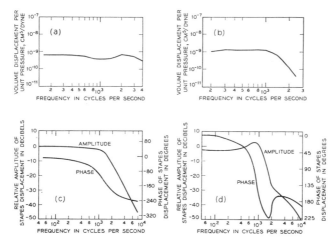

Fig. 4.3 a–d. Data on middle ear transmission; effective stapes displacement for a constant sound pressure at the eardrum. (a) BÉKÉSY (1960) (one determination); (b) BÉKÉSY (1960) (another determination); (c) measured from an electrical analog circuit (after ZWISLOCKI, 1959); (d) measured from an electrical analog circuit (after MØLLER, 1961)

MØLLER'S result in Fig. 4.3d is near 1000 cps. The common indication is that the middle-ear transmission has a low-pass characteristic. The effective cut-off frequency and the skirt slope are apparently subject to considerable variation.

4.13. The Inner Ear

As illustrated in Fig. 4.1, the inner ear is composed of the cochlea (normally coiled like a snail shell in a flat spiral of two and one-half turns), the vestibular apparatus and the auditory nerve terminations. It is in the cochlea that auditory mechanical-to-neural transduction takes place. The vestibular components (semi-circular canals, saccule and utricle) serve the sense of spatial orientation and apparently are not normally used for detecting audio vibrations.

If the cochlea is uncoiled and stretched out, it appears schematically as in Fig. 4.4. The cochlear chamber is filled with a colorless liquid, perilymph, which has a viscosity about twice that of water and a specific gravity of about 1.03. The length of the canal in the spiral conch is about 35 mm. The cross-sectional area at the stirrup end is about 4 mm^2 and the area decreases to about 1 mm^2 at the tip.

Fig. 4.4. Simplified diagram of the cochlea uncoiled

The cochlear chamber is divided along almost its whole length by a partition. The half which receives the stapes is called the scala vestibuli; the other half is the scala tympani. The cochlear partition is itself a channel — the scala media — bounded partly by a bony shelf, a gelatinous membrane called the basilar membrane, and another membrane known as REISSNER's membrane. The partition is filled with a different liquid, the endolymph. The basilar membrane and bony shelf both terminate a mm or two short of the ends of the scalas, permitting them to communicate at the helicotrema. The area of the connecting passage is about 0.3 to 0.4 mm^2 (BÉKÉSY and ROSENBLITH). The basilar membrane is about 32 mm in length and tapers from a width of about 0.05 mm at the base (stirrup) to about 0.5 mm at the apex (DAVIS, 1951).

The inner ear is connected to the middle ear at the stapes footplate. The latter, supported by a ring-shaped ligament, seats into the oval window (about 3 mm^2 in area). In vibrating, the stapes acts as a piston and produces a volume displacement of the cochlear fluid. Because the cochlea is essentially rigid and its fluid incompressible, fluid displacements caused by inward motion of the stapes must be relieved. This function is accomplished at the round window which is covered by a compliant membrane (about 2 mm^2). Very slow vibrations of the stapes (say less than 20 cps) result in a to-and-fro flow of fluid between the scala vestibuli and scala tympani through the opening at the helicotrema. Higher frequency vibrations are transmitted through the yielding cochlear partition at a point which depends uqon the frepuency content of the stimsound ulation.

A cross-section of the cochlea and its partition is shown in Fig. 4.5. The main functions and dynamical properties of the partition reside in

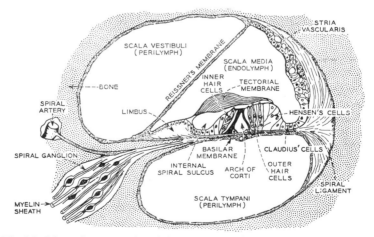

Fig. 4.5. Schematic cross section of the cochlear canal. (Adapted from DAVIS, 1957)

the basilar membrane. It is upon the latter that the organ of Corti rests. Among several types of supporting cells, the organ of Corti contains some 30000 sensory cells (or hair cells), on which the endings of the auditory nerve (entering from the lower left in Fig. 4.5) terminate. The basilar membrane is stiffer and less massive at its narrow, basal end and more compliant and massive at the broad, apical end. Its resonant properties therefore vary continuously along its length. At low frequencies, REISSNER's membrane normally moves cophasically with the basilar membrane.

Current knowledge of the acoustic-mechanical properties of the basilar membrane is due almost exclusively to the efforts of VON BÉKÉSY. In physiological preparations, he vibrated the stapes footplate sinusoidally and measured the amplitude and phase of the membrane displacements along the length of the cochlea. The mechanical characteristics of the basilar membrane, as determined in these experiments, are shown in Fig. 4.6. Figs. 4.6a and b show the amplitude and phase of specific membrane points as functions of frequency. Fig. 4.6c shows the amplitude and phase as a function of membrane place with frequency as the parameter.

The amplitude and phase response of a given membrane point is much like that of a relatively broad band-pass filter. The amplitude responses of successive points are roughly constant-Q in nature. Because of this constant percentage bandwidth property, the frequency resolution is best at the low-frequency (apical) end of the membrane, and the time resolution is best at the higher-frequency (basal) end [1].

All the amplitude responses of Fig. 4.6 are normalized to unity. BÉKÉSY's measurements suggest, however, that for constant amplitude of stapes displacement, the peak membrane response increases at about 5 db/octave for points resonant at frequencies up to about 1000 cps, and is approximately constant in peak displacement for points resonant at higher frequencies. Linear increments of distance along the basilar membrane correspond approximately to logarithmic increments of peak frequency, at least for frequencies less than about 1000 cps.

Excitation at the stapes is propagated down the membrane in the form of a travelling wave of displacement. Because of the taper of the distributed constants with distance, essentially no reflection takes place at the helicotrema, and no standing wave of displacement is created. The membrane is a dispersive transmission medium. The travelling wave loses more and more of its high frequency components as it progresses toward the helicotrema, and its group delay increases.

---

[1] Recent measurements of basilar membrane vibration in animals, using the Mössbauer effect (JOHNSTONE and BOYLE; RHODE), suggest that the mechanical response is sharper (higher in Q) than shown in Fig. 4.6. Also, the measurements suggest that the mechanical response is somewhat dependent upon sound intensity.

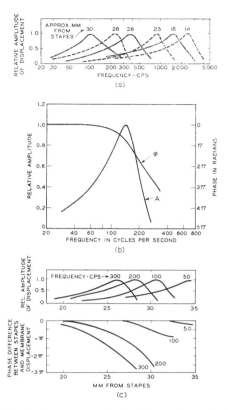

Fig. 4.6 a–c. Amplitude and phase responses for basilar membrane displacement. The stapes is driven sinusoidally with constant amplitude of displacement. (After Békésy, 1960.) (a) Amplitude *vs* frequency responses for successive points along the membrane. (b) Amplitude and phase responses for the membrane place maximally responsive to 150 cps. (c) Amplitude and phase of membrane displacement as a function of distance along the membrane. Frequency is the parameter

4.14. Mechanical-to-Neural Transduction

Mechanical motion of the membrane is converted into neural activity in the organ of Corti. An enlarged view of this structure is shown in Fig. 4.7. The organ of Corti contains a collection of cells among which are the hair cells. The hairs emanating from these sensory cells protrude upward through the reticular lamina and contact a third membrane of the cochlear partition, the tectorial membrane. One set of cells lies in a single row, longitudinal to the basilar membrane and toward the axis of the cochlear spiral (left of the arch of Corti). They are termed the inner hair cells. Another set lies in three or four longitudinal rows, radially away from the center of the spiral. These are the outer hair

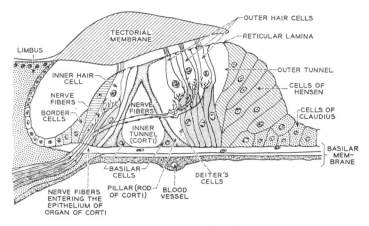

Fig. 4.7. Cross section of the organ of Corti. (After DAVIS, 1951)

cells. Estimates fix the number of the former at about 5000 and the latter at about 25000.

The tectorial and basilar membranes are anchored at their inner edges at spatially separate points. A deformation of the basilar membrane causes relative motion between the tectorial membrane and the reticular lamina and a resultant stress on the hairs passing between. By a process that presently is not understood, a bending of the hairs produces an electrical discharge in the cochlear portion of the VIIIth nerve[1]. The first-order fibers of this cochlear branch, or auditory nerve, enter from the lower left in Fig. 4.7 and run to the inner and outer hair cells.

Electrophysiological experiments suggest that the outer and inner hair cells of the organ of Corti differ in their sensitivities to mechanical stimulation (BÉKÉSY, 1953; DAVIS, 1958). The outer hair cells appear to be sensitive to bending only in a direction transverse to the long dimension of the membrane. Moreover, only outward bending of the hairs (away from the arch of Corti) produces an electrical potential in the scala media favorable for exciting the auditory nerve endings. This outward bending is produced on (unipolar) upward motions of the basilar membrane, that is, motions which drive it toward the tectorial membrane.

The inner hair cells, on the other hand — residing between the arch of Corti and the axis of the cochlear spiral — appear sensitive to bending in a direction parallel to the long dimension of the membrane (BÉKÉSY, 1953; DAVIS, 1958). In this case bending only toward the apex of the cochlea produces a scala media potential favorable for stimulating the

[1] The VIIIth nerve also serves the vestibular apparatus. See Fig. 4.1.

nerve. So far as a given point on the membrane is concerned, the inner hair cells are essentially sensitive to the longitudinal gradient of displacement, that is, to the spatial derivative in the long dimension. Furthermore, the inner cells fire only on the polarity of the gradient which corresponds to bending toward the apex. The threshold for firing of the inner cells appears to be appreciably higher than that for the outer cells. Exactly how the pattern of mechanical displacement of the basilar membrane is reflected in the "transducer" potentials of the sensory cells and in the electrical pulses elicited in the auditory nerve has yet to be put on a firm basis.

The sensory cells of the ear connect to the brain via the bundle of nerve cells — or neurons — comprising the auditory nerve. The auditory nerve passes down the axis of the cochlear spiral — collecting more nerve fibers as it runs from apex to base — until it contains some 30000 neurons. Neurons presumably have only two states, namely, active or inactive. When excited by an electrical input above a particular threshold, they produce a standard electrical pulse of about a millisecond duration and are desensitized for a period of about one to three milliseconds thereafter. They consequently can be excited to maximum discharge rates on the order of 300 to 1000 sec^{-1}.

The connections between the nerve cells and the hair cells in the organ of Corti are complex. Each inner hair cell is innervated by one or two nerve fibers, and each fiber connects with one or two hair cells. Innervation of the outer cells is more compound. Most nerve fibers make connections with a number of outer cells, and each outer cell usually receives connections from several nerve fibers (DAVIS, 1957). The exact functional significance of this complex multiple distribution of the nerve supply is not presently known. One study has suggested that it contributes to the great intensity range of the ear (VAN BERGEIJK).

The fibers of the auditory nerve twist like strands of rope about a central core. The nerve itself is short and enters the lower brain stem (medulla oblongata) after a run of about 5 mm (DAVIS, 1957). The incoming fibers divide, and the branches run respectively to the dorsal and to the vertral portions of the cochlear nucleus. Here the first synapses (junctions connecting one nerve cell to another) of the auditory system reside. The fibers of the auditory nerve, and the cells of the cochlear nucleus to which they join, essentially preserve the orderly arrangement of the corresponding sensory cells on the basilar membrane. The same general tendency toward orderly arrangement, with respect to membrane place of origin, seems to be maintained throughout the auditory system.

Relatively little is known about the mechanism by which the basilar membrane displacements are converted into neural activity. Still less is known about how information is coded in nerve pulses and assimilated into an auditory percept by the brain. Qualitatively, however, several deductions seem to be generally accepted. First, the hairs of the sensory cells, in experiencing a lateral shear owing to relative motion of basilar membrane and tectorial membrane (see Fig. 4.7), generate local electrical potentials which represent the local basilar membrane displacement. More precisely, the shearing forces on the sensory hairs "modulate" (as would a variable resistor) a current passing between the scala media and the base of the hair cell (DAVIS, 1965).

Second, this facsimile alternating potential, acting at the base of the hair cell, modulates the liberation of a chemical mediator about some quiescent rate. The mediator, in sufficient quantity, stimulates the dendritic endings of the first-order nerve fibers and causes the fibers to fire. Because of its quiescent bias rate, the hypothesized chemical mediator is secreted more on one phase of the sensory potential than on the other; that is, a rectifying function is implied in triggering the nerve fiber.

Lastly, the chemical stimulation of the nerve endings produces an all-or-none electrical firing, which is propagated axonally to subsequent higher-order fibers in the central nervous system.

There are two basic electrical phenomena in the cochlea: the resting (dc) polarization of the parts, and the ac output of the organ of Corti (which, as stated, appears to reflect the displacement of the cochlear partition). Current thinking holds that the ac output, or the cochlear microphonic[1], is a potential produced by the sensory or receptor cells and is derived from the pre-existing resting polarization of the receptor cells by a change in the ohmic resistance of a mechanically-sensitive portion of the cell membrane. "This change in resistance is presumably brought about by a deformation, however slight, of a critical bit of the polarized surface" (DAVIS, 1965).

Energy considerations argue for an active (power-amplifying) type of transduction, as in a carbon microphone. The biasing current (power supply) for the transducer is produced by the biological battery which is the resting polarization of the hair cell. The mechanical energy of the basilar membrane is not transduced into electrical current, rather it controls or modulates the flow of current across the interface (cell membrane) which separates the negative polarization inside the hair cell from the positive, endo-cochlear potential of the endolymph inside the cochlear partition.

A map of the cochlear resting potentials is shown in Fig. 4.8. The scala tympani is taken as the zero reference potential, and regions of similar potential are often found within the organ of Corti. Other areas,

---

[1] This potential is typically observed by an electrode placed at the round window or inserted into a scala.

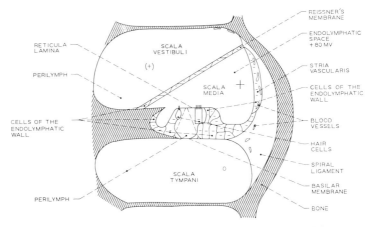

Fig. 4.8. Distribution of resting potentials in the cochlea. Scala tympani is taken as the zero reference. The tectorial membrane is not shown. The interiors of all cells are strongly negative. (After TASAKI, DAVIS and ELDREDGE)

presumably intracellular, are strongly negative. The endolymphatic space (scala media) is strongly positive. (Refer to Fig. 4.5 for more details on the organ of Corti.)

If a microelectrode penetrates upward through the basilar membrane, recording simultaneously the dc potentials (which serve to locate the electrode tip) and the cochlear microphonic response to a 500 cps tone, the result is shown in Fig. 4.9. The conclusion is that the electrical interface at which the phase reversal of the cochlear microphonic occurs is

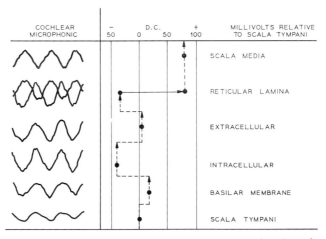

Fig. 4.9. Cochlear microphonic and dc potentials recorded by a microelectrode penetrating the organ of Corti from the scala tympani side. The cochlear microphonic is in response to a 500 cps tone. (After DAVIS, 1965)

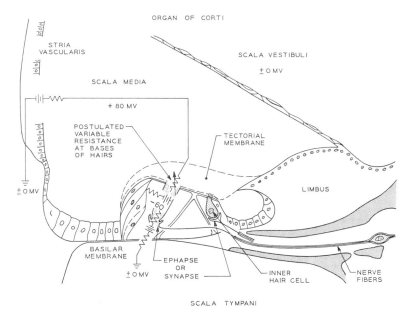

Fig. 4.10. A "resistance microphone" theory of cochlear transduction. (After DAVIS, 1965)

the hair-bearing surface of the hair cell (although one cannot differentiate between the surface and base location of the hair cell).

Two biological batteries therefore act in series: the internal (negative) polarization of the hair cells and the (positive) dc polarization of the endocochlear voltage (which is probably generated by the stria vascularis). This action leads to the conception of the equivalent circuit for cochlear excitation shown in Fig. 4.10.

The cochlear microphonic, as already mentioned, is viewed as the fluctuating voltage drop across the cell membrane due to alternating increase or decrease in its ohmic resistance. It appears to be a facsimile representation of the local displacement of the basilar membrane (TEAS et al.). The dynamic range of the microphonic is relatively large. Its amplitude appears linearly related to input sound pressure over ranges greater than 40 dB (TEAS et al.).

Although the functional link between the cochlear microphonic (or the facsimile membrane displacement) and the all-or-none electrical activity in the fibers of the auditory nerve remains obscure, it is nevertheless clear that a local deformation of the membrane (of sufficient amplitude), and a consequent bending of the sensory hairs in the area, causes the sensory cells to generate a scala media potential favorable for triggering the neurons in that region. The greater the displacement magnitude, the greater the number of neurons activated. A periodic displacement of sufficiently low frequency elicits neural firing synchronous with the stimulus. The periodicity of tones of frequencies less than about 1000 cps may therefore be represented by the periodicity of the neural volleys. This mechanism may be one method of coding for the subjective attribute of pitch. The fact that the neurons leading away from a given region of the frequency-selective basilar membrane maintain their identity in the auditory nerve offers a further possibility for the coding of pitch, namely, in terms of membrane place of maximum stimulation.

4.15. Neural Pathways in the Auditory System

A schematic representation of the ascending neural pathways associated with one ear are shown in Fig. 4.11. Beginning in the organ of Corti, the roughly 30000 individual neurons innervate singly or multiply about the same number of sensory (hair) cells. (In general, the inner

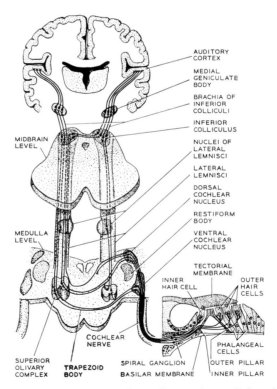

Fig. 4.11. Schematic diagram of the ascending auditory pathways. (Adapted from drawings by NETTER)

hair cells are served by only one or two neurons, the outer cells by several.) The dendritic arbors of the first-order neurons bear on the sensory cells. The cell bodies of the first-order neurons are located in the spiral ganglion, and their axons pass via the cochlear nerve (about 5 mm) to the dorsal and ventral cochlear nuclei in the medulla. Here the first synapses of the auditory pathway are located. From these nuclei, some second-order neurons pass to the superior olive on the same side, some decussate to the opposite side. Some pass upward to the medial geniculate body, with or without intermediate synapses with other neurons located in the lateral lemnisci and the inferior colliculi. The latter nuclei are located in the midbrain, and a second, smaller pathway of decussation runs between them. Thus, stimuli received at the two ears may interact both at the medulla and midbrain levels. The last stage in the pathway is the auditory cortex. The exact neuro-electrical representation of sound stimuli at these various levels is not well understood, and considerable research effort is presently aimed at studying these processes.

The first-order fibers of the auditory nerve connect to different places along the cochlear partition. Starting at the point (apex) of the cochlea, they are progressively collected in the internal auditory meatus until, at the base, the whole nerve trunk is formed. Because the basilar membrane is a mechanical frequency analyzer, it is not surprising that individual fibers exhibit frequency specificity. Owing to the way in which the fibers are collected and the trunk formed, those fibers which have greatest sensitivity to high frequencies lie on the outer part of the whole nerve, while those more sensitive to low frequencies tend to be found toward the core. This "tonotopic" organization of the auditory system (that is, its place-frequency preserving aspect) seems to be maintained at least to some degree all the way to the cortical level (TUNTURI).

The electrical response of individual fibers is a standard pulse. Characteristically, the pulse exhibits a duration on the order of a millisecond. The activity is statistical in two senses. First, the firing patterns of an individual fiber are not identical in successive repetitions of a given stimulus. Second, individual fibers exhibit spontaneous firing (electrical output) of a random nature. The latter appears to be much the same for all first-order fibers.

Comprehensive investigation of first-order electrical behavior in cats has been carried out by KIANG *et al.* Since the structure of the cochlea and auditory nerve follows the same general plan in all mammals, data from these studies should give insight into the human auditory system.

Typical microelectrode recordings from single primary fibers are illustrated in Fig. 4.12. In this instance, the signal comprises 50 msec tone bursts of a 2.3 kcps frequency. The upper recording is from a fiber that is maximally sensitive to this frequency, while the lower is from a fiber maximally sensitive to 6.6 kcps. The electrical output of the former is highly correlated with the stimulus, while the electrical output of the latter is not. The nerve response potential is recorded with respect to a convenient reference potential, in this case the head holder for the preparation. A positive voltage is indicated by a downward deflection.

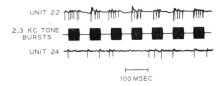

Fig. 4.12. Electrical firings from two auditory nerve fibers. The characteristic frequency of unit 22 is 2.3 kcps and that for unit 24 is 6.6 kcps. The stimulus is 50 msec bursts of a 2.3 kcps tone. (After KIANG et al.)

By choosing a suitable criterion of response, the frequency characteristic (tuning curve) of an individual first-order fiber can be measured. Results of such measurements are illustrated for several fibers in Fig. 4.13. The frequency for which the threshold is lowest (the minimum of each curve) is called the characteristic frequency (CF) of the fiber (unit). These minima appear to match well the shape of the audiogram determined from behavioral measurements. An interesting aspect of these data is that while over the low-frequency range the shapes of the tuning curves appear to be nearly constant percentage bandwidth in character (constant Q) and display a bandwidth which correlates reasonably well with BÉKÉSY's mechanical responses, the tuning curves of high-frequency units are much sharper and display Q increasing with frequency. (BÉKÉSY's

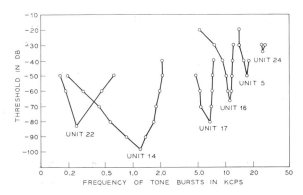

Fig. 4.13. Frequency sensitivities for six different fibers in the auditory nerve of cat. (After KIANG et al.)

observations on human basilar membrane were, of course, limited to
the low end of the spectrum − 2400 cps and down.)

KIANG *et al.* have also observed the electrical response of primary
units to punctuate signals, namely, broadband clicks. Individual responses
to 10 successive rarefaction clicks of 100-μsec duration are plotted in
Fig. 4.14. The figure shows the electrical response recorded at the round
window (RW, primarily the cochlear microphonic) and the response of
the individual fiber. The time origin is taken as the time the pulse is
delivered to the earphone. The characteristic frequency of the unit is
540 cps. The pattern of firing differs in successive stimulations, but the
responses show a consistent periodic aspect. Multiple firings in response
to a single click are apparent.

Fig. 4.14. Electrical response of a single auditory nerve fiber (unit) to 10 successive rarefaction pulses of 100 μsec duration. *RW* displays the cochlear microphonic response at the
round window. *CF* = 540 cps. (After KIANG *et al.*)

A convenient way to analyze this periodic feature is, in successive presentations of the signal, to measure the number of times the fiber fires at a prescribed time after the signal onset. This number plotted against the time of firing forms the post-stimulus time (PST) histogram. Some quantization of the time scale is implied and this quantization (or "bin width") is made sufficiently small to resolve the periodicities of interest. (For click signals, a bin width of 0.063 msec was customarily used.) A digital computer is a valuable tool for calculating and displaying the histogram. One minute of data from the conditions in Fig. 4.14 produces the histogram of Fig. 4.15. (Since the clicks are

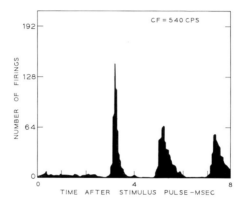

Fig. 4.15. Post stimulus time (PST) histogram for the nerve fiber shown in Fig. 4.14. $CF = 540$ cps. Stimulus pulses 10 sec^{-1}. (After KIANG *et al.*)

delivered at a rate of 10 sec^{-1}, this histogram is the result of 600 signal presentations.) The times of firings show a periodic structure, or "preferred" times for firing. In the midfrequency range for the animal, the histogram may exhibit as many as five or six distinct peaks or preferred times. At the upper end of the animal's frequency range, the tendency is for the histogram to display a single major peak.

The preferred times for firing appear to be intimately linked to the characteristic frequency of the unit, and the interval between peaks in the PST histogram is approximately equal to 1/CF. Higher frequency units consequently show smaller intervals between the PST histogram peaks. The interval between peaks in the histogram and 1/CF are related as shown in Fig. 4.16. Data for 56 different units are plotted. The multiple responses of single primary units to single clicks almost certainly reflect the mechanical response of the cochlea. (See the derivations of Section 4.2 for the impulse response of the basilar membrane.)

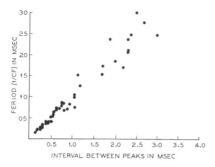

Fig. 4.16. Characteristic period $(1/CF)$ for 56 different auditory nerve fibers plotted against the interpeak interval measured from PST histograms. (After KIANG *et al.*)

Microelectrode studies of the electrical activity of single neurons at other levels in the auditory pathway have been, and are being, carried out. Varying experimental techniques and methods of anesthesia have sometimes led to disagreements among the results, but as research progresses the neural schema is becoming increasingly better understood.

According to at least one investigation on cat, the rate of single unit firings is monotonically related to stimulus intensity at all neural stages from the periphery up to the medial geniculate body (KATSUKI). This is exemplified for sinusoidal tones in Figs. 4.17 and 4.18. Fig. 4.17 shows the spikes (firings) of a single neuron in the trapezoidal body of cat in response to tone bursts of 9000 cps, delivered at four different levels. The spike duration is on the order of the conventional 1 msec, and the firings are more numerous for the more intense sounds.

Fig. 4.18 shows a monotone relation between firing rate and intensity for different neural stages. The firing rate for the first-order single neuron (the top curve for the cochlear nerve) has a maximum value close to its best (characteristic) frequency, namely 830 cps. This suggests that for the sinusoidal stimulation, the first-order neuron fires at most once per period. The rates at the higher neural stages appear substantially less than their characteristic frequencies.

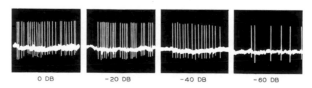

Fig. 4.17. Responses of a single auditory neuron in the trapezoidal body of cat. The stimulus was tone bursts of 9000 cps produced at the indicated relative intensities. (After KATSUKI)

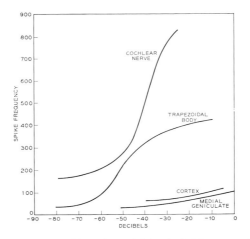

Fig. 4.18. Relation between sound intensity and firing (spike) frequency for single neurons at four different neural stages in the auditory tract of cat. Characteristic frequencies of the single units: Nerve: 830 cps; Trapezoid: 9000 cps; Cortex: 3500 cps; Geniculate: 6000 cps. (After KATSUKI)

Microelectrode recordings from single first-order neurons often show appreciable spontaneous activity. At higher neural stages and in the cortex, spontaneous activity apparently is not as pronounced (KATSUKI).

The cochlear nucleus complex of cat has been another particular area of study (ROSE, GALAMBOS and HUGHES). Strong evidence for a distinct tonotopical organization is found in the major subdivision of the cochlear nucleus. Typical of this finding is the sagittal section through the left cochlear complex shown in Fig. 4.19. The frequency scale indicates the best (most sensitive) frequencies of the neurons located along the ruled axis.

Some tonotopical organization appears to exist at the cortical level, although its degree and extent seems to be controversial (for example, KATSUKI; TUNTURI).

The relations between threshold sound amplitude and tone frequency (that is, the tuning curves) for single units at the cochlear nucleus level have been found to vary in shape (ROSE, GALAMBOS and HUGHES). Some appear broad, others narrow. All, however, resemble roughly the mechanical resonance characteristic of the basilar membrane. That is, the tuning curve (or threshold amplitude) rises more steeply on the high-frequency side than on the low-frequency side. Typical narrow and broad tuning curves obtained from single units in the cochlear nucleus are shown in Fig. 4.20a and b, respectively. For tones up to about 60 db above the threshold, the frequency range of response for both narrow and broad units does

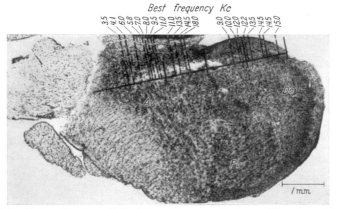

Fig. 4.19. Sagittal section through the left cochlear complex in cat. The electrode followed the track visible just above the ruled line. Frequencies of best response of neurons along the track are indicated. (After ROSE, GALAMBOS and HUGHES)

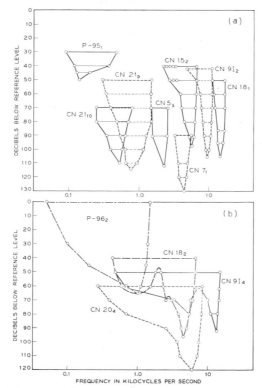

Fig. 4.20a and b. Intensity *vs* frequency "threshold" responses for single neurons in the cochlear nucleus of cat. The different curves represent the responses of different neurons. (a) Units with narrow response areas; (b) units with broad response areas. (After ROSE, GALAMBOS and HUGHES)

not extend over more than about 0.3 of an octave above the best frequency. The frequency range below the best frequency can range from about 0.4 to 3.8 octaves for the narrow units, to almost the whole lower frequency range for the broad units. Single units at this level display adaptive and inhibitory behavior which is strongly intensity dependent.

The mechanism of neural transmission across a synapse also remains to be firmly established. A temporal delay—typically on the order of 1 msec—is usually incurred at the junction. Response latencies at the level of the cochlear nucleus have minimum times on the order of 2 to 3 msec, but latencies as great as 6 to 8 msec have been measured. At the cortical level, latencies as great as 20 to 30 msec and as small as 6 to 8 msec are possible.

4.2. Computational Models for Ear Function

It has been emphasized in the preceding discussion that the complete mechanism of auditory perception is far from being adequately understood. Even so, present knowledge of ear physiology, nerve electrophysiology, and subjective behavior make it possible to relate certain auditory functions among these disparate realms. Such correlations are facilitated if behavior can be quantified and analytically specified. As a step in this direction, a computational model has been derived to describe basilar membrane displacement in response to an arbitrary sound pressure at the eardrum (FLANAGAN, 1962a).

The physiological functions embraced by the model are shown in the upper diagram of Fig. 4.21. In this simplified schematic of the peripheral

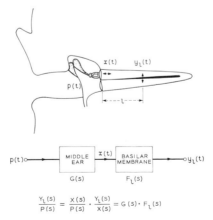

Fig. 4.21. Schematic diagram of the peripheral ear. The quantities to be related analytically are the eardrum pressure, $p(t)$; the stapes displacement, $x(t)$; and the basilar membrane displacement at distance l from the stapes, $y_l(t)$

ear, the cochlea is shown uncoiled. $p(t)$ is the sound pressure at the ear-drum, $x(t)$ is the equivalent linear displacement of the stapes footplate, and $y_l(t)$ is the linear displacement of the basilar membrane at a distance l from the stapes. The desired objective is an analytical approximation to the relations among these quantities. It is convenient to obtain it in two steps. The first step is to approximate the middle-ear transmission, that is, the relation between $x(t)$ and $p(t)$. The second is to approximate the transmission from the stapes to the specified point l on the membrane. The approximating functions are indicated as the frequency-domain (LAPLACE) transforms $G(s)$ and $F_l(s)$, respectively, in the lower part of Fig. 4.21.

The functions $G(s)$ and $F_l(s)$ must be fitted to available physiological data. If the ear is assumed to be mechanically passive and linear over the frequency and amplitude ranges of interest, rational functions of frequency with stable normal modes (left half-plane poles) can be used to approximate the physiological data. Besides computational convenience, the rational functions have the advantage that they can be realized in terms of lumped-constant electrical circuits, if desired. Because the model is an input-output or "terminal" analog, the response of one point does not require explicit computation of the activity at other points. One therefore has the freedom to calculate the displacement $y_l(t)$ for as many, or for as few, values of l as are desired.

4.21. Basilar Membrane Model

The physiological data upon which the form of $F_l(s)$ is based are those of BÉKÉSY, shown in Fig. 4.6[1]. If the curves of Fig. 4.6 are normalized with respect to the frequency of the maximum response, one finds that they are approximately constant percentage bandwidth responses. One also finds that the phase data suggest a component which is approximately a simple delay, and whose value is inversely proportional to the frequency of peak response. That is, low frequency points on the membrane (nearer the apex) exhibit more delay than high frequency (basal) points. A more detailed discussion of these relations and the functional fitting of the data has been given previously (FLANAGAN, 1962a). [In this earlier work, the fit afforded by three different forms of $F_l(s)$ was considered. For purpose of the present discussion, only the results for the first, a fifth-degree function, will be used.]

The physiological data can, of course, be approximated as closely as desired by selecting an appropriately complex model. The present model

---

[1] More recent data on basilar membrane vibration, determined in animal experiments using the Mössbauer effect (JOHNSTONE and BOYLE; RHODE), may also serve as this point of departure.

is chosen to be a realistic compromise between computational tractability and adequacy in specifying the physiological data. One function
which provides a reasonable fit to BÉKÉSY's results is

$$F_l(s) = c_1 \beta_l^4 \left(\frac{2000\pi\beta_l}{\beta_l + 2000\pi} \right)^{0.8} \left(\frac{s + \varepsilon_l}{s + \beta_l} \right) \left[\frac{1}{(s + \alpha_l)^2 + \beta_l^2} \right]^2 e^{\frac{-3\pi s}{4\beta_l}}, \quad (4.1)$$

where

$s = \sigma + j\omega$ is the complex frequency,

$\beta_l = 2\alpha_l$ is the radian frequency to which the point l-dis-
tance from the stapes responds maximally,

c_1 is a real constant that gives the proper absolute
value of displacement,

$e^{\frac{-3\pi s}{4\beta_l}}$ is a delay factor of $3\pi/4\beta_l$ seconds which brings
the phase delay of the model into line with the
phase measured on the human ear. This factor is
primarily transit delay from stapes to point l on
the membrane,

$\left(\dfrac{2000\pi\beta_l}{\beta_l + 2000\pi} \right)^{0.8} \beta_l^4$ is an amplitude factor which matches the variations in peak response with resonant frequency β_l,
as measured physiologically by BÉKÉSY (1943).

$\varepsilon_l/\beta_l = 0.1$ to 0.0 depending upon the desired fit to the
response at low frequencies.

The membrane response at any point is therefore approximated in
terms of the poles and zeros of the rational function part of $F_l(s)$. As
indicated previously in Fig. 4.6, the resonant properties of the membrane are approximately constant-Q (constant percentage bandwidth) in
character. The real and imaginary parts of the critical frequencies can
therefore be related by a constant factor, namely, $\beta_l = 2\alpha_l$. To within
a multiplicative constant, then, the imaginary part of the pole frequency,
β_l, completely describes the model and the characteristics of the membrane at a place l-distance from the stapes. The pole-zero diagram for
the model is shown in Fig. 4.22a.

The real-frequency response of the model is evidenced by letting
$s = j\omega$. If frequency is normalized in terms of $\zeta = \omega/\beta_l$, then relative
phase and amplitude responses of $F_l(j\zeta)$ are as shown in Fig. 4.22b.
Because of the previously mentioned relations, $F_l(\zeta)$ has (except for the
multiplicative constant) the same form for all values of l.

The inverse Laplace transform of (4.1) is the displacement response
of the membrane to an impulse of displacement by the stapes. The
details of the inverse transformation are numerically lengthy, but if the

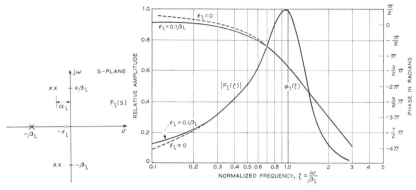

Fig. 4.22a. Pole-zero diagram for the approximating function $F_l(s)$. (After FLANAGAN, 1962a)

Fig. 4.22b. Amplitude and phase response of the basilar membrane model $F_l(s)$. Frequency is normalized in terms of the characteristic frequency β_l

mathematics is followed through it is found to be

$$
\begin{aligned}
f_l(t) = c_1 & \left(\frac{2000\,\pi}{\beta_l + 2000\,\pi} \right)^{0.8} \beta_l^{1+r} \left\{ [0.033 + 0.360\,\beta_l(t-T)] \right. \\
& \times e^{-\frac{\beta_l(t-T)}{2}} \sin \beta_l(t-T) + [0.575 - 0.320\,\beta_l(t-T)] \\
& \left. \times e^{-\frac{\beta_l(t-T)}{2}} \cos \beta_l(t-T) - 0.575\,e^{-\beta_l(t-T)} \right\} = 0
\end{aligned} \tag{4.2}
$$

$$
\text{for } t \geqq T \quad \text{and} \quad \varepsilon_l/\beta_l = 0.1,
$$

where the delay $T = 3\pi/4\beta_l$, as previously stated. A plot of the response (4.2) is shown in Fig. 4.23.

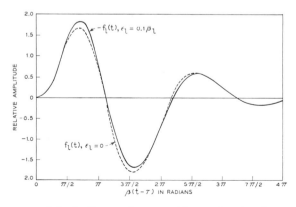

Fig. 4.23. Response of the basilar membrane model to an impulse of stapesdisplacement

Note, too, from the form of (4.1) that the complex displacement response can be determined as a function of the place frequency β_l for a given stimulating frequency $s = j\omega_n$. The radian frequency β_l can, in turn, be related directly to the distance l (in mm) from the stapes by

$$(35 - l) = 7.5 \log \beta_l / 2\pi \quad (20)$$

(see FLANAGAN, 1962a). Therefore (4.1) can be used to compute $F(s, l)|_{s = j\omega_n} = A(l) e^{j\varphi(l)}$ to give spatial responses of amplitude and phase similar to those shown in Fig. 4.6c.

4.22. Middle Ear Transmission

To account for middle ear transmission, an analytical specification is necessary of the stapes displacement produced by a given sound pressure at the eardrum (see Fig. 4.21). Quantitative physioacoustical data on the operation of the human middle ear are sparse. The data which are available are due largely to BÉKÉSY and, later, to ZWISLOCKI and to MØLLER. These results have been shown in Fig. 4.3. The data suggest appreciable variability and uncertainty, particularly in connection with the critical (roll-off) frequency and damping of the characteristic. All agree, however, that the middle ear transmission is a low-pass function. BÉKÉSY's results were obtained from physiological measurements. ZWISLOCKI's and MØLLER's data are from electrical analogs based upon impedance measurements at the eardrum, a knowledge of the topology of the middle ear circuit, and a knowledge of some of the circuit constants. In gross respects the data are in agreement[1].

If ZWISLOCKI's results in Fig. 4.3 are used, they can be approximated reasonably well by a function of third degree. Such an approximating function is of the form

$$G(s) = \frac{c_0}{(s+a)\left[(s+a)^2 + b^2\right]}, \quad (4.3)$$

where c_0 is a positive real constant. [When combined with $F_l(s)$, the multiplying constants are chosen to yield proper absolute membrane displacement. For convenience, one might consider $c_0 = a(a^2 + b^2)$ so that the low-frequency transmission of $G(s)$ is unity.] When the pole frequencies of $G(s)$ are related according to

$$b = 2a = 2\pi(1500) \text{ rad/sec}, \quad (4.4)$$

the fit to ZWISLOCKI's data is shown by the plotted points in Fig. 4.24.

The inverse transform of (4.3) is the displacement response of the stapes to an impulse of pressure at the eardrum. It is easily obtained and

---

[1] Recent measurements on middle-ear transmission in cat (GUINAN and PEAKE) also correspond favorably with these data.

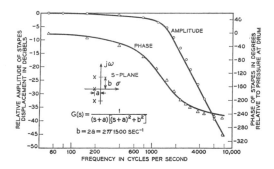

Fig. 4.24. Functional approximation of middle ear transmission. The solid curves are from an electrical analog by ZWISLOCKI (see Fig. 4.3 c). The plotted points are amplitude and phase values of the approximating function $G(s)$. (FLANAGAN, 1962 a)

will be useful in the subsequent discussion. Let

$$G(s) = G_1(s) G_2(s),$$

where

$$G_1(s) = \frac{c_0}{s+a}; \qquad G_2(s) = \frac{1}{(s+a)^2 + b^2}. \tag{4.5}$$

The inverses of the parts are

$$g_1(t) = c_0 e^{-at}; \qquad g_2(t) = \frac{e^{-at}}{b} \sin bt. \tag{4.6}$$

The inverse of $G(s)$ is then the convolution of $g_1(t)$ and $g_2(t)$

$$g(t) = \int_0^t g_1(\tau) g_2(t-\tau) d\tau,$$

or

$$g(t) = c_0 \frac{e^{-at}}{b} (1 - \cos bt) = \frac{c_0 e^{-bt/2}}{b} (1 - \cos bt). \tag{4.7}$$

Also for future use, note that the time derivative of the stapes displacement is

$$\dot{g}(t) = \frac{c_0 e^{-bt/2}}{2} (2 \sin bt + \cos bt - 1). \tag{4.8}$$

Plots of $g(t)$ and $\dot{g}(t)$ are shown in Fig. 4.25. For this middle ear function, the response is seen to be heavily damped. Other data, for example MØLLER's in Fig. 4.3, suggest somewhat less damping and the possibility of adequate approximation by a still simpler, second-degree

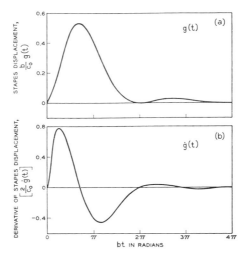

Fig. 4.25a and b. Displacement and velocity responses of the stapes to an impulse of pressure at the eardrum

function. For such a transmission, the stapes impulse response would be somewhat more oscillatory[1].

4.23. Combined Response of Middle Ear and Basilar Membrane

The combined response of the models for the middle ear and basilar membrane is

$$H_l(s) = G(s) F_l(s)$$
$$h_l(t) = g(t) * f_l(t).$$

(4.9)

For the $F_l(s)$ model described here, the combined time response is easiest obtained by inverse transforming $H_l(s)$. [For other $F_l(s)$ models, the combined response may be more conveniently computed from time-domain convolution.]

The details of the inverse transform of $H_l(s)$ are numerically involved and only the result is of interest here. When the inverse transform is calculated, the result has the form

$$h_l(\tau) = A e^{-b\tau/2} + B e^{-b\tau/2}(\cos b\tau - \tfrac{1}{2}\sin b\tau) + C(e^{-b\tau/2}\sin b\tau)$$

$$+ D e^{-\eta b\tau} + E(e^{-\eta b\tau/2}\sin \eta b\tau) + F(\eta b\tau e^{-\eta b\tau/2}\sin \eta b\tau) \qquad (4.10)$$

$$+ G(e^{-\eta b\tau/2}\cos \eta b\tau) + H(\eta b\tau e^{-\eta b\tau/2}\cos \eta b\tau); \quad \text{for } \tau \geqq 0,$$

---

[1] The modelling technique does not of course depend critically upon the particular set of data being modeled. When more complete physiological measurements are forthcoming, the rational function can be altered to fit the new data.

where $\tau=(t-T)$; $T=3\pi/4\beta_l$; $\eta=\beta_l/b$; $\beta_l=2\alpha_l$; $b=2a$; $\varepsilon_l=0$; and the A, B, C, D, E, F, G, H are all real numbers which are functions of β_l and b (see FLANAGAN, 1962a, for explicit description).

The form of the impulse response is thus seen to depend upon the parameter $\eta=\beta_l/b$. Values of $\eta<1.0$ refer to (apical) membrane points whose frequency of maximal response is less than the critical frequency of the middle ear. For these points, the middle-ear transmission is essentially constant with frequency, and the membrane displacement is very nearly that indicated by $f_l(t)$ in Eq. (4.2). On the other hand, values of $\eta>1.0$ refer to (basal) points which respond maximally at frequencies greater than the critical frequency of the middle ear. For these points, the middle-ear transmission is highly dependent upon frequency and would be expected to influence strongly the membrane displacement. To illustrate this point, Eq. (4.10) has been evaluated for $\eta=0.1$, 0.8, and 3.0. The result is shown in Fig. 4.26.

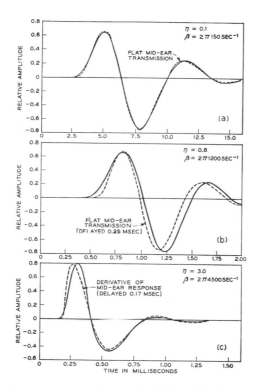

Fig. 4.26a–c. Displacement responses for apical, middle and basal points on the membrane to an impulse of pressure at the eardrum. The responses are computed from the inverse transform of $[G(s)\,F_l(s)]$

For an impulse of pressure delivered to the eardrum, the three solid curves represent the membrane displacements at points which respond maximally to frequencies of 150, 1200, and 4500 cps, respectively. Each of the plots also includes a dashed curve. In Figs. 4.26a and 4.26b, the dashed curve is the membrane displacement computed by assuming the middle-ear transmission to be constant, or flat, and with zero phase. This is simply the response $[\mathscr{L}^{-1} F_l(s)]$. In Fig. 4.26c the dashed curve is the time derivative of the stapes displacement, $g(t)$, taken from Fig. 4.25. Fig. 4.25c therefore suggests that the form of the membrane displacement in the basal region is very similar to the derivative of the stapes displacement.

The individual frequency-domain responses for $G(s)$ and $F_l(s)$ have been shown in Figs. 4.22 and 4.24, respectively. The combined response in the frequency domain is simply the sum of the individual curves for amplitude (in db) and phase (in radians). The combined amplitude and phase responses for the model $G(s) F_l(s)$ are shown in Figs. 4.27a and 4.27b, respectively.

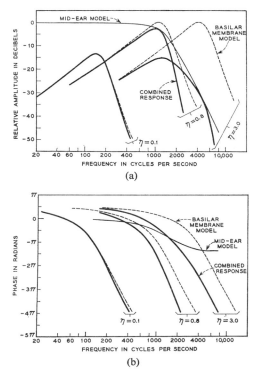

Fig. 4.27a and b. (a) Amplitude *vs* frequency responses for the combined model. (b) Phase *vs* frequency responses for the combined model

As already indicated by the impulse responses, the response of apical (low-frequency) points on the membrane is given essentially by $F_l(s)$, while for basal (high-frequency) points the response is considerably influenced by the middle-ear transmission $G(s)$. Concerning the latter point, two things may be noted about the frequency response of the membrane model [i.e., $F_l(\omega)$]. First, the low-frequency skirt of the amplitude curve rises at about 6 db/octave. And second, the phase of the membrane model [i.e. $\underline{/F_l(\omega)}$] approaches $+\pi/2$ radians at frequencies below the peak amplitude response[1]. In other words, at frequencies appreciably less than its peak response frequency, the membrane function $F_l(\omega)$ behaves crudely as a differentiator. Because the middle-ear transmission begins to diminish in amplitude at frequencies above about 1 500 cps, the membrane displacement in the basal region is roughly the time derivative of the stapes displacement. The waveform of the impulse response along the basal part of the membrane is therefore approximately constant in shape. Along the apical part, however, the impulse response oscillates more slowly (in time) as the apex is approached. This has already been illustrated in Fig. 4.26.

One further point may be noted from Fig. 4.27. Because the amplitude response of the middle-ear declines appreciably at high frequencies, the amplitude response of a basal point is highly asymmetrical. (Note the combined response for $\eta = 3.0$.) The result is that a given basal point—while responding with greater amplitude than any other membrane point at its characteristic frequency—responds with greatest amplitude (but not greater than some other point) at some lower frequency.

4.24. An Electrical Circuit for Simulating Basilar Membrane Displacement

On the basis of the relations developed in the previous sections [Eqs. (4.1) and (4.3)], it is possible to construct electrical circuits whose transmission properties are identical to those of the functions $G(s)$ and $F_l(s)$. This is easiest done by representing the critical frequencies in terms of simple cascaded resonant circuits, and supplying the additional phase delay by means of an electrical delay line. Such a simulation for the condition $\varepsilon_l = 0$ is shown in Fig. 4.28.

The voltage at an individual output tap represents the membrane displacement at a specified distance from the stapes. The electrical

---

[1] This phase behavior is contrary to the physiological phase measurements shown in Fig. 4.6b. Nevertheless, calculations of minimum phase responses for the basilar membrane indicated that the low-frequency phase behavior must approach $\pi/2$ radians *lead* (FLANAGAN and BIRD). This earlier analytical prediction (and hence justification for the choice $\varepsilon_l = 0$) has been confirmed by recent measurements. These measurements, using the Mössbauer effect, in fact reveal a leading phase at low frequencies (JOHNSTONE and BOYLE; RHODE).

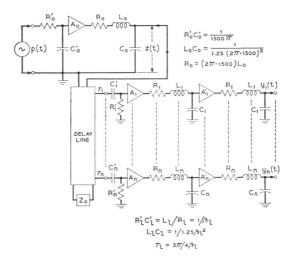

Fig. 4.28. Electrical network representation of the ear model

voltages analogous to the sound pressure at the eardrum and to the stapes displacement are also indicated. The buffer amplifiers labelled A have fixed gains which take account of the proper multiplicative amplitude constants.

The circuit elements are selected according to the constraints stated for $G(s)$ and $F_l(s)$. The constraints are represented by the equations shown in Fig. 4.28 and, together with choice of impedance levels, completely specify the circuit. For each membrane point the relative gains of the amplifiers are set to satisfy the amplitude relations implied in Fig. 4.27a. The gains also take account of the constant multiplying factors in the rational function models.

Some representative impulse responses of the analog circuit of Fig. 4.28 are shown in Fig. 4.29a. One notices the degradation in time resolution as the response is viewed at points more apicalward. That is, the frequency resolution of the membrane increases as the apex is approached.

The electrical circuit can also be used in a simple manner to provide an approximation to the spatial derivative of displacement. This function, like the displacement, may be important in the conversion of mechanical-to-neural activity. As mentioned earlier, it has been noted that the inner hair cells in the organ of Corti appear sensitive to longitudinal bending of the membrane, whereas the outer cells are sensitive to transverse bending (BÉKÉSY, 1953). The former may therefore be more sensitive to the spatial gradient or derivative of membrane displacement, while the latter may be primarily sensitive to displacement.

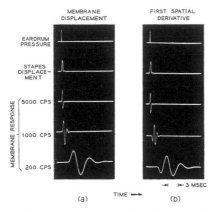

Fig. 4.29 a and b. (a) Impulse responses measured on the network of Fig. 4.28. (b) First difference approximations to the spatial derivative measured from the network of Fig. 4.28

The differences between the deflection of adjacent, uniformly-spaced points can be taken as an approximation to the spatial derivative. Fig. 4.29 b shows the first spatial difference obtained from the analog circuit by taking

$$\frac{\partial y}{\partial x} = \frac{y(t, x + \Delta x) - y(t, x)}{\Delta x},$$

where

$$\Delta x = 0.3 \text{ mm}.$$

The similarity to the displacement is considerable.

4.25. Computer Simulation of Membrane Motion

If it is desired to simulate the membrane motion at a large number of points and to perform complex operations upon the displacement responses, it is convenient to have a digital representation of the model suitable for calculations in a digital computer. One such digital simulation represents the membrane motion at 40 points (FLANAGAN, 1962b).

As might be done in realizing the analog electrical circuit, the digital representation of the model can be constructed from sampled-data equivalents of the individual complex pole-pairs and the individual real poles and zeros. The sampled-data equivalents approximate the continuous functions over the frequency range of interest. The computer operations used to simulate the necessary poles and zeros are shown in Fig. 4.30. All of the square boxes labelled D are delays equal to the time between successive digital samples. The input sampling frequency, $1/D$, in the present simulation is 20 Kcps, and the input data is quantized

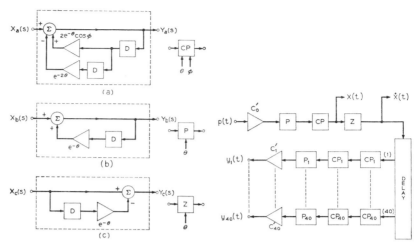

Fig. 4.30. Sampled-data equivalents for the conjugate complex poles, real-axis pole, and real-axis zero

Fig. 4.31. Functional block diagram for a digital computer simulation of basilar membrane displacement

to 11 bits. All of the triangular boxes are "amplifiers" which multiply their input samples by the gain factors shown next to the boxes.

Each of the digital operations enclosed by dashed lines is treated as a component block in the program. The block shown in Fig. 4.30a is labelled CP for conjugate-pole. It has the transfer function

$$\frac{Y_a(s)}{X_a(s)} = [e^{-2\vartheta} e^{-2sD} - 2e^{-\vartheta} \cos \Phi \, e^{-sD} + 1]^{-1} \qquad (4.11)$$

which has poles at

$$e^{-(\vartheta + sD)} = \cos \Phi \pm j \sin \Phi,$$

or

$$s = \frac{1}{D} [-\vartheta \pm j(\Phi + 2n\pi)], \qquad n = 0, 1, 2, \dots,$$

so that

$$\vartheta_l = \alpha_l D \quad \text{and} \quad \Phi_l = \beta_l D,$$

where α_l and β_l are the real and imaginary parts of the pole-pair to be simulated The pole constellation of the sampled-data function repeats at $\pm j 2n\pi/D$ (or at $\pm j 2n\pi/5 \times 10^{-5}$ for the 20 kcps sampling frequency).

Single real-axis poles are approximated as shown by the P block in Fig. 4.30b. The transfer function is

$$\frac{Y_b(s)}{X_b(s)} = [1 - e^{-(\vartheta + sD)}]^{-1} \qquad (4.12)$$

and has poles at

$$s = \frac{1}{D}(-\vartheta \pm j2n\pi), \qquad n = 0, 1, 2, \ldots.$$

The single zero is simulated by the Z block in Fig. 4.30c. Its transfer function is the reciprocal of the P block and is

$$\frac{Y_c(s)}{X_c(s)} = 1 - e^{-(\vartheta + sD)} \tag{4.13}$$

with zeros at

$$s = \frac{1}{D}(-\vartheta \pm j2n\pi), \qquad n = 0, 1, 2, \ldots.$$

In the present simulation the zero is placed at the origin, so that $\vartheta = 0$ (i.e., $\varepsilon_l = 0$).

The computer operations diagrammed by these blocks were used to simulate the model $G(s) F_l(s)$ for 40 points along the basilar membrane. The points represent 0.5 mm increments in distance along the membrane, and they span the frequency range 75 to 4600 cps. The blocks are put together in the computer program as shown in Fig. 4.31[1]. The amplifier boxes c_0' and c_l' in Fig. 4.31 take into account not only the model amplitude constants c_0 and c_1 and the $(2000\pi\beta_l/\beta_l + 2000\pi)^{0.8}$ factor, but also the amplitude responses of the digital component blocks. For example, it is convenient to make the zero-frequency gain of the CP boxes unity, so each c_l' amplifier effectively includes a $[e^{-2\vartheta} - 2e^{-\vartheta} \times \cos\varPhi + 1]^2$ term. The overall effect of the c_0' and c_l' gain adjustments is to yield the amplitudes specified by $G(s) F_l(s)$. The delay to each membrane point, $3\pi/4\beta_l$, is simulated in terms of integral numbers of sample intervals. In the present simulation it is consequently represented to the nearest 50 μsec.

An illustrative impulse response from the simulation, plotted automatically by the computer, is shown in Fig. 4.32. The displacement response of the membrane at 40 points is shown as a function of time. The characteristic frequencies of the membrane points are marked along the y-axis, starting with 4600 cps at the lower (basal) end and going to 75 cps at the upper (apical) end. Time is represented along the x-axis. The input pressure signal $p(t)$ is a single positive pulse 100 μsec in duration and delivered at $t = 0$. The responses show that the basal points respond with short latency and preserve a relatively broad-band version of the input pulse. The apical points display increasingly greater latency and progressive elimination of high-frequency content from the signal.

---

[1] In the present case the simulation was facilitated by casting the operations in the format of a special compiler program (see KELLY, VYSSOTSKY and LOCHBAUM).

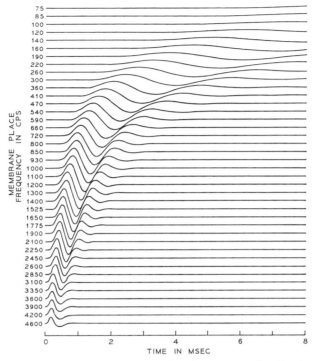

Fig. 4.32. Digital computer simulation of the impulse responses for 40 points along the basilar membrane. The input signal is a single rarefaction pulse, 100 μsec in duration, delivered to the eardrum at time $t = 0$. (After FLANAGAN, 1962b)

These same attributes of the membrane are put in evidence by a periodic pulse signal, which will be of interest in the subsequent discussion. Fig. 4.33 shows the reponse to an input signal composed of alternate positive and negative pulses of 100 μsec duration, produced at a fundamental frequency of 100 cps and initiated at $t = 0$. The time between alternate pulses is therefore 5 msec. At the apical (low-frequency) end of the membrane, the frequency resolution is best, and the displacement builds up to the fundamental sinusoid. At the basal (high-frequency) end, the membrane resolves the individual pulses in time. The responses also reflect the transit delay along the membrane.

The utility of the computation model depends equally upon its mathematical tractability and its adequacy in approximating membrane characteristics. Given both, the model can find direct application in relating subjective and physiological auditory behavior. More specifically, it can be useful in relating psychoacoustic responses to patterns of membrane displacement and in establishing an explanatory framework for the neural representation of auditory information.

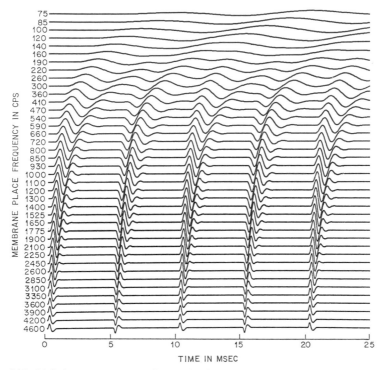

Fig. 4.33. Digital computer output for 40 simulated points along the basilar membrane. Each trace is the displacement response of a given membrane place to alternate positive and negative pressure pulses. The pulses have 100 μsec duration and are produced at a rate of 200 sec^{-1}. The input signal is applied at the eardrum and is initiated at time zero The simulated membrane points are spaced by 0.5 mm. Their characteristic frequencies are indicated along the ordinate. (After FLANAGAN, 1962b)

4.26. Transmission Line Analogs of the Cochlea

The preceding discussion has concerned an "input-output" formulation of the properties of the middle ear and basilar membrane. This approach, for computational and applicational convenience, treats the mechanism in terms of its terminal characteristics. A number of derivations have been made, however, in which the distributed nature of the inner ear is taken into account, and the detailed functioning of the mechanism is examined (PETERSON and BOGERT; BOGERT, 1951; RANKE; ZWISLOCKI, 1948; OETINGER and HAUSER). At least two of these treatments have yielded transmission line analogs for the inner ear.

The simplifying assumptions made in formulating the several treatments are somewhat similar. By way of illustration, they will be indicated for one formulation (PETERSON and BOGERT). The cochlea is idealized as shown in Fig. 4.34. The oval window is located at O and the round window at R. The distance along the cochlea is reckoned from the base and denoted as x. The cross-sectional areas of the scalas vestibuli and tympani are assumed to be identical functions of distance, $S_0(x)$. The width of the basilar membrane is taken as $b(x)$, and the per-unit-area distributed mass, resistance and stiffness of the basilar membrane (or, more precisely, of the cochlear duct separating the scalas) are respectively $m(x)$, $r(x)$ and $k(x)$. The mechanical constants used are deduced from the physiological measurements of BéKéSY.

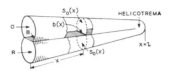

Fig. 4.34. Idealized schematic of the cochlea. (After PETERSON and BOGERT)

The following simplifying assumptions are made. All amplitude are small enough that non-linear effects are excluded. The stapes produces only plane compressional waves in the scalas. Linear relations exists between the pressure difference across the membrane at any point and the membrane displacement, velocity and acceleration at that point. The vertical component of particle velocity in the perilymph fluid is small and is neglected. A given differential element of the membrane exerts no mutual mechanical coupling on its adjacent elements.

The relations necessary to describe the system are the equations for a plane compressional wave propagating in the scalas and the equation of motion for a given membrane element. For a plane wave in the scalas, the sound pressure, p, and particle velocity, u, are linked by the equation of motion

$$\rho \frac{\partial u}{\partial t} = -\frac{\partial p}{\partial x}, \tag{4.14}$$

where ρ is the average density of the perilymph fluid. If the membrane displacements are small, the equations of continuity (mass conservation) for the two scalas are

$$\frac{\partial(u_v S)}{\partial x} = -\frac{S}{\rho c^2} \frac{\partial p_v}{\partial t} - v b$$

$$\frac{\partial(u_t S)}{\partial x} = -\frac{S}{\rho c^2} \frac{\partial p_t}{\partial t} + v b, \tag{4.15}$$

where v is the membrane velocity and the subscripts v and t denote vestibuli and tympani, respectively. These relations state that the rate of mass accumulation for an elemental volume in the scala is equal to the temporal derivative of the fluid density.

The equation of motion for the membrane is

$$(p_v - p_t) = m \frac{dv}{dt} + rv + k \int v \, dt, \qquad (4.16)$$

where the pressure difference between the scalas $(p_v - p_t)$ is the forcing function for a membrane element.

Eqs. (4.14) to (4.16) can be solved simultaneously for the pressures and velocities involved. A typical solution for the instantaneous pressure difference produced across the membrane by an excitation of 1 000 cps is shown in Fig. 4.35. The pressure difference is shown at $\frac{1}{8}$ msec intervals (every $\pi/4$ radians of phase) for one cycle. The traveling wave nature of the excitation is apparent, with the speed of propagation along the membrane being greater at the basal end and becoming slower as the apex (helicotrema) is approached.

From the pressure and velocity solutions, an equivalent four-pole network can be deduced for an incremental length of the cochlea. Voltage can be taken analogous to sound pressure and current analogous

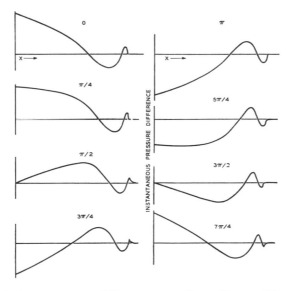

Fig. 4.35. Instantaneous pressure difference across the cochlear partition at successive phases in one period of a 1 000 cps excitation. (After PETERSON and BOGERT)

to volume velocity. Such a network section is shown in Fig. 4.36 (Bo-
GERT). Here L_1 represents the mass of the fluid in an incremental length
of the scalas; C_1 the compressibility of the fluid; and L_2, R_1, C_2, C_3,
and C_4 represent the mechanical constants of the membrane. The voltage
$P(x, \omega)$ represents the pressure difference across the membrane as a
function of distance and frequency, and the voltage $Y(x, \omega)$ represents
the membrane displacement.

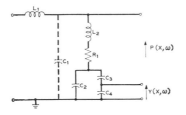

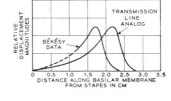

Fig. 4.36. Electrical network section for representing an incremental length of the
cochlea. (After BOGERT)

Fig. 4.37. Comparison of the displacement response of the transmission line
analog of the cochlea to physiological
data for the ear. (After BOGERT)

A set of 175 such sections has been used to produce a transmission
line analog of the cochlea (BOGERT). The displacement responses exhibited by the line compare well in shape with those measured by
BÉKÉSY on real cochleas. An illustrative response is shown in Fig. 4.37.
Some differences are found in the positions of peak response and in the
lowest frequencies which exhibit resonance phenomena. Probable origins
of the differences are the uncertainties connected with the spatial variation of the measured mechanical constants of the membrane and the
neglect of mutual coupling among membrane elements. Despite the uncertainties in the distributed parameters, the transmission line analog
provides a graphic demonstration of the traveling-wave nature of the
basilar membrane motion.

4.3. Illustrative Relations between Subjective and Physiological Behavior

The ear models discussed above describe only the mechanical functions of the peripheral ear. Any comprehensive hypothesis about auditory
perception must provide for the transduction of mechanical displacement into neural activity. As indicated earlier, the details of this process
are not well understood. The assumptions that presently can be made
are of a gross and simplified nature. Three such assumptions are useful,

however, in attempting to relate physiological and subjective behavior. Although oversimplifications, they do not seem to violate known physiological facts.

The first is that sufficient local deformation of the basilar membrane elicits neural activity in the terminations of the auditory nerve. A single neuron is presumably a binary (fired or unfired) device. The number of neurons activated depends in a monotonic fashion upon the amplitude of membrane displacement[1]. Such neural activity may exist in the form of volleys triggered synchronously with the stimulus, or in the form of a signalling of place localization of displacement. Implicit is the notion that the displacement — or perhaps spatial derivatives of displacement — must exceed a certain threshold before nerve firings take place.

Second, neural firings occur on only one "polarity" of the membrane displacement, or of its spatial derivative. In other words, some process like half-wave rectification operates on the mechanical response. Third, the membrane point displacing with the greatest amplitude originates the predominant neutral activity. This activity may operate to suppress or inhibit activity arising from neighboring points.

These assumptions, along with the results from the models, have in a number of instances been helpful in interpreting auditory subjective behavior. Without going into any case in depth, several applications can be outlined.

4.31. Pitch Perception

Pitch is that subjective attribute which admits of a rank ordering on a scale ranging from low to high. As such, it correlates strongly with objective measures of frequency. One important facet of auditory perception is the ability to ascribe a pitch to sounds which exhibit periodic characteristics.

Consider first the pitch of pure (sinusoidal) tones. For such stimuli the basilar membrane displacements are, of course, sinusoidal. The frequency responses given previously in Fig. 4.27a indicate the relative amplitudes of displacement versus frequency for different membrane points. At any given frequency, one point on the membrane responds with greater amplitude than all others. In accordance with the previous assumptions, the most numerous neural volleys are elicited at this maximum point. For frequencies sufficiently low (less than about 1000 cps), the volleys are triggered once per cycle and at some fixed epoch on the displacement waveform. Subsequent processing by higher

---

[1] Psychological and physiological evidence suggests that the intensity of the neural activity is a power-law function of the mechanical displacement. A single neuron is also refractory for a given period after firing. A limit exists, therefore, upon the rate at which it can fire.

centers presumably appreciates the periodicity of the stimulus-locked volleys.

For frequencies greater than about 1000 to 2000 cps, electro-physiological evidence suggests that synchrony of neural firings is not maintained (GALAMBOS). In such cases, pitch apparently is perceived through a signalling of the place of greatest membrane displacement. The poorer frequency resolution of points lying in the basal part of the basilar membrane probably also contributes to the psychoacoustic fact that pitch discrimination is less acute at higher frequencies.

Suppose the periodic sound stimulus is not a simple sinusoidal tone but is more complex, say repeated sharp pulses. What pitch is heard? For purpose of illustration, imagine the stimulus to be the alternately positive and negative impulses used to illustrate the digital simulation in Fig. 4.33. Such a pulse train has a spectrum which is odd-harmonic. If the pulses occur slowly enough, the membrane displacement at all points will resolve each pulse in time. That is, the membrane will have time to execute a complete, damped impulse response at all places for each pulse, whether positive or negative. Such a situation is depicted by the analog membrane responses shown in the left column of Fig. 4.38. The fundamental frequency of excitation is 25 cps (50 pps). The waveforms were measured from analog networks such as illustrated in Fig. 4.28.

For this low pulse rate condition, one might imagine that neural firings synchronous with each pulse – regardless of polarity – would be triggered at all points along the membrane. The perceived pitch might

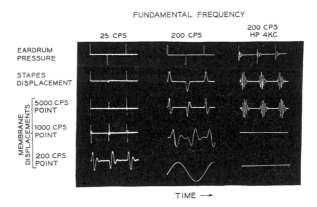

Fig. 4.38. Membrane displacement responses for filtered and unfiltered periodic pulses. The stimulus pulses are alternately positive and negative. The membrane displacements are simulated by the electrical networks shown in Fig. 4.28. To display the waveforms more effectively, the traces are adjusted for equal peak-to-peak amplitudes. Relative amplitudes are therefore not preserved

then be expected to be equal to the pulse rate. Measurements show this to be the case (FLANAGAN and GUTTMAN). Furthermore, the model indicates that a pulse signal of this low rate causes the greatest displacements near the middle portion of the membrane, that is, in the vicinity of the place maximally responsive to about 1 500 cps.

If, on the other hand, the fundamental frequency of excitation is made sufficiently high, say 200 cps or greater, the fundamental component will be resolved (in frequency) at the most apically-responding point. This situation is illustrated for a 200 cps fundamental by the traces in the second column of Fig. 4.38. The 200 cps place on the membrane displaces with a nearly pure sinusoidal motion, while the more basal points continue to resolve each pulse in time. At the apical end, therefore, neural volleys might be expected to be triggered synchronously at the fundamental frequency, while toward the basal end the displacements favor firings at the pulse rate, that is, twice per fundamental period. Psychoacoustic measurements indicate that the apical, fundamental-correlated displacements are subjectively more significant than the basal, pulse-rate displacements. The fundamental-rate volleys generally predominate in the percept, and the pitch is heard as 200 sec^{-1}. At some frequency, then, the pitch assignment switches from pulse rate to fundamental.

The pulse pattern illustrating the computer simulation in Fig. 4.33 is the same positive-negative pulse alternation under discussion, but it is produced at a fundamental frequency of 100 cps. This frequency is immediately in the transition range between the fundamental and pulse-rate pitch modes. One notices in Fig. 4.33 that the ear is beginning to resolve the fundamental component in relatively low amplitude at the apical end of the membrane, while the pulse rate is evident in the basal displacements. One might suppose for this condition that the pulse rate *and* fundamental cues are strongly competing, and that the pitch percept is ambiguous. Subjective measurements bear this out.

Another effect becomes pronounced in and near the pitch-transition region corresponding to the conditions of Fig. 4.33. A fine structure in the perception of pulse pitch becomes more evident. The membrane region where displacement amplitude is greatest is in the place-frequency range 600 to 1 500 cps. In this region the displacement response to a pulse has a period which is an appreciable fraction of the pulse repetition period. That is, the half-period time of the pulse response is a significant percentage of the pulse period. Assume as before that neural firings occur only on positive deflections of the membrane. The intervals between firings on fibers originating from a given place in this region should, therefore, be alternately lengthened and shortened. The change in interval (from strict periodicity) is by an amount equal to the half-period of the pulse response at that place. One might expect, therefore, a bimodality in the pitch percept. If f_d is the place-frequency of dominant membrane motion and r the signal pulse rate, the perceived pitch f_p should correspond to

$$f_p = \left[\frac{1}{r} \pm \frac{1}{2 f_d} \right]^{-1} .$$

This bimodality in the pitch percept is in fact found (ROSENBERG; RITSMA).

If the 200 cps stimulus in the middle column of Fig. 4.38 is high-pass filtered at a sufficiently high frequency, only the basal displacements remain effective in producing the pitch percept. For example, the membrane displacements for a high-pass filtering at 4000 cps are shown in the third column of Fig. 4.38. If the present arguments continue to hold, such a filtering should change the percept from the fundamental mode back to the pulse-rate mode. The reason, of course, is that the time resolution of the basal end separates each pulse, whether positive or negative. This hypothesis is in fact sustained in psychoacoustic measurements (GUTTMAN and FLANAGAN, 1964).

A somewhat more subtle effect is obtained if the high-pass filtering is made at a fairly small harmonic number, for example, at the second harmonic, so as to remove only the fundamental component. Under certain of these conditions, the membrane may generate displacements which favor a difference-frequency response. For a stimulus with odd and even components, the pitch percept can be the fundamental, even though the fundamental is not present in the stimulus.

4.32. Binaural Lateralization

Another aspect of perception is binaural lateralization. This is the subjective ability to locate a sound image at a particular point inside the head when listening over earphones. If identical clicks (impulses of sound pressure) are produced simultaneously at the two ears, a normal listener hears the sound image to be located exactly in the center of his head. If the click at one ear is produced a little earlier or with slightly greater intensity than the other, the sound image shifts toward that ear. The shift continues with increasing interaural time or intensity difference until the image moves completely to one side and eventually breaks apart. One then begins to hear individual clicks located at the ears.

Naively we suppose the subjective position of the image to be determined by some sort of computation of coincidence between neural volleys. The volleys originate at the periphery and travel to higher centers via synaptic pathways. The volley initiated earliest progresses to a point in the neural net where a coincidence occurs with the later volley. A subjective image appropriately off-center is produced. To the extent that intensity differences can shift the image position, intensity must be coded—at least partially—in terms of volley timing. As has been the case in pitch perception, there are several research areas in binaural phenomena where the computational model described in Section 4.2 has been helpful in quantifying physiological response and relating it to subjective behavior. One such area concerns the effects of phase and masking upon the binaural lateralization of clicks.

If a pulse of pressure rarefaction is produced at the eardrum, the drum is initially drawn outward. The stapes is also initially drawn outward, and the membrane is initially drawn upward. The stapes and membrane displacements (as described by the model) in response to a rarefaction pulse of 100 μsec duration are shown by the waveforms at the right of Fig. 4.39. The pulse responses of three different membrane points are shown, namely, the points maximally responsive to 2400 cps, 1200 cps, and 600 cps, respectively. The stapes displacement is a slightly integrated version of the input. The membrane responses reflect the vibratory behavior of the particular points as well as the traveling-wave transit delay to the points.

According to the model, broadband pulses produce the greatest displacements near the middle of the membrane, roughly in the region

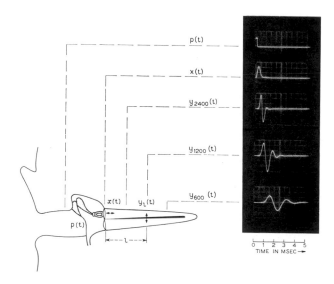

Fig. 4.39. Basilar membrane responses at the 2400, 1200 and 600 cps points to a pressure-rarefaction pulse of 100 μsec duration. The responses are measured on the electrical analog circuit of Fig. 4.28. Relative amplitudes are preserved

maximally responsive to about 1 500 cps. The magnitude of displacement is less at places either more toward the base or more toward the apex. It has been hypothesized that the most significant neural activity is generated at the membrane point displacing with the greatest amplitude. Further, electro-physiological data suggest that neural firings occur at some threshold only on unipolar motions of the basilar membrane. (For the outer hair cells, these are motions which drive the basilar membrane toward the tectorial membrane.) The oscillatory behavior of the pulse response suggests, too, that multiple or secondary neural firings might be elicited by single stimulus pulses.

If pulses are supplied to both ears, a centered sound image is heard if the significant neural activity is elicited simultaneously. Suppose that the input pulses are identical rarefaction pulses. The maximum displacements occur near the middle of the membrane. For simplicity imagine that the neural firings are triggered somewhere near the positive crests of the displacement waves. For this cophasic condition, a centered image is heard if the input pulses are produced simultaneously, or if the interaural time is zero. Suppose now that the pulse to one of the ears is reversed in phase to a pressure condensation. The membrane responses for this ear also change sign and are the negatives of those shown in Fig. 4.39. Their first positive crests now occur later by about one-half cycle of the displacement at each point. At the middle of the membrane this half-cycle amounts to about 300 to 400 μsec. To produce a centered image for the antiphasic condition, then, one would expect that the condensation pulse would have to be advanced in time by this amount.

The membrane point which displaces with the greatest coherent amplitude can be manipulated by adding masking noise of appropriate frequency content. That is, the place which normally responds with greatest amplitude can be obscured by noise, and the significant displacement caused to occur at a less sensitive place. For example, suppose that the basal end of the membrane in one ear is masked by high-pass noise, and the apical end of the membrane in the other ear is masked by low-pass noise. If the listener is required to adjust stimulus pulses to produce a centered image, the fusion must be made from apical-end information in one ear and basal-end in the other. The resulting interaural time would then reflect both the oscillatory characteristics of the specific membrane points and the traveling-wave delay between them.

Experiments show these time dependencies to be manifest in subjective behavior (FLANAGAN, DAVID, and WATSON). The test procedure to measure them is shown in Fig. 4.40. Identical pulse generators produce 100 μsec pulses at a rate of 10 per second. Pulse amplitude is set to produce a 40 db sensation level. The subject, seated in a sound-

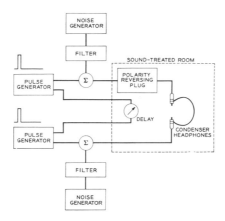

Fig. 4.40. Experimental arrangement for measuring the interaural times that produce centered sound images. (After Flanagan, David and Watson)

treated room, listens to the pulses over condenser earphones. (Condenser phones are used because of the importance of good acoustic reproduction of the pulses.) He has a switch available to reverse the polarity of the pulses delivered to the right ear so that it can be made a condensation instead of the normal rarefaction. The subject also has a delay control which varies the relative times of occurrence of the two pulses over a range of ± 5 msec. Two uncorrelated noise generators supply masking noise via variable filters. (A separate experiment was conducted to determine the filtered noise levels necessary to mask prescribed spectral portions of the pulse stimuli.)

For a given masking and pulse polarity condition, the subject is required to adjust the delay to produce a centered sound image in his head. Multiple images are frequently found, with the more subtle, secondary images apparently being elicited on secondary bounces of the membrane.

Fig. 4.41 shows the results for principal-image fusions under a variety of masking conditions. Fig. 4.41a gives results for unmasked and symmetrically-masked conditions, and Fig. 4.41b gives the results for asymmetrical masking. The data are for four subjects, and each point is the median of approximately 15 principal-image responses. Each two sets of points is bracketed along the abscissa. The set labelled C is the cophasic response and that labelled A is the antiphasic. The cophasic conditions are rarefaction pulses in both ears. The antiphasic conditions are rarefaction in the left ear and condensation in the right ear.

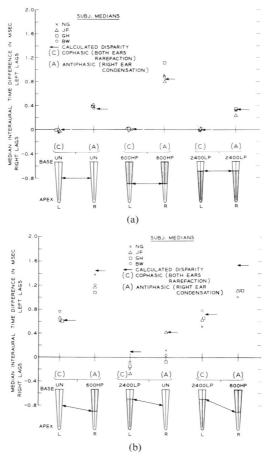

Fig. 4.41 a and b. Experimentally measured interaural times for lateralizing cophasic and antiphasic clicks. Several conditions of masking are shown. (a) Unmasked and symmetrically masked conditions. (b) Asymmetrically masked conditions. The arrows indicate the interaural times predicted from the basilar membrane model

Each bracket corresponds to the masking conditions represented by the schematic cochleas drawn below the brackets. The labelling at the top of each cochlea gives the masking condition for that ear. For example, the UN means unmasked. The dark shading on the cochleas indicates the membrane regions obscured by masking noise. The double arrow between each pair of cochleas indicates approximately the points of maximum, unmasked displacement. For example, in the first case of Fig. 4.41a, which is the unmasked case, the maximum displacements occur near the middles of the two membranes.

The single arrows in the vicinity of the plotted responses are estimates of the interaural times calculated from the basilar membrane model. The estimates are made by assuming the neural firings to be produced at the positive crest of the displacement at the most significant place. The arrows therefore represent the time differences between the first positive crests at the places indicated in the cochlear diagrams. As such, they include the transit time to the particular place, plus the initial quarter-cycle duration of the pulse response.

The actual threshold for neural firing is of course not known, and is very likely to be dependent upon place. In the symmetrically-masked conditions, an actual knowledge of the threshold is not of much consequence since the threshold epoch, whether it is at the crest or down from the crest, should be about the same in the two ears. For these cases, therefore, it is the half-cycle time of the displacement wave that is important. Fig. 4.41a shows that the measured responses do, in fact, agree relatively well with this simple estimate of the interaural time. All of the principal cophasic fusions are made for essentially zero time, and the antiphasic lateralizations reflect the half-cycle disparity of the appropriate places, with the condensation pulse always leading.

The agreement is not as good for the asymmetrically-masked cases shown in Fig. 4.41b. Signal loudnesses are different in the two ears, and the neural thresholds probably vary with place. The times of the initial positive crests would not be expected to give very realistic estimates of the interaural times. It becomes much more important to have a knowledge of the actual threshold levels and the relative amplitudes of the displacements. Even so, it is interesting to note to what extent the simple positive-crest estimates follow the data.

In the first condition, the left ear is unmasked and the right ear has masking noise high-pass filtered at 600 cps (600 HP). The cophasic interaural time is predicted to be on the order of 600 μsec, and the measurements do give essentially this figure. The antiphasic condition is expected to be on the order or 1450 μsec, but the measured median response is a little less, about 1200 μsec.

The next case has the left ear masked with noise low-pass filtered at 2400 cps (2400 LP), and the right ear is unmasked. The cophasic condition is expected to yield an interaural time of slightly less than 100 μsec, with the left ear lagging, but the experimental measurements actually give a right ear lag of about 150 μsec. The relatively wide spread of the subject medians in the asymmetrical cases, and in particular for the cases involving 2400 LP, show that these lateralizations are considerably more difficult and more variable than the symmetrical cases. The antiphasic response for this same condition is estimated to give an interaural time on the order of 400 μsec, but again the responses are variable with the median falling at about 100 µsec. One subject's median actually falls on the right-lag side of the axis.

The final condition has 2400 LP in the left ear and 600 HP in the right ear. The cophasic fusion is expected to be in the neighborhood of 700 µsec, and the measured response is found about here. The anti-phasic condition should yield an interaural time on the order of 1 550 µsec, but the measurements produce a median slightly greater than 1 100 µsec.

Clearly, the simple assumption of neural firing at the positive crests (or some other fixed epoch) of the displacement is not adequate to specify all of the interaural times. The real thresholds for firing are likely to vary considerably with place. In fact, by taking data such as these, plus the displacement waves from the model, the possibility exists for working backwards to deduce information about neural threshold epochs. More broadly than this, however, the present results suggest strong ties between subjective response and the detailed motion of the basilar membrane.

4.33. Threshold Sensitivity

The combined response curves in Fig. 4.27a indicate that the ear is mechanically more sensitive to certain frequencies than to others. A similar frequency dependence exists subjectively. To what extent are the variations in the threshold of audibility accounted for simply by the mechanical sensitivity of the ear?

The envelope of the peak displacement responses in Fig. 4.27a can be compared with the subjectively determined minimum audible pressure for pure (sine) tones. Fig. 4.42 shows this comparison. The agreement

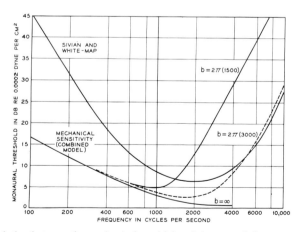

Fig. 4.42. Relation between the mechanical sensitivity of the ear and the monaural minimum audible pressure threshold for pure tones

is generally poor, although the gross trends are similar. One curve in the figure is based on the 1 500 cps critical frequency for the middle ear. The earlier discussion has pointed up the uncertainty and variability of this figure. If a critical frequency of 3 000 cps is taken for the middle ear, the fit to the threshold curve at high frequencies is more respectable[1]. The match at low frequencies, however, is not improved, but this is of less concern for a different reason.

At the low frequencies, the disparity between the mechanical and subjective sensitivity may be partially a neural effect. According to the earlier assumptions, the number of neurons activated bears some monotonic relation to amplitude of membrane displacement. Perception of loudness is thought to involve possibly temporal and spatial integrations of neural activity. If a constant integrated neural activity were equivalent to constant loudness, the difference between mechanical and subjective sensitivities might be owing to a sparser neural density in the apical (low-frequency) end of the cochlea. There is physiological evidence to this effect.

In histological studies, GUILD et al. counted the number of ganglion cells per mm length of the organ of Corti. Their results for normal ears are summarized in Fig. 4.43. These data show a slight decrease in the number of cells at the basal end, and a substantial decrease in the density as the apex is approached. The innervation over the middle of the membrane is roughly constant.

One can pose similar questions about threshold sensitivity to short pulses or clicks of sound. For pulses of sufficiently low repetition rate, the maximal displacement of the membrane — as stated before — is near

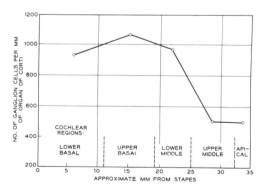

Fig. 4.43. Average number of ganglion cells per mm length of organ of Corti.
(After GUILD et al.)

---

[1] Note, too, that the membrane velocity response $\dot{y}(t)$ provides a better fit to the tone threshold than does the displacement, $y(t)$. $\dot{y}(t)$ includes an additional +6 db/oct. component.

the middle. According to the model, the place of maximum displacement remains near the middle for pulse rates in excess of several hundred per second. In its central region, the resonance properties of the membrane permit temporal resolution of individual exciting pulses for rates upwards of $1000\ \mathrm{sec}^{-1}$. If the predominant displacement takes place in one vicinity for a large range of pulse rates, polarity patterns and pulse durations, how might the subjective threshold vary with these factors, and how might it be correlated with the membrane motion? At least one examination of this question has been made (FLANAGAN, 1961a). The results can be briefly indicated.

Binaural thresholds of audibility for a variety of periodic pulse trains with various polarity patterns, pulse rates and durations are shown in Fig. 4.44. The data show that the thresholds are relatively independent of polarity pattern. For pulse rates less than 100 pps, the thresholds are relatively independent of rate, and are dependent only upon duration. Above 100 pps, the thresholds diminish with increasing pulse rate. The amplitude of membrane displacement would be expected to be a function of pulse duration and to produce a lower threshold for the longer pulses, which is the case. For rates greater than $100\ \mathrm{sec}^{-1}$, however, some other nonmechanical effect apparently is of importance. The way in which audible pulse amplitude diminishes suggests a temporal integration with a time constant of the order of 10 msec.

Using the earlier assumptions about conversion of mechanical to neural activity, one might ask "what processing of the membrane displacement at the point of greatest amplitude would reflect the constant loudness percept at threshold." One answer is suggested by the operations illustrated in Fig. 4.45. The first two blocks represent middle ear transmission [as specified in Eq. (4.3)] and basilar membrane displacement [vicinity of the 1000 cps point, as specified in Eq. (4.1)]. The

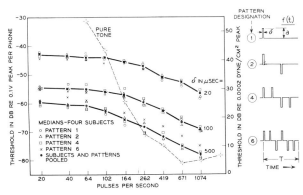

Fig. 4.44. Binaural thresholds of audibility for periodic pulses. (After FLANAGAN, 1961a)

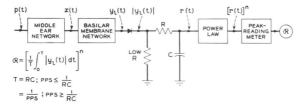

Fig. 4.45. Model of the threshold of audibility for the pulse data shown in Fig. 4.44

diode represents the half-wave rectification associated with neural firings on unipolar motions of the membrane. The *RC* integrator has a 10 msec time constant, as suggested by the threshold data. The power-law element (exponent$=0.6$) represents the power-law relation found in loudness estimation[1]. A meter indicates the peak value of the output of the power-law device. When the stimulus conditions represented by points on the threshold curves in Fig. 4.44 are applied to this circuit, the output meter reads the same value, namely, threshold.

One can also notice how this simple process might be expected to operate for sine wave inputs. Because the integration time is 10 msec, frequencies greater than about 100 cps produce meter readings proportional to the average value of the half-wave rectified sinusoid. In other words, the meter reading is proportional to the amplitude of the sine wave into the rectifier. Two alterations in the network circuitry are then necessary. First, the basilar membrane network appropriate to the point maximally responsive to the sine frequency must be used. This may be selected from an ensemble of networks. And second, to take account of the sparser apical innervation, the signal from the rectifier must be attenuated for the low-frequency networks in accordance with the difference between the mechanical and subjective sensitivity curves in Fig. 4.42. The power-law device is still included to simulate the growth of loudness with sound level.

4.34. Auditory Processing of Complex Signals

The preceding discussions suggest that the extent to which subjective behavior can be correlated with (and even predicted by) the physiological operation of the ear is substantial. Recent electrophysiological data link neural activity closely with the detailed mechanical motion of the basilar membrane. Subjective measurements, such as described in the foregoing

---

[1] The power-law device is not necessary for simple threshold indications of "audible-inaudible". It is necessary, however, to represent the growth of loudness with sound level, and to provide indications of subjective loudness above threshold.

sections, lend further support to the link. Psychological and physiological experimentation continue to serve jointly in expanding knowledge about the processes involved in converting the mechanical motions of the inner ear into intelligence-preserving neural activity.

The physiological-psychoacoustic correlations which have been put forward here have involved only the simplest of signals — generally, signals that are temporally punctuate or spectrally discrete, or both. Furthermore, the correlations have considered only gross and salient features of these signals, such as periodicity or time of occurrence. The primary aim has been to outline the peripheral mechanism of the ear and to connect it with several phenomena in perception. Little has been said about classical psychoacoustics or about speech perception. As the stimuli are made increasingly complex — in the ultimate, speech signals — it seems clear that more elaborate processing is called into play in perception. Much of the additional processing probably occurs centrally in the nervous system. For such perception, the correlations that presently can be made between the physiological and perceptual domains are relatively rudimentary. As research goes forward, however, these links will be strengthened.

The literature on hearing contains a large corpus of data on subjective response to speech and speech-like stimuli. There are, for example, determinations of the ear's ability to discriminate features such as vowel pitch, loudness, formant frequency, spectral irregularity and the like. Such data are particularly important in establishing criteria for the design of speech transmission systems and in estimating the channel capacity necessary to transmit speech data. Instead of appearing in this chapter, comments on these researches have been reserved for a later, more applied discussion where they have more direct application to transmission systems.

V. Techniques for Speech Analysis

The earlier discussion suggested that the encoding of speech information might be considered at several stages in the communication chain. On the transmitter side, the configuration and excitation of the vocal tract constitute one description. In the transmission channel, the transduced acoustic waveform is a signal representation commonly encountered. At the receiver, the mechanical motion of the basilar membrane is still another portrayal of the information. Some of these descriptions exhibit properties which might be exploited in communication.

Efforts in speech analysis and synthesis frequently aim at the efficient encoding and transmission of speech information[1]. Here the goal is the transmission of speech information over the smallest channel capacity adequate to satisfy specified perceptual criteria. Acoustical and physiological analyses of the vocal mechanism suggest certain possibilities for efficient description of the signal. Psychological and physiological experiments in hearing also outline certain bounds on perception. Although such analyses may not necessarily lead to totally optimum methods for encoding and transmission, they do bring to focus important physical constraints. Transmission economies beyond this level generally must be sought in linguistic and semantic dependencies.

The discussions in Chapters II and III set forth certain fundamental relations for the vocal mechanism. Most of the analyses presumed detailed physical knowledge of the tract. In actual communication practice, however, one generally has knowledge only of some transduced version of the acoustic signal. (That is, the speaker does not submit to measurements on his vocal tract.) The acoustic and articulatory parameters of the preceding chapters must therefore be determined from the speech signal if they are to be exploited.

This chapter proposes to discuss certain speech analysis techniques which have been found useful for deriving so-called "information-bearing elements" of speech. Subsequent chapters will consider synthesis of speech from these low information-rate parameters, perceptual criteria appropriate to the processing of such parameters, and application of analysis, synthesis and perceptual results in complete transmission systems.

5.1. Spectral Analysis of Speech

Frequency-domain representation of speech information appears advantageous from two standpoints. First, acoustic analysis of the vocal mechanism shows that the normal mode or natural frequency concept permits concise description of speech sounds. Second, clear evidence exists that the ear makes a crude frequency analysis at an early stage in its processing. Presumably, then, features salient in frequency analysis are important in production and perception, and consequently hold promise for efficient coding. Experience supports this notion.

Further, the vocal mechanism is a quasi-stationary source of sound. Its excitation and normal modes change with time. Any spectral measure applicable to the speech signal should therefore reflect temporal features of perceptual significance as well as spectral features. Something other then a conventional frequency transform is indicated.

---

[1] Other motivating objectives are: basic understanding of speech communication, voice control of machines, and voice response from computers.

5.11. Short-Time Frequency Analysis

The conventional mathematical link between an aperiodic time function $f(t)$ and its complex amplitude-density spectrum $F(\omega)$ is the Fourier transform-pair

$$F(\omega) = \int_{-\infty}^{\infty} f(t) e^{-j\omega t} dt$$

$$f(t) = \frac{1}{2\pi} \int_{-\infty}^{\infty} F(\omega) e^{j\omega t} d\omega. \tag{5.1}$$

For the transform to exist, $\int_{-\infty}^{\infty} |f(t)| \, dt$ must be finite. Generally, a continuous speech signal neither satisfies the existence condition nor is known over all time. The signal must consequently be modified so that its transform exists for integration over known (past) values. Further, to reflect significant temporal changes, the integration should extend only over times appropriate to the quasi-steady elements of the speech signal. Essentially what is desired is a *running* spectrum, with real-time as an independent variable, and in which the spectral computation is made on weighted past values of the signal.

Such a result can be obtained by analyzing a portion of the signal "seen" through a specified time window, or weighting function. The window is chosen to insure that the product of signal and window is Fourier transformable. For practical purposes, the weighting function $h(t)$ usually is the impulse response of a physically-realizable linear system. Then, $h(t) = 0$; for $t < 0$. Generally $h(t)$ is desired to be unipolar and is essentially the response of a low-pass filter. The Fourier transform (5.1) can therefore be modified by transforming that part of the signal seen through the window at a given instant of time. The desired operation is

$$F(\omega, t) = \int_{-\infty}^{t} f(\lambda) h(t - \lambda) e^{-j\omega\lambda} d\lambda,$$

or,

$$F(\omega, t) = e^{-j\omega t} \int_{0}^{\infty} f(t - \lambda) h(\lambda) e^{j\omega\lambda} d\lambda. \tag{5.2}$$

The signal, with its past values weighted by $h(t)$, is illustrated for a given instant, t, in Fig. 5.1.

The short-time transform, so defined, is the convolution

$$[f(t) e^{-j\omega t} * h(t)], \quad \text{or alternatively,} \quad e^{-j\omega t}[f(t) * h(t) e^{j\omega t}].$$

If the weighting function $h(t)$ is considered to have the dimension sec^{-1} (i.e., the Fourier transform of $h(t)$ is dimensionless), then $|F(\omega, t)|$ is a

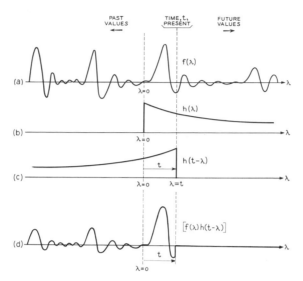

Fig. 5.1. Weighting of an on-going signal $f(t)$ by a physically realizable time window $h(t)$. λ is a dummy integration variable for taking the Fourier transform at any instant, t

short-time amplitude spectrum with the same dimension as the signal. Like the conventional Fourier transform, $F(\omega, t)$ is generally complex with a magnitude and phase, namely $|F(\omega, t)|e^{-j\vartheta(\omega, t)}$, where $\vartheta(\omega, t)$ is the short-time phase spectrum.

By definition, the inverse relation also holds

$$[f(\lambda)\,h(t-\lambda)] = \frac{1}{2\pi} \int_{-\infty}^{\infty} F(\omega, t)\,e^{j\omega\lambda}\,d\omega.$$

Note that at any time $t=t_1$, the product $[f(\lambda)\,h(t_1-\lambda)]$ is determined for all $\lambda \leq t_1$. If the window function $h(t_1-\lambda)$ is known, then the original function over the interval $-\infty \leq \lambda \leq t_1$ can be retrieved from the product. For a value of λ equal to t_1

$$[f(t)\,h(0)] = \frac{1}{2\pi} \int F(\omega, t_1)\,e^{j\omega t_1}\,d\omega,$$

or in general for $\lambda = t$

$$f(t) = \frac{1}{2\pi\,h(0)} \int_{-\infty}^{\infty} F(\omega, t)\,e^{j\omega t}\,d\omega.$$

The short-time transform is therefore uniquely invertible if one non-zero value of the window function is known. Typically $h(t)$ can be chosen so that $h(0)=1$ and

$$f(t)=\frac{1}{2\pi}\int_{-\infty}^{\infty}F(\omega,t)\,e^{j\omega t}\,d\omega$$

which bears a pleasing parallel to the conventional infinite-time Fourier transform.

The inversion implies that $f(t)$ can be determined for the same points in time that $F(\omega,t)$ is known, provided $F(\omega,t)$ is known as a continuous function of frequency. However, in cases where the product function $[f(\lambda)\,h(t-\lambda)]$ is of finite duration in λ (say owing to a finite duration window) then samples of the waveform $f(t)$ may be recovered exactly from samples in ω of $F(\omega,t)$ (WEINSTEIN). Discrete-frequency, continuous-time values of the short-time transform, $F(\omega_n,t)$, are of particular interest and will find applications in later discussions.

5.12. Measurement of Short-Time Spectra

We notice that (5.2) can be rewritten

$$F(\omega,t)=\int_{-\infty}^{t}f(\lambda)\cos\omega\lambda\,h(t-\lambda)\,d\lambda-j\int_{-\infty}^{t}f(\lambda)\sin\omega\lambda\,h(t-\lambda)\,d\lambda \tag{5.3}$$

$$=[a(\omega,t)-j\,b(\omega,t)].$$

Further,

$$|F(\omega,t)|=[F(\omega,t)\,F^*(\omega,t)]^{\frac{1}{2}}$$
$$=(a^2+b^2)^{\frac{1}{2}} \tag{5.4}$$

and

$$\vartheta(\omega,t)=\tan^{-1}b/a,$$

where $F^*(\omega,t)$ is the complex conjugate of $F(\omega,t)$. Note that $|F(\omega,t)|$ is a scalar, whereas $F(\omega,t)\,F^*(\omega,t)$ is formally complex, and that $|F(\omega,t)|^2$ is the short-time power spectrum. The measurement of $|F(\omega,t)|$ can therefore be implemented by the operations shown in Fig. 5.2.

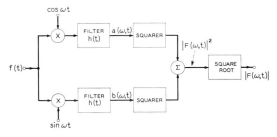

Fig. 5.2. A method for measuring the short-time amplitude spectrum $|F(\omega,t)|$

The frequency-domain interpretation of these operations is apparent. The heterodyning (or multiplication by $\cos \omega t$ and $\sin \omega t$) shifts (or translates) the spectrum of $f(t)$ across the pass-band of filter $h(t)$. The latter is normally a low-pass structure. Frequency components of $f(t)$ lying close to ω produce difference-frequency components inside the low-pass band and yield large outputs from the $h(t)$ filter. Quadrature versions of the shifted signals are squared and added to give the short-time power spectrum $|F(\omega, t)|^2$.

Alternatively, Eq. (5.2) can be written

$$F(\omega, t) = e^{-j\omega t} \left\{ \int_0^\infty f(t-\lambda) h(\lambda) \cos \omega \lambda \, d\lambda + j \int_0^\infty f(t-\lambda) h(\lambda) \sin \omega \lambda \, d\lambda \right\}$$

$$= [a'(\omega, t) + j b'(\omega, t)] e^{-j\omega t}. \tag{5.5}$$

The alternative measurement of $|F(\omega, t)| = [a'^2 + b'^2]^{\frac{1}{2}}$ can therefore be effected by the operations in Fig. 5.3.

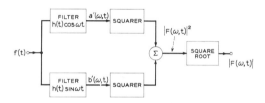

Fig. 5.3. Alternative implementation for measuring the short-time amplitude spectrum $|F(\omega, t)|$

Again, in terms of a frequency-domain interpretation, the measurement involves filtering by phase-complementary band-pass filters centered at ω and having bandwidths twice that of the low-pass $h(t)$ function. The outputs are squared and added to produce the short-time power spectrum $|F(\omega, t)|^2$. Both filters have impulse responses whose envelopes are the time window, $h(t)$. As many pairs of filters are required as the number of frequency values for which the spectrum is desired. Notice, too, that for both methods of measurement (i.e., Figs. 5.2 and 5.3) if the input signal $f(t)$ is a unit impulse the short-time amplitude spectrum is simply $h(t)$, the weighting function.

It is common, in experimental practice, to minimize equipment complexity by making an approximation to the measurements indicated in Figs. 5.2 and 5.3. The desired measurement $|F(\omega, t)| = [a'^2(\omega, t) + b'^2(\omega, t)]^{\frac{1}{2}}$ is essentially the time envelope of either $a'(\omega, t)$ or $b'(\omega, t)$.

The time envelope of a Fourier-transformable function $u(t)$ can be defined as

$$e(t)=[u^2(t)+\hat{u}^2(t)]^{\frac{1}{2}}, \quad \text{where } \hat{u}(t)=\left[u(t)*\frac{1}{\pi t}\right]$$

is the Hilbert transform of $u(t)$. One can show that $\widehat{u(t)\,v(t)}=u(t)\,\hat{v}(t)=\hat{u}(t)\,v(t)$, provided the spectra of $u(t)$ and $v(t)$ do not overlap.

Making use of these relations, and the possibilities for interchanging orders of integration in the convolutions, one notices that

$$a'(\omega, t)=[f(t)*h(t)\cos\omega t]$$

$$\hat{a}'(\omega, t)=\left[a'(\omega, t)*\frac{1}{\pi t}\right]$$

$$=f(t)*\left[h(t)\cos\omega t*\frac{1}{\pi t}\right] \tag{5.6}$$

$$=f(t)*[h(t)\sin\omega t]$$

$$=b'(\omega, t),$$

provided the spectrum of $h(t)$ does not overlap ω. The quantity $|F(\omega, t)|$ is therefore essentially the time envelope of either $a'(\omega, t)$ or $b'(\omega, t)$. The envelope can be approximated electrically by developing the envelope of either filter branch in Fig. 5.3. This is conventionally done by the linear rectification and low-pass filtering indicated in Fig. 5.4. If the impulse response of the low-pass filter is appropriately chosen, the output $|f(t)*p(t)|*q(t)$ approximates $|F(\omega, t)|$.

The measurement method of Fig. 5.4 is precisely the one used in the well-known Sound Spectrograph and in most filter-bank spectrum analyzers. In particular, it is usually the method used to develop the short-time spectrum in vocoders and in several techniques for automatic formant analysis. All of these applications will be discussed in further detail subsequently. As a present example, however, Fig. 5.5 shows successive short-time spectra of a voiced speech sample as produced by a bank of 24 filters. The filters are approximately 150 cps wide, and cover the frequency range 150 to 4000 cps. Each filter is followed by a rectifier and an R-C network. The filter bank is scanned every 10 msec and the short-time spectrum plotted. High-frequency emphasis is used on the input signal to boost its level in the high-frequency end of the

Fig. 5.4. Practical measurement of the short-time spectrum $|F(\omega, t)|$ by means of a band-pass filter, a rectifier and a smoothing network

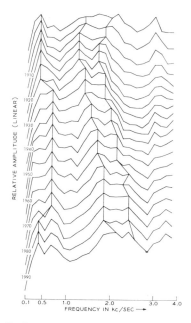

Fig. 5.5. Short-time amplitude spectra of speech measured by a bank of 24 band-pass filters. A single filter channel has the configuration shown in Fig. 5.4. The spectral scans are spaced by 10 msec in time. A digital computer was used to plot the spectra and to automatically mark the formant frequencies. (After FLANAGAN, COKER and BIRD)

spectrum. The filter-bank output is fed into a digital computer through an analog-to-digital converter, and the spectral scans are plotted automatically by the computer (FLANAGAN, COKER, and BIRD). The lines connecting the peaks represent speech formant frequencies which were automatically determined by computer processing of the short-time spectrum.

5.13. Choice of the Weighting Function, $h(t)$

In speech applications, it usually is desirable for the short-time analysis to discriminate vocal properties such as voiced and unvoiced excitation, fundamental frequency, and formant structure. The choice of the analyzing time window $h(t)$ determines the compromise made between temporal and frequency resolution. A time window short in duration corresponds to a broad band-pass filter. It may yield a spectral analysis in which the temporal structure of individual vocal periods is resolved. A window with a duration of several pitch periods, on the other hand, corresponds to a narrower bandpass filter. It may produce

an analysis in which individual harmonic spectral components are resolved in frequency.

In order to illustrate applicable orders of magnitude for filter widths
and time windows, imagine the analyzing bandpass filter to be ideal
(and nonrealizable) with a rectangular amplitude-frequency response
and with zero (or exactly linear) phase response. Let the frequency-
domain specification be

$$P(\omega) = 1; \quad (\omega_0 - \omega_1) \leq \omega \leq (\omega_0 + \omega_1)$$
$$= 1; \quad -(\omega_0 + \omega_1) \leq \omega \leq -(\omega_0 - \omega_1) \tag{5.7}$$
$$= 0; \quad \text{elsewhere.}$$

The impulse response of the filter is therefore

$$p(t) = \left(\frac{2\omega_1}{\pi}\right) \left(\frac{\sin \omega_1 t}{\omega_1 t}\right) \cos \omega_0 t \tag{5.8}$$
$$= h(t) \cos \omega_0 t,$$

and the time window for this ideal filter is the $\sin x/x$ envelope of the
impulse response. If the time between initial zeros of the envelope is
arbitrarily taken as the effective duration, D, of the time window, then
$D = 2\pi/\omega_1 = 4\pi/\Delta\omega$, where $\Delta\omega = 2\omega_1$ is the bandwidth of the filter[1]. The
D's corresponding to several $\Delta\omega$'s are

Condition	$\Delta\omega/2\pi$ (cps)	D (msec)
(1)	50	40
(2)	100	20
(3)	250	8

Condition (1) is an analyzing bandwidth commonly used to resolve
the harmonic spectral components in voiced portions of speech. For this
bandwidth, the duration of the time window spans about four or five
pitch periods of a man's voice.

The broad filter condition (3), on the other hand, produces a weighting
function comparable in duration with a single pitch period of a man's
voice. The time resolution of this analysis therefore resolves amplitude
fluctuations whose temporal courses are of the order of a pitch period.
Filter conditions analogous to both (1) and (3) are employed in the well-
known Sound Spectrograph which will be discussed in the following
section.

---

[1] Sometimes one-half this value is taken as the effective window duration.

The middle condition (2) is a sort of time-frequency compromise for speech. It is a filter width which has been found useful in devices such as vocoders and formant trackers. The short-time spectra already shown in Fig. 5.5 are representative of this resolution.

In passing, it is relevant to estimate the effective time window for the mechanical short-time analysis made by the basilar membrane in the human ear. From the earlier discussion in Chapter IV[1], a reasonably good approximation to the displacement impulse response of the basilar membrane, at a point maximally responsive to radian frequency β, is

$$p(t) = (\beta t)^2 \, e^{-\beta t/2} \sin \beta t$$
$$= h_{bm}(t) \sin \beta t. \tag{5.9}$$

The time window for the basilar membrane, according to this modeling[2], is the "surge" function plotted in Fig. 5.6. One notices that the

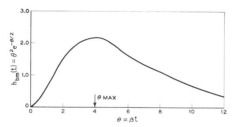

Fig. 5.6. The effective time window for short-time frequency analysis by the basilar membrane in the human ear. The weighting function is deduced from the ear model discussed in Chapter IV

time window has a duration inversely related to β. It has its maximum at $t_{max} = 4/\beta$. If, as a crude estimate, $2 t_{max}$ is taken as the effective duration D of the window, then for several membrane places:

$\beta/2\pi$ (cps)	$D = 2 t_{max}$ (msec)
100	12.0
1 000	1.2
5 000	0.2

For most speech signals, therefore, the mechanical analysis of the ear apparently provides better temporal resolution than spectral resolu-

[1] See also the "third" model described in FLANAGAN (1962a).

[2] Eq. (5.9) does not include the effects of the middle ear. See Chapter IV for these details.

tion. Generally, the only harmonic component resolved mechanically is the fundamental frequency of voiced segments. This result is borne out by observations on the models described in Chapter IV.

5.14. The Sound Spectrograph

Spectral analysis of speech came of age, so to speak, with the development of the Sound Spectrograph (KOENIG, DUNN and LACEY). This device provides a convenient means for permanently displaying the short-time spectrum of a sizeable duration of signal. Its method of analysis is precisely that shown in Fig. 5.4. Its choice of time windows (see preceding section) is made to highlight important acoustic and perceptual features such as formant structure, voicing, friction, stress and pitch. Many other devices for spectrum analysis have also been developed, but the relative convenience and ease of operation of the sound spectrograph has stimulated its wide acceptance in speech analysis and phonetic science. Because it is such a widely used tool, this section will give a brief description of the device and its principles of operation.

Fig. 5.7 shows a functional diagram of one type of sound spectrograph (commonly known as the Model *D* Sonagraph). With the microphone switch (SW1) in the *record* position, a speech sample (generally about 2.5 sec in duration) is recorded on a magnetic disc. The microphone switch is turned to *analyze*, and a spectral analysis of the sample is made by playing it repeatedly through a bandpass filter. Upon successive playings the bandpass filter is, in effect, scanned slowly across the frequency band of the signal. The result is therefore equivalent to an analysis by many such filters. For practical reasons it is more convenient to use a fixed bandpass filter and to "slide" the spectrum of the signal past the filter. This is accomplished by modulating the signal onto a high frequency carrier and sliding one sideband of the signal past the fixed bandpass filter. The translation is accomplished by varying the

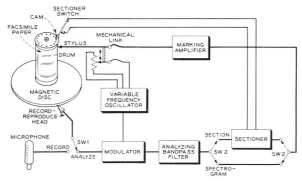

Fig. 5.7. Functional diagram of the sound spectrograph

frequency of the carrier. The carrier frequency control is mechanically geared to the magnetic disc so the signal spectrum is progressively analyzed upon repeated rotations of the disc.

With SW 2 in the *spectrogram* position, the output current of the bandpass filter is amplified and passed to a stylus whose vertical motion is geared to the magnetic disc and the carrier control (or to the effective frequency position of the bandpass filter). The stylus is in contact with an electrically sensitive facsimile paper which is fixed to a drum mounted on the same shaft as the magnetic disc. Electrical current from the stylus burns the paper in proportion to the current magnitude. The paper therefore acts as the full-wave rectifier of Fig. 5.4, and the finite size and spreading of the burned trace perform the low-pass filtering. The density of the burned mark is roughly proportional to the logarithm of the current magnitude. Because of the mechanical linkage, the stylus and carrier move slowly across the frequency range of the signal as the magnetic disc rotates, and a time-intensity-frequency plot of the signal is "painted" on the paper.

Two widths of the bandpass filter are conventionally used with the instrument, 300 cps and 45 cps. The time-frequency resolution of the analysis is essentially determined by these widths. As discussed in the preceding section, the wide pass-band provides better temporal resolution of speech events, while the narrow band yields a frequency resolution adequate to resolve harmonic lines in voiced utterances. A typical spectrogram made with the 300 cps wide analyzing filter is shown in the upper diagram of Fig. 5.8. As previously indicated, the abscissa is time, the ordinate is frequency, and darkness of the pattern represents in-

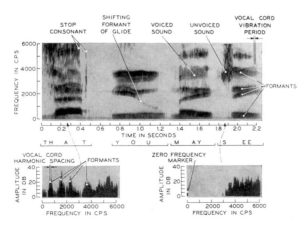

Fig. 5.8 a and b. (a) Broadband sound spectrogram of the utterance "That you may see". (b) Amplitude *vs* frequency plots (amplitude sections) taken in the vowel portion of "that" and in the fricative portion of "see". (After Barney and Dunn)

tensity. Several speech features are indicated. Note that the time resolution is such that vertical striations in the voiced portions show the fundamental period of the vocal cords.

The facsimile paper is capable of depicting an intensity range (from lightest gray to darkest black) of only about 12 db (PRESTIGIACOMO, 1957). It often is desirable to examine amplitude spectra over a greater intensity range. A means is therefore provided for making a frequency-versus-amplitude portrayal at any given instant along the time scale. For this operation, SW2 in Fig. 5.7 is put to the *section* position. A cam is placed on the drum periphery at the time of occurrence of the sound whose amplitude section is desired. The functions of the carrier and stylus are as previously described.

The sectioner contains a full-wave rectifier, an R-C integrator and a biased multivibrator. In one version of the apparatus, as the magnetic disc and drum rotate, the cam closes the section switch at the desired instant in the utterance. The value of the short-time spectrum at this instant is effectively "read" and stored on a capacitor in the input circuit of a biased multivibrator. The multivibrator is held on (i.e., free runs) until the capacitor charge decays to a threshold value. The multivibrator then turns off. During its on-time, it delivers a marking current to the stylus and (because of the exponential decay) the length of the marked trace is proportional to the logarithm of the smoothed output of the analyzing filter. Because the stylus is scanning the frequency scale with the filter, an amplitude (*db*)-versus-frequency plot is painted for the prescribed instant.

Amplitude sections are usually made with the 45 cps (narrow band) filter. Typical sections taken in a vowel and in a fricative are shown in the lower half of Fig. 5.8.

Because the speech sample must be played repeatedly as the analyzing filter scans its band, the time to produce the complete spectrogram is appreciable. Common practice is to shorten the analyzing time by playing back at several times the recording speed. A typical value, for example, is a speed-up of three-to-one. A recorded bandwidth of 100 to 4000 cps is therefore multiplied to 300 to 12000 cps. If the analyzing bandpass filter is centered at, say, 15000 cps, then the carrier oscillator may scan from 15000 to 27000 cps. Depending upon frequency range and technique, one to several minutes may be required to analyze a 2.5 sec speech sample. In the course of the analysis the sample may be played back several hundred times. A common figure for the filter advance is of the order of 20 cps/playback.

The manner in which broadband spectrograms highlight vocal modes, or formants, for various articulatory configurations is illustrated in Fig. 5.9. Articulatory diagrams for four vowels, /i, æ, a, u/ and their cor-

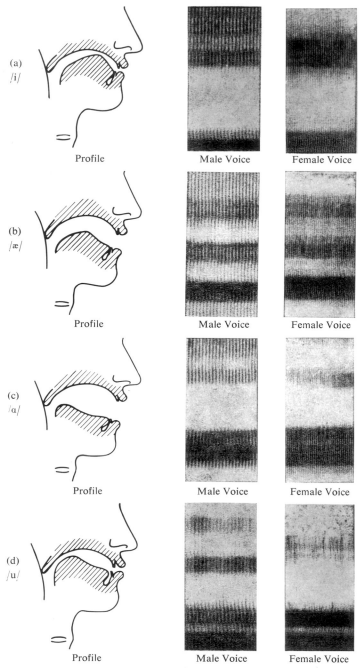

| | Profile | Male Voice | Female Voice |

Fig. 5.9 a–d. Articulatory diagrams and corresponding broad-band spectrograms for the vowels /i, æ, ɑ, u/ as uttered by adult male and female speakers. (After POTTER, KOPP and GREEN)

responding broadband (300 cps) spectrograms are shown. The dark bands indicate the spectral energy concentrations and reflect the vocal modes for a given configuration. (These spectrograms can be compared with the calculated mode patterns for similar vowels in Figs. 3.28 and 3.29 of Chapter III.)

Typical of the research uses to which this type of spectrographic display has been put is a large-scale study of vowel formant frequencies, amplitudes, and pitches for a number of different speakers (PETERSON and BARNEY). The results of this study for 33 men give the mean formant frequencies for the English vowels as plotted in Fig. 5.10. The vowels were uttered in an /h−d/ environment.

Numerous "relatives" of the sound spectrograph − both predecessors and successors − have been designed and used, each usually with a specific purpose in mind. These devices range from scanned filter banks to correlation instruments. In a short space it is not possible to mention many of them. One variation in the spectrographic technique is the so-called "resonagraph" (HUGGINS, 1952). This device is designed to delineate formant frequencies and to suppress nonformant energy. Another modification displays the time derivative of the spectral amplitude, rather than simply the amplitude (MEYER-EPPLER, 1951; KOCK and MILLER). The effect is to emphasize dynamic time changes in the spectrum and to suppress quasi-steady portions. Features such as stop consonants or formant transitions are therefore more sharply delineated.

An even closer relative is the so-called visible speech translator (DUDLEY and GRUENZ; RIESZ and SCHOTT) in which the conventional sound spectrogram is painted electronically in real time, either on a moving belt coated with luminescent phosphor, or on a rotating cathode

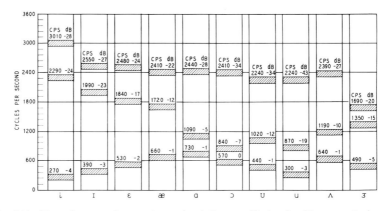

Fig. 5.10. Mean formant frequencies and relative amplitudes for 33 men uttering the English vowels in an /h–d/ environment. Relative formant amplitudes are given in db *re* the first formant of /ɔ/. (After PETERSON and BARNEY as plotted by Haskins Laboratories)

ray tube. A still different variation is the correlatograph (BENNETT, 1953; BIDDULPH) which plots the magnitude of the short-time autocorrelation function of the signal in trace density, the delay parameter on the ordinate, and time along the abscissa.

Several schemes for quantizing the intensity dimension of the conventional spectrogram have also been described (KERSTA, 1948; PRESTIGIACOMO, 1957). The result is to yield a "topological map" of the signal in which intensity gradients are indicated by the closeness of the contour lines.

5.15. Short-Time Correlation Functions and Power Spectra

If $x(t)$ is an on-going stationary random signal, its autocorrelation function $\varphi(\tau)$ and its power density spectrum $\Phi(\omega)$ are linked by Fourier transforms (WIENER; LEE).

$$\varphi(\tau) = \lim_{T \to \infty} \frac{1}{2T} \int_{-T}^{T} x(t)\, x(t+\tau)\, dt$$

$$= \frac{1}{2\pi} \int_{-\infty}^{\infty} \Phi(\omega)\, e^{j\,\omega\,\tau}\, d\omega$$

and

$$\Phi(\omega) = \int_{-\infty}^{\infty} \varphi(\tau)\, e^{-j\,\omega\,\tau}\, d\tau. \tag{5.10}$$

[Note that $\varphi(0)$ is the mean square value, or average power, of the signal.]

For an aperiodic Fourier-transformable signal, $y(t)$, parallel relations link the autocorrelation function $\psi(\tau)$ and the energy density spectrum $\Psi(\omega)$.

$$\psi(\tau) = \int_{-\infty}^{\infty} y(t)\, y(t+\tau)\, dt$$

$$= \frac{1}{2\pi} \int_{-\infty}^{\infty} \Psi(\omega)\, e^{j\,\omega\,\tau}\, d\omega \tag{5.11}$$

$$\Psi(\omega) = \int_{-\infty}^{\infty} \psi(\tau)\, e^{-j\,\omega\,\tau}\, d\tau,$$

where

$$\Psi(\omega) = Y(\omega)\, Y^{*}(\omega), \quad \text{and} \quad Y(\omega) = \int_{-\infty}^{\infty} y(t)\, e^{-j\omega t}\, dt.$$

[Note that

$$\psi(0) = \frac{1}{2\pi} \int_{-\infty}^{\infty} \Psi(\omega)\, d\omega$$

is the total energy of the signal.]

In both cases the correlation functions are real and even functions of the delay parameter τ, and the spectra are real and even functions of the frequency ω. All of the transforms can therefore be written as cosine transforms. These transform-pairs suggest the possibility of determining short-time spectral information by means of correlation techniques, provided the latter can be extended to the short-time case.

In the preceding discussion on short-time spectral analysis, the approach was to analyze a Fourier-transformable "piece" of the signal obtained by suitably weighting the past values. The correlation relations for aperiodic functions can be similarly extended to this description of the speech signal. According to the earlier derivations, at any instant t the following transforms are presumed to hold for the speech signal $f(t)$,

$$F(\omega, t) = \int_{-\infty}^{t} f(\lambda) h(t-\lambda) e^{-j\omega\lambda} d\lambda$$

$$[f(\lambda) h(t-\lambda)] = \frac{1}{2\pi} \int_{-\infty}^{\infty} F(\omega, t) e^{j\omega\lambda} d\omega,$$

(5.12)

where $h(t)$ is the weighting function. Then, formally,

$$\psi(\tau, t) = \int_{-\infty}^{t} f(\lambda) h(t-\lambda) f(\lambda+\tau) h(t-\lambda-\tau) d\lambda$$

$$\psi(\tau, t) = \frac{1}{2\pi} \int_{-\infty}^{\infty} \Psi(\omega, t) e^{j\omega\tau} d\omega$$

(5.13)

$$\Psi(\omega, t) = [F(\omega, t) F^*(\omega, t)] = \int_{-\infty}^{\infty} \psi(\tau, t) e^{-j\omega\tau} d\tau.$$

Practically, for real time measurement at time t, $f(t+\tau)$ for $\tau > 0$ is not known. [For a fixed over-all delay (comparable to the window duration) τ may be considered to be a differential delay.] However, $\psi(\tau, t)$ is formally an even function of τ. It can therefore be defined in terms of negative τ so that

$$\Psi(\omega, t) = \int_{-\infty}^{\infty} \psi(\tau, t) e^{-j\omega\tau} d\tau = 2 \int_{-\infty}^{0} \psi(\tau, t) \cos \omega\tau d\tau, \quad (5.14)$$

where $\Psi(\omega, t)$ is also an even function of ω.

Thus a short-time autocorrelation measure, related to the short-time power spectrum $|F(\omega, t)|^2$ by the aperiodic transform, can be made. Techniques for the measurement of $|F(\omega, t)|^2$ have already been described in Section 5.12. Measurement of $\psi(\tau, t)$ for negative τ can be effected by the arrangement shown in Fig. 5.11. The individual output taps from the delay lines are weighted according to $h(t)$. Corresponding points (in the running variable λ) are multiplied, and the integration is

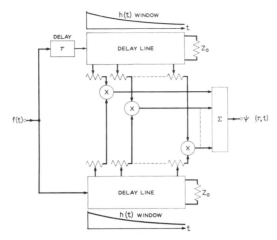

Fig. 5.11. Method for the measurement of the short-time correlation function $\psi(\tau, t)$

approximated as a finite sum[1]. $\psi(\tau, t)$ is therefore a running correlation which is related to $|F(\omega, t)|^2$ or $\Psi(\omega, t)$ by a Fourier transform.

It is also possible to define a short-time correlation function produced by weighting the product of the original signal and the signal delayed (FANO). The defining relation is

$$\varphi(\tau, t) = \int_{-\infty}^{t} f(\lambda) f(\lambda + \tau) k(t - \lambda) d\lambda, \qquad (5.15)$$

where $k(t) = 0$, $t < 0$ is the weighting function. The measure is easily implemented for $\tau \leq 0$ by the circuit shown in Fig. 5.12. This technique has been used experimentally to measure correlation functions for speech sounds (STEVENS, 1950; KRAFT; BIDDULPH).

In general, no simple transform relation exists between $\varphi(\tau, t)$ and a measurable short-time power spectrum. Under the special condition

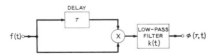

Fig. 5.12. Circuit for measuring the running short-time correlation function $\varphi(\tau, t)$

---

[1] The operations of Fig. 5.11 compute

$$\psi(\tau, t) = \int_{0}^{\infty} f(t - \lambda) h(\lambda) f(t - \lambda - \tau) h(\lambda + \tau) d\lambda,$$

for negative τ, instead of the form given in Eq. (5.13).

$k(t) = 2\alpha e^{-2\alpha t} = [h(t)]^2$, however, $\varphi(\tau, t)$ can be related to $\Psi(\omega, t) = |F(\omega, t)|^2$.

$$\psi(\tau, t) = \int_{-\infty}^{t} f(\lambda) h(t-\lambda) f(\lambda+\tau) h(t-\lambda-\tau) d\lambda$$

$$= e^{\alpha \tau} \int_{-\infty}^{t} 2\alpha f(\lambda) f(\lambda+\tau) e^{-2\alpha(t-\lambda)} d\lambda \qquad (5.16)$$

$$= e^{\alpha \tau} \varphi(\tau, t); \quad \tau \leq 0.$$

But as previously argued, $\psi(\tau, t)$ is an even function of τ, and if $\varphi(\tau, t)$ is defined as an even function, then $\psi(\tau, t) = e^{-\alpha|\tau|} \varphi(\tau, t)$ for all τ, or

$$\varphi(\tau, t) = e^{\alpha|\tau|} \psi(\tau, t)$$

$$= \frac{e^{\alpha|\tau|}}{2\pi} \int_{-\infty}^{\infty} \Psi(\omega, t) e^{j\omega\tau} d\omega,$$

and

$$\Psi(\omega, t) = \int_{-\infty}^{\infty} e^{-\alpha|\tau|} \varphi(\tau, t) e^{-j\omega\tau} d\tau$$

$$= \int_{-\infty}^{\infty} e^{-\alpha|\tau|} \varphi(\tau, t) \cos \omega\tau \, d\tau. \qquad (5.17a)$$

It also follows that

$$\Psi(\omega, t) = \frac{1}{2\pi} [\mathscr{F}\{e^{-\alpha|\tau|}\} * \mathscr{F}\{\varphi(\tau, t)\}]$$

$$= \frac{1}{2\pi} \left[\left(\frac{2\alpha}{\alpha^2 + \omega^2} \right) * \Phi(\omega, t) \right] \qquad (5.17b)$$

$$= \frac{1}{2\pi} [|H(\omega)|^2 * \Phi(\omega, t)],$$

where $\mathscr{F}$ denotes the Fourier transform.

Thus the short-time power spectrum $\Psi(\omega, t)$ is the real convolution of the power spectrum $\Phi(\omega, t)$ with the low-pass energy spectrum $(2\alpha/\alpha^2 + \omega^2)$. $\Psi(\omega, t)$ therefore has poorer spectral resolution than the Fourier transform of $\varphi(\tau, t)$ [i.e., $\Phi(\omega, t)$]. Note also that for $h(t) = (2\alpha)^{\frac{1}{2}} e^{-\alpha t}$, $|F(\omega, t)|$ is essentially measured by single-resonant circuits with impulse responses $[(2\alpha)^{\frac{1}{2}} e^{-\alpha t} \cos \omega t]$ and $[(2\alpha)^{\frac{1}{2}} e^{-\alpha t} \sin \omega t]$. (See Fig. 5.3.)

Weighting functions different from the exponential just discussed do not lead to simple transform relations between $\varphi(\tau, t)$ and a power spectrum. Other definitions, however, can be made of measurable correlations and short-time power spectra, and these can be linked by specially defined transforms (SCHROEDER and ATAL). For example, one

can define a short-time spectrum

$$\Omega(\omega, t) = \int_{-\infty}^{\infty} \varphi(\tau, t) \, m(|\tau|) \cos \omega \tau \, d\tau, \qquad (5.18a)$$

in which $\varphi(\tau, t)$, as given in Eq. (5.15), is defined as an even function of τ (but is measured for delays only) so that,

$$\varphi(\tau, t) = \int_{-\infty}^{t} f(\lambda) f(\lambda - |\tau|) \, n(t - \lambda) \, d\lambda, \qquad (5.18b)$$

where $m(t)$ and $n(t)$ are physically realizable weighting functions and are zero for $t < 0$[1]. $\Omega(\omega, t)$ and $\varphi(\tau, t)$ are then linked by the definitions (5.18). $\varphi(\tau, t)$ can be measured according to Fig. 5.12, and a straightforward measure of $\Omega(\omega, t)$ can also be made. Substituting for $\varphi(\tau, t)$ in the definition of $\Omega(\omega, t)$ gives

$$\Omega(\omega, t) = 2 \int_{-\infty}^{t} f(\lambda) \, n(t - \lambda) \, d\lambda \int_{0}^{\infty} f(\lambda - \tau) \, m(\tau) \cos \omega \tau \, d\tau \qquad (5.19)$$

$$= 2 \{ n(t) * f(t) [f(t) * m(t) \cos \omega t] \}.$$

The operations indicated in (5.19) are a filtering of the signal $f(t)$ by a (normally bandpass) filter whose impulse response is $[m(t) \cos \omega t]$; a multiplication of this output by the original signal; and a (normally low pass) filtering by a filter whose impulse response is $n(t)$. The measurement is schematized in Fig. 5.13.

Fig. 5.13. Arrangement for measuring the short-time spectrum $\Omega(\omega, t)$. (After SCHROEDER and ATAL)

For the case $m(t) = n(t) = e^{-\alpha t}$, $\Omega(\omega, t)$ reduces to $\Psi(\omega, t)$. From the definition of $\Omega(\omega, t)$, the inverse relation follows

$$\varphi(\tau, t) = \frac{1}{2\pi m(|\tau|)} \int_{-\infty}^{\infty} \Omega(\omega, t) \cos \omega \tau \, d\omega. \qquad (5.20)$$

The defining relations of Eq. (5.18) also imply that

$$\Omega(\omega, t) = M(\omega) * \Phi(\omega, t), \qquad (5.21)$$

---

[1] If $\Omega(\omega, t)$ is to be a positive quantity, some further restrictions must be placed on $n(t)$.

where

$$M(\omega) = \int_{-\infty}^{\infty} m(|\tau|) e^{-j\omega\tau} d\tau,$$

and

$$\Phi(\omega, t) = \int_{-\infty}^{\infty} \varphi(\tau, t) e^{-j\omega\tau} d\tau.$$

This result can be compared with Eq. (5.17), where

$$|H(\omega)|^2 = \int_{-\infty}^{\infty} e^{-\alpha|\tau|} e^{-j\omega\tau} d\tau$$

$$H(\omega) = \int_{0}^{\infty} (2\alpha)^{\frac{1}{2}} e^{-\alpha\tau} e^{-j\omega\tau} d\tau = \int_{0}^{\infty} h(\tau) e^{-j\omega\tau} d\tau.$$

Since $\Omega(\omega, t)$ is obtained from $\Phi(\omega, t)$ by convolution with the (low pass) spectrum $M(\omega)$, it has poorer spectral definition than $\Phi(\omega, t)$.

5.16. Average Power Spectra

The spectral measuring schemes of the previous discussion use windows which are relatively short in duration to weight past values of the signal. They yield spectra in which brief temporal fluctuations are preserved. A long-term mean value of the spectrum, say $\overline{|F(\omega, t)|^2}$, might also be of interest if average spectral distribution is of more importance than short-time variations. Such an average can be written as

$$\lim_{T\to\infty} \frac{1}{2T} \int_{-T}^{T} F(\omega, t) F^*(\omega, t) dt = \overline{|F(\omega, t)|^2} = \overline{\Psi(\omega, t)}$$

$$= \lim_{T\to\infty} \frac{1}{2T} \int_{-T}^{T} dt \int_{-\infty}^{t} f(\lambda) h(t-\lambda) e^{-j\omega\lambda} d\lambda \int_{-\infty}^{t} f(\eta) h(t-\eta) e^{j\omega\eta} d\eta. \tag{5.22}$$

Changing variables and rearranging

$$\overline{|F(\omega, t)|^2}$$

$$= \int_{0}^{\infty} d\lambda\, h(\lambda) e^{j\omega\lambda} \int_{0}^{\infty} d\eta\, h(\eta) e^{-j\omega\eta} \lim_{T\to\infty} \frac{1}{2T} \int_{-T}^{T} f(t-\lambda) f(t-\eta) dt. \tag{5.23}$$

According to Eqs. (5.10), the latter integral is simply $\varphi(\lambda-\eta)$, which is the Fourier transform of $\Phi(\omega)$. That is,

$$\varphi(\lambda-\eta) = \frac{1}{2\pi} \int_{-\infty}^{\infty} \Phi(\delta) e^{j\delta(\lambda-\eta)} d\delta$$

$$= \frac{1}{2\pi} \int_{-\infty}^{\infty} \Phi(\delta) e^{-j\delta(\lambda-\eta)} d\delta,$$

because $\Phi(\omega)$ is real and even. Then

$$\overline{|F(\omega,t)|^2} = \frac{1}{2\pi} \int_{-\infty}^{\infty} \Phi(\delta)\,d\delta \int_0^{\infty} h(\lambda)\,e^{j\lambda(\omega-\delta)}\,d\lambda \int_0^{\infty} h(\eta)\,e^{-j\eta(\omega-\delta)}\,d\eta$$

$$= \frac{1}{2\pi} \int_{-\infty}^{\infty} \Phi(\delta)\,H(\omega-\delta)\,H^*(\omega-\delta)\,d\delta \qquad (5.24)$$

$$\overline{|F(\omega,t)|^2} = \frac{1}{2\pi}\left[\Phi(\omega) * |H(\omega)|^2\right].$$

Therefore, the long-time average value of the power spectrum $|F(\omega,t)|^2$ is the real convolution of the power density spectrum $\Phi(\omega)$ and the energy density spectrum of the time window $h(t)$. The narrower the $|H(\omega)|^2$ spectrum, the more nearly $\overline{|F(\omega,t)|^2}$ represents the power density spectrum $\Phi(\omega)$. A narrow $H(\omega)$ corresponds to a long time window and to narrow bandpass filters in the circuits of Figs. 5.3 and 5.4. In the limit $H(\omega)$ is an impulse at $\omega=0$, the time window is a unit step function and $\overline{|F(\omega,t)|^2}$ has the same spectral characteristics as $\Phi(\omega)$. For any value of ω, $\overline{|F(\omega,t)|^2}$ is the integral of the power density spectrum "seen" through the aperture $|H(\omega)|^2$ positioned at ω. It is therefore the average power of the signal in the pass band of the filter in Fig. 5.4.

It was previously demonstrated [Eq. (5.17)] that for the special condition $h(t) = [(2\alpha)^{\frac{1}{2}}\,e^{-\alpha t}]$,

$$\Psi(\omega,t) = \frac{1}{2\pi}\left[|H(\omega)|^2 * \Phi(\omega,t)\right].$$

Notice that for this situation, the long-time average is

$$\overline{\Psi(\omega,t)} = \lim_{T\to\infty} \frac{1}{2T} \int_{-T}^{T} \int_{-\infty}^{\infty} e^{-\alpha|\tau|}\,\varphi(\tau,t)\cos\omega\tau\,d\tau\,dt$$

$$= \int_{-\infty}^{\infty} e^{-\alpha|\tau|}\,\overline{\varphi(\tau,t)}\cos\omega\tau\,d\tau. \qquad (5.25)$$

Substituting for $\varphi(\tau,t)$ from (5.15) and interchanging variables leads to

$$\overline{\Psi(\omega,t)} = \int_0^{\infty} e^{-\alpha|\tau|}\,\varphi(\tau)\cos\omega\tau\,d\tau \int_0^{\infty} k(\beta)\,d\beta. \qquad (5.26)$$

Since

$$\int_0^{\infty} k(t)\,dt = \int_0^{\infty} h^2(t)\,dt = 1,$$

then

$$\overline{\Psi(\omega,t)} = \frac{1}{2\pi}\left[|H(\omega)|^2 * \Phi(\omega)\right],$$

which corresponds to the result (5.24).

5.17. Measurement of Average Power Spectra for Speech

A number of experimental measurements of the average power spectrum of speech have been made (for example, SIVIAN; DUNN and WHITE). The technique frequently used is essentially the bandpass filter arrangement shown previously in Fig. 5.4, with the exception that a square-law rectifier and a long-time integrator (averager) are used. This arrangement is shown is Fig. 5.14. If the switch closes at time $t=0$ and

Fig. 5.14. Circuit for measuring the long-time average power spectrum of a signal

remains closed for T sec, the accumulated capacitor voltage is an approximation to $\overline{|F(\omega, t)|^2}$ and is,

$$V_c(T) = \int_0^T a'^2(\omega, \lambda) \frac{1}{RC} e^{-\frac{1}{RC}(T-\lambda)} d\lambda. \qquad (5.27)$$

If $RC \gg T$, then the exponential is essentially unity for $0 \leq \lambda \leq T$, and

$$V_c(T) \cong \frac{1}{RC} \int_0^T a'^2(\omega, \lambda) d\lambda \qquad (5.28)$$

$$\sim \overline{|F(\omega, t)|^2}.$$

The measurement described by (5.28) has been used in one investigation of speech spectra. Bandpass filters with bandwidths one-half octave wide below 500 cps and one octave wide above 500 cps were used. The integration time was $\frac{1}{8}$ sec (DUNN and WHITE). Distributions of the absolute root-mean-square speech pressure in these bands — measured 30 cm from the mouth of a talker producing continuous conversational speech — are shown in Fig. 5.15. The data are averages for six men. The distribution for the unfiltered speech is shown by the marks on the left ordinate.

If the integration time is made very long, say for more than a minute of continuous speech (all natural pauses between syllables and sentences being included), or if many short-time measurements are averaged, one obtains a long-time power spectrum in which syllabic length variations are completely smoothed out. Assuming that the speech power is uniformly distributed in the octave and half-octave filter bands the measured longtime power density spectrum, $\Phi(\omega)$, for speech is shown in

Fig. 5.16. The ordinate here is given in terms of mean-square sound pressure per cycle. In both Figs. 5.15 and 5.16, the detailed formant structure of individual sound is averaged out.

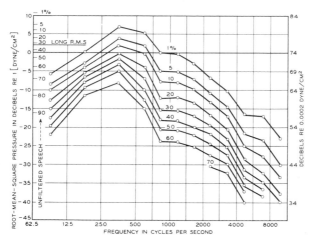

Fig. 5.15. Root mean square sound pressures for speech measured in $\frac{1}{8}$ sec intervals 30 cm from the mouth. The analyzing filter bands are one-half octave wide below 500 cps and one octave wide above 500 cps. (After DUNN and WHITE.) The parameter is the percentage of the intervals having levels greater than the ordinate

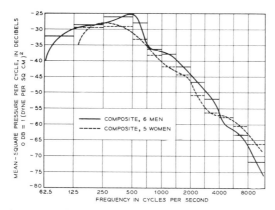

Fig. 5.16. Long-time power density spectrum for continuous speech measured 30 cm from the mouth. (After DUNN and WHITE)

5.2. Formant Analysis of Speech

Formant analysis of speech can be considered a special case of spectral analysis. The objective is to determine the complex natural frequencies of the vocal mechanism as they change temporally. The changes are, of course, conditioned by the articulatory deformations of the vocal tract. One approach to such analysis is to consider how the modes are exhibited in the short-time spectrum of the signal. As an initial illustration, the temporal courses of the first three speech formants are traced in an idealized form on the spectrogram of Fig. 5.17. Often, for bandwidth compression application, an automatic, real-time determination of these data is desired.

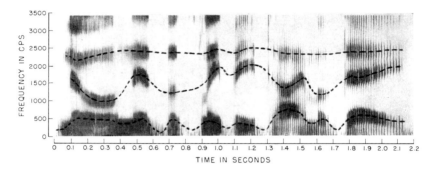

"NOON IS THE SLEEPY TIME OF DAY"

Fig. 5.17. Sound spectrogram showing idealized tracks for the first three speech formants

As certain of the results in Chapter III imply, the damping or dissipation characteristics of the vocal system are relatively constant and predictable, especially over the frequency range of a given formant. Generally, therefore, more interest attaches to the temporal variations of the imaginary parts of the complex formant frequencies than to the real parts. Nevertheless, an adequate knowledge of the real parts, or of the formant bandwidths, is important both perceptually and in spectral analysis procedures.

The "system function" approach to speech analysis, as discussed in Chapter III, aims at a specification of the signal in terms of a transmission function and an excitation function. If the vocal configuration is known, the mode pattern can be computed, and the output response to a given excitation can be obtained. In automatic analysis for encoding and transmission purposes, the reverse situation generally exists. One has available only the acoustic signal and desires to analyze it in terms of the properties of the source and the modes of the system. One main difficulty is in not knowing how to separate uniquely the source and the system.

The normal modes of the vocal system move continuously with time, but they may not, for example, always be clearly manifest in a short-time spectrum of the signal. A particular pole may be momentarily obscured or suppressed by a source zero or by a system zero arising from a side-branch element (such as the nasal cavity). The short-time spectrum generally exhibits the prominent modes, but it is often difficult to say with assurance where the low-amplitude poles or significant pole-zero pairs might lie.

Further complicating the situation is the fact that the output speech signal is generally not a minimum-phase function (that is, it may not have all its zeros in the left half of the complex frequency plane). If it were, its phase spectrum would be implied by its amplitude spectrum. The vocal-tract transmission is, of course, minimum phase for all conditions where radiation takes place from only one point, i.e., mouth or nostril. For simultaneous radiation from these points it is not. It can be shown that the glottal source, provided the volume velocity wave is zero at some time during its period, possesses only finite-frequency zeros and no poles (MATHEWS, MILLER and DAVID, 1961 b). Further, it can be shown that the zeros can lie in either the right or left half planes, or in both (DUNN, FLANAGAN and GESTRIN). These factors conspire to make accurate automatic formant analysis a difficult problem. The present section outlines a number techniques for the automatic measurement of formant frequency and formant bandwidth, and indicates the performance they achieve.

5.21. Formant-Frequency Extraction

In its simplest visualization, the voiced excitation of a vocal resonance is analogous to the excitation of a single-tuned circuit by brief, periodic pulses. The output is a damped sinusoid repeated at the pulse rate. The envelope of the amplitude spectrum has a maximum at a frequency equal essentially to the imaginary part of the complex pole frequency. The formant frequency might be measured either by measuring the axis-crossing rate of the time waveform, or by measuring the frequency of the peak in the spectral envelope. If the bandwidth of the resonance is relatively small, the first moment of the amplitude spectrum,

$$\bar{f} = \frac{\int f A(f)\,df}{\int A(f)\,df}$$

might also be a reasonable estimate of the imaginary part of the pole frequency.

The resonances of the vocal tract are, of course, multiple. The output time waveform is therefore a superposition of damped sinusoids and the amplitude spectrum generally exhibits multiple peaks. If the individual resonances can be suitably isolated, say by appropriate filtering, the axis-crossing measures, the spectral maxima and the moments might all be useful indications of formant frequency. If, on the other hand, the more subtle properties of the source and the system are to be accounted for — say the spectral zeros produced by the glottal source or by a sidebranch resonator — a more sophisticated measure of the normal modes generally is necessary. One such approach is the detailed fitting of an hypothesized spectral model to the real speech spectrum. For analyses of this type, it is often advantageous to employ the storage and rapid logical operations of a digital computer.

5.211. Axis-Crossing Measures of Formant Frequency. One of the earliest attempts at automatic tracking of formant frequencies was an average zero-crossing count (E. PETERSON). The idea was to take the average density of zero-crossings of the speech wave and of its time derivative as approximations to the first and second formants, respectively. The reasoning was that in the unfiltered, voiced speech the first formant is the most prominent spectral component. It consequently is expected to have the strongest influence upon the axis-crossing rate. In the differentiated signal, on the other hand, the first formant is de-emphasized and the second formant is dominant. The results of these measures, however, were found to be poor, and the conclusion was that the method did not give acceptable precision.

A number of refinements of the zero-crossing technique have been made. In one (MUNSON and MONTGOMERY; DAVIS, BIDDULPH, and BALASHEK), the speech signal is pre-filtered into frequency ranges appropriate to individual formants. The axis-crossing rate and the amplitude are measured for the signal in each of the bands. A remaining disadvantage, however, is that the method is still subject to the overlapping of the formant frequency ranges.

A more elaborate implementation of the same basic idea, but with a feature designed to minimize deleterious overlap, has also been made (CHANG). The notion is to employ an iterative measure of the average rate of zero-crossing in a given frequency range and to successively narrow the frequency range on the basis of the measured rate. The expectation is for rapid convergence. Fig. 5.18 illustrates the method. The signal is pre-filtered by fixed filters into ranges roughly appropriate to the first two formants. An axis-crossing measure, ρ_0, of the lower band is made and its value is used to tune automatically a narrower, variable band-pass filter. The axis-crossing output of this filter is, in turn, taken as an indication of the first formant frequency ($F1$). Its value is used to adjust the cut-off frequency of a variable HP filter. The average axis-crossing output of the latter is taken as an estimate of the second formant frequency ($F2$).

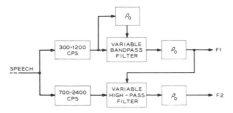

Fig. 5.18. Automatic formant measurement by zero-crossing count and adjustable pre-filtering. (After CHANG)

If the spectral distribution of the signal is continuous, as in the case of unvoiced sounds, the average axis-crossing rate for a given spectral element is approximately twice the first moment of the spectral piece (CHANG, PIHL and ESSIGMAN). However, other more direct methods for measuring spectral moments have been considered.

5.212. Spectral Moments. The n-th moment of an amplitude spectrum $A(\omega)$ is $M_n = \int \omega^n A(\omega)\, d\omega$, where ω is the radian frequency. If a suitable pre-filtering or partitioning of the spectrum can be made, then a formant frequency can be approximated by

$$\bar{\omega} = \frac{M_1}{M_0} \cong \frac{\sum\limits_i \omega_i A(\omega_i)}{\sum\limits_i A(\omega_i)}.$$

A number of formant measures based upon this principle have been examined (POTTER and STEINBERG; GABOR; SCHROEDER, 1956; CAMPANELLA). The spectral partitioning problem remains of considerable importance in the accuracy of these methods. However, certain moment ratios have been found useful in separating the frequency ranges occupied by formants (SUZUKI, KADOKAWA and NAKATA). Another difficulty in moment techniques is the asymmetry or skewness of the spectral resonances. The measured formant frequency may be weighted toward the "heavier" side of the spectrum, rather than placed at the spectral peak.

5.213. Spectrum Scanning and Peak-Picking Methods. Another approach to real-time automatic formant tracking is simply the detection and measurement of prominences in the short-time amplitude spectrum. At least two methods of this type have been designed and implemented (FLANAGAN, 1956a). One is based upon locating points of zero slope in the spectral envelope, and the other is the detection of local spectral maxima by magnitude comparison. In the first — illustrated in Fig. 5.19 —

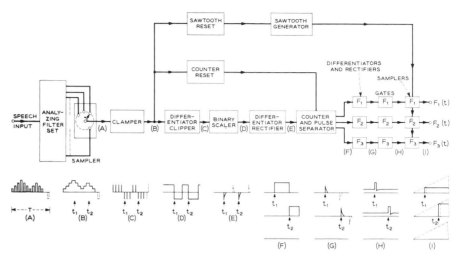

Fig. 5.19. Spectrum scanning method for automatic extraction of formant frequencies.
(After FLANAGAN, 1956a)

a short-time amplitude spectrum is first produced by a set of bandpass filters, rectifiers and integrators. The analysis is precisely as described earlier in Section 5.12. The outputs of the filter channels are scanned rapidly (on the order of 100 times per second) by a sample-and-hold circuit. This produces a time function which is a step-wise representation of the short-time spectrum at a number (36 in this instance) of frequency values. For each scan, the time function is differentiated and binary-scaled to produce pulses marking the maxima of the spectrum. The marking pulses are directed into separate channels by a counter where they sample a sweep voltage produced at the scanning rate. The sampled voltages are proportional to the frequencies of the respective spectral maxima and are held during the remainder of the scan. The resulting stepwise voltages are subsequently smoothed by low-pass filtering.

The second method segments the short-time spectrum into frequency ranges that ideally contain a single formant. The frequency of the spectral maximum within each segment is then measured. The operation is illustrated in Fig. 5.20. In the simplest form the segment boundaries are fixed. However, additional control circuitry can automatically adjust the boundaries so that the frequency range of a given segment is contingent upon the frequency of the next lower formant. The normalizing circuit "clamps" the spectral segment either in terms of its peak value or its mean value. This common-mode rejection enables the

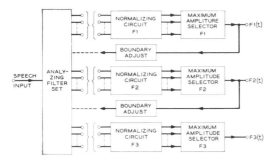

Fig. 5.20. Peak-picking method for automatic tracking of speech formants.
(After FLANAGAN, 1956a)

following peak-selecting circuitry to operate over a wide range of amplitudes. The maxima of each segment are selected at a rapid rate — for
example, 100 times per second — and a voltage proportional to the frequency of the selected channel is delivered to the output. The selections
can be time-phased so that the boundary adjustments of the spectral
segments are made sequentially and are set according to the measured
position of the next lower formant. A number of improvements on the
basic method have been made by providing frequency interpolation
(SHEARME, 1959), more sophisticated logic for adjusting the segment
boundaries (HOLMES and KELLY), and greater dynamic range for the
peak selectors (STEAD and JONES). The objective in all these designs has
been the realization of a real-time, practicable hardware device for direct
application in a transmission system.

A typical output from the device of Fig. 5.20, using fixed boundaries,
is shown in Fig. 5.21. It is clear that the operation is far from perfect.

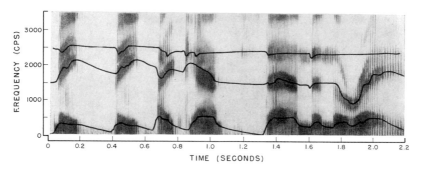

"BEAT, BEAT, I CAN'T STAND IN THE RAIN"

Fig. 5.21. Formant outputs from the tracking device shown in Fig. 5.20. In this instance
the boundaries of the spectral segments are fixed

In this example a large third formant error occurs in the /r/ of "rain."
Automatic control of the $F2$–$F3$ boundary, however, eliminates this
error. As a rough indication of the performance, one evaluation shows
that its output follows $F1$ of vowels within ± 150 cps greater than 93%
of the time, and $F2$ within ± 200 cps greater than 91% of the time
(FLANAGAN, 1956a). Although one desires greater precision, this method
– because of its simplicity and facility for real-time analysis – has proved
useful in several investigations of complete formant-vocoder systems
(FLANAGAN and HOUSE; STEAD and JONES; SHEARME, SMITH and KELLY).

5.214. Digital Computer Methods for Formant Extraction. The development of digital computers has enabled application of more sophisticated strategies to speech processing. The more esoteric processings are
made possible by the ability of the computer to store and rapidly manipulate large quantities of numerical data. A given data sample can be
held in the machine while complex tests and measures are applied to
analyze a particular feature and make a decision. This advantage extends not only to formant tracking, but to all phases of speech processing.
The relations between sampled-data systems and continuous systems
(see, for example, RAGAZZINI and FRANKLIN) permit simulation of complete transmission systems within the digital computer. This is a topic
in itself, and we will return to it in a later chapter.

The digital analyses which have been made for speech formants have
been primarily in terms of operations on the spectrum. The spectrum
either is sampled and read into the computer from an external filter
bank, or is computed from a sampled and quantized version of the speech
waveform. One approach along the latter line has been a pitch-synchronous analysis of voiced sounds (MATHEWS, MILLER and DAVID,
1961b). Individual pitch periods are determined by visual inspection of
the speech oscillogram. The computer then calculates the Fourier series
for each pitch period as though that period were one of an exactly
periodic signal. The envelope of the calculated spectrum is then fitted
by a synthetic spectrum in successive approximations and according to
a weighted least-square error criterion. A pole-zero model for the vocal
tract and the glottal source, based upon acoustic relations for the vocal
tract (see Chapter III), produces the synthetic spectrum.

The fitting procedure is initiated by guessing a set of poles and zeros
appropriate to the calculated real spectrum. The computer then successively increments the frequency and damping of each individual pole
and zero to minimize the weighted mean-square error (in log-amplitude
measure). After about 10 to 20 complete cycles, a close fit to the speech
spectrum can be obtained. Typical rms log-amplitude errors range from
about 1.5 to 2.5 db. A typical result of the fitting procedure is shown in

Fig. 5.22. The measured formant frequencies and bandwidths are then taken as the frequencies and bandwidths of the best fitting spectral model.

A computer system for non-pitch-synchronous formant analysis, in which spectral data are produced external to the computer, can also be summarized (HUGHES; FORGIE and HUGHES). A bank of 35 contiguous bandpass filters with rectifiers and integrators produces a short-time spectrum of the running speech. The filter outputs are scanned at a rapid rate ($180 \sec^{-1}$) to produce a framed time function which represents successive spectral sections (essentially the same as that shown in Fig. 5.5). This time function is sampled every 154 µsec and quantized to 11 bits by an analog-to-digital converter. A certain amount of the data is then held in the computer storage for processing.

One analysis procedure for which the computer is programmed (1) locates the fricative sounds in a word and classifies them; (2) locates the first and second formants in voiced segments; and (3) calculates the overall sound level. The formant tracking procedure is basically a peak-picking scheme similar to that shown previously in Fig. 5.20. However, a number of detailed, programmed constraints are included to exploit vocal tract characteristics and limitations. In principle, the procedure for a given spectral scan is as follows. Find the peak filter in the frequency range appropriate to the first formant. Store the frequency and ampli-

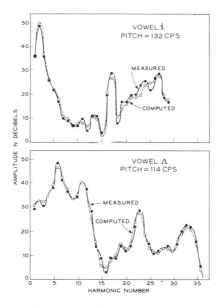

Fig. 5.22. Spectral fit computed for one pitch period of a voiced sound.
(After MATHEWS, MILLER and DAVID, 1961 b)

tude values of this channel. On the basis of the $F1$ location, adjust the frequency range for locating $F2$. Locate the peak filter in the adjusted $F2$ range and store its frequency and amplitude values. Finally, examine the next spectral scan and find $F1$ and $F2$, subject to continuity constraints with previously determined values. Large, abrupt changes in $F1$ and $F2$ of small time duration are ignored. Typical results, described as "good" and "average" from this procedure are shown in Fig. 5.23.

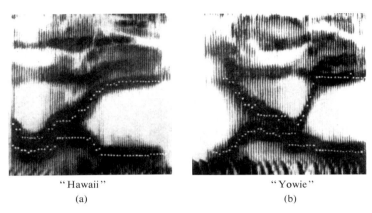

"Hawaii"   "Yowie"

(a)   (b)

Fig. 5.23 a and b. Tracks for the first and second formant frequencies obtained from a computer-analysis of real-time spectra. The speech samples are (a) "Hawaii" and (b) "Yowie" uttered by a man. (After HUGHES)

A real-time spectral input to a computer has also been applied in a spectral-fitting technique for formant location (BELL *et al.*). The procedure — termed "analysis-by-synthesis" by its originators — is illustrated in Fig. 5.24. As before, a filter bank produces a short-time spectrum which is read into the digital computer via an analog-to-digital converter. Inside the computer, speech-like spectra are generated from a pole-zero model of the vocal tract and its excitation. (The filter bank characteristics are also applied to the synthetic spectra.) As in the pitch-synchronous analysis, the model is based upon the acoustical principles discussed in Chapter III. The real and synthetic spectra at a given instant are compared, and a weighted square error is computed. The nature of the comparison is illustrated in Fig. 5.25. The effect of an error in formant frequency is indicated by Fig. 5.25a. An error in formant bandwidth is illustrated in Fig. 5.25b.

On the basis of error computations for the immediate and for adjacent spectral samples, a programmed automatic control strategy determines the procedure for adjusting the pole-zero positions of the fitting

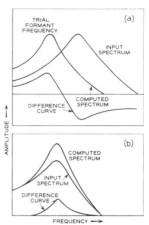

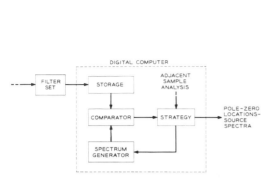

Fig. 5.24. Computer procedure for formant location by the "analysis-by-synthesis" method. (After BELL *et al.*)

Fig. 5.25 a and b. Idealized illustration of formant location by the "analysis-by-synthesis" method shown in Fig. 5.24

synthetic spectrum to reduce the weighted error. When a minimum-error fit is obtained, the computer automatically stores the pole-zero locations of the vocal tract model and the source characteristics chosen for that spectrum. Five operations are carried out by the computer: (1) storage of real input speech spectra; (2) generation of synthetic spectra; (3) control and adjustment of the synthetic spectra; (4) calculation of spectral difference according to a prescribed error criterion; and (5) storage and display of the parameters which yield minimum error. Provisions are made so that, if desired, the comparison and control functions can be performed by an human operator instead of by the automatic procedure.

In principle the programmed matching procedure is applicable both to vowel and consonant spectra, but the matching model for consonants is generally more complex. A typical result of the procedure is shown for the first three formants in Fig. 5.26. The (a) part of the figure shows a sound spectrogram of the utterance /h ə b I b/ with sample intervals laid off along the top time axis. The (b) part of the figure shows the computer-determined formant tracks for essentially the vowel portion of the second syllable (i.e., /I/). The sample numbers on the abscissa of the (b) part correspond with those at the top of (a). The top diagram in part (b) is the square error for the spectral fit. The "analysis-by-synthesis" technique has also been implemented using a gradient-climbing calculation for matching the short-time spectrum (OLIVE). Other implementations have used sequential algorithms for fitting the spectrum (FUJISAKI).

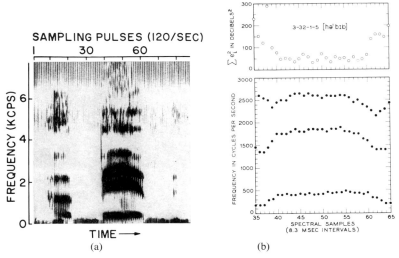

Fig. 5.26a and b. Computer-determined formant tracks obtained by the "analysis-by-synthesis" method. (a) Spectrogram of original speech. (b) Extracted formant tracks and square error measure. (After BELL *et al.*)

Another computer formant tracker uses a principle related to the pole-zero model of speech (COKER). The analyzing strategy is a combined peak-picking and spectral fitting approach. A filter bank, associated rectifiers and lowpass filters produce a short-time spectrum. The filter outputs are scanned by an electronic commutator, and the time waveform representing the spectral sections is led to an analog-to-digital converter. The output digital signal describing the successive spectra is read into the computer, and the short-time spectra are stored in the memory.

The automatic analyzing procedure, prescribed by a program, first locates the absolute maximum of each spectrum. A single formant resonance is then fitted to the peak. The single resonance is positioned at a frequency corresponding to the first moment of that spectral portion lying, say, from zero to 6 db down from the peak on both sides. The single formant resonance is then inverse filtered from the real speech spectrum by subtracting the log-amplitude spectral curves. The operation is repeated on the remainder until the required number of formants are located. Since the peakpicking is always accomplished on the whole spectrum, the problem of formant segmentation is obviated! Proximate formants can also be resolved and accurate results can be obtained on running speech. The formant selections can be displayed directly on the spectral sections in a manner similar to that shown in Fig. 5.5. Again, the ability of the computer to store large amounts of data and to perform relatively complex operations at high speed permits a detailed fitting of the spectrum. The analysis is easily accomplished in real time, and the computer can essentially be used as the formant-tracking element of a complete formant-vocoder system (COKER and CUMMISKEY).

A still different method for formant analysis (SCHAFER and RABINER) makes use of a special digital transform — the Chirp-Z transform (RABINER, SCHAFER and RADER). The method also incorporates Fast Fourier Transform methods for spectral analysis (COOLEY and TUKEY). In its complete form, the method depends upon relations prescribed by a 3-pole model of voiced sounds and a single pole-zero model of voiceless sounds.

The point of departure is a short-time transform of the speech waveform for both voiced an voiceless sounds. The steps in the spectral analysis are depicted in Fig. 5.27.

The upper part of the figure shows the analysis of voiced speech. The waveform at the top left is a segment of voiced speech of approximately 40 msec duration, which has been multiplied by a Hamming window[1]. Over such a short time interval, the speech waveform looks

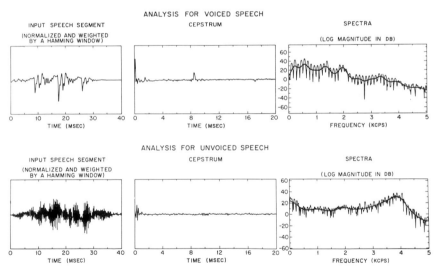

Fig. 5.27. Spectrum and cepstrum analysis of voiced and unvoiced speech sounds.
(After SCHAFER and RABINER)

---

[1] The Hamming window is specified by the function

$$h(t) = \left\{0.54 + 0.46 \cos\left(\frac{2\pi t}{\tau}\right)\right\} \quad \text{for} \quad -\frac{\tau}{2} \leqq t \leqq \frac{\tau}{2},$$

where τ is the window duration. This data window is attractive because the side lobes of its Fourier transform remain more than 40 db down at all frequencies (BLACKMAN and TUKEY).

like a segment of a periodic waveform. The detailed time variation of the waveform during a single period is primarily determined by the vocal tract response, while the fundamental period (pitch period) reflects the vocal-cord vibration rate.

The logarithm of the magnitude of the Fourier transform of this segment of speech is the rapidly-varying spectrum plotted at the top right of Fig. 5.27. This function can be thought of as consisting of an additive combination of a rapidly-varying periodic component, which is associated primarily with the vocal-cord excitation, and a slowly-varying component primarily due to the vocal-tract transmission function. Therefore, the excitation and vocal-tract components are mixed and must be separated to facilitate estimation of formant values. The standard approach to the problem of separating a slowly-varying signal and a rapidly-varying signal is to employ linear filtering. Such an approach applied to the log magnitude of the short-time Fourier transform leads to the computation of the *cepstrum* (BOGERT, HEALY and TUKEY).

The cepstrum is a Fourier transform of a Fourier transform. To compute the cepstrum the Fourier transform of the time waveform is computed. The logarithm is taken of the magnitude of this transform. Inverse Fourier transformation of this log-magnitude function produces the cepstrum. (See also Section 5.3.)

The cepstrum is plotted in the middle of the top row of Fig. 5.27. The rapidly-varying component of the log-magnitude spectrum contributes the peak in the cepstrum at about 8 msec (the value of the pitch period). The slowly-varying component corresponds to the low-time portion of the cepstrum. Therefore, the slowly-varying component can be extracted by first smoothly truncating the cepstrum values to zero above about 4 msec, and then computing the Fourier transform of the resulting truncated cepstrum. This yields the slowly-varying curve which is superimposed on the short-time spectrum, shown at the right of the top row in Fig. 5.27.

The formant frequencies correspond closely with the resonance peaks in the smoothed spectrum. Therefore, a good estimate of the formant frequencies is obtained by determining which peaks in the smoothed spectrum are vocal tract resonances. Constraints on formant frequencies and amplitudes, derived from a three-pole model of voiced sounds, are incorporated into an alogrithm which locates the first three formant peaks in the smoothed spectrum.

The analysis of unvoiced speech segments is depicted in the bottom row of Fig. 5.27. In this case, the input speech resembles a segment of a random noise signal. As before, the logarithm of the magnitude of the Fourier transform of the segment of speech can be thought of as consisting of a rapidly-varying component, due to the excitation, plus a slowly-varying component due to the spectral shaping of the vocal-tract transfer function. In this case, however, the rapidly-varying component is not periodic but is random. Again the low-time part of the cepstrum corresponds to the slowly-varying component of the transform, but the high-time peak present in the cepstrum of voiced speech is absent for unvoiced speech. Thus, the cepstrum can also be used in deciding whether an input speech segment is voiced or unvoiced, and if voiced, the pitch period can be estimated from the location of the cepstral peak. Low-pass filtering of the logarithm of the transform, by truncation of the cepstrum and Fourier transformation, produces the smoothed spectrum curve which is again superimposed on the short-time transform at the lower right of Fig. 5.27. In this case, an adequate specification of the spectrum shape can be achieved by estimating the locations of a single wide-bandwidth resonance and a single anti-resonance, i.e., a single pole and zero.

Continuous speech is analyzed by performing these operations on short segments of speech which are selected at equally-spaced time intervals, typically 10–20 msec apart. Fig. 5.28 illustrates this process for a section of speech which, as evidenced by the peaks in the cepstra, is voiced throughout. The short-time spectrum and smoothed spectrum corresponding to each cepstrum are plotted adjacent to the cepstrum. In going from top to bottom in Fig. 5.28, each set of curves corresponds to the analysis of segments of speech selected at 20 msec increments in time. The formant peaks determined automatically by the program are connected by straight lines. Occasionally the formants come close together in frequency and pose a special problem in automatic extraction.

In the third and fourth spectra from the top, the second and third formants are so close together that there are no longer two distinct peaks. A similar situation occurs in the last four spectra where the first and second formants are not resolved. A procedure for detecting such situations has been devised and a technique for enhancing the resolution of the formants has been developed. An example of the technique is shown in Fig. 5.29.

The curve shown in Fig. 5.29a is the smooth spectrum as evaluated along the $j\omega$-axis of the complex frequency s-plane. (The lowest three vocal tract eigen-frequencies corresponding to this spectrum are depicted by the x's in the s-plane at the left.) Because formants two and three ($F2$ and $F3$) are quite close together, only one broad peak is observed in the conventional Fourier spectrum. However, when the spectrum is evaluated on a contour which passes closer to the poles, two distinct peaks are in evidence, as shown in Fig. 5.29b. The Chirp z-transform alogrithm facilitates this additional spectral analysis by allowing a fast

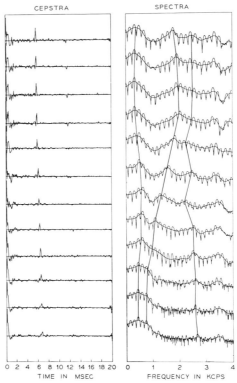

Fig. 5.28. Cepstrum analysis of continuous speech. The left column shows cepstra of con-
secutive segments of speech separated by 20 ms. The right column shows the corresponding
short-time spectra and the cepstrally-smoothed spectra

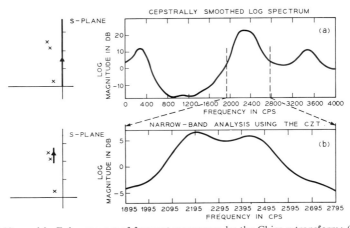

Fig. 5.29a and b. Enhancement of formant resonances by the Chirp-z transform: (a) Cepstrally-smoothed spectrum in which F_2 and F_3 are not resolved. (b) Narrow-band analysis
along a contour passing closer to the poles. (After SCHAFER and RABINER)

computation of the spectrum along an s-plane contour shown at the left of Fig. 5.29 b.

Once the vocal excitation and formant functions are determined, they can be used to synthesize a waveform which resembles the original speech signal. (Systems for speech synthesis from formant data are discussed in Section 6.2.) Comparison of the formant-synthesized signal with the original speech signal is an effective means for evaluating the automatic formant tracking. Fig. 5.30 shows a typical result of automatic analysis and synthesis of a voiced sentence. The upper curves show the pitch period and formant parameters as automatically estimated from a natural utterance whose spectrogram is also shown in the figure. The bottom of the figure shows the spectrogram of speech synthesized from the automatically estimated pitch and formant parameters. Comparison of the spectograms of the original and synthetic speech indicates that the spectral properties are reasonably well preserved.

Another approach using computer processing is the analysis of real speech spectra in terms of a model of articulation (HEINZ, 1962a, b).

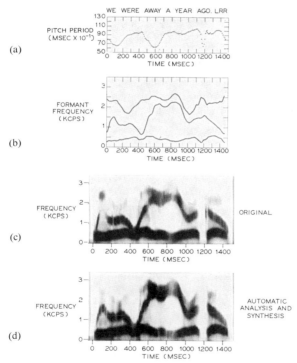

Fig. 5.30 a–d. Automatic formant analysis and synthesis of speech. (a) and (b) Pitch period and formant frequencies analyzed from natural speech. (c) Spectrogram of the original speech. (d) Spectrogram of synthesis speech. (After SCHAFER and RABINER)

This approach differs from the preceding techniques essentially in the spectrum-generation and control strategy operations. The vocal tract poles and zeros are obtained from an articulatory or area function specification of the tract. These are obtained by solving the Webster horn equation (see Chapter III). A spectrum corresponding to the computed poles and zeros is generated and compared to the real speech spectrum. The error in fit is used to alter the synthetic spectrum by adjusting, on the articulatory level, the vocal tract area function. A modification of a three-parameter description of vocal configuration is used to specify the area function (DUNN, 1950; STEVENS and HOUSE, 1955; FANT, 1960).

This formulation, provided the area function can be specified accurately enough, offers an important advantage over pole-zero models of the vocal system. The latter have as their input parameters the locations in the complex plane of the poles and zeros of the vocal transmission. The poles of the system are independent of source location and depend only on the configuration (see Chapter III). They move in a continuous manner during the production of connected speech, even though the source may change in character and location. The zeros, however, depend upon source location as well as upon tract configuration. They may move, appear and disappear in a discontinuous fashion. This discontinuous behavior of the zeros — and the resulting large changes in the speech spectrum — makes pole-zero tracking difficult.

An articulatory description of the signal obviates these difficulties to a considerable extent. More realistic continuity constraints can be applied to the articulators. The location of the unvoiced source is generally implied by the configuration, and the vocal zero specification is an automatic by-product of the specification of configuration and excitation. In terms of articulatory parameters, the spectra of consonants and consonant-vowel transitions can be matched with little more difficulty than for vowels. A typical result of this articulatory fitting procedure is shown in Fig. 5.31.

The left diagram shows the temporal courses of the poles and zeros in the /ʃ ɛ/ portion of the bisyllabic utterance /h ə′ ʃ ɛ ʃ/ (the time scale is the sample number multiplied by 8.3 msec). The vertical line, where the zero tracks disappear, represents the consonant-vowel boundary. (Only the first three formants are computed in the vowel part of the utterance.) The diagram to the right shows the corresponding temporal courses of the four articulatory parameters that were adjusted to make the spectral matches. They are:

r_0, the effective radius at the tongue constriction,

d_0, the location of the tongue constriction measured from the glottis,

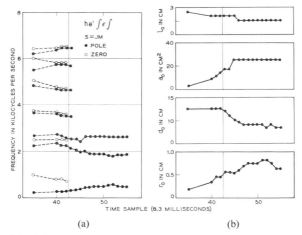

Fig. 5.31 a and b. Pole-zero computer analysis of a speech sample using an articulatory model for the spectral fitting procedure. The (a) diagram shows the pole-zero positions calculated from the articulatory model. The (b) diagram shows the articulatory parameters which describe the vocal tract area function. (After HEINZ, 1962a)

a_0, the cross-sectional area of the mouth opening, and

l_0, the length of the lip tube (or mouth section).

Their trajectories are essentially continuous as the match proceeds across the consonant-vowel boundary. In going from the fricative /ʃ/ to the vowel /ε/, the mouth section becomes shorter and more open. The position of the constriction moves back toward the glottis, and the radius of the constriction becomes larger. The position of the unvoiced sound source during the fricative is taken 2.5 cm anterior to the constriction (i.e., $d_0 + 2.5$). The manner in which these relatively simple motions describe the more complicated pole-zero pattern is striking. Success of the method depends directly upon the accuracy with which the articulatory parameters describe the vocal-tract shape. Derivation of sophisticated articulatory models is an important area for research. (See Section 5.4.)

5.22. Measurement of Formant Bandwidth

The bandwidths of the formant resonances — or the real parts of the complex poles — are indicative of the losses associated with the vocal system. Not only are quantitative data on formant bandwidths valuable in corroborating vocal tract calculations (for example, those made in Chapter III for radiation, viscous, heat-conduction, cavity-wall and glottal losses), but a knowledge of the damping is important in the proper synthesis of speech.

A number of measurements have been made of vocal tract damping and formant bandwidth[1]. The measurements divide mainly between two techniques; either a measure of a resonance width in the frequency domain, or a measure of a damping constant (or decrement) on a suitably filtered version of the speech time waveform. In the former case the formant is considered as a simple resonance, and the half-power frequencies of the spectral envelope are determined. In the latter case the formant is considered a damped sinusoid, having amplitudes A_1 and A_2 at times t_1 and t_2. The damping constant, σ, for the wave and its half-power bandwidth, Δf, are related simply as

$$\sigma = \pi \Delta f = \frac{\ln A_2/A_1}{(t_2 - t_1)}.$$

The results of one of the more extensive formant bandwidth studies are summarized in Fig. 5.32 (DUNN, 1961). Part (a) of the figure shows the formant bandwidths measured by fitting a simple resonance curve to amplitude sections of vowels uttered in an /h–d/ syllable. The data are averages for 20 male voices producing each vowel. The second

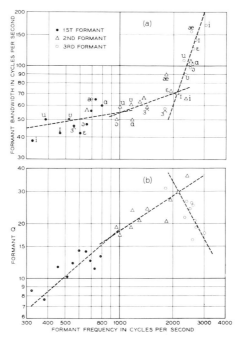

Fig. 5.32a and b. Measured formant bandwidths for adult males. (After DUNN, 1961)

---

[1] For a good summary and bibliography of earlier investigations, see DUNN (1961), Also, see FANT (1958, 1959a, b).

curve (b) represents the same data plotted in terms of $Q=f/\Delta f$. The upper graph shows that over the frequency ranges of the first and second formants, the nominal bandwidths are generally small — on the order of 40 to 70 cps. Above 2000 cps the bandwidth increases appreciably. The lower plot of formant-Q *vs* formant frequency shows that resonant Q's are largest in the frequency region around 2000 cps.

Formant bandwidths can also be effectively measured from a frequency response of the actual vocal-tract (FUJIMURA). A sine wave of volume velocity is introduced into the vocal-tract at the glottal end by means of a throat vibrator. The pressure output at the mouth is measured as the input source is changed in frequency. A typical vocal-tract frequency response is shown in Fig. 5.33a. The variation in first-formant bandwidth, as a function of first-formant frequency, is shown in 5.33b.

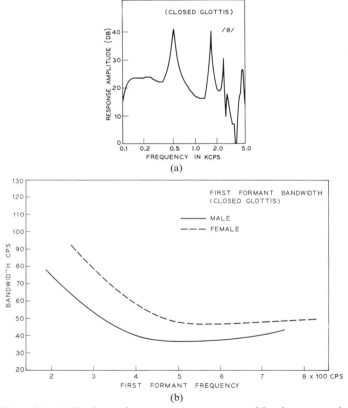

Fig. 5.33a and b. (a) Vocal-tract frequency response measured by sine-wave excitation of an external vibrator applied to the throat. The articulatory shape is for the neutral vowel and the glottis is closed. (After FUJIMURA and LINDQUIST). (b) Variation in first-formant bandwidth as a function of formant frequency. Data for men and women are shown for the closed-glottis condition. (After FUJIMURA and LINDQUIST)

These data are for a closed-glottis condition. The bandwidth is seen to increase as first formant frequency diminishes, owing primarily to the influence of cavity-wall loss. (See calculations of cavity-wall loss in Section 3.37.)

The origins of the principal contributions to vocal-tract damping have already been indicated by the theory derived in Chapter III. These are glottal loss and cavity-wall loss for the lower formants, and radiation, viscous and heat-conduction loss for the higher formants.

5.3. Analysis of Voice Pitch

Fundamental frequency analysis—or "pitch extraction"—is a problem nearly as old as speech analysis itself. It is one for which a complete solution remains to be found. The main difficulty is that voice pitch has yet to be adequately defined. Qualitatively, pitch is that subjective attribute that admits of rank ordering on a scale ranging from low to high. The voiced excitation of the vocal tract is only quasi-periodic. Not only does the exciting glottal waveform vary in period and amplitude, but it also varies in shape. Precisely what epochs on the speech waveform, or even on the glottal waveform, should be chosen for interval or period measurement is not clear. Furthermore, the relation between an interval, so measured, and the perceived pitch is not well established.

Most pitch-extracting methods take as their objective the indication of the epoch of each glottal puff and the measurement of the interval between adjacent pulses. Still, exactly how this relates to the pitch percept with all the random jitter and variation of the glottal wave is a question worthy of inquiry.

Most automatic or machine pitch extractors attempt either to describe the periodicity of the signal waveform (GRÜTZMACHER and LOTTERMOSER; GRUENZ and SCHOTT; DOLANSKY, 1955; GILL) or to measure the frequency of the fundamental component if it is present (DUDLEY, 1939 b). Computer efforts at pitch extraction essentially do the same, but usually more elaborate constraints and decisions are applied (INOMATA; GOLD; SUGIMOTO and HASHIMOTO).

One particularly useful method for machine pitch extraction utilizes properties of the cepstrum to reveal signal periodicity (NOLL; OPPENHEIM, SCHAFER and STOCKHAM). As described in Section 5.214, the cepstrum is defined as the Fourier transform of the logarithm of the amplitude spectrum of a signal. Since it is a transform of a transform, and since the resulting independent variable is reciprocal frequency, or time, the terms "cepstrum" and "quefrency" were coined by its inventors

(BOGERT, HEALY and TUKEY) to designate the transform and its independent variable.

The log-taking operation has the desirable property of separating source and system characteristic (at least to the extent that they are spectrally multiplicative). If the output speech wave, $f(t)$, is the convolution of the vocal tract impulse response, $v(t)$, and the vocal excitation source, $s(t)$, the magnitudes of their Fourier transforms are related as

$$|F(\omega)| = |V(\omega)| \cdot |S(\omega)|,$$

where all the amplitude spectra are even functions. Taking the logarithm of both sides gives

$$\ln|F(\omega)| = \ln|V(\omega)| + \ln|S(\omega)|.$$

Similarly, taking the Fourier transform[1] of both sides yields

$$\mathscr{F}\ln|F(\omega)| = \mathscr{F}\ln|V(\omega)| + \mathscr{F}\ln|S(\omega)|.$$

For voiced sounds, $|S(\omega)|$ is approximately a line spectrum with components spaced at the pitch frequency $1/T$. $\mathscr{F}\ln|S(\omega)|$ therefore exhibits a strong component at the "quefrency", T. $|V(\omega)|$, on the other hand, exhibits the relatively "slow" formant maxima. Consequently $\mathscr{F}\ln|V(\omega)|$ has its strongest component at a very low quefrency.

Because of the additive property of the transforms of the log amplitude spectra, the characteristics of the source and system are well separated in the cepstrum. The cepstrum is therefore also a valuable tool for formant analysis as well as pitch measurement (SCHAFER and RABINER). (See Section 5.21.) Measurement of pitch and voiced-unvoiced excitation is accomplished by using a suitable strategy to detect the quefrency components associated with $\mathscr{F}\ln|S(\omega)|$. Because the method does not require the presence of the fundamental component, and because it is relatively insensitive to phase and amplitude factors (owing to the log-magnitude operations) it performs well in vocoder applications. In one test with a complete channel vocoder, it demonstrated superior performance in extracting the pitch and voiced-unvoiced control data (NOLL). Because a large amount of processing is necessary, the method is most attractive for special purpose digital implementations where Fast Fourier Transform hardware can be used. An illustration of pitch determination by cepstrum computation has been shown previously in Figs. 5.28a and 5.30.

Perhaps a more basic measurement of voiced excitation is that of the glottal volume-velocity wave (R. L. MILLER, 1959; FANT, 1959b; MATHEWS, MILLER and DAVID, 1961a; HOLMES, 1962). Approximations

---

[1] Formally an inverse Fourier transform.

to this function can be obtained by so-called inverse-filtering techniques. The idea is to pass the speech signal through a network whose transmission function is the reciprocal of that of the vocal tract for the particular sound. Zeros of the network are adjusted to nullify vocal tract poles, and the resulting output is an approximation to the input glottal volume current.

The inverse-filtering analysis presumes that the source and system relations for the speech-producing mechanism do not interact and can be uniquely separated and treated independently. This assumption is a treacherous one if the objective is an accurate estimate of the glottal volume velocity. In the real vocal tract they interact to a certain extent (particularly at the first-formant frequency). Another difficulty is that it is not always clear whether to ascribe certain properties (primarily, zeros) to the tract or to the source. The estimate obtained for the glottal wave obviously depends upon the vocal-tract model adopted for the inverse filter. The criterion of adjustment of the inverse filter also influences the answer. Under certain conditions, for example, ripples on the inverse wave which may be thought to be formant oscillations might in fact be actual glottal variations.

One question often raised is "where in the pitch period does the excitation occur." Presumably if such an epoch could be determined, the pulse excitation of a synthesizer could duplicate it and preserve natural irregularities in the pitch period. Because the glottal wave frequently changes shape, such a datum is difficult to describe. One claim is that this epoch commonly is at the close of the cords (R. L. MILLER, 1959), while another (HOLMES, 1962) is that it can occur at other points in the wave. To a first approximation, such an epoch probably coincides with the greatest change in the derivative of the glottal waveform. Often this point can occur just about anywhere in the period. For a triangular wave, for example, it would be at the apex.

A perceptual study has been made of the effects of the glottal waveform on the quality of synthetic speech. The results support the notion that the significant vocal excitation occurs at the point of greatest slope change in the glottal wave (ROSENBERG, 1971 b). Natural speech was analyzed pitch-synchronously. The vocal-tract transmission and the glottal waveform were determined and separated by inverse filtering. Artificial glottal waveforms were substituted and the speech signal was regenerated. Listening tests showed that good quality speech can be obtained from an excitation function fixed in analytical form. The absence of temporal detail, period-to-period, does not degrade quality. A preferred glottal pulse shape has but a single slope discontinuity at closing. It is intrinsically asymmetric, so its spectral zeros never fall on or near the $j\omega$-axis for any combination of opening and closing times (ROSENBERG, 1971 b).

5.4. Articulatory Analysis of the Vocal Mechanism

The discussion of Chapter III showed that if the vocal tract configuration is known, the system response can be computed and the mode structure specified. The cross-sectional area as a function of distance is sufficient to compute the lower eigenfrequencies of the tract. An accurate account of losses along the tract requires knowledge of the cross-sectional shape or the circumference. [See Eq. 3.33).] Because the vocal mechanism is relatively inaccessible, the necessary dimensions are obviously difficult to obtain. Even at best, present methods of measurement yield incomplete descriptions of tract dimensions and dynamics.

X-ray techniques for motion and still pictures have provided most of the articulatory information available to date. The X-ray data generally are supplemented by other measures. Conventional moving pictures can be made of the external components of the vocal system. Palatograms, molds of the vocal cavities, and electromyographic recordings are also useful techniques for "filling in the picture." Much of the effort in X-ray analysis is directed toward therapeutic goals, such as cleft palate repair and laryngeal treatment. Consequently, the results are often left in only a qualitative form. Several investigations, however, have aimed at measuring vocal dimensions and articulatory movements. (FANT, 1960; CHIBA and KAJIYAMA; PERKELL; FUJIMURA *et al.*; HOUDE.)

One of the main problems in obtaining such data is keeping the radiation dose of the subject within safe limits. This usually means that only a very limited amount of data can be taken on a single individual. One ingenious solution to this problem utilizes a computer-controlled X-ray beam which, under program control, is made to irradiate and track only the physiological areas of interest (FUJIMURA *et al.*).

Another problem is the detail of the X-ray photograph. This is particularly a problem in moving X-ray photography, even with the best image-intensifier tubes. Detail which looks deceptively good in the (visually-integrated) moving picture, disappears when one stops the film to study a single frame. Sound recordings are usually made simultaneously for analysis, but often are of poor quality because of the noise of the proximate movie camera.

The detail in still pictures is somewhat better but nevertheless lacking. An example of a typical medical X-ray is shown in Fig. 5.34. The tongue and lips of the subject were coated with a barium compound to make them more visible. The vocal tract position is appropriate to the production of a high-front vowel close to /i/.

The typical procedure for obtaining an area function from the X-ray picture can be illustrated. An axial line through the centers of gravity of the cross sectional areas is first located, as shown in Fig. 5.35a

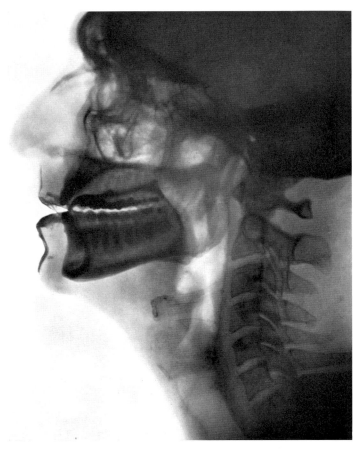

Fig. 5.34. Sagittal plane X-ray of adult male vocal tract

(FANT, 1960). The shape and area of the cross-sections at a number of locations are estimated, as shown in Fig. 5.35b. The shape estimates are deduced on the basis of all available data, including dental molds of the vocal and nasal cavities, conventional photographs and X-ray photographs from the front. These sections provide anchor points for an estimate of the whole area curve. Intermediate values are established both from the sagittal plane X-ray tracing and from continuity considerations to give the complete area function, as shown in Fig. 5.35c. Typical results for several sounds produced by one man are shown in Fig. 5.36.

Even under best conditions, some of the vocal dimensions during natural speech are impossible to measure. For example, one often can

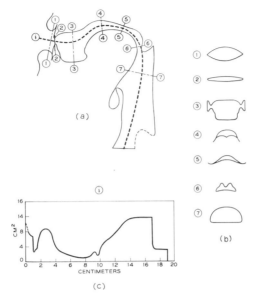

Fig. 5.35 a–c. Method of estimating the vocal tract area function from X-ray data. (After FANT, 1960)

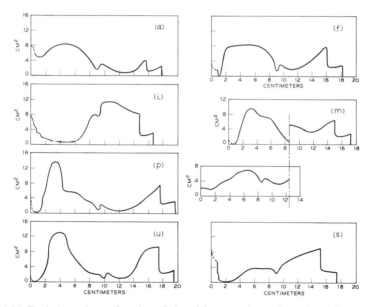

Fig. 5.36. Typical vocal area functions deduced for several sounds produced by one man. (After FANT, 1960)

only make crude estimates of the true shape and lateral dimensions of the
pharynx cavity. In the same vein, the true dimensions of the constrictions for fricatives and affricates and the lateral pathways in /l/ are
often very uncertain.

Similarly, the vocal source of excitation cannot be studied easily by
direct methods. For sustained, open vowels, however, the vocal cord
source can be examined by high-speed moving pictures. Measurements
of subglottal pressure are also possible and give insight into vocal cord
operation. Characteristics of the unvoiced sources, on the other hand,
i.e., location, spectral properties and internal impedance, are best in-
ferred from physiological configuration, air flow measurements and
spectral analysis of the output sound.

Research interest in better methods for physiological measurements
remains high. One active research area centers on the possibilities for
relating electromyographic recordings of muscle potentials to the articu-
lator movements observed in X-ray pictures. Several "exotic" schemes
for vocal measurement have also been proposed, half humorously. They
may, however, hold some promise. For example, a conducting dag
loop might be painted around the circumference of the tract at a given
position and electrical leads attached. The cross sectional area at that
point could be measured by placing the subject in a magnetic field
normal to the section and measuring the flux which links the dag loop.
Other possibilities might be the attachment of miniature strain gauges
at significant points, or the placement of inflatable annular cuffs or
catheters at given positions in the tract. Still other possibilities include
miniature ultrasonic transducers fixed to the articulators.

Acoustic measurements directly on the vocal-tract also promise useful estimation of the cross-sectional area function (MERMELSTEIN and
SCHROEDER; GOPINATH and SONDHI). In one method the acoustic impedance of the tract is periodically sampled at the mouth (GOPINATH
and SONDHI). While the subject silently articulates into an impedance
tube, pulses of sound pressure are produced periodically (typically at
100 sec^{-1}) and the volume velocity response is measured. The pressure
and volume velocity along the tract are assumed to obey WEBSTER's
horn equation [Eq. (3.1)], which is valid for frequencies below about
4000 cps. An asymptotic high-frequency behavior of the tract is assumed.
No assumptions are made about the termination at the glottal end or
about the length of the tract. Solution of an integral equation yields the
integral of the cross-sectional area of an equivalent lossless, hard-walled
pipe as a function of distance. Differentiation gives the area function.
Typical results, compared to area functions from X-ray measurements,
are shown in Fig. 5.37. The impedance tube calculations are made for
hard-walled vocal-tracts having the shapes given by the X-ray data.

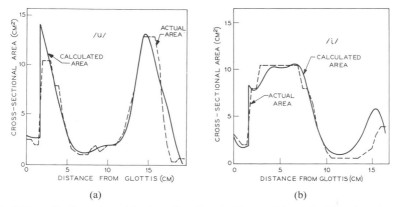

Fig. 5.37 a and b. Typical vocal-tract area functions (solid curves) determined from impedance measurements at the mouth. The actual area functions (dashed curves) are derived from X-ray data. (After GOPINATH and SONDHI)

A question of considered importance is the influence of wall-yielding (as is present in the real vocal tract) upon the calculated area function. Present efforts aim to include wall vibration and wall loss into the area determination method. Further research is needed to test the method with real speakers and real speech, and to account for real vocal-tract conditions, including loss, yielding side walls and nasal coupling.

Vocal-tract models, electrical vocal-tract analogs and computational analyses have all been useful in inferring articulatory data and tract dynamics from acoustic measurements of speech sounds and from X-ray data. One articulatory model, which has an important application in synthesis (see Section 6.26), has also been useful in establishing physiological constraints and time constants associated with major articulators (COKER, 1968). The articulatory model describes the vocal area function in terms of seven parameters, shown in Fig. 5.38. The coordinates are: the position of the tongue body, X, Y; the lip protrusion, L; the lip rounding W; the place and degree of tongue tip constriction, R and B; and the degree of velar coupling, N. No nasal tract is incorporated in this version of the model, and velar coupling exerts its influence solely through the tract area function.

The area function described by the model can be used to synthesize connected speech, which in turn can be compared in spectral detail to real speech. Also, because of its correspondence to major vocal elements, the seven-parameter model can be used to duplicate articulatory motions observed from X-ray motion pictures. Further, its description of vocal-tract area can be compared with X-ray area data, as shown in Fig. 5.39. Such comparisons have been useful in analyzing priorities

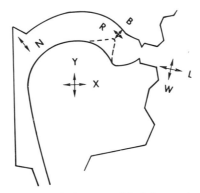

Fig. 5.38. Seven-parameter articulatory model of the vocal tract. (After Coker)

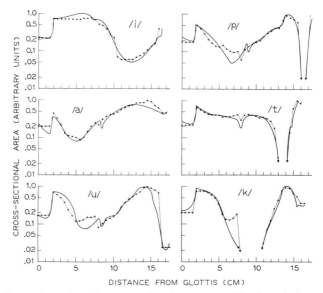

Fig. 5.39. Comparison of vocal tract area functions generated by the articulatory model of Fig. 5.38 and human area data measured from X-rays. (After Coker)

and time-constants for the motions of the articulators in real speech and in quantifying these effects for speech synthesis (Coker, Umeda and Browman; Flanagan, Coker, Rabiner, Schafer and Umeda).

5.5. Automatic Recognition of Speech

A human can listen to meaningful speech of a given language and set down a written equivalent of what he hears. He performs a transformation on the acoustic input signal wherein distinctive linguistic elements (phonemes) are recognized and re-encoded into a sequence of letter symbols. Recognition of the linguistic elements is based upon a knowledge of the contextual, grammatical and semantic constraints of the given language. It does not take much examination of sound spectrograms to convince oneself that a unique relation generally does not exist between a given segment of the acoustic signal and a linguistic element. Neither are phonemic boundaries necessarily apparent in the acoustic signal.

Automatic recognition of speech implies phonemic analysis by machine. It is possible to simulate crudely the initial operations performed on the acoustic signal by the human (see the frequency analysis and neural encoding performed at the ear's periphery in Chapter IV) but, to date, not even the most elaborate mechanical recognizers have been able to apply linguistic constraints comparable in effectiveness to the human. This latter area represents an active field of research in theory of grammar, semantics, and mechanical translation.

The difference (or, more precisely, the gulf) between phoneme recognition for a given language and a straight-forward encoding of the acoustic signal, say in terms of vocal modes and excitation, cannot be overemphasized. The former implies complete linguistic knowledge, the latter only that the signal is produced by the human vocal mechanism. The latter is within the scope of present speech analysis techniques. The former, as yet, is not. If phoneme recognition ultimately proves possible, the import to efficient transmission is, of course, immense. (Recall it was suggested in Section 1.2, Chapter I, that the information rate associated with the utterance of independent, equiprobable phonemes is on the order of 50 bits/sec. A coding exists for transmitting information at this rate over a channel of about 5 cps bandwidth and 30 db signal-to-noise ratio, with as small an error as desired.)

A number of research investigations have treated machines which are capable of recognizing limited ensembles of speech sounds uttered by limited numbers of speakers (often only one). Generally these devices make decisions about either the short-time spectrum of the acoustic signal or about features of the time waveform. The constraints usually employed are ones more appropriate to the vocal mechanism (i.e., acoustical constraints) than to linguistic structure. Without attempting to be exhaustive, the state of the art can be outlined by several examples.

One effort toward a recognizer for a limited ensemble of sounds is a recognizer for spoken digits, called Audrey (DAVIS, BIDDULPH and BALASHEK). The principle of operation is to make a rough measure of the first and second formant frequencies as functions of time, and to compare the measured temporal patterns (in the $F1-F2$ plane) with a set of stored reference patterns. The stored pattern affording the best correlation is then chosen as the uttered digit.

The procedure is illustrated in Fig. 5.40. The speech signal is filtered into two bands, 900 cps low pass and 1000 cps high pass. Limiting amplifiers in both channels peak clip the signals. Axis-crossing measures approximate the frequencies of the first and second formants as

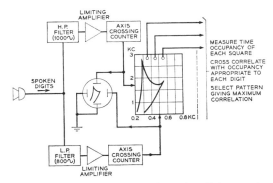

Fig. 5.40. Principle of operation of a spoken digit recognizer.
(After DAVIS, BIDDULPH and BALASHEK)

functions of time. The first-formant frequency range (from 200 to 800 cps) is quantized into six 100-cps segments. The second-formant range (from 500 to 2500 cps) is quantized into five 500-cps steps. An $F1$–$F2$ plane with 30 matrix elements is thereby produced. For a given digit utterance, the time that the $F1$–$F2$ trajectory occupies each elemental square is determined.

A reference "time-occupancy" pattern for each digit is stored in the machine. The storage mechanism is 10 weighting resistors associated with each square. Through these resistors, charges are accumulated on 10 separate condensers during the time the square is occupied. A cross correlation of the stored and incoming patterns is effected by weighting the 10 conductances associated with each square according to the average time-occupancy of that square by the respective digits. That is, for each of the 30 squares, there are 10 relays which close charging paths to the 10 fixed condensers. The conductance of a given path is weighted proportional to the time occupancy of that square by a given digit. The condenser left with the greatest charge at the end of the utterance indicates the pattern affording the highest correlation, and hence the spoken digit.

The machine does not have provisions for automatically adjusting its stored patterns to a given speaker's voice. This must be done manually.

When it is done, however, the accuracy in recognizing telephone quality utterances of the digits ranges between 97 and 99% correct.

An extension of this technique is to correlate—on an instant-by-instant basis—a measured short-time amplitude spectrum with stored spectral patterns (DUDLEY and BALASHEK). Instead of the $F1$–$F2$ trackers, a set of bandpass filters (10 in this case, each 300 cps wide) is used to produce a short-time spectrum. Stored spectral patterns (again, 10) are continuously cross-correlated with the short-time spectrum produced by the filters. The maximum correlation is taken as an indication of the particular speech sound being produced. The pattern-matching procedure is illustrated in Fig. 5.41. If $F_0(\omega_n)$ is the short-time amplitude spectrum produced by the n filter channels for a given speech input, and $F_j(\omega_n)$ the j-th stored pattern, the circuit, in principle, approximates the correlation quantity

$$\varphi_{0j}(0) = \frac{1}{\Omega} \int_0^\Omega F_0(\omega) F_j(\omega)\, d\omega \qquad j = 1, 2, 3, \ldots,$$

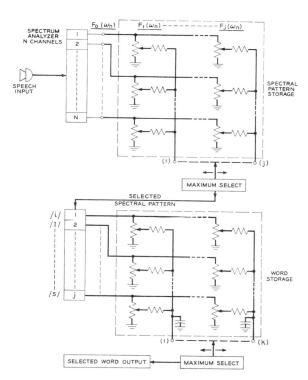

Fig. 5.41. Scheme for automatic recognition of spectral patterns and spoken digits.
(After DUDLEY and BALASHEK)

by

$$\varphi_{0j}(0) \cong \frac{1}{n} \sum_n F_0(\omega_n) F_j(\omega_n) \qquad j = 1, 2, 3, \dots,$$

and selects the j that produces a maximum $\varphi_{0j}(0)$. The 10 sound patterns stored in this particular development are all continuants and are /i, I, ε, a, o, u, n, r, f, s/.

A word recognizing device follows the spectral pattern recognizer to recognize the 10 digits. Similar to the Audrey device, each selected spectral pattern is weighted according to its duration in a given digit (see the lower part of Fig. 5.41). Again a maximum selection is made to recognize the uttered digit. The word indication is developed as follows. When a particular spectral pattern is energized, 10 charge paths are set up to 10 fixed condensers. The conductance of a given path is proportional to the average time for which that spectral pattern appears in a given digit. The 10 condensers therefore accumulate charges proprotional to the correlation between the 10 stored word patterns and the measured pattern. At the end of the utterance, a maximum selection indicates the best-fitting word. This device – designed as an elaboration upon the previous one – provides digit recognition with good accuracy when set for a particular voice. In both devices the sequence of spectral patterns and the recognized digits are displayed on electrical panel lights. Despite its early date of conception and implementation, this device and the previously-described digit recognizer, Audrey, still reflect present limitations in automatic speech recognition; namely, one can achieve success if the vocabulary is isolated words, sufficiently small in number, and if the number of speakers is sufficiently constrained.

Another speech recognizing device also compares spectral patterns with stored patterns representative of specific speech phonemes (FRY and DENES). The comparison however, is made in a different way, and the machine types out the identification in terms of special symbols. Selection of a match is asynchronous and is initiated by the rate of change of the spectral patterns. More important, however, an attempt is made to exploit elementary linguistic constraints. A block diagram of the device is shown in Fig. 5.42.

A filter-bank analyzer (20 channels) produces a short-time amplitude spectrum. Spectral patterns appropriate to a given sound are produced by multiplying the outputs of two channels. The products are scanned by a selector, and the maximum is chosen. The choice is typed out by the machine and is remembered by a storage circuit. On the basis of the choice, the ensemble of stored patterns is biased according to digram statistics for the language. Selection of the next phoneme is biased in favor of its being the most probable one to follow the previous choice.

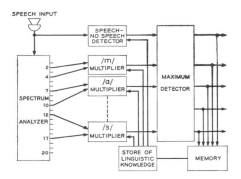

Fig. 5.42. Block diagram of speech sound recognizer employing elementary linguistic constraints. (After FRY and DENES)

In the present machine 14 phonemes are recognized; four vowels, nine consonants and silence. A new selection is made whenever the product voltages have a rate of change greater than a given threshold value. With the machine adjusted for a given speaker, the spoken input and printed output have been compared. When the digram constraints are not used, the percentage correct response on individual sounds and on words is 60% and 24%, respectively. When the digram constraints are connected, these same scores rise to 72% and 44% for the single speaker. For a second and third speaker, without readjusting the machine, the sound articulation scores fall to about 45%.

The linguistic information clearly improves the recognition when scored to give all phonemes equal weight. If scored on the basis of information per phoneme, however, the digram constraints could, under certain conditions, be detrimental. The most probable phoneme is favored, but it is also the conveyor of the least information. The constraints also raise the question of sequential errors and how they might be propagated. A certain level of accuracy in the acoustic recognition is certainly necessary if the use of linguistic constraints is to lead to a decrease, rather than to an increase, in error rate. Sequential errors of course occur in the human listener. A listener, once embarked upon the wrong set of constraints in a particular sequence, may add one error to another for quite a long stretch. In the machine, severe restriction of vocabulary reduces this possibility.

If the linguistic constraints to be incorporated into the recognition process are at all realistic, the storage and processing functions become complex. Also if elaborate processings are to be carried out on the acoustic signal, large storage and rapid computation are requisite. The digital computer is adept at this, and a number of efforts have been made to capitalize upon its ability. One effort in this direction is the programming of a digit recognizer (DENES and MATHEWS). Short-time amplitude spectra are produced from a filter bank. The filter outputs are scanned sequentially, and the spectral data are read into and stored in the machine. A speech spectrogram — quantized in time, frequency and intensity — is laid down in the storage. Amplitude values are normalized so that the sum of the squares over all time-frequency blocks is unity. The measured time-frequency-intensity pattern is then cross-correlated with stored spectrographic patterns. The correlation is effected by multiplying the amplitude values of corresponding time-frequency elements and summing the products over all elements of the time-frequency plane. The stored pattern yielding the maximum correlation is chosen.

Provisions are made to time-normalize the data if desired. The beginning and the end of the digit utterance are located, and the data are, in effect, stretched to fit a standard time duration (actually 60 scans of the filter bank at $70 \sec^{-1}$). Without time normalization only the beginning of each utterance is located, and the first 60 scans are used.

The reference pattern for each digit is obtained by averaging the spectral data for three utterances of that digit by five men. These patterns are used to recognize different utterances by the same and by different speakers. For different utterances by the same five speakers, the error rates are found to be 6% with time normalization and 13% without. When the reference patterns are set for a single speaker, the digits uttered by that speaker are recognized essentially with no error.

A more linguistically-based approach, using a large on-line computer facility, performs a feature analysis of segments of the speech waveform (REDDY, 1967). The wave is first divided into minimal segments, 10-msec in duration. Minimal segments which are acoustically similar are grouped to form larger segments representing either sustained parts or transitional parts. Features such as voiced-unvoiced, pitch, intensity, formant frequency and amplitude are used to classify each segment into four phoneme groups: stop, fricative, nasal-liquid and vowel. A very detailed algorithm is then used to assign a phoneme label to each segment of a phoneme group. The object, literally, is a speech to phoneme-like translation. This system, while recognizing the potential advantages of phonetic feature classification and language element probabilities, is nevertheless faced with the same problems of linguistic and semantic constraints that confront all recognizers. Its sophistication pays off, however, in enlarging the speaker population and vocabularly which can be successfully handled. The system has been demonstrated to yield 98% correct recognition on 500 isolated words spoken by one individual (REDDY, 1969).

At least one similar word-recognition experiment has been carried out for the Russian language (VELICHKO and ZAGORUYKO). In this case the energy-time-frequency dimensions of individually spoken words are quantized. A distance functional between the unknown word and the stored references for a word library of 203 words is computed. For two speakers, producing approximately 5000 utterances chosen from the 203 word library, the recognition accuracy was found to be about 95%. Computation time for each utterance was 2 to 4 sec.

The preceding discussion has attempted to indicate by example several stages of development in automatic speech recognition. A sizeable number of related efforts have not been mentioned (for example, SMITH, 1951; BAUMANN, LICKLIDER and HOWLAND; OLSON and BELAR; FORGIE and FORGIE; FRICK; DREYFUS-GRAF; MARTIN; LINDGREN). Most share a common point of departure, namely, the short-time spectrum. It is clear from the discussion that none of the schemes tells us very much about how the human processes speech information, nor about how he recognizes linguistic elements. None of the methods works well on an unrestricted number of voices, nor on a large contextual vocabulary. The human, however, is proficient at handling both. Nevertheless, the investigations do indicate what can be realized in the way of voice-actuated devices for special applications — specifically, applications where vocabulary and number of voices may be suitably restricted. It is clear, too, that for a given accuracy of recognition, a trade can be made between the necessary linguistic constraints, the complexity of the vocabulary, and the number of speakers.

Automatic speech recognition — as the human accomplishes it — will probably be possible only through the proper analysis and application of grammatical, contextual, and semantic constraints. These constraints, as yet, are largely unknown. Perhaps not surprisingly, research in speech synthesis seems to be providing more insight into linguistic constraints than is speech recognition work. One view of speech recognition (PIERCE) makes the point that success will be very limited until the recognizing device understands what is being said with something of the facility of a native speaker.

5.6. Automatic Recognition and Verification of Speakers

The previous discussion pointed up the notion that the spectral patterns of one speaker are not always adequate to recognize the speech of another. This fact suggest that spectral data might be used to recognize or identify different speakers. A number of efforts along these lines have been made — mainly with the use of digital computers. By way of illustration, one study produced quantized time-frequency-intensity (spectrographic) patterns from a 17-channel filter bank scanned at a rate of 100 sec^{-1} (PRUZANSKY). Ten key words were excerpted from context for 10 different speakers (three women, seven men). For each talker, three utterances of the 10 key words were used to establish the reference patterns for that individual.

For talker identification, the spectrographic pattern of a different key-word utterance by an unknown speaker of the ten-member group was cross-correlated with the reference patterns (again by multiplying amplitudes at each time-frequency element of the spectrogram), and the maximum correlation was taken. Because the utterances varied in length, alignment of patterns was done by matching them at the maximum overall amplitude points. Results showed that among the 10 speakers for whom the reference library was formed, the identification was correct in 89% of the cases.

In the same study, the three dimensional time-frequency-intensity patterns were reduced to two dimensions by summing over the time of the utterance for each filter channel. The summation produces a graph of integrated intensity-versus-frequency for each utterance. It was found that this operation still afforded a recognition score of 89%.

It is of course difficult to draw conclusions about human recognition of speakers from such an experiment. Again, however, for a limited, specific application, where speaker ensemble and vocabulary are restricted, such a technique could be effectively applied.

A few experiments have measured human recognition of speakers from visual inspection of speech spectrograms. In one of these (KERSTA, 1948, 1962a) a group of speakers (either 5, 9 or 12) was asked to utter 10 key words four times. Conventional bar spectrograms and contour spectrograms were made of their utterances (see Section 5.14). For each word a randomized matrix of spectrograms consisting of four utterances of each speaker was displayed. Subjects were asked to identify the utterances of each individual speaker. The errors in grouping the prints according to speaker ranged from 0.35% to 1.0% for bar prints and from 0.37% to 1.5% for contour spectrograms. When the test words were excerpted from context, the error was still about the same order of magnitude.

A second experiment was modeled after fingerprint identification procedures, although the analogy is a tenous one. A file of "voice prints" of five key words was compiled for 12 speakers. Subjects then identified a different set of utterances by an unknown member of the group through comparisons to the reference sets. Using the groups of five cue words, the misidentifications were less than 1%. Identifications based upon two 5-word groups in tandem gave errors of about one-half percent. Preliminary investigations were also made into the ability to recognize disguised voices. The results suggest that adults have certain invariant linguistic and physiological characteristics which the spectrograph may display even when an effort is made to alter the voice.

These experiments, through a combination of publicity and private development, captured the notice of various law-enforcing organizations, who saw in the method a new means for identifying criminals. Several efforts were made to introduce the technique into legal proceedings with controversial results. Independent experiments were conducted to test the method, and the findings were at variance with the original experiments (YOUNG and CAMPBELL). Most opinion holds that more research is needed to accurately establish the utility of human recognition of speakers from sound spectrograms (FLANAGAN et al.; BOLT et al.). Subsequent efforts continue in this direction (TOSI). These latter experiments have treated a variety of experimental conditions (for example, closed sets versus open sets) and the error rates in visual identification vary from 1% to 30%, depending upon the experimental constraints. This error range, when analyzed in terms of experimental conditions, appears consistent with previous data.

A problem perhaps more interesting and presently more tractable than speaker recognition is automatic verification of speakers (DODDINGTON; LUMMIS; DAS and MOHN). In the usual context of this problem one has a restricted population of "customers" who want to be verified (i.e., a cooperative situation), and they are willing to state a prearranged phrase (secret if desired) chosen to be advantageous for the machine. (The voice banking, and voice validation of credit cards are applications in point). In the verification situation unknown caller, x, claims to be customer, C_i. The machine must decide to accept or reject x as C_i. The decision can be weighted according to the importance of the verification (for example, whether the sum charged is large or small) and a predetermined mix of error types (i.e., rejecting a true speaker versus accepting a false speaker) can be specified.

The most important aspect of the verification problem, and the one which distinguishes it from the recognition problem, is that no matter what the size of the impostor population, the average percent correct verification tends to be constant. The performance is determined by the average consistencies of the known speakers and by how each of them differs from the average of the impostor population. In a recognition situation, on the other hand, where the unknown must be identified by successive comparisons to all members of a known set, the probability of error is monotonely related to the number of speakers in the set, and the probability of a recognition error approaches unity as the user population becomes large.

One experiment on verification (DODDINGTON) has made use of pitch, formant and intensity data to form reference patterns for the known speakers. Frequency data (i.e., formants and pitch) were considered attractive because they are resistant to variations in the amplitude-frequency characteristics of a voice communication link. A novel non-linear time-warping of the utterance of an unknown speaker was used to compare (register) it with a stored reference pattern corresponding to the claimed identity. The non-linear warp was achieved on a digital computer by a steepest-ascent algorithm. The algorithm warped the pattern of the unknown speaker to maximize its correlation with the stored reference pattern. A mean square error measure was then made for the registered patterns and the speaker was accepted or rejected depending upon whether the mean square error was less than or greater than a threshold chosen for a specified mix of errors (i.e., reject true versus accept false).

Fig. 5.43 shows how the formant, pitch and intensity (gain) data are compared for a verification phrase; namely, the voiced sentence "We were away a year ago". In Fig. 5.43a the unknown utterance (solid curve) has been given a linear time stretch to make its duration equal to the reference (dashed curve). Poor internal registration is evident. In Fig. 5.44b, the non-linear warp has been applied to register the second formant tracks with maximum correlation. The registration of the other parameters is similarly improved. The remaining differences and the amount of non-linear warp applied are indicative of the similarities of the two patterns. A square error measure is formulated to indicate a "distance" between the registered patterns.

Using this technique, with a population of 40 male speakers, correct verification was achieved 98.5% of the time on the verification phrase "We were away a year ago" used by all subjects. Identical twins included in the experiment were differentiated 100% of the time.

If more sophisticated "distance measures" are used to characterize the differences between the registered patterns for the unknown and reference, a comparable performance can be obtained on simple measures, easily made in real time. A subsequent experiment on the same population of 40 speakers, and using more elaborate distance measures on only intensity, pitch and non-linear warp, achieved 99% correct verification (LUMMIS).

A natural query is "How good would human listeners do in the same task?" To answer this, a completely parallel auditory experiment was conducted with the same 40 speakers, but using human listeners instead of a computer to make the verification decision. The listeners performed with greater error rate than the machine and achieved approximately 96% correct verification (ROSENBERG, 1971 a).

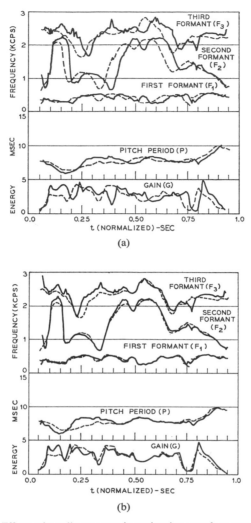

Fig. 5.43 a and b. Effects of nonlinear warp in registering speech parameter patterns. The dashed curves are reference data for an individual. The solid curves are a sample utterance from the same individual. (a) Linear stretch to align end points only. (b) Nonlinear warp to maximize the correlation of the $F2$ patterns. (After DODDINGTON)

Results of these and related verification experiments suggest that automatic machine verification may have practical value. An obvious and further question is how easily might accomplished mimics deceive the machine and be erroneously accepted. Continuing research is aimed at this question.

A number of features seem to distinguish one speaker from another. The size and shape of the vocal tract vary considerably among persons. Characteristic damping, mouth and glottal dimensions also vary. Individual nasal coupling, size and damping of the nasal tract are other relevant features. Temporal patterns of intensity (stress) and pitch (inflection) are still others. Vocal obstructions and variations in dental work may contribute still further differences. Some or all these factors might be used to recognize or verify a speaker. It is probable that machine and human do not use the same features to equal effect. The machine, for example, might make use of data the human ear cannot assimilate.

As suggested earlier, the speech-recognition and speaker-identification experiments described here tell us little about the perceptual processing which the human accomplishes. They do not, for example, suggest the temporal span of the recognition unit used by the human. Neither do they indicate subjective techniques for measuring whether the unit is the phoneme, word, sentence, or something larger. The automatic machine methods deal mainly with advantageous processings of essentially the acoustic signal, and not with perception as the human practices it.

The mechanism of human perception of speech is difficult to analyze and present understanding is meager. The discussion of Chapter IV showed that for signals with simple temporal and spectral structure, reasonably close correlations can be made between subjective behavior and the known physiology of the peripheral ear. To a modest extent, similar relations can be established for speech signals. (For example, one can identify features such as voice pitch, formant frequency and voiced-unvoiced excitation in terms of the basilar membrane motion.) But how the neural data are stored and processed after leaving the periphery is a completely open question. Continued research on the electrophysiology of the auditory tract, and on human response to meaningful speech signals, will hopefully provide some of the answers.

VI. Speech Synthesis

Ancient man often took his ability of speech as a symbol of divine origin. Not unnaturally, he sometimes ascribed the same ability to his gods. Pagan priests, eager to fulfill great expectations, frequently tried to make their idols speak directly to the people. Talking statues, miraculous voices and oracles were well known in the Greek and Roman civilizations—the voice usually coming to the artificial mouth via cleverly concealed speaking tubes. Throughout early times the capacity of "artificial speech" to amaze, amuse and influence its listeners was remarkably well appreciated and exploited.

As the civilized world entered the Renaissance scientific curiosity developed and expanded. Man began to inquire more seriously into the nature of things. Human life and physiological functions were fair targets of study, and the physiological mechanism of speech belonged in this sphere. Not surprisingly, the relatively complex vocal mechanism was often considered in terms of more tractable models. These early models were invariably mechanical contrivances, and some were exceedingly clever in design.

6.1. Mechanical Speaking Machines; Historical Efforts

One of the earliest documented efforts at speech synthesis was by KRATZENSTEIN in 1779. The Imperial Academy of St. Petersburg offered its annual prize for explaining the physiological differences between five vowels, and for making apparatus to produce them artificially. As the winning solution, KRATZENSTEIN constructed acoustic resonators similar in shape to the human vocal tract. He activated the resonators with vibrating reeds which, in a manner analogous to the human vocal cords, interrupted an air stream.

A few years later (1791), VON KEMPELEN constructed and demonstrated a more elaborate machine for generating connected utterances. [Apparently VON KEMPELEN's efforts antedate KRATZENSTEIN's, since VON KEMPELEN purportedly began work on his device in 1769 (VON KEMPELEN; DUDLEY and TARNÓCZY).] Although his machine received considerable publicity, it was not taken as seriously as it should have been. VON KEMPELEN had earlier perpetrated a deception in the form of a mechanical chess-playing machine. The main "mechanism" of the machine was a concealed, legless man – an expert chess player.

The speaking machine, however, was a completely legitimate device. It used a bellows to supply air to a reed which, in turn, excited a single, hand-varied resonator for producing voiced sounds. Consonants, including nasals, were simulated by four separate constricted passages, controlled by the fingers of the other hand. An improved version of the machine was built from VON KEMPELEN's description by Sir CHARLES WHEATSTONE (of the Wheatstone Bridge, and who is credited in Britain with the invention of the telegraph). It is shown in Fig. 6.1.

Briefly, the device was operated in the following manner. The right arm rested on the main bellows and expelled air through a vibrating reed to produce voiced sounds. (See the lower diagram in Fig. 6.1.) The fingers of the right hand controlled the air passages for the fricatives /ʃ/ and /s/, as well as the "nostril" openings and the reed on-off control.

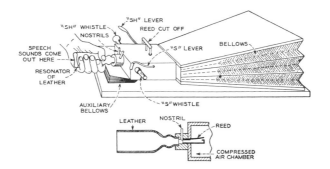

Fig. 6.1. WHEATSTONE'S construction of VON KEMPELEN'S speaking machine

For vowel sounds, all the passages were closed and the reed turned on. Control of vowel resonances was effected with the left hand by suitably deforming the leather resonator at the front of the device. Unvoiced sounds were produced with the reed off, and by a turbulent flow through a suitable passage. In the original work, VON KEMPELEN claimed that approximately 19 consonant sounds could be made passably well.

VON KEMPELEN'S efforts probably had a more far-reaching influence than is generally appreciated. During ALEXANDER GRAHAM BELL'S boyhood in Edinburgh, Scotland (latter 1800's), BELL had an opportunity to see the reproduction of VON KEMPELEN'S machine which had been constructed by WHEATSTONE. He was greatly impressed with the device. With stimulation from his father (ALEXANDER MELVILLE BELL, an elocutionist like his own father), and his brother MELVILLE'S assistance, BELL set out to construct a speaking automaton of his own.

Following their father's advice, the boys attempted to copy the vocal organs by making a cast from a human skull and molding the vocal parts in gutta-percha. The lips, tongue, palate, teeth, pharynx, and velum were represented. The lips were a frame-work of wire, covered with rubber which had been stuffed with cotton batting. Rubber checks enclosed the mouth cavity, and the tongue was simulated by wooden sections—likewise covered by a rubber skin and stuffed with batting. The parts were actuated by levers controlled from a keyboard. A larynx "box" was constructed of tin and had a flexible tube for a windpipe. A vocal cord orifice was made by stretching a slotted rubber sheet over tin supports.

BELL says the device could be made to say vowels and nasals and could be manipulated to produce a few simple utterances (apparently well enough to attract the neighbors). It is tempting to speculate how this boyhood interest may have been decisive in leading to U.S. patent

No. 174,465, dated February 14, 1876—describing the telephone, and which has been perhaps one of the most valuable patents in history.

BELL's youthful interest in speech production also led him to experiment with his pet Skye terrier. He taught the dog to sit up on his hind legs and growl continuously. At the same time, BELL manipulated the dog's vocal tract by hand. The dog's repertoire of sounds finally consisted of the vowels /ɑ/ and /u/, the diphthong /ou/ and the syllables /mɑ/ and /gɑ/. His greatest linguistic accomplishment consisted of the sentence, "How are you Grandmamma?" The dog apparently started taking a "bread and butter" interest in the project and would try to talk by himself. But on his own, he could never do better than the usual growl. This, according to BELL, is the only foundation to the rumor that he once taught a dog to speak.

Interest in mechanical analogs of the vocal system continued to the twentieth century. Among those who developed a penetrating understanding of the nature of human speech was Sir RICHARD PAGET. Besides making accurate plaster tube models of the vocal tract, he was also adept at simulating vocal configurations with his hands. He could literally "talk with his hands" by cupping them and exciting the cavities either with a reed, or with the lips made to vibrate after the fashion of blowing a trumpet.

Around the same time, a different approach to artificial speech was taken by people like HELMHOLTZ, D. C. MILLER, STUMPF, and KOENIG. Their view was more from the point of perception than from production. HELMHOLTZ synthesized vowel sounds by causing a sufficient number of tuning forks to vibrate at selected frequencies and with prescribed amplitudes. MILLER and STUMPF, on the other hand, accomplished the same thing by sounding organ pipes. Still different, KOENIG synthesized vowel spectra from a siren in which air jets were directed at rotating, toothed wheels.

At least one more-recent design for a mechanical talker has been put forward (RIESZ, unpublished, 1937). The arrangement is shown in Fig. 6.2. Air under pressure is brought from a reservoir at the right. Two valves, V_1 and V_2 control the flow. Valve V_1 admits air to a chamber L_1 in which a reed is fixed. The reed vibrates and interrupts the air flow much like the vocal cords. A spring-loaded slider varies the effective length of the reed and changes its fundamental frequency. Unvoiced sounds are produced by admitting air through valve V_2. The configuration of the vocal tract is varied by means of nine movable members representing the lips (1 and 2), teeth (3 and 4), tongue (5, 6, and 7), pharynx (8), and velar coupling (9).

To simplify the control, RIESZ constructed the mechanical talker with finger keys to control the configuration, but with only one control

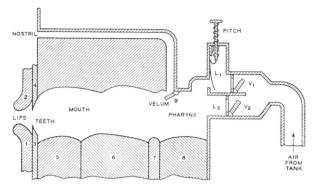

Fig. 6.2. Mechanical vocal tract of RIESZ

each for lips and teeth (i.e., members 1–2 and 3–4 of Fig. 6.2 worked as opposing pairs). The simplified arrangement with control keys is shown in Fig. 6.3. The dark surface regions indicate soft rubber linings to accomplish realistic closures and dampings. Keys 4 and 5 operate excitation valves V_4 and V_5, arranged somewhat differently from V_1 and V_2 in Fig. 6.2. Valve V_4 admits air through a hole forward in the tract (below element 6) for producing unvoiced sounds. Valve V_5 supplies air to the reed chamber for voiced excitation. In this case pitch is controlled by the amount of air passed by valve V_5. When operated by a skilled person, the machine could be made to simulate connected speech. One of its particularly good utterances was reported to be "cigarette"[1].

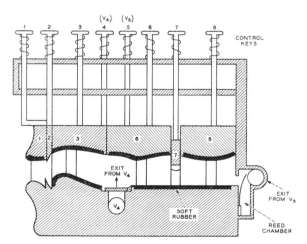

Fig. 6.3. Key control of RIESZ's mechanical talker

---

[1] Personal communication, R. R. RIESZ.

Interest in mechanical analogs continues to the present day. The motivation is mainly that of simulating and measuring nonlinear vocal effects. The latter are generally difficult to analyze computationally and cannot, of course, be represented with linear circuitry. One of the difficult parameters to measure in the real vocal tract is the location, intensity, spectrum, and internal impedance of the sound source for unvoiced sounds. One way of gaining knowledge about this source is with a mechanical analog. The technique for making such measurements is shown in Fig. 6.4a (HEINZ, 1958).

The size of the spherical baffle is taken to represent the human head. A constricted tube in the baffle represents the vocal tract. Air is blown through the constriction to produce turbulence. The sound radiated is measured with a spectrum analyzer. A typical spectrum obtained when the constriction is placed 4 cm from the "mouth", is plotted in Fig. 6.4b. The sound is roughly similar to the fricative /ʃ/. Because the constriction size for fricative consonants tends to be small, the spectral resonances are conditioned primarily by the cavities in front of the constriction. The antiresonances occur at frequencies where the impedance looking into the constriction from the mouth side is infinite. (Recall the discussion of Section 3.75, Chapter III.) The spectrum of the source is

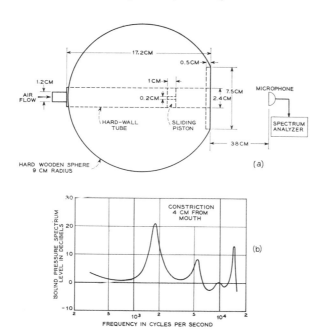

Fig. 6.4a and b. (a) Mechanical model of the vocal tract for simulating fricative consonants. (b) Measured sound spectrum for a continuant sound similar to /ʃ/. (After HEINZ, 1958)

deduced to be relatively flat. Its total power is found to be roughly proportional to the fifth power of the flow velocity.

A number of other mechanical analogs have been used in recent studies of nonlinear flow phenomena in the vocal tract (VAN DEN BERG, ZANTEMA and DOORNENBAL; MEYER-EPPLER, 1953; WEGEL). At least two of these have simulated the air flow in the glottis.

6.2. Electrical Methods for Speech Synthesis

With the evolution of electrical technology, interest in speech synthesis assumed a broader basis. Academic interest in the physiology and acoustics of the signal-producing mechanism was supplemented by the potential for communicating at a distance. Although "facsimile waveform" transmission of speech was the first method to be applied successfully (i.e., in the telephone), many early inventors appreciated the resonance nature of the vocal system and the importance to intelligibility of preserving the short-time amplitude spectrum[1]. Analytical formulation and practical application of this knowledge were longer in coming.

---

[1] Prominent among this group was ALEXANDER GRAHAM BELL. The events—in connection with his experiments on the "harmonic telegraph"—that led BELL, in March of 1876, to apply the facsimile waveform principle are familiar to most students of communication. Less known, perhaps, is BELL's conception of a spectral transmission method remarkably similar to the channel vocoder.

BELL called the idea the "harp telephone". It consisted of an elongated electromagnet with a row of steel reeds in the magnetic circuit. The reeds were to be arranged to vibrate in proximity to the pole of the magnet, and were to be tuned successively to different frequencies. BELL suggested that "—they might be considered analogous to the rods in the harp of Corti in the human ear". Sound uttered near the reeds would cause to vibrate those reeds corresponding to the spectral structure of the sound. Each reed would induce in the magnet an electrical current which would combine with the currents produced by other reeds into a resultant complex wave. The total current passing through a similar instrument at the receiver would, BELL thought, set identical reeds into motion and reproduce the original sound (WATSON).

The device was never constructed. The reason, WATSON says, was the prohibitive expense! Also, because of the lack of means for amplification, BELL thought the currents generated by such a device might be too feeble to be praticable. (BELL found with his harmonic telegraph, however, that a magnetic transducer with a diaphragm attached to the armature could, in fact, produce audible sound from such feeble currents.)

The principle of the "harp telephone" carries the implication that speech intelligibility is retained by preserving the short-time amplitude spectrum. Each reed of the device might be considered a combined electro-acoustic transducer and band-pass filter. Except for the mixing of the "filter" signals in a common conductor, and the absence of rectifying and smoothing means, the spectrum reconstruction principle bears a striking resemblance to that of the channel Vocoder (see Section 8.1).

6.21. Spectrum Reconstruction Techniques

Investigators such as HELMHOLTZ, D. C. MILLER, R. KOENIG and STUMPF had earlier noted that speech-like sounds could be generated by producing an harmonic spectrum with the correct fundamental frequency and relative amplitudes. In other words, the signal could be synthesized with no compelling effort at duplicating the vocal system, but mainly with the objective of producing the desired percept. Among the first to demonstrate the principle electrically was STEWART, who excited two coupled resonant electrical circuits by a current interrupted at a rate analogous to the voice fundamental. By adjusting the circuit tuning, sustained vowels could be simulated. The apparatus was not elaborate enough to produce connected utterances. Somewhat later, WAGNER devised a similar set of four electrical resonators, connected in parallel, and excited by a buzz-like source. The outputs of the four resonators were combined in the proper amplitudes to produce vowel spectra.

Probably the first electrical synthesizer which attempted to produce connected speech was the Voder (DUDLEY, RIESZ and WATKINS). It was basically a spectrum-synthesis device operated from a finger keyboard. It did, however, duplicate one important physiological characteristic of the vocal system, namely, that the excitation can be voiced or unvoiced. A schematic diagram of the device is shown in Fig. 6.5.

The "resonance control" box of the device contains 10 contiguous band-pass filters which span the speech frequency range and are connected in parallel. All the filters receive excitation from either the noise source or the buzz (relaxation) oscillator. The wrist bar selects the excitation source, and a foot pedal controls the pitch of the buzz oscillator. The outputs of the band-pass filters pass through potentiometer gain controls and are added. Ten finger keys operate the potentiometers. Three additional keys provide a transient excitation of selected filters to simulate stop-consonant sounds.

This speaking machine was demonstrated by trained operators at the World's Fairs of 1939 (New York) and 1940 (San Francisco). Although the training required was quite long (on the order of a year or more), the operators were able to "play" the machines—literally as though they were organs or pianos—and to produce intelligible speech[1]. More recently, further research studies based upon the Voder principle have been carried out (OIZUMI and KUBO).

---

[1] H. W. DUDLEY retired from Bell Laboratories in October 1961. On the completion of his more than 40 years in speech research, one of the Voder machines was retrieved from storage and refurbished. In addition, one of the original operators was invited to return and perform for the occasion. Amazingly, after an interlude of twenty years, the lady was able to sit down to the console and make the machine speak.

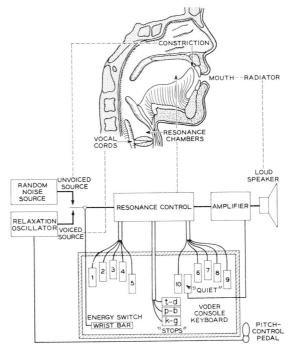

Fig. 6.5. Schematic diagram of the Voder synthesizer. (After DUDLEY, RIESZ and WATKINS)

Speech analysis by the sound spectrograph was described at some length in Chapter V. Since — as HELMHOLTZ and others observed — intelligibility is largely preserved in the short-time amplitude spectrum, speech synthesis from spectrographic plots is immediately suggested. Coupled with this notion is the question of the extent to which spectrograms of real speech might be abstracted or "caricatured" without destroying intelligibility. Several devices for automatically "playing" sound spectrograms have been designed. One uses a line source of light, parallel to the frequency axis of the spectrogram, to illuminate a variable density spectrographic pattern (SCHOTT). Contiguous photocells behind the pattern develop amplitude control signals for a set of band-pass filters (such as in the Voder). Voiced-unvoiced selection and pitch control information are represented in additional tracks. A similar scheme has been used to control a Voder-type synthesizer in an arrangement called Voback (BORST and COOPER).

A somewhat different type of spectrogram playback has been used in extensive studies on speech synthesis (COOPER; COOPER, LIBERMAN, and BORST). The speech wave is effectively simulated by a Fourier series $\sum_n A_n \cos(n\omega_0 t + \Phi_n)$. The coefficients A_n are time varying and are determined by the spectrogram intensity at a given instant. The sound generation is accomplished by the arrangement shown in Fig. 6.6a.

The regular time-frequency-intensity pattern is illuminated by 50 contiguous light spots. The spots are sinusoidally modulated in intensity at harmonically related frequencies. The contiguous spots are produced by illuminating a "tone-wheel" with a line source. The tone wheel has 50 concentric, variable-density bands. The innermost band has four sinusoidal cycles, the next 8, the next 12, and on up to 200 for the 50th band. The tone wheel is rotated at 1800 rpm so the fundamental frequency is 120 cps. Light from the tone wheel can be either reflected from the spectrographic pattern or transmitted by it. The reflected (or transmitted) light is sensed by a collector and photocell which effectively

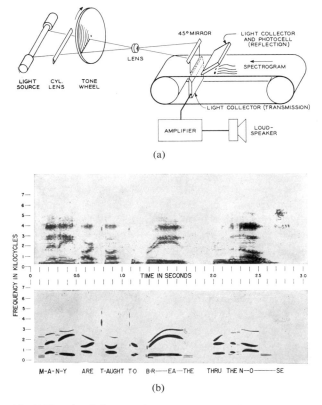

(a)

(b)

Fig. 6.6a and b. (a) Functional diagram of a spectrogram play-back device. (After Cooper.) (b) Spectrograms of real speech and an abstracted, hand-painted version of the same. Both displays can be synthesized on the pattern play-back machine. (After Borst)

sums the fifty terms of the Fourier series. The collected components are amplified and transduced.

Because of the constant rotation of the tone wheel, the pitch is monotone. Also, the phase relations of the harmonic components are fixed by the tone-wheel bands. Unvoiced sounds are simulated from a random time and intensity modulation of the frequency components — similar to the spectrographic representation of a noise burst. Spectrograms of both real speech and its abstracted version can be played on the machine. A sample of each is shown in Fig. 6.6b. In the abstracted spectrogram, in the lower part of the figure, the dark bars represent the speech formants, and the patches of fine, irregular dots produce the noise bursts. Intelligible monotone speech can be produced by the machine, and it has been used in extensive perceptual studies. Some of these results will discussed in Chapter VII.

6.22. "Terminal Analog" Synthesizers

In Chapter III linear circuit theory was applied to the acoustic analysis of the vocal tract. The results show that for simple geometries the transmission properties can be stated in a straightfoward form. Complex geometries, on the other hand, may be approximated by quantizing the vocal tube as short, abutting cylindrical sections. Effects of losses and yielding walls can be included as discussed in Section 3.73.

The tract behavior can be considered either in terms of its over-all transmission, or in terms of its detailed distributed properties. Speech synthesis may be based upon either view. The former approach attempts to duplicate — usually with a unilateral electrical circuit — the transmission properties of the tract as viewed from its input and output terminals. Synthesizers designed in this manner have, for lack of a better term, been named "terminal-analogs" (FLANAGAN, 1957c). The second view attempts to duplicate, on a one-for-one basis, the geometry and distributed properties of the tract. Electrical synthesizers designed according to this approach are bilateral, nonuniform transmission-line models of the system. The present section proposes to discuss the terminal analog approach, while the following section will treat the transmission-line device.

Both approaches to synthesis must take account of sound radiation and the vocal sources of excitation. These factors, common to both modellings of speech production, will be discussed subsequently.

6.221. Terminal Properties of the Vocal Tract.
The unconstricted, glottally-excited tract can be approximated as a straight pipe, closed at the vocal cords ($Z_g = \infty$) and open at the mouth ($Z_r = 0$). For such a case the results of Chapter III show that the ratio of mouth and glottal

volume velocities has a frequency-domain representation

$$\frac{U_m}{U_g} = \frac{1}{\cosh \gamma l},\qquad(6.1)$$

where l is the length of the tube, $\gamma = (\alpha + j\beta) = [(R_a + j\omega L_a)(G_a + j\omega C_a)]^{\frac{1}{2}}$ and R_a, L_a, G_a and C_a are the per-unit-length acoustical parameters of the pipe (see Fig. 3.22 and Eq. (3.61)].

It will be convenient in the subsequent discussion to treat frequency as a complex variable. Let $j\omega \to s = \sigma + j\omega$ and rewrite γ as

$$\gamma(s) = [(R_a + s L_a)(G_a + s C_a)]^{\frac{1}{2}},$$

which for low-loss conditions is

$$\gamma(s) \cong \left(\alpha + \frac{s}{c}\right),$$

where $c = 1/\sqrt{L_a C_a}$ is the sound velocity [see Eq. (3.8)].

Since the vocal tract is a distributed system, its transmission characteristics involve transcendental functions. However, to represent the terminal behavior by lumped-constant electrical networks, it is necessary to describe the vocal transmission in terms of rational, meromorphic functions. Because the transcendental transfer functions for the vocal tract are meromorphic, and because their numerator and denominator components are generally integral functions (i.e., analytic for all finite values of the complex variable), it is possible to approximate the transmission by rational functions.

A relation in function theory (TITCHMARSH) says that if $f(z)$ is an integral function of the complex variable z, and meets certain restrictions, it can be represented by the product series

$$f(z) = f(0) e^{z \frac{f'(0)}{f(0)}} \prod_{m=1}^{\infty} \left(1 - \frac{z}{a_m}\right) e^{z/a_m},\qquad(6.2)$$

where the a_m's are the ordered, simple zeros of $f(z)$.

For the vocal transmission (6.1), the zeros of the denominator (or the poles of the transmission) occur for

$$\gamma(s) = \pm j \frac{(2n-1)\pi}{2l}, \qquad n = 1, 2, \dots[1]$$

---

[1] In Chapter III this result was written

$$\gamma = \pm j \frac{(2n+1)\pi}{2l}, \qquad n = 0, 1, 2, \dots$$

[see Eq. (3.62)]. For the present discussion it will be convenient to write $(2n-1)$ $n = 1, 2, \dots$. This has the mnemonic nicety that n may also represent the formant number.

or,

$$\gamma^2(s) = -\frac{(2n-1)^2 \pi^2}{4l^2} = (R_a + sL_a)(G_a + s\,C_a),$$

or, dropping the subscript a's,

$$s_n = -\left(\frac{R}{2L} + \frac{G}{2C}\right) \pm j\left[\frac{(2n-1)^2 \pi^2}{4l^2 LC} - \left(\frac{R}{2L} - \frac{G}{2C}\right)^2\right]^{\frac{1}{2}}, \qquad n = 1, 2, \dots.$$

$$= -\sigma_n \pm j\,\omega_n. \tag{6.3}$$

For small loss

$$s_n \cong -\alpha c \pm j\,\frac{(2n-1)\pi c}{2l}, \qquad n = 1, 2, \dots. \tag{6.4}$$

which [except for the change to $(2n-1)$, $n=1, 2, \dots$] is the same as Eq. (3.63) in Chapter III. Substituting the result (6.3) in (6.2) gives

$$\cosh z = \prod_{n=1}^{\infty} \left[1 - \frac{z}{\pm j\,\dfrac{(2n-1)\pi}{2}}\right], \tag{6.5}$$

where $z = \gamma(s)l$. [The initial two terms of (6.2) yield unity, and the final term multiplies to unity because the roots of $f(z)$ are conjugate imaginaries.] For small loss $\gamma(s)l \cong (\alpha + s/c)l$ and

$$\frac{1}{\cosh \gamma(s)\,l} = \prod_n \frac{\pm j(2n-1)\pi c/2l}{s + \alpha c \pm j\,\dfrac{(2n-1)\pi c}{2l}}$$

$$= \prod_n \frac{\omega_n^2}{(s - s_n)(s - s_n^*)} \tag{6.6}$$

$$\cong \prod_n \frac{s_n\,s_n^*}{(s - s_n)(s - s_n^*)}$$

which is Eq. (3.64) in Chapter III.

As (6.4) indicates, the poles for the straight pipe are uniformly spaced at $\pi c/l$ intervals along the $j\omega$-axis. In this particular case, a very simple electrical circuit will realize the transmission function, namely the feedback circuit shown in Fig. 6.7. Its transmission is

$$\frac{e_0}{e_i} = H(s) = 1 - a\,e^{-sD} + a^2\,e^{-2sD} - \cdots$$

$$= \frac{1}{1 + a\,e^{-sD}}, \tag{6.7}$$

Fig. 6.7. Feedback circuit for producing a transmission having uniformly spaced complex conjugate poles

where a is a positive-real gain less than unity, and D is a simple delay equal to twice the sound transit time through the pipe. The impulse response therefore simulates the multiple reflections, with some loss, that occur at the ends of the pipe. The poles of $H(s)$ occur at

$$s_n = -\frac{1}{D}\ln\frac{1}{a} \pm j\frac{(2n-1)\pi}{D}, \qquad n=1, 2, \ldots. \tag{6.8}$$

If $D=2l/c$ and $a=e^{-2\alpha l}$, the poles are identical to (6.4).

For a nonuniform pipe, the transmission (6.6) will generally have its poles spaced nonuniformly in frequency. In such a case, one simple way to realize the vocal transmission with electrical circuits is by "building up" the function in terms of the individual pole-pairs. This can be done by cascading individual, isolated electrical resonators, suitably tuned. This approach has the advantage of a one-to-one relation between speech formants and resonator poles, and it provides for non-interacting control of the resonances.

6.221a. Spectral Contribution of Higher-Order Poles. On perceptual grounds it is usually sufficient to simulate only the first several (three to five) modes of the tract. The remaining modes can be accounted for by a single multiplicative term representing their summed influence upon the amplitude (magnitude) spectrum (FANT, 1960). This factor, following the technique of FANT, then becomes simply a frequency-equalizing network. Assuming the higher modes to be approximately those of a straight pipe, the nature of the equalizer can be set down directly.

Write Eq. (6.6) as two product series:

$$P(s) = \prod_{n=1}^{k}\frac{s_n s_n^*}{(s-s_n)(s-s_n^*)} \cdot \prod_{n=k+1}^{\infty}\frac{s_n s_n^*}{(s-s_n)(s-s_n^*)} \tag{6.9}$$

$$= P_k(s) \cdot Q_k(s),$$

where $s_n = (-\sigma_n + j\omega_n)$. For $s=j\omega$,

$$Q_k(j\omega) = \prod_{n=k+1}^{\infty}\frac{\omega_{0n}^2}{(\omega_{0n}^2-\omega^2)+j 2\sigma_n\omega}, \tag{6.10}$$

where $\omega_{0n}^2 = (\sigma_n^2 + \omega_n^2)$.

Taking the magnitude,

$$|Q_k(j\omega)| = \prod_{n=k+1}^{\infty} \frac{\omega_{0n}^2}{[(\omega_{0n}^2 - \omega^2)^2 + (2\sigma_n\omega)^2]^{\frac{1}{2}}} . \qquad (6.11)$$

For low loss $\sigma_n \ll \omega_n$, and

$$|Q_k(j\omega)| \cong \prod_{n=k+1}^{\infty} \frac{1}{\left(1 - \dfrac{\omega^2}{\omega_n^2}\right)} . \qquad (6.12)$$

Taking the logarithm of both sides gives

$$\ln|Q_k(j\omega)| = -\sum_{n=k+1}^{\infty} \ln\left(1 - \frac{\omega^2}{\omega_n^2}\right) .$$

Expanding the logarithm as a series and taking only the first term (to approximate the behavior at frequencies $\omega < \omega_n$) yields

$$\ln|Q_k(j\omega)| \cong \omega^2 \sum_{n=k+1}^{\infty} \frac{1}{\omega_n^2} ,$$

where

$$\omega_n = (2n-1)\omega_1 = \frac{(2n-1)\pi c}{2l} , \qquad n = 1, 2, \ldots$$

(that is, the modes for the straight pipe of length l). Alternatively, the logarithm may be written

$$\ln|Q_k| \cong \left(\frac{\omega}{\omega_1}\right)^2 \sum_{n=k+1}^{\infty} \frac{1}{(2n-1)^2} . \qquad (6.13)$$

But

$$\sum_{1}^{\infty} \frac{1}{(2n-1)^2} = \frac{\pi^2}{8} ,$$

and the sum in (6.13) may be written

$$\sum_{1}^{\infty} \frac{1}{(2n-1)^2} = \frac{\pi^2}{8} - \sum_{1}^{k} \frac{1}{(2n-1)^2} . \qquad (6.14)$$

Therefore,

$$\ln|Q_k| \cong \left(\frac{\omega}{\omega_1}\right)^2 \left[\frac{\pi^2}{8} - \sum_{1}^{k} \frac{1}{(2n-1)^2}\right] = \left(\frac{\omega}{\omega_1}\right)^2 [R(k)]$$

or,

$$|Q_k| \cong e^{(\omega/\omega_1)^2 R(k)} , \qquad (6.15)$$

where $R(k)$ is a positive-real function of k, the highest pole accounted for on an individual basis.

6.221b. Non-Glottal Excitation of the Tract. The discussion of Chapter III showed that if the vocal excitation occurs at some point other than at the end of the tract, the transmission function will exhibit zeros as well as poles. This can be simply illustrated for front excitation of a straight pipe by a pressure source, as shown in Fig. 6.8. The ratio of

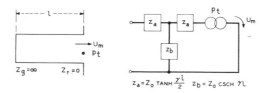

Fig. 6.8. Front excitation of a straight pipe by a pressure source

mouth current to the source pressure is simply the driving point impedance of the mouth, or

$$\frac{U_m(s)}{p_t(s)} = \frac{1}{Z_0} \tanh \gamma(s)\, l$$

$$= \frac{1}{\cosh \gamma(s)\, l} \cdot \frac{\sinh \gamma(s)\, l}{Z_0} \tag{6.16}$$

$$= P(s) \cdot Z(s).$$

Since $P(s)$ has no zeros, the zeros of the transmission are the zeros of $Z(s)$ and occur for

$$(e^{2\gamma l} - 1) = 0$$

$$\gamma = \pm j \frac{m\pi}{l}, \qquad m = 0, 1, 2, \dots \tag{6.17}$$

$$\gamma^2 = \frac{-m^2 \pi^2}{l^2} = [(R + sL)(G + sC)].$$

The zeros therefore lie at

$$s_m = -\left(\frac{R}{2L} + \frac{G}{2C}\right) \pm j \left[\frac{m^2 \pi^2}{l^2 LC} - \left(\frac{R}{2L} - \frac{G}{2C}\right)^2\right]^{\frac{1}{2}},$$

or, again for small losses,

$$s_m \cong \left(-\alpha c \pm j \frac{m\pi c}{l}\right) \qquad m = 0, 1, 2, \dots \tag{6.18}$$

The poles of the transmission are the same as given in Eq. (6.4), and the poles and zeros in this instance alternate in the $j\omega$-direction.

Applying the product series formula in Eq. (6.2) gives

$$\sinh z = z \prod_{m=1}^{\infty} \left(1 - \frac{z}{\pm jm\pi}\right),$$

where

$$z = \gamma l \cong \left(\alpha l + s\frac{l}{c}\right). \tag{6.19}$$

Then

$$\sinh \gamma l = \left(\alpha l + s\frac{l}{c}\right) \prod_{m=1}^{\infty} \left(1 - \frac{\alpha l + s\dfrac{l}{c}}{\pm jm\pi}\right)$$

$$= \frac{l}{c}(\alpha c + s) \prod_{m=1}^{\infty} \left(\frac{s + \alpha c \pm jm\pi c}{\pm j\dfrac{m\pi c}{l}}\right) \tag{6.20}$$

$$\cong \frac{l}{c}(s + s_0) \prod_{m=1}^{\infty} \frac{(s - s_m)(s - s_m^*)}{s_m s_m^*},$$

where $s_0 = -\alpha c$.

6.221c. Spectral Contribution of Higher-Order Zeros. The series for the zero terms can be "truncated" as described previously for pole terms, and a spectral correction factor can be obtained for higher-order zeros. Following the technique of Eq. (6.9),

$$Z(s) \cong \frac{l}{cZ_0}(s + s_0) \prod_{m=1}^{k} \frac{(s - s_m)(s - s_m^*)}{s_m s_m^*} \cdot |Y_k(s)|,$$

where

$$\ln |Y_k(j\omega)| \cong -\sum_{m=k+1}^{\infty} \frac{\omega^2}{\omega_m^2}$$

$$\cong -\frac{\omega^2}{\omega_1^2} \sum_{m=k+1}^{\infty} \frac{1}{m^2}, \tag{6.21}$$

and where $\omega_1 = \pi c/l$.

The summation may be rewritten as

$$\ln |Y_k(j\omega)| \cong -\frac{\omega^2}{\omega_1^2}\left[\frac{\pi^2}{6} - \sum_{m=1}^{k} \frac{1}{m^2}\right],$$

or

$$|Y_k(j\omega)| \cong e^{-(\omega^2/\omega_1^2) T(k)}, \tag{6.22}$$

where $T(k)$ is a positive-real function of the zero number k. Except for the sign of the exponent, this is the same form as (6.15). The factor $|Y_k(j\omega)|$ can therefore be realized by a frequency-equalizing network in conjunction with the variable poles and zeros of a formant synthesizer.

This simple example of front excitation illustrates that the vocal transmission, in general, involves poles $[P(s)]$ as well as zeros $[Z(s)]$. In the example, the zeros (like the poles) are uniformly distributed in frequency. For the nonuniform vocal tract, the mode frequencies will generally be irregularly distributed. Besides being dependent upon source location, zeros of transmission can also arise from side-branch paths coupled to the main transmission path. Cases in point are nasal consonants, nasalized vowels and perhaps liquids such as /l/[1]. In all cases where the sound radiation is from a single port (i.e., either mouth or nostril), the vocal transmission is minimum phase. For simultaneous radiation from mouth and nostril (as in a nasalized vowel) the transmissions to individual ports are minimum phase, but the combined response at a fixed point in front of the speaker may be nonminimum phase.

6.221 d. Effects of a Side-Branch Resonator. The effect of a nasal or oral side branch can be simply illustrated by the circuit of Fig. 6.9a. For very low frequencies the circuit may be treated in terms of lumped-constant approximations to the major cavities and constrictions, as illustrated in Fig. 6.9b. The poles occur at frequencies where the sum of the admittances at any network node is zero. The velar junction is a convenient point to consider. Neglecting losses, the respective admit-

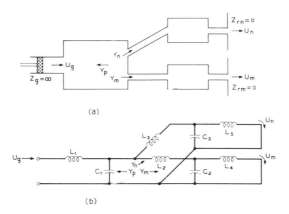

Fig. 6.9 a and b. Simplified configuration illustrating coupling between oral and nasal cavities

---

[1] The cul-de-sac formed by the tongue can act as a side-branch resonator.

tances for the low-frequency approximation are

$$Y_n = \frac{s^2 + \dfrac{1}{L_5 C_3}}{s L_3 \left[s^2 + \dfrac{1}{C_3}\left(\dfrac{1}{L_3} + \dfrac{1}{L_5}\right)\right]}$$

$$Y_m = \frac{s^2 + \dfrac{1}{L_4 C_2}}{s L_2 \left[s^2 + \dfrac{1}{C_2}\left(\dfrac{1}{L_2} + \dfrac{1}{L_4}\right)\right]} \qquad (6.23)$$

$$Y_p = s C_1,$$

or for real frequencies $s \to j\omega$,

$$Y_n = \frac{\omega_{n0}^2 - \omega^2}{j\omega L_3(\omega_{np}^2 - \omega^2)}$$

$$Y_m = \frac{\omega_{m0}^2 - \omega^2}{j\omega L_2(\omega_{mp}^2 - \omega^2)} \qquad (6.24)$$

$$Y_p = j\omega C_1,$$

where ω_{n0} and ω_{m0} are the zeros of the nasal and mouth admittances respectively, and ω_{np} and ω_{mp} are the poles of the nasal and mouth admittances.

The poles of the system occur at frequencies for which

$$\Sigma Y = Y_n + Y_m + Y_p = 0$$

or

$$\omega^2 C_1 = \frac{\omega_{n0}^2 - \omega^2}{L_3(\omega_{np}^2 - \omega^2)} + \frac{\omega_{m0}^2 - \omega^2}{L_2(\omega_{mp}^2 - \omega^2)}. \qquad (6.25)$$

The low-frequency zero of U_n/U_g is ω_{mp}, and the zero of U_m/U_g is ω_{np}.

It is instructive to consider the loci of the low frequency modes for a highly simplified situation. Suppose the pharyngeal, oral and nasal cavities (C_1, C_2, C_3) are held fixed in size, and the mouth and velar constrictions (L_2, L_3, L_4) are varied. Suppose the velar areas are such that $(A_n + A_m) = A_0 = $ constant, so that L_2 and L_3 are inversely related. Assume that all tube lengths are held fixed so that area variations alone constitute the lumped element variation. Consider the low frequency mode behavior corresponding to the sequence: vowel → nasalized vowel → nasal, as in /am/. The simplified articulatory sequence is: vowel, with the nasal tract decoupled and sealed off and the mouth open; nasalized vowel, with the velum partially open and the mouth still open; and nasal, with the velum full open and the mouth closed.

For the vowel, the nasal coupling is nil and $L_3 \cong \infty$. The frequencies ω_{n0} and ω_{np} are equal (i.e., the pole and zero are coincident) and $Y_n = 0$. The poles of the glottis-to-mouth transmission occur at frequencies where $Y_m = Y_p$. As the vowel is nasalized, the velum opens, L_3 diminishes and L_2 increases. ω_{n0} remains fixed, but ω_{np} parts from ω_{n0} and moves up in frequency. ω_{np} becomes the zero of glottis-to-mouth transmission. In a similar manner ω_{m0} remains fixed, but ω_{mp} moves down. The exact trajectories of the system modes depend upon the relative sizes of the nasal and oral cavities, but, in general, the original vowel poles move up in frequency. A new pole is introduced in the region above ω_{n0} by the parting of ω_{n0} and ω_{np}.

As the mouth closes to produce the nasal, L_4 becomes infinite and all sound radiation transfers to the nostril. The closed oral cavity now acts as a side branch resonator for the glottis-to-nostril transmission. ω_{m0} now goes to zero, and ω_{mp} becomes lower. ω_{mp} is the zero of glottis-to-nostril transmission. The first system pole is relatively low in frequency, and the second resides in the vicinity of ω_{mp}. The third is generally somewhat higher than ω_{np}. A more detailed computation, using an idealized vocal configuration, has been given previously in Fig. 3.37. Representative frequency positions for a nasal such as /m/ are approximately 250, 1 100, 1 350 and 2 000 cps for the first four poles and 1 300 cps for the zero. More extensive analyses of nasals can be found in the literature (FUJIMURA, 1962a).

So long as the radiation is from a single port, the dc transmission to that port is essentially unity. For simultaneous radiation from mouth and nostril, the sound energy divides according to the oral and nasal admittances, and the dc transmission to a single port is determined by the respective branch losses.

6.222. Cascade Type Synthesizers. The intent of these elementary considerations is to indicate that for all configurations and excitations, the vocal transmission $T(s)$ may be approximated in terms of its first few (low-frequency) poles and zeros, that is, the first several roots of $P(s)$ and $Z(s)$. A straightforward means for simulating the vocal transmission electrically is to build up the product functions in terms of the individual poles and zeros by cascading individual electrical resonators. As the preceding discussion showed, the transmission function for a vowel sound can be written

$$T(s) = P(s) = \prod_n \frac{s_n s_n^*}{(s - s_n)(s - s_n^*)} .$$

Such a function can be represented in terms of its individual poles by the isolated, cascaded, series RLC resonators shown in Fig. 6.10a. Here the

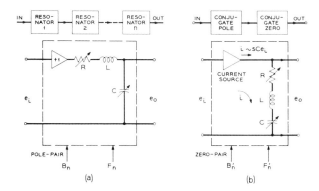

Fig. 6.10a and b. (a) Cascade connection of isolated RLC resonators for simulation of vocal transmission for vowel sounds. Each pole-pair or vocal resonance is simulated by a series circuit. (b) Cascaded pole and zero circuit for simulating low frequency behavior of a side branch resonator. The zero pair is approximated by the transmission of a simple series circuit

transmission of a single resonant circuit is

$$\frac{e_0(s)}{e_i(s)} = \frac{\dfrac{1}{LC}}{s^2 + \dfrac{R}{L}s + \dfrac{1}{LC}} = \frac{s_n s_n^*}{(s - s_n)(s - s_n^*)},$$

where

$$\omega_n = \sqrt{\frac{1}{LC} - \frac{R^2}{4L^2}},$$

$$\sigma_n = \frac{R}{2L}, \tag{6.26}$$

and

$$s_n = -\sigma_n + j\omega_n.$$

Control of the formant tuning is effected by changes in the tuning capacitor C. Control of formant bandwidth is accomplished by variation of R. For the serial connection of resonators, specification of the pole frequencies s_n implies specification of the spectral peaks, or formant amplitudes, as well. This point has been treated in some detail in the literature (FANT, 1956; FLANAGAN, 1957c).

The results of Chapter III and the preceding discussion (Fig. 6.9) suggest that sounds such as unvoiced consonants, nasals, nasalized vowels, and perhaps liquids, may have at least one low-frequency zero which might be perceptually significant[1]. In particular, a pole-zero pair additional to the usual vowel formants is commonly associated with nasals and nasalized vowels. The transmission of the vowel resonator string of Fig. 6.10a can be simply modified to accomodate this condition. A resonance and an antiresonance—as shown in the upper part of Fig. 6.10b—can be included in the synthesizer circuit (FLANAGAN, COKER and BIRD). So long as a pure vowel is to be produced, the added pole and zero are made coincident in frequency, and their transmission is unity. For nasal production they are pulled apart and set to appropriate values corresponding to the relations for the side branch resonator.

Practically, the complex conjugate zero can be approximated by the electrical circuit shown in the lower part of Fig. 6.10b. Its transmission is

$$\frac{e_0(s)}{e_i(s)} = LC\left(s^2 + s\frac{R}{L} + \frac{1}{LC}\right), \tag{6.27}$$

which is the reciprocal of the conjugate pole. As in the pole-pair resonator, the low frequency (dc) gain is made unity—which is proper so long as radiation occurs from a single port, and is approximately correct for the mouth radiation of nasalized vowels.

The front-excited voiceless sounds can also be approximated in terms of their poles and zeros. Following the results of the previous discussion and of Chapter III, a reasonable approximation is given by

$$T(s) = P(s) \cdot Z(s) = K \cdot s \cdot \frac{\prod\limits_m (s - s_m)(s - s_m^*)}{\prod\limits_n (s - s_n)(s - s_n^*)}, \tag{6.28}$$

where an m and n of order 1 or 2 often suffice perceptually (in addition to higher-order pole and zero corrections). The zero at zero frequency arises because of the essentially closed back cavity (see Fig. 3.31). The amplitude scale factor K is accounted for by an over-all amplification.

6.223. Parallel Synthesizers. The vocal tract transmission has been represented as a ratio of product series which, when truncated, produce rational meromorphic functions. Because the poles are simple, the transmission can be expanded as a partial fraction with first-degree terms

$$T(s) = P(s)Z(s) = \sum_n \frac{A_n}{(s - s_n)} + \frac{A_n^*}{(s - s_n^*)}, \qquad n = 1, 2, \dots$$
$$= \sum_n \frac{2a_n s + 2(\sigma_n a_n + \omega_n b_n)}{s^2 + s\sigma_n s + (\sigma_n^2 + \omega_n^2)}, \tag{6.29}$$

---

[1] The perceptual effects of spectral zeros—both of the excitation and of the system—have not been throughly established. The extent to which the quality of synthetic speech depends upon these factors is a current problem in research. It will be discussed further in a later section.

where $s_n = (-\sigma_n + j\omega_n)$, and $A_n = (s - s_n)T(s)|_{s \to s_n} = (a_n + jb_n)$ is the residue in the n-th pole and is a function of all the poles and zeros. The inverse transform is

$$h(t) = \sum_n 2|A_n| e^{-\sigma_n t} \cos(\omega_n t + \varphi_n),$$

where

$$A_n = |A_n| e^{j\varphi_n}.$$

Expanding the cosine term, $h(t)$ may be rewritten

$$h(t) = \sum_n 2|A_n| e^{-\sigma_n t} [\cos \varphi_n \cos \omega_n t - \sin \varphi_n \sin \omega_n t]. \tag{6.30}$$

Each term of the latter expression can be realized by the operations shown in Fig. 6.11, where the filters represented by the boxes are simple resonant circuits.

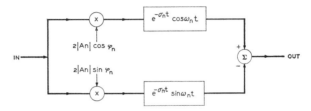

Fig. 6.11. Circuit operations for simulating the time-domain response of Eq. (6.30)

If the transmission function is for pure vowels, $Z(s) \to 1$ and $T(s) \to P(s)$ and the transmission has only poles. Its numerator is not a function of s, but only of the s_n, that is, $\prod_n s_n s_n^* = f(s_n)$. The residue in the q-th pole is then

$$A_q = \frac{f(s_n)}{2j\omega_q \prod_{n \neq q} [(\sigma_n - \sigma_q)^2 + (\omega_n^2 - \omega_q^2) + 2j\omega_q(\sigma_q - \sigma_n)]}. \tag{6.31}$$

If the σ's are essentially equal (a reasonable approximation for the lower modes of the vocal tract), then

$$A_q \cong \frac{f(s_n)}{2j\omega_q \prod_{n \neq q} (\omega_n^2 - \omega_q^2)},$$

or

$$A_q \cong \frac{f(s_n)}{2j\omega_q(-1)^{q-1}} \frac{1}{\prod_{n \neq q} |\omega_n^2 - \omega_q^2|}. \tag{6.32}$$

The residues are therefore pure imaginary (i.e., $\cos \varphi_n = 0$) and their signs alternate with pole number. The inverse transform (impulse response) for this transmission is

$$h(t) = \sum_n (-1)^{n-1} 2 |A_n| e^{-\sigma_n t} \sin \omega_n t, \tag{6.33}$$

where each term can by synthesized by the electrical operations in Fig. 6.12. This circuit is essentially the lower branch of the previous circuit where now $-\sin \varphi_n = -\sin[(-1)^n(\pi/2)] = (-1)^{n-1}$, and the RCL resonator has an impulse response $(\omega_n e^{-\sigma_n t} \sin \omega_n t)$. Summation of the outputs of similar circuits, one for each n, produces the response (6.33).

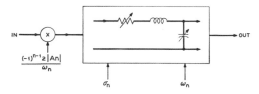

Fig. 6.12. Circuit for simulating the vowel function impulse response [see Eq. (6.33)]

The magnitude of the residue bears a simple approximate relation to the spectral magnitude at the formant frequency. Recall the residue magnitude is

$$|A_n| = |(s - s_n) T(s)|_{s \to s_n},$$

which for small damping $(\sigma \ll \omega_n)$ is approximately

$$|(s - s_n) T(s)|_{s \to j\omega_n} = |(j\omega_n - s_n) T(j\omega_n)| \approx |A_n|,$$

or,

$$\sigma_n |T(j\omega_n)| \approx |A_n|. \tag{6.34}$$

If the transmission function exhibits zeros, as exemplified by Eq. (6.28), the residues are then

$$A_q' = (s - s_q) T(s)|_{s \to s_q} = Z(s) \cdot (s - s_q) P(s)|_{s \to s_q}$$

$$= Z(s_q) \cdot A_q = K s_q [\prod_m (s_q - s_m)(s_q - s_m^*)] A_q \tag{6.35}$$

$$= A_q K s_q \cdot \prod_m [(\sigma_q - \sigma_m)^2 + (\omega_m^2 - \omega_q^2) + j 2 \omega_q (\sigma_q - \sigma_m)].$$

Again, if the σ's are nearly the same,

$$A_q' = A_q K s_q \cdot \prod_m (\omega_m^2 - \omega_q^2), \tag{6.36}$$

and the sign of A'_q is determined by the relative magnitudes ω_m and ω_q. Or,

$$A'_q = A_q(-1)^p K s_q \prod_m |\omega_m^2 - \omega_q^2|,\qquad(6.37)$$

where p is the number of zeros lying below the pole ω_p. Or, substituting for A_q from Eq. (6.32),

$$A'_q = \frac{f(s_n)(-1)^p K s_q \prod_m |\omega_m^2 - \omega_q^2|}{2j\,\omega_q(-1)^{q-1} \prod_{n \neq q} |\omega_n^2 - \omega_q^2|},\qquad(6.38)$$

and the net sign of the residue is determined by the difference between the numbers of poles and zeros lying below the q-th pole.

Again the residue bears a simple approximate relation to the real-frequency spectrum evaluated at the pole frequency. That is,

$$A_n = (s - s_n)\,T(s)|_{s \to s_n},$$

but for low damping $s_n \to j\omega_n$.

$$A_n \cong (j\,\omega_n - s_n)\,T(j\,\omega_n)$$

$$A_n \cong \sigma_n\,T(j\,\omega_n) = \sigma_n|T(j\,\omega_n)|\underline{/T(j\,\omega_n)}\qquad(6.39)$$

$$A_n = |A_n|\,e^{j\,\varphi_n}.$$

A number of terminal-analog synthesizers, both of the parallel and cascade types, have been constructed and operated. (See for example, FANT, 1959a; STEVENS, BASTIDE and SMITH; LAWRENCE, 1953; STEAD and JONES; CAMPANELLA; CHANG; FLANAGAN, 1956a, 1960b.) Most of the devices utilize one or more of the relations discussed—either by overt recognition of the principles or by qualitative implication. The transmission relations commonly exploited involve the formant frequency and the magnitude of the residue, or the formant frequency and amplitude.

At least one study has considered use of the complex residue, that is, the angle or sign of the residue. In this case, analysis of the short-time phase spectrum of speech[1]—in conjunction with the short-time amplitude spectrum—is used to gain naturalness. Specification of the complex residues, as implied by Eq. (6.29), is equivalent to specification of spectral zeros. A parallel formant synthesizer, implemented as described by Eq. (6.30) and using pitch-synchronous spectral analysis to obtain formant frequency and *complex* residue, produced speech of improved quality (FLANAGAN, 1965).

---

[1] See Eq. (5.4), Chapter 5, for a definition of the short-time phase spectrum.

6.23. Transmission-Line Analogs of the Vocal System

A different method for simulating the vocal transmission is the non-uniform electrical transmission line. The discussion in Chapter III indicated how the nonuniform acoustic tubes of the vocal and nasal tracts can be represented by abutting right-circular cylinders (see Fig. 3.35). The approximation to the nonuniform tract is better the more numerous the cylindrical elements.

Each cylindrical section of length l can be represented by its T-equivalent as shown in Fig. 6.13a, where $z_a = Z_0 \tanh \gamma l/2$ and $z_b = Z_0 \operatorname{csch} \gamma l$.

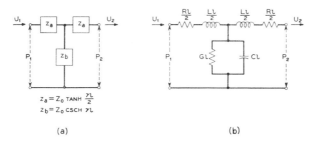

$$z_a = Z_0 \text{ TANH } \frac{\gamma L}{2}$$
$$z_b = Z_0 \text{ CSCH } \gamma L$$

(a)   (b)

Fig. 6.13a and b. T-circuit equivalents for a length l of uniform cylindrical pipe. (a) Exact circuit, (b) first-term approximations to the impedance elements

A practical electrical realization of the individual T-section is obtained by taking the first terms in the series expansions of the hyperbolic quantities. For a hard-walled tube this gives $z_a \cong \frac{1}{2}(R+j\omega L)\,l$ and $z_b^c \cong 1/(G+j\omega C)\,l$ where the R, L, G and C are the per-unit-length acoustic parameters of the tube, as previously discussed. The resulting network is Fig. 6.13b[1].

For practical realization, the characteristic impedance of the analogous electrical line may be scaled from the acoustic value by a convenient constant, i.e., $Z_{0e} = k Z_{0a}$, where the superscripts e and a distinguish electrical and acoustical quantities. For low-loss conditions, $Z_{0a} \cong \sqrt{L_a/C_a} = \rho c/A$. Since $L_a = \rho/A$ and $C_a = A/\rho c^2$, a given simulated cross-sectional area is equal $\rho c \sqrt{C_a/L_a}$. The losses R and G require knowledge of the circumference as well as the cross-sectional area of the tract [see Eq. (3.33)]. They can also be introduced into the electrical circuit and their impedances scaled after the fashion just indicated. Given the shape factor, all analogous electrical elements can be determined from the A and l data-pairs, or from area data for a given number of fixed-length cylindrical sections.

---

[1] Section 3.73 derives a technique for including the effects of a yielding wall.

   A vocal tract representation in terms of equivalent electrical sections
forms the ladder networks of Fig. 6.14. The upper circuit is for glottal
excitation of the tract by a volume-velocity source U_g and with internal
impedance Z_g. The lower circuit is for forward fricative excitation by a
pressure source P_t with internal impedance Z_t. Both circuits can be
solved — at least in principle — by straightforward matrix methods. If
voltage (pressure) equations are written for each circuit loop, beginning
at the glottis and ending at the mouth and nose, the number of independent equations is equal the number of loops. The transmissions from

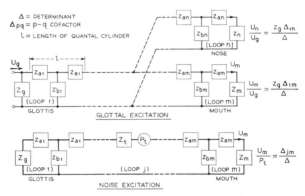

Fig. 6.14. Ladder network approximations to the vocal tract. The impedance elements of
the network are those shown in Fig. 6.13 b

glottis to mouth, from glottis to nostril, and from front noise source to
mouth are, respectively,

$$\frac{U_m}{U_g} = \frac{Z_g \, \Delta_{1m}}{\Delta}$$

$$\frac{U_n}{U_g} = Z_g \frac{\Delta_{1n}}{\Delta} \tag{6.40}$$

$$\frac{U_m}{P_t} = \frac{\Delta_{jm}}{\Delta},$$

where Δ is the impedance determinant (characteristic equation) for the
network having impedance members z_{11}, z_{12}, etc., where z_{11} is the
self-impedance of loop 1, z_{12} is the mutual impedance between loops 1
and 2, etc., and Δ_{xy} is the cofactor of the x-th row and y-th column of
the determinant Δ. As mentioned earlier, all the transmissions of
Eq. (6.40) are minimum phase functions[1].

_____

   [1] The functions are the responses of passive ladder networks. They can have
zeros of transmission only for zeros of a shunt element or for poles of a series element.
All these poles and zeros must lie in the left half of the complex-frequency plane.

Several electrical transmission-line synthesizers have been constructed. The first such device consisted of 25 uniform T-sections (DUNN, 1950). Each section represented a tract length of 0.5 cm and a nominal area of 6 cm². A variable inductance could be inserted between any two sections to simulate the tongue construction. Another variable inductance at the mouth end of the line represented the lip constriction. Radiation from the mouth was simulated by taking the output voltage across a small series inductance. For voiced sounds, the synthesizer was excited by a high-impedance sawtooth oscillator whose fundamental frequency could be controlled. The source spectrum was adjusted to fall at about -12 db/octave (recall Fig. 3.17). To simulate unvoiced and whispered sounds, a white noise source was applied at an appropriate point along the line.

At least two other passive line analogs, similar to DUNN's device, have been constructed (STEVENS, KASOWSKI and FANT; FANT, 1960). These synthesizers incorporate network sections which can be varied independently to simulate the tract geometry in detail. At least one effort has been made to develop a continuously-controllable transmission-line analog. Continuous variation of the network elements by electronic means permits the device to synthesize connected speech (ROSEN; HECKER). This device utilizes saturable-core inductors and electronically-variable capacitors as the line elements. A nasal tract is also provided. The number of network sections and their control points are shown in Fig. 6.15. Control of the synthesizer can be effected either from an electronic data-storage circuit (ROSEN) of from a digital computer (DENNIS).

The transmission-line synthesizer has outstanding potential for directly incorporating the constraints that characterize the vocal mechanism. Success in this direction, however, depends directly upon deriving a realistic model for the area and for the dynamic motions of the vocal tract. Research on one such model has been described in Section 5.4. Also, the usefulness of a transmission-line synthesizer in a

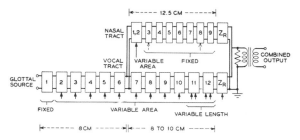

Fig. 6.15. Continuously controllable transmission line analog of the vocal system.
(After ROSEN; HECKER)

complete analysis-synthesis system depends upon how accurately vocal tract area data, or its equivalent, can be derived automatically from connected speech. Some progress has been made toward analyzing speech signals in articulatory terms from which area and length numbers can be derived (see Section 5.4, Chapter 5).

Besides obvious application in a bandwidth compression system, the transmission-line synthesizer, along with other synthesis devices, has potential use as a computer output device for man-machine communication; as a stimulus generator for psychoacoustic and bioacoustic experimentation; or, as a standard sound generator for speech pathology, therapy or linguistics studies. The possibility of specifying the control functions in articulatory terms makes applications such as the latter particularly attractive.

All transmission-line synthesizers of early design have been implemented as analog network devices. Digital techniques, on the other hand, offer many advantages in stability and accuracy. One of the first digital transmission-line synthesizers was programmed on a computer in terms of the reflection coefficients at the junctions of cylindrical tube-elements (KELLY and LOCHBAUM).

Another computer implementation has duplicated the bilateral properties of the transmission line by a difference-equation equivalent. Because absolute impedance relations are preserved in this formulation, it has been useful in studying the acoustic interaction between the vocal tract and the vocal cords. The same formulation has also been used as a complete synthesizer for voiced and unvoiced sounds (FLANAGAN and LANDGRAF; FLANAGAN and CHERRY).

Further discussion of digital representation of transmission-line synthesizers is given in Section. 6.26.

6.24. Excitation of Electrical Synthesizers

The preceding sections have discussed simulation of the vocal transmission both from the transfer-function point of view and from the transmission-line approach. Having implemented one or the other for electrical synthesis of speech, the system must be excited from signal sources analogous to those of the vocal tract. This section considers vocal source characteristics that appear relevant in synthesis.

6.241. Simulation of the Glottal Wave. The results of Chapter III suggested that the vocal cord source is approximately a high-impedance, constant volume-velocity generator. Hence, to a first-order approximation, the vocal tract and glottal source can be assumed not to interact greatly. To the extent that this is true (and we shall subsequently discuss this matter further), the source and system can be analyzed independently, and their characteristics can be simulated individually.

The shape and periodicity of the vocal cord wave can vary considerably. This is partially illustrated by the single periods of glottal area and volume-velocity waves shown in Fig. 6.16. The extent to which variability in period and shape affect speech naturalness and quality is an important research question. In many existing electrical synthesizers, the properties of the vocal cord source are approximated only in a gross form. It is customary to specify the vocal pitch as a smooth, continuous time function and to use a fixed glottal wave shape whose amplitude spectrum falls at about -12 db/octave. In many synthesizers the source is produced by repeated impulse excitation of a fixed, spectral-shaping network. Such lack of fidelity in duplicating actual glottal characteristics

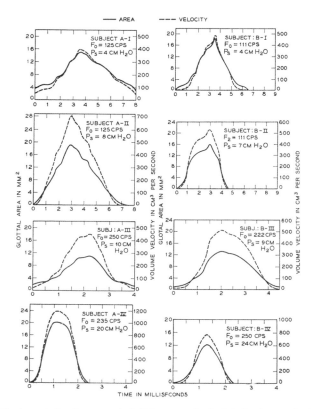

Fig. 6.16. Single periods of measured glottal area and calculated volume velocity functions for two men (A and B) phonating the vowel /æ/ under four different conditions of pitch and intensity. F_0 is the fundamental frequency and P_s the subglottal pressure. The velocity wave is computed according to the technique described in Section 3.52.
(After FLANAGAN, 1958)

undoubtedly detracts from speech naturalness and the ability to simulate a given voice.

6.241 a. Spectral Properties of Triangular Waves. Under some conditions of voicing (commonly, mid-range pitch and intensity), the glottal wave is roughly triangular in shape. The spectral properties of triangular waves therefore appear to have relevance to voiced excitation. They have been studied in some detail with a view toward better understanding the relations between waveform and spectrum in real glottal waves (DUNN, FLANAGAN and GESTRIN)[1].

Fig. 6.17 shows a triangular approximation to the glottal wave. The opening time is τ_1, the closing time $\tau_2 = k\tau_1$, and the total open time

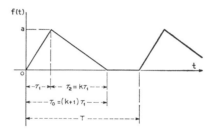

Fig. 6.17. Triangular approximation to the glottal wave. The asymmetry factor is k

$\tau_0 = (1+k)\tau_1$. The amplitude of the wave is a and its period T. Its Laplace transform is

$$F(s) = \frac{a}{s^2}\left[\frac{1}{\tau_1} - \left(\frac{1}{\tau_1} + \frac{1}{\tau_2}\right)e^{-s\tau_1} + \frac{1}{\tau_2}e^{-s(\tau_1+\tau_2)}\right]. \qquad (6.41)$$

The spectral zeros are the complex values of s which make $F(s) = 0$. Except for the $s = 0$ root, the zeros are the roots of the bracketed expression, or the roots of

$$[e^{-(k+1)s\tau_1} - (k+1)e^{-s\tau_1} + k] = 0. \qquad (6.42)$$

Because the equation is transcendental it can be solved exactly only for special values of the asymmetry constant, k. In particular, solutions are straightforward for values of k which can be expressed as the ratio of small whole numbers. In less simple cases, the roots can be obtained by numerical solution.

---

[1] It should be emphasized again that the implication here is not that the glottal pulse is a neat triangular wave, but only that this analytical simplification permits tractable and informative calculations. These data are included because they are not avaliable elsewhere.

Let
$$x = e^{-s\tau_1} = e^{-(\sigma + j\omega)\tau_1} = e^{-\sigma\tau_1}(\cos\omega\tau_1 - j\sin\omega\tau_1). \tag{6.43}$$

The (6.42) becomes
$$x^{(k+1)} - (k+1)x + k = 0. \tag{6.44}$$

When k is an integer, (6.44) will yield $(k+1)$ values of x. These can then be put into (6.43), and both $\sigma\tau_1$ and $\omega\tau_1$ found by equating real and imaginary parts in separate equations.

For integers up to $k=5$, (6.44) can be solved by straightforward algebraic methods. In the case $k=5$, (6.44) is a sixth degree equation in x, but a double root exists at $x=1$, and a fourth degree equation is left when these are removed. For higher values of k, roots can be approximated by known methods.

However, k need not be an integer. Suppose only that it is a rational number (and it can always be approximated as such). Then $(k+1)$ is also rational. Let
$$k + 1 = \frac{p}{q}, \tag{6.45}$$

where p and q are positive integers, and $p \geq q$, since k cannot be less than zero. Then (6.44) can be written
$$x^{\frac{p}{q}} - \frac{p}{q}x + \frac{p-q}{p} = 0. \tag{6.46}$$

Let $y = x^{1/q}$, so that (6.46) becomes
$$y^p - \frac{p}{q}y^q + \frac{p-q}{q} = 0, \tag{6.47}$$

and by (6.43)
$$y = e^{-\frac{1}{q}\sigma\tau_1}\left(\cos\frac{1}{q}\omega\tau_1 - j\sin\frac{1}{q}\omega\tau_1\right). \tag{6.48}$$

Eq. (6.47) has integer exponents, and can be solved for y. Then (6.48) can be solved for
$$\frac{1}{q}\sigma\tau_1 \quad \text{and} \quad \frac{1}{q}\omega\tau_1,$$

which need only to be multiplied by p to get $\sigma\tau_0$ and $\omega\tau_0$.

The preceding methods become awkward when p is larger than 6. The following is more suitable for numerical approximation by digital computer. Equating the real and imaginary parts of (6.42) separately to zero gives the equations
$$e^{-(k+1)\sigma\tau_1}\cos(k+1)\omega\tau_1 - (k+1)e^{-\sigma\tau_1}\cos\omega\tau_1 + k = 0, \tag{6.49}$$
$$e^{-(k+1)\sigma\tau_1}\sin(k+1)\omega\tau_1 - (k+1)e^{-\sigma\tau_1}\sin\omega\tau_1 = 0. \tag{6.50}$$

Both of these equations must be satisfied by the pair of values of $\sigma\tau_1$ and $\omega\tau_1$ which represent a zero. Eq. (6.50) can be solved for $\sigma\tau_1$

$$\sigma\tau_1 = \frac{1}{k}\log\frac{\sin(k+1)\omega\tau_1}{(k+1)\sin\omega\tau_1}. \tag{6.51}$$

A series of values of $\omega\tau_1$ is put into (6.51) and the $\sigma\tau_1$ computed for each. Each pair of values is substituted into (6.49) to find those which satisfy it. The solutions can be approximated as closely as desired by choosing suitably small increments of $\omega\tau_1$, and by interpolation. A modest amount of computation time on a digital computer produces the first half-dozen roots.

6.241b. Repetition and Symmetry of the Zero Pattern. Let ω be the imaginary part of a zero that (together with its real part σ) simultaneously satisfies (6.49) and (6.50). Also let k be related to integers p and q as in (6.45). Consider another imaginary part ω' such that

$$\omega'\tau_1 = 2q\pi + \omega\tau_1.$$

Then

$$\omega'\tau_0 = (k+1)\omega'\tau_1 = \frac{p}{q}\omega'\tau_1 = 2p\pi + (k+1)\omega\tau_1. \tag{6.52}$$

Both sines and cosines of $\omega'\tau_1$ and $(k+1)\omega'\tau_1$ are the same as those of $\omega\tau_1$ and $(k+1)\omega\tau_1$. Hence, with no change in σ, ω' also represents a zero. The pattern of zeros between $\omega\tau_0 = 0$ and $\omega\tau_0 = 2p\pi$ will be repeated exactly in each $2p\pi$ range of $\omega\tau_0$, to infinity, with an unchanged set of σ's.

Again supposing ω is the imaginary part of a zero, let ω' be a frequency such that

$$\omega'\tau_1 = 2q\pi - \omega\tau_1. \tag{6.53}$$

Then

$$\omega'\tau_0 = (k+1)\omega'\tau_1 = 2p\pi - (k+1)\tau_1. \tag{6.54}$$

Now the cosines of $\omega'\tau_1$ and $(k+1)\omega'\tau_1$ are the same as those of $\omega\tau_1$ and $(k+1)\omega\tau_1$, while the sines are both of opposite sign. Both (6.49) and (6.50) will still be satisfied, and ω' represents a zero having the same σ as that of ω. In each $2p\pi$ interval of $\omega\tau_0$, the zeros are symmetrically spaced about the center of the interval (an odd multiple of $p\pi$), each symmetrical pair having equal values of σ. There may or may not be a zero at the center of symmetry, depending upon whether p is odd or even.

6.241c. Zeros of the Reversed Triangle. If $f(t)$ is the triangular wave, then $f(-t)$ is the wave reversed in time, and

$$\mathscr{L}[f(t)] = F(s)$$

and,

$$\mathscr{L}[f(-t)]=F(-s). \tag{6.55}$$

Therefore, the zeros of the reversed triangle are the negatives of those for the original triangle. Since the zeros of the original triangle occur in complex conjugate pairs, the reversed triangle has the same zeros as the original triangle, but with the signs of the real parts reversed.

Also, the asymmetry constant for the reversed triangle, is $1/k$, where k is the asymmetry of the original triangle.

6.241d. Zeros of the Right Triangle. When $k=0$, the triangle is right and has a transform

$$F(s)=\frac{a}{s^2\tau_0}\left[1-e^{-s\tau_0}(1+s\tau_0)\right]. \tag{6.56}$$

Its zeros occur for

$$(1+s\tau_0)=e^{s\tau_0}. \tag{6.57}$$

Equating real and imaginary parts,

$$1+\sigma\tau_0=e^{\sigma\tau_0}\cos\omega\tau_0, \tag{6.58}$$

$$\omega\tau_0=e^{\sigma\tau_0}\sin\omega\tau_0. \tag{6.59}$$

[Note the solution $\omega=0$, $\sigma=0$ cannot produce a zero because of the s^2 in the denominator of (6.56).]

As before, the roots can be approximated numerically with the computer. Note that with σ and ω real, and taking only positive values of ω, $\sin\omega\tau_0$ is positive according to (6.59). Also, since $\omega\tau_0$ is larger than $\sin\omega\tau_0$, $\sigma\tau_0$ must be positive and the real parts of the zeros must be positive, or they must lie in the right half s-plane. Then by (6.58) $\cos\omega\tau_0$ is also positive which means that all zeros must occur for $\omega\tau_0$ in the first quadrant.

For $k=\infty$, the triangle is also right, but reversed in time. Its zeros are therefore the same as those for $k=0$, but with the signs of the real parts reversed.

6.241e. Loci of the Complex Zeros. Using the foregoing relations, enough zeros have been calculated to indicate the low-frequency behavior of the triangular wave. A complex-frequency plot of the zero loci – normalized in terms of $\omega\tau_0$ and $\sigma\tau_0$ and with the asymmetry k as the parameter – is shown in Fig. 6.18. In this plot the asymmetry is restricted to the range $0\leq k\leq1$. For $k>1$, these loci would be mirrored in the vertical axis, that is, the signs of σ would be reversed.

For the symmetrical case ($k=1$), the zeros are double and fall on the $j\omega$-axis at even multiples of 2π; i.e., at 4π, 8π, 12π, etc. They are re-

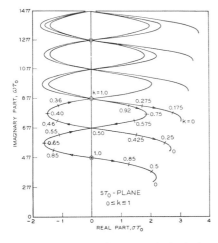

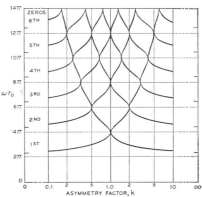

Fig. 6.18. Complex frequency loci of the zeros of a triangular pulse. The s-plane is normalized in terms of $\omega\tau_0$ and $\sigma\tau_0$. The asymmetry constant k is the parameter. (After DUNN, FLANAGAN and GESTRIN)

Fig. 6.19. Imaginary parts of the complex zeros of a triangular pulse as a function of asymmetry. The imaginary frequency is normalized in terms of $\omega\tau_0$ and the range of asymmetry is $0 \leqq k \leqq \infty$. (After DUNN, FLANAGAN and GESTRIN)

presented by the small concentric circles at these points. In terms of cps, the double zeros lie at $2/\tau_0$, $4/\tau_0$, etc., and the amplitude spectrum is $(\sin^2 x/x^2)$. As k is made smaller than unity, the double zeros part — one moving initially into the right half plane and the other into the left. Their paths are plotted.

As the order of the zero increases, the s-plane trajectory also increases in length and complexity for a given change in k. A given reduction in k from unity causes the first zero to move into the right half plane where it remains. The same change in k may cause a higher order zero, say the sixth, to make several excursions between right and left half planes. For the first, second and third zeros, values of k from 1.0 to 0.0 are laid off along the paths. For $k=0$, the triangle is right, with zero closing time, and all zeros have terminal positions in the right half plane. Note, too, that in the vicinity of the $j\omega$-axis, a relatively small change in symmetry results in a relatively large change in the damping of the zeros.

All imaginary-axis zeros are double and the degree of the zeros never exceeds two. This point is further emphasized in a plot of the loci of the imaginary parts of the zeros as a function of the asymmetry factor k. The pattern is shown in Fig. 6.19. It is plotted for values of k between 0.1 and 10. All points of tangency represent double $j\omega$-axis zeros. The average number of zeros is one per every 2π interval of $\omega\tau_0$. The pattern of imaginary parts is symmetrical about the $k=1$ value, with the right and left ordinates showing the zeros of the right triangles, i.e., for $k=0$ and $k=\infty$.

To illustrate the sensitivity of the amplitude spectrum to a specific change in the asymmetry constant, Fig. 6.20 shows amplitude spectra $|F(j\omega)|$ for two values of asymmetry, namely, $k=1$ and $k=11/12$ (or $12/11$). For $k=1$ the zeros are double and are spaced at cps frequencies of $2/\tau_0$, $4/\tau_0$, $6/\tau_0$, etc. The spectrum is $\sin^2 x/x^2$ in form. A change in k to $11/12$ (or to $12/11$) causes each double zero to part, one moving into the right half plane and the other into the left. Their $j\omega$-positions

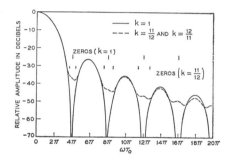

Fig. 6.20. Amplitude spectra for two triangular pulses, $k = 1$ and $k = 11/12$. (After DUNN, FLANAGAN and GESTRIN)

are indicated by the ticks on the diagram. The increase in real parts is such as to provide the spectral "fill" indicated by the dotted curve. In this case a relatively small change in symmetry results in a relatively large spectral change.

6.241 f. Other approximations to the Glottal Pulse. The preceding comments have exclusively concerned triangular approximations to the glottal wave. In reality the glottal wave can take on many forms, and it is instructive to consider the zero patterns for other simple approximations. The triangle has three points where slope is discontinuous. What, for example, might be the effect of eliminating one or more of these discontinuities by rounding or smoothing the wave?

There are several symmetrical geometries that might be considered realistic approximations to glottal waves with more rounding. Three, for example, are pulses described respectively by a half (rectified) sine wave, a half ellipse, and a raised cosine. The waveforms are plotted in the top part of Fig. 6.21. The first two have two points of discontin-

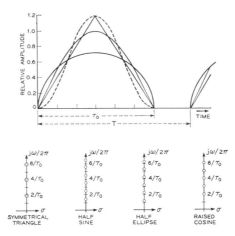

Fig. 6.21. Four symmetrical approximations to the glottal pulse and their complex zeros

uous slope; the latter has none. They can be described temporally and spectrally as follows.

Half-sine wave

$$f(t) = a \sin \beta t, \quad 0 \leq t \leq \frac{\pi}{\beta}, \quad \beta = \frac{\pi}{\tau_0}$$

$$= 0, \quad \text{elsewhere} \tag{6.60}$$

$$F(\omega) = \left(\frac{\beta a}{\beta^2 - \omega^2}\right)(1 + e^{-j\pi\omega/\beta}),$$

where the zeros occur at:

$$\omega = \pm \frac{(2n+1)\pi}{\tau_0} = \pm(2n+1)\beta, \quad n = 1, 2, \ldots[1].$$

Half-ellipse

$$f(t) = \frac{4}{\pi\tau_0}\left[1 - \left(\frac{2t}{\tau_0}\right)^2\right]^{\frac{1}{2}}, \quad |t| \leq \tau_0/2$$

$$= 0, \quad \text{elsewhere} \tag{6.61}$$

$$F(\omega) = \frac{2J_1(\omega\tau_0/2)}{\omega\tau_0/2},$$

where, except for $\omega = 0$, the zeros occur at the roots of $J_1(\omega\tau_0/2)$.

----

[1] For all these symmetrical waves, the zeros lie on the $j\omega$-axis.

Raised Cosine

$$f(t) = a(1 - \cos \beta t), \qquad 0 \leqq t \leqq \frac{2\pi}{\beta}, \qquad \beta = \frac{2\pi}{\tau_0}$$

$$= 0, \qquad \text{elsewhere} \tag{6.62}$$

$$F(\omega) = a \left[\frac{\beta^2}{j\omega(\beta^2 - \omega^2)} \right] [1 - e^{-j 2\pi \omega/\beta}],$$

and the zeros occur at:

$$\omega = \pm n\beta = \pm \frac{2n\pi}{\tau_0}, \qquad n = 2, 3, \dots .$$

The complex zeros for these functions are plotted in the lower part of Fig. 6.21. The plots suggest that relatively small changes in rounding and pulse shape can have appreciable influence upon the zero pattern and upon the low-frequency behavior of the glottal spectrum. Although the zeros may shift around, the average number of zeros in a given frequency interval (above a frequency of about $1/\tau_0$) still remains the same for all the waves, namely one per $1/\tau_0$ cps[1].

6.241g. Asymptotic Density of Source Zeros. This average density of zeros also holds at high frequencies. Consider an arbitrary glottal pulse, $f(t)$, which is finite and nonzero in the interval $0 < t < \tau_0$ and zero elsewhere. Since $\int_0^{\tau_0} f(t) e^{-st} dt$ must be finite, the function can have no poles. Suppose the second derivative of $f(t)$ is bounded inside the same interval and that the slope is discontinuous at $t = 0$ and $t = \tau_0$. Except at $s = 0$, two differentiations of $f(t)$ leave the zeros the same, and produce impulses of areas $f'(0_+)$ and $f'(\tau_{0-})$ at the leading and trailing edges of the pulse. The transform of the twice-differentiated pulse is therefore

$$s^2 F(s) = \int_0^\infty f''(t) e^{-st} dt = f'(0_+) + f'(\tau_{0-}) e^{-s\tau_0} + \int_{0_+}^{\tau_{0-}} f''(t) e^{-st} dt.$$

Since $f''(t)$ is bounded in $0 < t < \tau_0$, the integral of the third term must be of order $1/s$ or less. At high frequencies it becomes small compared to the first two terms and the transform is approximately

$$s^2 F(s) \cong [f'(0_+) + f'(\tau_{0-}) e^{-s\tau_0}],$$

---

[1] The spectra given here are for single pulses, that is, continuous spectra given by the Laplace or Fourier transforms of the pulses. For periodically repeated pulses, the spectra are discrete harmonic lines whose amplitudes are given by $(1/T) F(m\Omega_0)$, where $F(m\Omega_0)$ is the Fourier transform of a single pulse evaluated at the harmonic frequencies $m\Omega_0 = m 2\pi/T$, $m = 1, 2, 3 \dots$.

with zeros at

$$s = -\frac{1}{\tau_0} \ln \left| \frac{f'(0_+)}{f'(\tau_{0-})} \right| \pm j \frac{(2n+1)\pi}{\tau_0}, \qquad n = 0, 1, \dots. \qquad (6.63)$$

At low frequencies, however, the zero positions may be much more irregular, as the previous computations show.

   6.241h. Perceptual Effects of Glottal Zeros. A relevant question concerns the effect of glottal zeros in real speech. Are they perceptually significant? Should they be taken into account in speech analysis techniques such as spectral pattern matching? Are they important for synthesizing natural speech? The complete answers to these questions are not clear and comprehensive subjective testing is needed. It is clear, however, that under particular conditions (which can sometimes be identified in sound spectrograms), a glottal zero may fall proximate to a speech formant and may alter both the spectrum and the percept.

   The formant nullifying potential of a glottal zero can easily be demonstrated in synthetic speech. Fig. 6.22 shows a four-resonance vowel synthesizer circuit. The circuit is excited by an approximately symmetrical, triangular glottal wave. The amplitude spectra actually measured with a wave analyzer are shown for two conditions of open time of the glottal wave. The vowel is $/\Lambda/$. In case (A), the open time is chosen to position the first double glottal zero near to the first formant ($\tau_0 \cong 4$ msec). In case (B), the first glottal zero is positioned between the first and second formants ($\tau_0 \cong 2.5$ msec). The relative pole-zero positions are shown for the first two formants in the s-plane diagrams. The first formant peak is clearly suppressed and flattened in the first

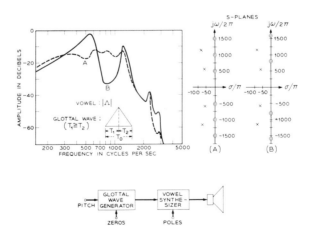

Fig. 6.22a and b. Effect of glottal zeros upon the measured spectrum of a synthetic vowel sound. (a) $\tau_0 = 4.0$ msec. (b) $\tau_0 = 2.5$ msec. (After FLANAGAN, 1961b)

case[1]. A significant difference in vowel quality is obvious in listening to the two conditions.

If an even more artificial situation is posed, the effect of source zeros can be made still more dramatic. For example, suppose the synthesizer is set for the vowel /ə/ which has nearly uniformly-spaced poles. Suppose also that the excitation is brief, double pulses described by $f(t) = a(t) + b(t-\delta)$, where $a(t)$ and $b(t)$ are impulses with areas a and b, respectively. The frequency transform of $f(t)$ is $F(s) = (a + be^{-s\delta})$ which has zeros at

$$ s = \left[-\frac{1}{\delta} \ln \frac{a}{b} \pm j \frac{(2n+1)\pi}{\delta} \right], \qquad n = 0, 1, \dots . \qquad (6.64) $$

That is, this excitation produces the same zero pattern as the asymptotic high frequency spacing given in Eq. (6.63). By suitable choice of a/b and δ, the source zeros can be placed near the formants. Three different excitation conditions (including a single pulse) are shown in three columns in Fig. 6.23. The input excitation and the resulting synthetic sound waveforms are also shown. In the first case the vowel is clearly heard and identified as /ə/. In the second and third cases, the vowel quality and color are substantially altered. Cases 2 and 3 differ very little perceptually, although the sound waveforms are greatly different. From the perceptual standpoint there appears to be a relatively narrow vertical strip, centered about the $j\omega$-axis, in which a glottal zero has the potential for substantially influencing the percept[2]. The double pulse excitation provides a simple means for manipulating the zero pattern for subjective testing. Also, to a very crude approximation, it is somewhat similar to the phenomenon of diplophonia (SMITH, S.).

As emphasized earlier in this section, the perceptual importance of glottal wave detail and of source zeros has not been thoroughly established. At least one speech analysis procedure, however, has taken glottal zeros into account to obtain more precise spectral analyses (MATHEWS, MILLER and DAVID, 1961b). A pole-zero model, with an average zero density of one per $1/\tau_0$ cps, is fitted in a weighted-least-square sense to real speech spectra (see Section 5.21). A typical pole-zero fit to the spectrum of a single pitch period of a natural vowels is shown in Fig. 6.24. The analysis procedure does not discriminate between right and left half-plane zeros, and all zeros are plotted in the left

---

[1] In neither case does the measured amplitude spectrum go to zero at the frequency of the zeros. The laboratory-generated glottal wave was not precisely symmetrical and its zeros did not lie exactly on the $j\omega$-axis.

[2] Symmetric glottal pulses produce zeros on the $j\omega$-axis, as described in the preceding discussion. In natural speech this region appears to be largely avoided through vocal-cord adjustments.

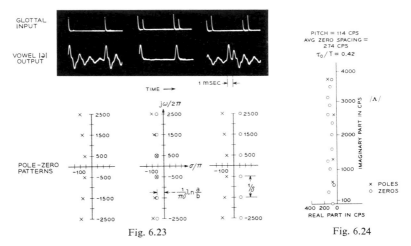

Fig. 6.23. Method for manipulating source zeros to influence vowel quality. Left column, no zeros. Middle column, left-half plane zeros. Right column, right-half plane zeros. (After FLANAGAN, 1961 b)

Fig. 6.24. Best fitting pole-zero model for the spectrum of a single pitch period of a natural vowel sound. (After MATHEWS, MILLER and DAVID, 1961 b)

half-plane. An open time of the glottal wave of about 0.4 times the pitch period is suggested by the result.

Whether the precise positions of source zeros are perceptually significant remains a question for additional study. Only their influence on over-all spectral balance and gross shape may be the important factor. The vocal excitation may vary in waveform so rapidly in connected speech that the zero pattern is not stationary long enough to influence the percept. A speaker also might adjust his glottal wave by auditory feedback to minimize unwanted suppression of formant frequencies.

One experiment leads to the view that the glottal wave can be represented by a fixed analytical form, and that period-to-period irregularities in the pitch function can be smoothed out (ROSENBERG, 1971). Natural speech was analyzed pitch-synchronously. Pitch, formant frequencies and an inverse-filter approximation to the glottal wave were determined for each period. The glottal wave shape was "cartoonized" and characterized by fixed, smooth, analytical functions, whose glottis-open times depended only upon pitch period[1]. Using the analyzed pitch and formant data, the speech was synthesized with this artificial characterization of the glottal wave. Listening tests were then conducted.

---

[1] Note that the spectral zeros of such waves vary in frequency position as the fundamental frequency changes. Only for monotone pitch are the spectral zeros constant in position.

Subjects preferred asymmetric wave characterizations with one slope discontinuity (corresponding to cord closure) and with opening and closing times equal to 40% and 16% of the pitch period. The subjects were relatively insensitive to variations in the precise shape and open-close times. Very small opening or closing times, and approximately equal opening and closing times were clearly not preferred. The latter, as discussed above, leads to spectral zeros near the $j\omega$-axis. The results also demonstrated that elimination of fine temporal detail in the glottal wave shape does not degrade speech quality. These results appear consistent with data on factors found important in formant-synthesized speech (HOLMES, 1961).

Another experiment, using the same analysis techniques, determined the amount of averaging of pitch and formant data that is perceptually tolerable in synthetic speech (ROSENBERG, 1971). In the vowel portions of syllables in connected speech, averaging over as much as four to eight pitch periods did not degrade quality. This averaging completely eliminated fine detail (period-to-period fluctuations) in the pitch and formant data. Longer averaging, which modified the underlying pitch and formant trajectories, did definitely impair quality.

Acoustic interaction between the vocal cords and vocal tract contributes some temporal details to the glottal volume flow waveform. This interaction also influences the temporal variation of voice pitch. These experiments suggest that the fine structure, both in wave shape and in pitch-period variation, is not perceptually significant, but that variations in values averaged over several pitch periods are significant.

One point should perhaps be emphasized in considering inverse-filter estimates of glottal wave shape. The fundamental hypothesis is that the source and system are linearly separable, and that the acoustic properties of each can be uniquely assigned. The glottal wave is usually obtained from the inverse filter according to some criterion such as minimum ripple. Such criteria are completely acceptable within the frame of a particular analysis model; that is, by specifically defining non-interactive source and system. On the other hand, if the objective is an accurate estimate of the real glottal flow, which in fact may have substantial ripple and detail, then the inverse-filter method can be treacherous. Properties justly belonging to the source might be assigned to the system, and vice versa.

6.242. Simulation of Unvoiced Excitation. The discussion of Chapter III pointed out the uncertainties in our present knowledge of unvoiced sources of excitation. Existing measurements (HEINZ, 1958) suggest that the source for voiceless continuants (fricatives) has a relatively flat spectrum in the mid-audio frequency range, and that the source impedance is largely resistive. In electrical synthesis of speech, these sounds are commonly generated by having a broadband random noise source excite the simulated vocal resonances. Stop sounds, on the other hand, are often produced by a transient excitation of the resonators, either with electrical pulses or brief noise bursts. Voiced fricatives, since they are excited by pitch-synchronous noise bursts in the real vocal tract, can be simulated by multiplying the simulated glottal wave with an on-going broadband noise signal.

6.243. Models for Sound Generation in the Vocal Tract. Increased insight into vocal-tract excitation can be obtained from efforts to model the acoustics of human sound generation (FLANAGAN and LANDGRAF; FLANAGAN and CHERRY; ISHIZAKA; FLANAGAN, 1969). Such efforts are also directly relevant to speech synthesis by vocal-tract simulation.

6.243a. Model for Voiced Excitation. Following the analyses of Chapter III, voiced excitation of the vocal system can be represented as in Fig. 6.25. The lungs are represented by the air reservoir at the left. The force of the rib-cage muscles raises the air in the lungs to subglottal pressure P_s. This pressure expels a flow of air with volume velocity U_g through the glottal orifice and produces a local Bernoulli pressure. The vocal cords are represented as a symmetric mechanical oscillator, composed of mass M, spring K and viscous damping, B. The cord oscillator is actuated by a function of the subglottal pressure and the glottal Bernoulli pressure. The sketched waveform illustrates the pulsive form of the U_g flow during voiced sounds. The vocal tract and nasal tract are shown as tubes whose cross-sectional areas change with distance. The acoustic volume velocities at the mouth and nostrils are U_m and U_n, respectively. The sound pressure P in front of the mouth is approximately a linear superposition of the time derivatives $\dot{U}_m$ and $\dot{U}_n$.

Following the transmission-line relations derived in Chapter III, the acoustic system of Fig. 6.25 can be approximated by the network of Fig. 6.26. The lung volume is represented by a capacity and loss

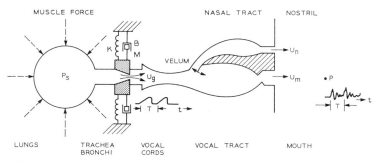

Fig. 6.25. Schematic diagram of the human vocal mechanism. (After FLANAGAN *et al.*, 1970.)

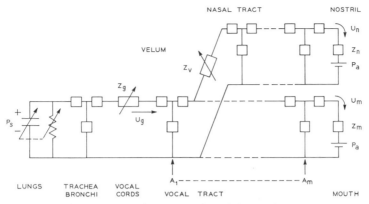

Fig. 6.26. Network representation of the vocal system

whose sizes depend upon the state of inflation. The lungs are connected to the vocal cords by the trachea and bronchi tubes, represented in the figure as a single T-section. The impedance of the vocal cords Z_g is both time-varying and dependent upon the glottal volume velocity U_g. The vocal tract is approximated as a cascade of T-sections in which the element impedances are determined by the cross-sectional areas $A_1 \ldots A_n$. The value of N is determined by the precision to which the area variation is to be represented. The line is terminated in a radiation load at the mouth Z_m, which is taken as the radiation impedance of a circular piston in a plane baffle. U_m is the mouth current and, for simulation of d.c. quantities, a battery P_a represents atmospheric pressure.

The nasal tract is coupled by the variable velar impedance Z_v. The nasal tract is essentially fixed in shape, and the nostril current U_n flows through the radiation impedance Z_n.

This formulation of the vocal system can simulate respiration as well as phonation. The glottis is opened (Z_g is reduced), the rib cage muscles enlarge the lung capacitor (volume), and the atmospheric pressure forces a charge of air through the tract and onto the capacitor. The glottis is then clenched and increased in impedance; the rib cage muscles contract, raising the voltage (pressure) across the lung capacity, and force out a flow of air. Under proper conditions, the vocal-cord oscillator is set into stable vibration, and the network is excited by periodic pulses of volume velocity. The lung pressure, cord parameters, velar coupling, and vocal tract area all vary with time during an utterance. A difference-equation specification of the network, with these variable coefficients, permits calculation of the Nyquist samples of all pressures and volume velocities, including the output sound pressure (FLANAGAN and LANDGRAF).

To simplify computation and to focus attention on the properties
of the vocal-cord oscillator, the cords can be represented by a single
moveable mass as shown in Fig. 6.27 (it being understood that the normal
movement is bilaterally symmetric with the opposing cord-mass experiencing identical displacement). The cords have thickness d and
length l. Vertical displacement x, of the mass changes the glottal area A_g,
and varies the flow U_g. At rest, the glottal opening has the phonation
neutral area A_{g0}.

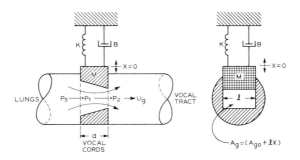

Fig. 6.27. Acoustic oscillator model of the vocal cords. (After FLANAGAN and LANDGRAF)

The mechanical oscillator is forced by a function of the subglottal
pressure and the Bernoulli pressure in the orifice. The Bernoulli pressure
is dependent upon U_g^2, which, in turn, is conditioned by the nonlinear,
time-varying acoustic impedance of the glottal opening. In qualitative
terms, the operation is as follows: the cords are set to the neutral or rest
area, and the subglottal pressure applied. As the flow builds up, so does
the negative Bernoulli pressure. The latter draws the mass down to inter-
rupt the flow. As the flow diminishes, so does the Bernoulli pressure,
and the spring acts to retrieve the mass. Under appropriate conditions,
stable oscillation results.

The undamped natural frequency of the oscillator is proportional
to $(K/M)^{\frac{1}{2}}$. It is convenient to define a vocal-cord tension parameter Q,
which scales the natural frequency by multiplying the stiffness and
dividing the mass. This is loosely analogous to the physiological tensing
of the cords, which stiffens them and reduces their distributed mass.
Since the trachea-bronchi impedance is relatively low (compared to that
of the glottal orifice), and since the large lung volume is maintained
at nearly constant pressure over short durations, a source of constant
pressure can approximate the subglottal system. For voiced, non-nasal
sounds, this modification to the network is shown in Fig. 6.28.

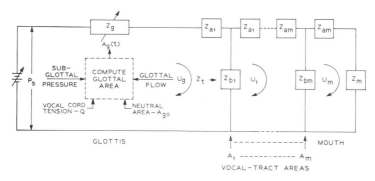

Fig. 6.28. Simplified network of the vocal system for voiced sounds.
(After FLANAGAN and LANDGRAF)

The acoustic impedance of the glottal orifice is characterized by two loss elements, R_v and R_k, and an inertance, L_g[1]. The values of these impedances depend upon the time-varying glottal area $A_g(t)$. In addition, R_k is dependent upon $|U_g|$. The glottal area is linked to P_s and to U_g through the differential equation that describes the vocal-cord motion and its forcing function. The values of the tension parameter Q and of the phonation-neutral area A_{g0} are also introduced into this equation. In other words, the dashed box of Fig. 6.28 represents iterative solutions to the differential equation for the system described in Fig. 6.27.

This continuous system can be represented by $(m+2)$ differential equations, which, in turn, can be approximated by difference equations. These difference equations are programmed for simultaneous solution on a digital computer. The program accepts as input data time-varying samples of the subglottal pressure P_s, the cord tension Q, the neutral area A_{g0} and the vocal tract areas $(A_1 \ldots A_m)$, and it computes sampled values of all volume velocities, including the glottal flow and mouth output. The resulting functions can be digital-to-analog converted and led to a display scope or loud-speaker. A typical glottal area and volume velocity, plotted by the computer for a vocal-tract shape corresponding to the vowel /a/, is shown in Fig. 6.29. This figure shows the initial 50 msec of voicing.

The top curve is the glottal area result, and the lower curve the glottal flow. The calculation is for a subglottal pressure of 8 cm H_2O, a neutral area of 0.05 cm² and a tension value that places the cord oscillation in the pitch range of a man. One notices that by about the fourth period a steady state is achieved. One sees, in this case, irregularities in the glottal flow that are caused by acoustic interaction at the first formant frequency

---

[1] See Section 3.52.

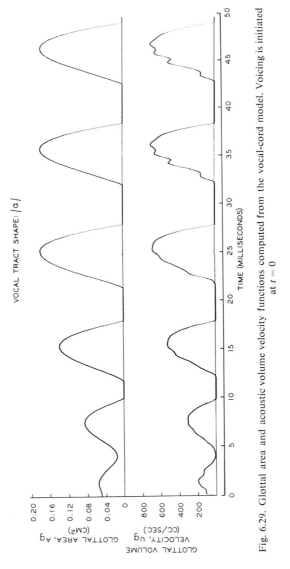

Fig. 6.29. Glottal area and acoustic volume velocity functions computed from the vocal-cord model. Voicing is initiated at $t = 0$

of the tract. One also notices that this temporal detail in the volume flow is not noticeably reflected in the mechanical behavior, that is in the area wave.

The behavior of the vocal-cord model over a range of glottal conditions suggests that it duplicates many of the features of human speech. Furthermore, the parameters necessary for complete synthesis of voiced sounds are now reduced to the articulatory quantities: tract areas,

$A_1 \ldots A_m$; subglottal pressure, P_s; cord tension, Q; and phonation neutral area A_{g0}. A spectrogram of the audible output for a linear transition in vocal tract shape from the vowel /i/ to the vowel /a/ is shown in Fig. 6.30. The glottal conditions in this case are constant and are: $P_s = 8$ cm H_2O, $A_{g0} = 0.05$ cm^2 and $Q = 2.0$. The resulting fundamental frequency of these sounds is not only a function of the glottal parameters, but also of the tract shape; this is, a function of the acoustic loading that the tract presents to the vocal cords. The spectral sections indicate realistic formant and pitch values.

The single-mass model of the cords, because of its simplicity and because it produces many features of human speech, is attractive for use in transmission-line synthesizers. It does not, however, represent physiological details such as phase differences between the upper and lower edges of the real cords. Also, its acoustic interaction with the vocal system is critically dependent upon the relations assumed for intraglottal pressure distribution. (The values determined by VAN DEN BERG were used in the above simulations.) If a more detailed simulation of the physiology and the acoustic interaction is needed, the acoustic oscillator concept can be extended to multiple mass-spring representations of the cord mass and compliance (FLANAGAN and LANDGRAF). A two-mass oscillator, stiffness coupled, has been found to represent with additional accuracy the real-cord behavior (ISHIZAKA and MATSUDAIRA; DUDGEON; ISHIZAKA and FLANAGAN). Continuing research aims to use this additional sophistication in synthesis.

6.243b. Voiceless Excitation. With slight modification, and with no additional control data, the system of Fig. 6.28 can be arranged to include fricative and stop excitation. Fricative excitation is generated by turbulent air flow at a constriction, and stop excitation is produced by making a complete closure, building up pressure and abruptly releasing it. The stop release is frequently followed by a noise excitation owing to turbulence generated at the constriction after the release.

Experimental measurements indicate that the noise sound pressure generated by turbulence is proportional to the square of the Reynolds number for the flow (see Section 3.6). To the extent that a one-dimensional wave treatment is valid, the noise sound pressure can be taken as proportional to the square of the volume velocity and inversely proportional to the constriction area. Measurements also suggest that the noise source is spatially distributed, but generally can be located at, or immediately downstream of the closure. Its internal impedance is primarily resistive, and it excites the vocal system as a series pressure source. Its spectrum is broadly peaked in the midaudio range and falls off at low and high frequencies (HEINZ, 1958).

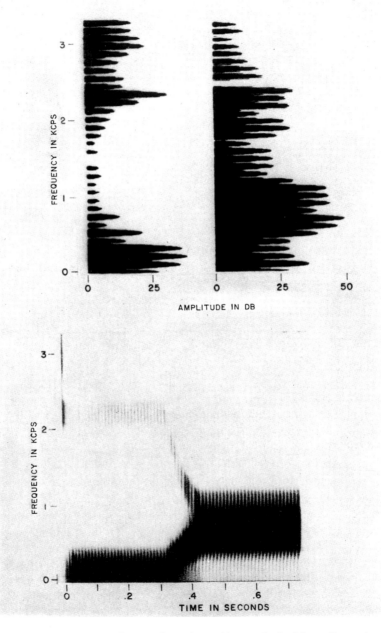

Fig. 6.30. Spectrogram of a vowel-vowel transition synthesized from the cord oscillator and vocal tract model. The output corresponds to a linear transition from the vowel /i/ to the vowel /a/. Amplitude sections are shown for the central portion of each vowel

The transmission-line vocal tract, including the vocal-cord model, can be modified to approximate the nonlinearities of turbulent flow (FLANAGAN and CHERRY). Fig. 6.31 shows a single section of the transmission line so modified. A series noise source P_n, with internal resistance R_n is introduced into each section of the line. The area of the section is A_n and the volume current circulating in the right branch is U_n. The level of the noise source and the value of its internal resistance are functions of U_n and A_n. The noise source is modulated in amplitude by a function proportional to the squared Reynolds number; namely, U_n^2/A_n. The source resistance

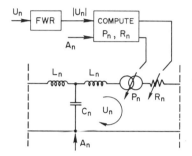

Fig. 6.31. Modification of network elements for simulating the properties of turbulent flow in the vocal tract. (After FLANAGAN and CHERRY)

is a flow-dependent loss similar to the glottal resistance. To first order, it is proportional to $|U_n|$ and inversely proportional to A_n^2. The diagram indicates that these quantities are used to determine P_n and R_n. In the computer simulation they are calculated on a sample-by-sample basis.

By continually noting the magnitudes of the volume currents in each section, and knowing the corresponding areas, the synthesizer detects conditions suitable to turbulent flow. Noise excitation and loss are therefore introduced automatically at any constriction. Small constrictions and low Reynolds numbers produce inaudible noise. The square-law dependence of P_n upon U_n has the perceptual effect of a noise threshold. (A real threshold switch can be used on the noise source, if desired.) The original control data, namely, vocal-tract shape, subglottal pressure, neutral area and cord tension, in effect, determine the place of the constriction and the loss and noise introduced there.

The P_n source is taken as Gaussian noise, bandpassed between 500 and 4000 Hz. Also, to ensure stability, the volume flow U_n is lowpass filtered to 500 Hz before it modulates the noise source. In other words, the noise is produced by the low-frequency components of U_n, including the dc flow.

This noise excitation works equally well for voiced and unvoiced sounds. The operation for voiced fricatives includes all features
of the formulation, and is a good vehicle for illustration. For example,
consider what happens in a vowel when the constriction is made substantially smaller than normal, giving rise to conditions favorable for
turbulent flow. Since we have already shown results for the vowel /a/,
consider the same vowel with the constriction narrowed. (This configuration is not proposed as a realistic English sound, but merely to
illustrate the effect of tightening the vowel constriction.) The situation
is shown in Fig. 6.32. All glottal conditions are the same as before,
but the constriction is narrowed to less than half the normal vowel
constriction (namely, to 0.3 cm^2).

The top trace shows the glottal area, and one notices that it settles
to a periodic oscillation in about four periods. The final pitch here is
somewhat less than that in Fig. 6.29 because the acoustic load is different.
The second trace from the top shows the glottal flow. The glottal flow
is about the same in peak value as before and is conditioned primarily
by the glottal impedance and not by the tract constriction. At about
the third period, noise that has been produced at the constriction by the
flow buildup has propagated back to the glottis and influences the U_g

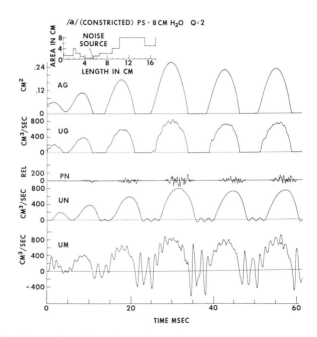

Fig. 6.32. Waveforms of vocal functions. The functions are calculated for a voiced fricative
articulation corresponding to the constricted vowel /a/. (After FLANAGAN and CHERRY)

flow. Note, too, that noise influence on the mechanical oscillator motion (i.e., the area function) is negligible.

The third trace shows the output of the noise source at the constriction. This output is proportional to the constriction current squared, divided by the constriction area. The fourth trace shows the low-passed constriction current that produces the noise. One sees that the tendency is for the noise to be generated in pitch-synchronous bursts, corresponding to the pulses of glottal volume flow. The result is a combined excitation in which the voicing and noise signals are multiplicatively related, as they are in the human.

The final trace is the volume flow at the mouth, and one can notice noise perturbations in the waveform. Note, too, that the epoch of greatest formant excitation corresponds to the falling phase of the glottal flow. A spectrogram of this audible output is compared with that for a normal /a/ in Fig. 6.33. The normal vowel is shown on the left; the constricted vowel on the right. Note in the constricted, noisy /a/ that: (1) the first formant has been lowered in frequency, (2) the fundamental frequency is slightly lower, and (3) pitch-synchronous noise excitation is clearly evident, particularly at the higher frequencies.

Voiceless sounds are produced in this cord-tract model simply by setting the neutral area of the vocal cords (A_{g0}) to a relatively large value, for example 1 cm^2. As this is done, the Bernoulli pressure in the glottal orifice diminishes, the oscillations of the vocal cords decay, and the cord displacement assumes a steady large value. Control of A_{g0} therefore corresponds to the voiced-voiceless distinction in the model. Measurements on real speech suggest this kind of effect in passing from voiced to voiceless sounds (SAWASHIMA; SAWASHIMA et al.). Corresponding exactly to this change, spectrograms of the audible output for the voiced-voiceless cognates /ʒ/ and /ʃ/ are compared in Fig. 6.34. The vocal-tract shape is the same for both sounds. One sees a pronounced voice bar in /ʒ/ (left spectrogram) that, of course, is absent in /ʃ/ (right spectrogram). The eigenfrequencies of the two systems are similar but not exactly the same because of the difference in glottal termination. Lower resonances are not strongly evident in the /ʃ/ output, because its transmission function, from point of constriction to mouth, exhibits low-frequency zeros.

The dynamics of continuous synthesis can be illustrated by a consonant-vowel syllable. Fig. 6.35 shows the syllable /ʒi/ synthesized by the system. In this case, the subglottal pressure the phonation neutral area and cord tension are held constant and the vocal tract area function is changed linearly from the configuration for /ʒ/ to that for /i/. Heavy noise excitation is apparent during the tightly constricted /ʒ/, and the noise diminishes as the articulation shifts to /i/. Also in this case, the high front vowel /i/ is characterized by a relatively tight constriction

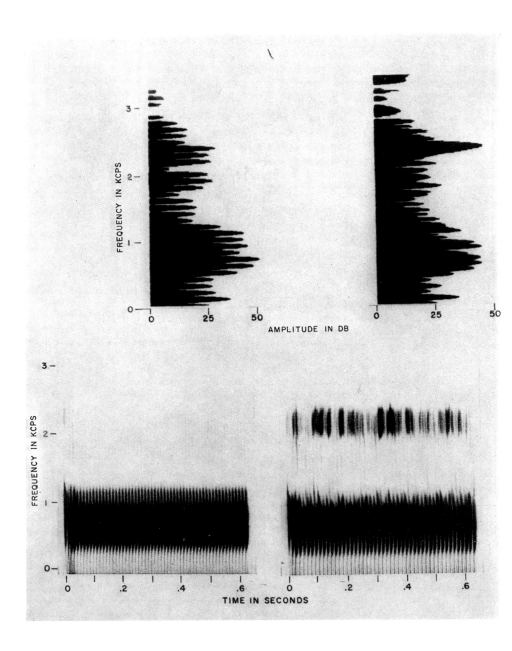

Fig. 6.33. Sound spectrograms of the synthesized output for a normal vowel /a/ (left) and the constricted /a/ shown in Fig. 6.32 (right). Amplitude sections are shown for the central portion of each vowel

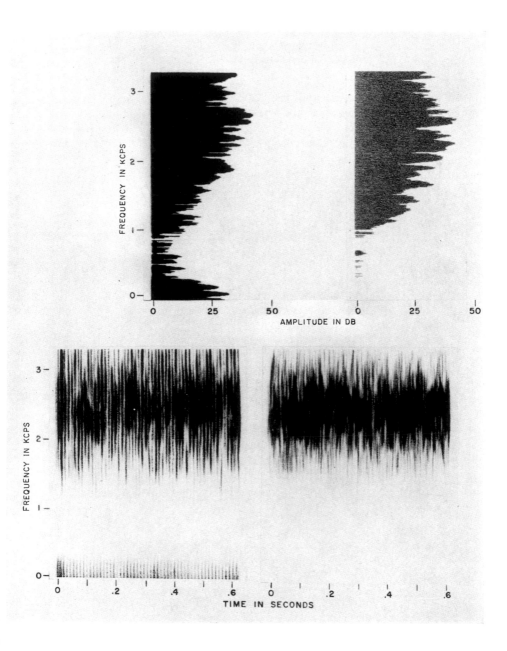

Fig. 6.34. Spectrograms for the voiced-voiceless cognates /ʒ/ and /ʃ/. Amplitude sections are shown for the central portion of each sound

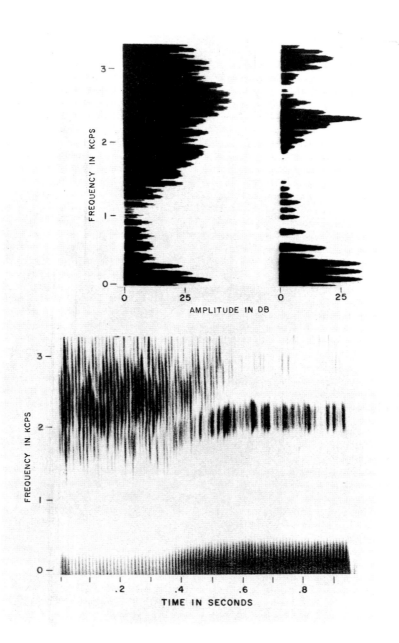

Fig. 6.35. Sound spectrogram for the synthesized syllable /ʒi/. Amplitude sections are shown for the central portion of each sound. (After FLANAGAN and CHERRY)

and a small amount of noise excitation continues in the /i/. This same effect can be seen in human speech.

This model also appears capable of treating sounds such as glottal stops and the glottal aspiration that accompanies /h/. In the former, the tension control can cause an abrupt glottal closure and cessation of voicing. Restoration to a normal tension and quiescent glottal opening permits voicing to again be initiated. In the latter, the flow velocity and area at the glottis can be monitored just as is done along the tract. When conditions suitable for turbulence exist, a noise excitation can be introduced at the glottal location. Note, too, that the central parameters for the voiceless synthesis are exactly the same as for voiced synthesis; namely, $A_1 \ldots A_m, P_s, Q$ and A_{g0}. No additional control data are necessary. Place and intensity of voiceless excitation are deduced from these data.

Although crude in its representations of acoustic non-linearities, this model for voiced and voiceless excitation appears to give realistic results. It is applicable to speech synthesis by vocal tract simulation and it provides a point of departure for further study of sound generation in the human vocal tract.

6.25. Vocal Radiation Factors

Electrical synthesizers usually attempt to account for source characteristics, vocal transmission and mouth-nostril radiation. In a terminal-analog synthesizer, the radiation factor is essentially the functional relation between sound pressure at a point in space and the acoustic volume current passing the radiating port. A transmission-line analog, on the other hand, should be terminated in an impedance actually analogous to the acoustic load on the radiating port. For most speech frequencies, the latter is adequately approximated as the radiation load on a piston in a large baffle (see Section 3.3). The former, for frequencies less than about 4000 cps, is adequately approximated by the relations for a small spherical source (see Section 3.4). That is, the pressure at a point in front of the speaker is proportional to the time derivative of the mouth volume velocity.

To simulate the radiation function in terminal-analog synthesizers, a frequency equalization proportional to frequency (i.e., a 6 db/oct boost) can be applied to the vocal transmission function. Similarly in the transmission-line analog, the current through the radiation load can be differentiated to represent the output sound pressure (alternatively, the voltage directly across the radiation load can be taken as the pressure). Because the mouth and nostrils are spatially proximate (a fraction of a wavelength apart at the lower speech frequencies), the effect of simultaneous radiation from these two points can be approximated by linearly superposing their volume currents or sound pressures.

6.26. Speech Synthesis by Computer Simulation

6.261. Digital Techniques for Formant Synthesis. The approximations made of vocal transmission in Section 6.22 can be represented by linear differential equations with constant coefficients. In turn, such equations can be approximated as linear difference equations. The difference equations can be programmed in a digital computer as arithmetic operations upon discrete values of the variables[1]. As an example, the input and output voltages for the series electrical resonator shown in Fig. 6.10a are related by

$$e_i = LC \frac{d^2 e_0}{dt^2} + RC \frac{de_0}{dt} + e_0 . \tag{6.65}$$

If the derivatives are approximated by differences between successive values of the dependent variable – sampled at uniform, discrete values of the independent variable – the equation can be written as

$$e_i = e_0 + RC \Delta e_0 + LC \Delta^2 e_0 ,$$

where Δ is the first backward difference divided by the sampling interval. Explicitly,

$$
\begin{aligned}
e_i(t_n) = e_0(t_n) &+ RC \left[\frac{e_0(t_n) - e_0(t_{n-1})}{(t_n - t_{n-1})} \right] \\
&+ LC \left[\frac{e_0(t_n) - 2e_0(t_{n-1}) + e_0(t_{n-2})}{(t_n - t_{n-1})(t_{n-1} - t_{n-2})} \right] .
\end{aligned} \tag{6.66}
$$

Collecting terms

$$
\begin{aligned}
e_{i_n} = e_{0_n} &\left[1 + \frac{RC}{D} + \frac{LC}{D^2} \right] - e_{0_{n-1}} \left[\frac{RC}{D} + \frac{2LC}{D^2} \right] + e_{0_{n-2}} \left[\frac{LC}{D} \right], \\
&= a\, e_{0_n} + b\, e_{0_{n-1}} + c\, e_{0_{n-2}} ,
\end{aligned} \tag{6.67}
$$

where $D = (t_n - t_{n-1})$ is the sampling interval and $e_{0_n} = e_0(t_n)$.

The theory of linear difference equations (HILDEBRAND, 1952) shows that the unforced homogeneous solution ($e_{i_n} = 0$) of Eq. (6.67) is a linear combination of exponential terms

$$e_{0_n} = K_1 \beta_1^n + K_2 \beta_2^n , \tag{6.68}$$

where β_1 and β_2 are the roots of the determinantal equation

$$a \beta^2 + b \beta + c = 0 ,$$

---

[1] Alternatively, special purpose digital hardware can accomplish the arithmetic operations.

K_1 and K_2 are arbitrary constants, and a, b and c are defined in (6.67). In the present instance the roots will be complex conjugate, and

$$\beta = -\frac{b \pm j\sqrt{4ac-b^2}}{2a} = e^{r_1 \pm j r_2}, \qquad (6.69)$$

where

$$e^{r_1} = \sqrt{\frac{c}{a}}$$

and

$$r_2 = \tan^{-1}\frac{\sqrt{4ac-b^2}}{-b}.$$

Therefore,

$$e_{0_n} = e^{r_1 n}(K_1' \cos r_2 n + K_2' \sin r_2 n),$$

where K_1' and K_2' are linear combinations of K_1 and K_2, and the response samples are those of a damped sinusoid. Following through the arithmetic gives

$$e^{r_1} = \left[\frac{1}{1+2\alpha D+\omega_0^2 D^2}\right]^{\frac{1}{2}},$$

where

$$\alpha = \frac{R}{2L} \quad \text{and} \quad \omega_0^2 = \frac{1}{LC},$$

and

$$r_1 = -\tfrac{1}{2}\ln\left[1+2\alpha D+\omega_0^2 D^2\right]. \qquad (6.70)$$

Expanding the logarithm as a series for $\ln(1+x)$, $-1<x<1$, and taking the first term yields

$$r_1 \cong -D\left(\alpha+\frac{\omega_0^2 D}{2}\right).$$

For a sufficiently small sampling interval D,

$$\frac{\omega_0^2 D}{2} \ll \alpha$$

and

$$r_1 \cong -\alpha D,$$

and the response samples are damped approximately as $e^{-\alpha n D}$, which is similar to the solution for the continuous equation.

In the same fashion

$$r_2 = \tan^{-1} D \left\{ \frac{\left(\dfrac{1}{LC} - \dfrac{R^2}{4L}\right)}{1 + \dfrac{RD}{L} + \dfrac{R^2 D^2}{4L^2}} \right\}^{\frac{1}{2}}$$

$$r_2 = \tan^{-1} D \left\{ \frac{(\omega_0^2 - \alpha^2)}{1 + 2\alpha D + \alpha^2 D^2} \right\}^{\frac{1}{2}} \tag{6.71}$$

$$r_2 = \tan^{-1} \frac{D\omega}{(1 + \alpha D)},$$

so that for small values of sampling interval

$$r_2 \cong \frac{D\omega}{1 + \alpha D}$$

and for small damping $r_2 \cong D\omega$. The response samples are then approximately those of a damped sinusoid with angular frequency ω, which is the continuous equation solution. One notices, however, that if the sampling is coarse the solution to the difference equation begins to depart substantially from the sampled values of the continuous system. This situation can be improved by more sophisticated approximations to the derivative (which of course require additional computation). The trades which can be made between sampling rate and derivative approximation is a topic area worthy of study.

A different approach permits one to compute exact samples of the continuous impulse response. If, in addition, the sampling rate exceeds twice the bandwidth of the continuous signal, the continuous response can be reconstructed by low-pass filtering. The approach employs the z-transform. Consider the same series RLC formant resonator used in the preceding discussion [see Fig. 6.10a]. Its transfer function, in terms of a Laplace transform, is

$$\frac{e_0(s)}{e_i(s)} = F(s) = \frac{s_1 s_1^*}{(s - s_1)(s - s_1^*)} = \frac{A_1}{(s - s_1)} + \frac{A_1^*}{(s - s_1^*)} \tag{6.72}$$

where

$s_1 = -\sigma_1 + j\omega_1$ is the pole frequency,

$A_1 = \lim\limits_{s \to s_1} (s - s_1) F(s)$ is the complex residue in pole s_1,

and the asterisk denotes complex conjugate. The inverse transform of $F(s)$ is the impulse response $f(t)$. Sampled values of the latter can be described as impulses with areas equal to the function at the sampling instants, that is,

$$f^\dagger(t) = \sum_{n=0}^{\infty} f(t)\delta(t-nD) \tag{6.73}$$

where $\delta(t)$ is a unit area impulse and $f^\dagger(t)$ is a periodic impulse train with period D representing the sample values $f(nD)$. The transform of $f^\dagger(t)$ is the complex convolution of the transform of its components, or

$$\mathcal{L}[f^\dagger(t)] = F^\dagger(s) = F(s) * \mathcal{L}\left\{\sum_n \delta(t-nD)\right\}.$$

But

$$\mathcal{L}\left[\sum_n \delta(t-nD)\right] = 1 + e^{-sD} + e^{-2sD} \cdots$$

$$= \Delta(s) = \frac{1}{1-e^{-sD}},$$

which has poles at $s = \pm j2m\pi/D$, $m = 0, 1, \dots$ The convolution to be computed is

$$F^\dagger(s) = \frac{1}{2\pi j} \int_{c-j\infty}^{c+j\infty} F(\lambda)\Delta(s-\lambda)d\lambda. \tag{6.74}$$

Using the residue theorem and recognizing that the circuit is linear and passive so that the poles of $F(s)$ lie in the left half plane, the integral can be evaluated for a contour of integration enclosing only the poles of $F(s)$.

$$F^\dagger(s) = \sum_{\substack{k \text{ poles} \\ \text{of } F(\lambda)}} \text{Res}[F(\lambda)\Delta(s-\lambda)]_{\lambda=\lambda_k},$$

or

$$F^\dagger(s) = \sum_k \left[\frac{1}{1-e^{-D(s-\lambda_k)}}\right] \text{Res}[F(\lambda)]_{\lambda=\lambda_k}. \tag{6.75}$$

Making the substitution $e^{sD} = z$, Eq. (6.75) can be rewritten

$$F(z) = \sum_k \frac{1}{1-e^{\lambda_k D}z^{-1}} \text{Res}[F(\lambda)]_{\lambda=\lambda_k}. \tag{6.76}$$

For the example at hand (that is, the single formant resonator)

$$\text{Res}[F(s)]_{s=s_1} = A_1 = \left(\frac{\sigma_1^2 + \omega_1^2}{j2\omega_1}\right),$$

and

$$F(z) = \frac{\sigma_1^2 + \omega_1^2}{\omega_1}\left\{\frac{e^{-\sigma_1 D}z^{-1}(\sin\omega_1 D)}{1-2e^{-\sigma_1 D}(\cos\omega_1 D)z^{-1} + e^{-2\sigma_1 D}z^{-2}}\right\}. \tag{6.77}$$

Notice also that Eq. (6.74) can be written

$$F^\dagger(s) = \frac{1}{2\pi j} \int_{-c-j\infty}^{-c+j\infty} F(s-\lambda)\,\varDelta(\lambda)\,d\lambda,$$

and that the poles of $\varDelta(\lambda)$ are

$$\lambda = \pm j\,\frac{2m\pi}{D}, \qquad m = 0, 1, 2, \ldots, \infty.$$

If the integration contour is selected to enclose the $j\omega$-axis poles of $\varDelta(\lambda)$, then the integral is

$$F^\dagger(s) = \frac{1}{D} \sum_{m=-\infty}^{+\infty} F\left(s - j\,\frac{2m\pi}{D}\right), \qquad (6.78)$$

because the residue in any pole of $\varDelta(\lambda)$ is $1/D$.

The system function represented by Eq. (6.75), or by Eq. (6.78), is a transform relating discrete samples of the input and output of the continuous system. Since $z^{-1} = e^{-sD}$ is a delay of one sample interval, D, the digital operations necessary to simulate the sampled response of the single formant resonator, given by Eq. (6.77), involve only delays, multiplications and summations. They are shown in Fig. 6.36a. If the $F(z)$ function in Eq. (6.77) is thought of in terms of the transmission of a common negative feedback amplifier,

$$G = \frac{K}{1+\beta K},$$

the return circuit connections in Fig. 6.36a become apparent.

The resonator of Fig. 6.36a has an impulse response equal to the sampled impulse response of the continuous function of Eq. (6.72).

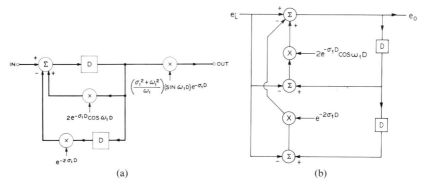

(a)   (b)

Fig. 6.36a and b. Digital operations for simulating a single formant resonance (pole-pair) (a) implementation of the standard z-transform; (b) practical implementation for unity dc gain and minimum multiplication

The frequency behavior for the two relations, however, are somewhat different. For example, their dc gains are

$$F(s)|_{s\to 0}=1$$

and

$$F^{\dagger}(s)|_{s\to 0}=\frac{1}{D}\sum_{m=-\infty}^{\infty}F\left(-j\frac{2m\pi}{D}\right),$$

respectively. Digital resonators can, however, be specified in terms of their frequency behavior and without direct reference to continuous resonators (GOLD and RADER). Since the formant resonance must correspond to prescribed bandwidth and frequency, and since its dc gain must be essentially unity, it is convenient in practice to modify (6.77) to

$$\frac{e_0(z)}{e_i(z)}=F(z)=\frac{1-2e^{-\sigma_1 D}\cos\omega_1 D+e^{-2\sigma_1 D}}{1-2e^{-\sigma_1 D}(\cos\omega_1 D)z^{-1}+e^{-2\sigma_1 D}z^{-2}}. \qquad (6.79)$$

This relation can be programmed for a minimum of two multiplications as shown in Fig. 6.36b. The origin of the configuration of Fig. 6.36b is easily seen by noting the output $e_0(z)$ is given by

$$e_0(z)=(2e^{-\sigma_1 D}\cos\omega_1 D)(z^{-1}e_0-e_i)$$
$$-(e^{-2\sigma_1 D})(z^{-2}e_0-e_i)+e_i,$$

where, as before, z^{-1} is the delay operator e^{-sD}.

The reciprocal of $F(z)$ has zeros where $F(z)$ has poles, so that the sampled-data equivalent of a simple complex conjugate zero is the reciprocal of Eq. (6.77)

$$\frac{1}{F(z)}=\left(\frac{\omega_1}{\sigma_1^2+\omega_1^2}\right)\left[\frac{1-2e^{-\sigma_1 D}(\cos\omega_1 D)z^{-1}+e^{-2\sigma_1 D}z^{-2}}{e^{-\sigma_1 D}z^{-1}\sin\omega_1 D}\right]. \qquad (6.80)$$

This response is physically unrealizable because the z^{-1} in the denominator implies an output prior to an input. Multiplication by z^{-1} to incur a unit sample delay does not alter the s-plane zero positions and makes the transmission function realizable by the digital operations shown in Fig. 6.37. As in the sampled data pole-pair, the frequency data ω_1 and the bandwidth control σ_1 are supplied to the multipliers. As with the digital resonator, it is practically convenient to have unity gain at zero frequency. The final gain multiplication in Fig. 6.37 can therefore be alternatively made $(1-2e^{-\sigma_1 D}\cos\omega_1 D+e^{-2\sigma_1 D})^{-1}$ to correspond to the reciprocal of the practical resonator shown in Fig. 6.36b and in Eq. (6.79).

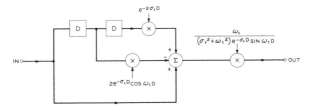

Fig. 6.37. Digital operations for simulating a single anti-resonance (zero-pair)

These basic pole and zero operations have been used to simulate a complete formant-vocoder synthesizer on a digital computer. One configuration of the synthesizer is shown in Fig. 6.38 (FLANAGAN, COKER, and BIRD). Voiced sounds are generated by the top branch which contains four variable poles and one variable zero. A fixed pole, not shown in the diagram, is included for high-frequency compensation. For vowels the final pole-zero pair is tuned coincidently so that its combined transmission is unity. Three poles therefore represent vowel spectra, in accordance with the acoustic relations developed in Section 3.7. For voiced nonvowels, such as the nasals, the final pole-zero pair is parted and positioned to represent relations given in Section 3.76. In general the pole-zero pair does not critically influence perception, provided the formant data are accurate, but is largely important to obtain realistic overall shape of the synthesized spectrum. Fundamental frequency, $F0$, and amplitude of voicing, A_v, are also controlled.

The unvoiced sounds are produced by the lower branch composed of one zero and either one or two poles. The amplitude of the noise is controlled by A_n. As Figs. 6.36 and 6.37 indicate, control of frequencies ω_n and bandwidths σ_n is effected by supplying these values to the multiplying elements in the digital circuits. Image poles, produced at multiples of the sampling frequency [see Eq. (6.78)] make further correction for higher vocal resonances unnecessary. This feature, which must be

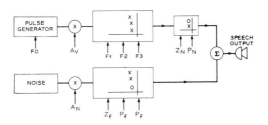

Fig. 6.38. Block diagram of a computer-simulated speech synthesizer.
(After FLANAGAN, COKER and BIRD)

treated explicitly in analog synthesizers (see Section 6.221), comes free in the digital representation.

A typical listing of control data — as supplied to the computer on punched cards — is shown in Table 6.1. The data represent approximately 1 sec of synthetic speech. The first column is time in tens of milliseconds; the second, pitch in cps; the next two columns, relative amplitudes of buzz and hiss; and finally, the pole and zero frequencies in cps. Each value entered in the table is held by the circuit until a new value is specified. The control functions are interpolated between specified values in 2.5 msec steps. The sampling rate for the simulation is

Table 6.1. *Typical listing of control data for the computer-simulated synthesizer of Fig. 6.38*

Time	Pitch	A_V	A_N	F_1	F_2	F_3	P_N	Z_N	Z_F	P_F
−20	107		0	170	1 290	2 190	750	1 000	1 750	3 500
4										
5		100								
7				180	1 260	2 170	850	950		
8				210	1 470	2 270	900	900		
9				390	1 550	2 300				
10				400	1 620	2 380				
11					1 690	2 410				
12					1 700	2 460				
19					1 690	2 500				
23				410	1 510	2 430				
24				350	1 490	2 410				
25				300	1 475	2 400				
26				250	1 490					
28				230	1 510					
32				215	1 620	2 390				
35				210	1 700	2 330				
36		0	25							
37							610	610		
41									1 655	3 310
46									1 500	2 950
47									1 400	2 800
48			0	320	1 420	1 800				
51										
52			25						975	1 950
54									960	1 920
56	120								925	1 850
57		100	0							
58	118				1 390	1 750				
61	112			450	1 200	1 700				
65	107			600	1 140	1 710				
70				690	1 115	1 910				
72				700	1 150	2 000				
78					1 305	2 070				

$1/D = 10$ KC. A spectrogram of synthetic speech produced from such data is shown in Fig. 6.39. Also shown is the original speech from which the control functions were derived.

Digitally-simulated formant synthesizers—implemented either by programmed operations in general-purpose computers or as special-purpose digital hardware—have been used in a variety of forms (for example, KELLY and GERSTMAN; FLANAGAN, COKER and BIRD; RABINER;

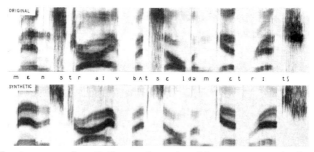

Fig. 6.39. Spectrograms of synthetic speech produced by a computer-simulated formant synthesizer and of the original utterance. (After FLANAGAN, COKER and BIRD)

RABINER, SCHAFER and FLANAGAN). Analog hardware synthesizers, controlled by digital computers, have over the past had even more extensive use (for example, COKER and CUMMISKEY; HOLMES, MATTINGLY and SHEARME; DIXON and MAXEY; LEE; KATO; NAKATA; FUJISAKI). Digital implementations, however, have distinct advantages in stability and accuracy, and current advances in digital circuitry make commitment to full digital operation irresistible (RABINER et al., 1971).

Much of the formant synthesis work over the past several years has made extensive use of interactive laboratory computers (see, for example, various work referenced in FLANAGAN et al., 1970). Especially valuable have been small interactive computers of integrated circuit design. Their ability for high-speed arithmetic and logic operations, and their ability to store sizeable amounts of information (both in primary and secondary memories) has substantially aided work in speech analysis and synthesis (FLANAGAN, 1971). The interactive computer has become a common laboratory tool, and as digital technology continues to develop, laboratory computers will expand in sophistication and utility.

Formant synthesizers, digitally implemented or controlled, have been used in many studies of speech synthesis-by-rule and in computer synthesis from stored formant data. In synthesis-by-rule, discrete symbols representing each speech phoneme, its duration and pitch are supplied as input. Each specified phoneme calls up from storage a set of formant values appropriate to that phoneme. Transitions of the formant and excitation functions from one phoneme to another are determined by stored rules designed to approximate the constraints of natural speech. The ultimate in synthesis-by-rule is to convert printed language to speech.

Several studies have treated the problem of converting printed English to continuous speech (TERANISHI and UMEDA; COKER and UMEDA; COKER, UMEDA and BROWMAN; LEE; ALLEN). In one of these (COKER, UMEDA and BROWMAN) a computer program uses a pronouncing dictionary to convert printed English text into discrete phonemic symbols, each carrying its own modifiers for pitch and duration. The text conversion is accomplished through a programmed syntax analysis and a prosodic feature determination. A dynamic model of the vocal tract (shown previously in Fig. 5.38) responds to the discrete phoneme commands to produce sequences of area changes similar to the real vocal tract. A difference equation solution of the Webster horn equation is periodically made to obtain continuous formant (eigenfrequency) data, and the latter are used to control a digital formant synthesizer to produce the synthetic speech.

A result of the automatic conversion of printed English into discrete control symbols for the synthesizer is shown in Table 6.2. These con-

Table 6.2. *Discrete control symbols for synthesis from printed text.* (After COKER, UMEDA and BROWMAN)

English text	Syntax and prosodic rules output
the	4dh 4a
north	6n $4aw 2er 6th
wind	6w *qq5i 4n 4d
and	4aa −n −d
the	−dh 4a
sun	6s *qq5uh 6n
were	4w 4er
arguing	4: $q6ah −r −g y 4uu 4i 6ng
one	4w &5uh 4n
day	6d *q9ay qq9<
,	$,
when	2h 2w &5eh 4n
a	4a
traveler	4t 4tr *q7aa −v 4o −l 4er
came	4k &4ay 4< 4m
along	4a 4l 8aw 4ng
,	$,
wrapped	6r $q8aa 4p 4t
in	4i −n
a	4a
warm	6w $5ah 2er 6m
coat	6k *q2oh qq2oh 6t

trol symbols actuate articulatory motions in the vocal tract model of
Fig. 5.38. The resulting synthetic output, compared with a similar
human utterance is shown in Fig. 6.40. Formant motions, word durations and pitch are seen to be realistically similar to natural speech.

In synthesis from stored formant data, libraries of formant-analyzed
words, phrases or syllables reside in the machine along with rules for
concatenating these elements into connected speech (RABINER, SCHAFER

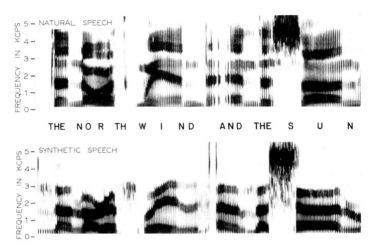

Fig. 6.40. Spectrograms comparing natural speech synthesized directly from printed text.
(After COKER, UMEDA and BROWMAN)

and FLANAGAN). This approach has the advantage of using naturally-
spoken signals to derive the so-called "segmental" information (i.e.,
the vocal resonances) rather than calculating these data. Additional
storage is the price paid.

Input to the system is the English text for the word string to be
generated, as illustrated in Fig. 6.41. From the library of words, stored
as control functions for a formant synthesizer, the program selects and
concatenates the sequence demanded. Formant functions must be interpolated naturally, word durations must be adjusted and pitch variations
must be calculated for the connected utterance. The resulting control
parameters are supplied to the formant synthesizer for conversion to
speech.

Fig. 6.42 illustrates one technique of concatenating formant-analyzed
words. At the top is a naturally-spoken sentence. At the bottom is a
sentence produced from the same words spoken in isolation, formant

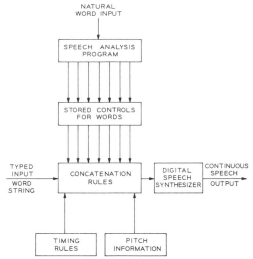

Fig. 6.41. Programmed operations for synthesis from stored formant data.
(After RABINER, SCHAFER and FLANAGAN)

WE WERE AWAY A YEAR AGO

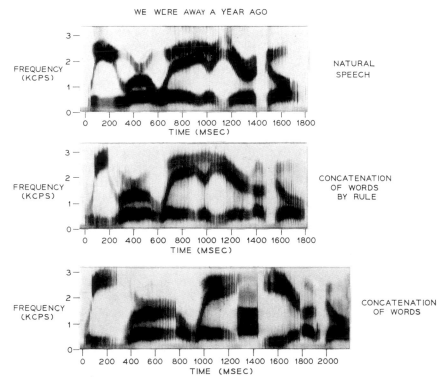

Fig. 6.42. Computer synthesis by concatenation of formant coded words.
(After RABINER, SCHAFER and FLANAGAN)

analyzed and synthesized, and merely abutted in sequence. The differences are obvious and marked. The center is the result of concatenation of the same isolated words, but where the program imposes formant interpolation, word duration and pitch according to stored rules. The result is much more like the natural signal. In particular one can examine the effects on the /ə/ vowel in "... away *a* year ...", seen at about 1000 msec in the top spectrogram. Mere abuttment renders this particularly badly at about 1400 msec in the bottom spectrogram. By rule, however, in the middle spectrogram, the sound is produced relatively well at about 1000 msec. This method of concatenation has been used successfully as an automatic answer back system for speaking seven-digit telephone numbers (RABINER, SCHAFER and FLANAGAN).

Synthesis-by-rule and concatenation methods both depend critically upon the adequacy of rules for calculating prosodic information; i.e., duration, pitch and intensity variations. This problem represents a whole field of study in itself, and it is the focus of considerable interest in phonetics research.

6.262. Digital Techniques for Vocal Tract Simulation. Formant synthesizers represent the input-output characteristics of the vocal tract. For this reason they are sometimes called "terminal" analogs. In many instances it is desirable to represent the distributed nature of the vocal system. Such representation is particularly important in efforts to model articulatory dynamics of speech (where the primary input data are physiological factors, such as the area function).

Distributed aspects of the system can be treated directly in terms of the wave-equation for one-dimensional wave propagation in a non-uniform pipe [i.e., WEBSTER's horn equation, Eq. (3.1)], or in terms of bilateral transmission-line models of the system (see Section 6.23). In the first instance, steady-state solutions can be used to obtain the un-damped eigen (formant) frequencies of non-nasal sounds, and transient solutions can be used to compute pressure and volume velocity distributions as functions of time. The Webster equation is

$$\frac{\partial^2 p}{\partial x^2} + \frac{1}{A} \frac{\partial p}{\partial x} \frac{\partial A}{\partial x} = \frac{1}{c^2} \frac{\partial^2 p}{\partial t^2}, \qquad (6.81)$$

where $p = p(x, t)$ is the sound pressure as a function of distance and time and $A(x)$ is the vocal tract area as a function of distance[1]. For steady-state behavior $p = p(x) e^{j\omega t}$.

---

[1] The volume velocity satisfies an analogous equation

$$A \frac{\partial}{\partial x} \left(\frac{1}{A} \frac{\partial U}{\partial x} \right) = \frac{1}{c^2} \frac{\partial^2 U}{dt^2}.$$

For convenient numerical solution on a computer, the differential equation can be approximated by a difference equation. A number of possibilities exist for making the approximation. Consider space to be quantized into uniform small intervals $\Delta x = l$. Let a central second difference approximate the second derivatives and a first back difference approximate the first derivative, i.e.,

$$\frac{d^2 f(x)}{dx^2}\bigg|_{x=x_i} = \left(\frac{f_{i+1} - 2f_i + f_{i-1}}{l^2}\right)$$

and

$$\frac{df(x)}{dx}\bigg|_{x=x_i} = \left(\frac{f_i - f_{i-1}}{l}\right). \tag{6.82}$$

Then the steady-state pressure at point $x = x_{i+1}$ can be written as the recursion formula

$$p_{i+1} = \left[p_i\left(1 - \frac{\omega^2 l^2}{c^2} + \frac{A_{i-1}}{A_i}\right) - \left(\frac{A_{i-1}}{A_i}\right)p_{i-1}\right]. \tag{6.83}$$

This formulation has been used to calculate the undamped eigenfrequencies of the non-uniform tract (COKER, 1968). Typical boundary conditions for the pressure are $p_{\text{glottis}} \neq 0$, $p_{\text{mouth}} = 0$. Assuming non-zero pressure at the glottis, the pressures at successive points along the tract are calculated from the recursion formula. By iteration, the value of ω is found that satisfies the mouth boundary. Convergence to the eigenfrequencies is facilitated by observing the number of pressure nodes along the tract which a given value of ω produces. That is, the first eigenfrequency corresponds to a quarter-wave resonance with no pressure nodes along tract; and the second formant to a three-quarter wave resonance with one node. This computation is repeated periodically as the $A(x)$ function changes with time.

It is relevant to note that the difference equation (6.83), so formulated, corresponds to representing the tract by a simple L-section ladder network with the LC elements shown in Fig. 6.43. The node equation relating the pressures p_{i-1}, p_i, p_{i+1} is identical to Eq. (6.83).

Another technique, useful for digital calculation of the transient sound pressure along the vocal tract, is a representation in terms of reflection coefficients (KELLY and LOCHBAUM). This approach depends upon initially approximating the non-uniform pipe by right-circular elements and assuming plane-wave propagation in each section, as discussed in Chapter 3.

Consider a plane wave moving from the left in the pipe shown in Fig. 6.44a and encountering an impedance discontinuity at $x = 0$. The

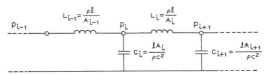

Fig. 6.43. Ladder network corresponding to a difference-equation approximation of the Webster wave equation

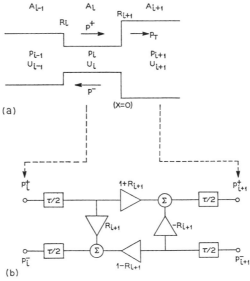

Fig. 6.44a and b. Representation of an impedance discontinuity in terms of reflection coefficients

steady-state pressure and volume velocity in the left tube must satisfy

$$p_i(x)=(p^+ e^{-jkx}+p^- e^{jkx})$$

$$U_i(x)=\frac{1}{Z_i}(p^+ e^{-jkx}-p^- e^{jkx}),\qquad(6.83)$$

where p^+ and p^- are the magnitudes of plane progressive waves moving to the right and the left respectively in the tube section with area A_i, $k=\omega/c$ and Z_i is the characteristic impedance of the left tube. (The pressure and particle velocity in a plane wave are linked by $dp/dx= -j\omega\rho u$.) Since pressure and volume velocity are continuous at the boundary,

$$p_i(0)=p_{i+1}(0)=(p^+ +p^-)$$

$$U_i(0)=U_{i+1}(0)=\frac{1}{Z_i}(p^+ -p^-),\qquad(6.84)$$

where the subscripts i and $i+1$ correspond to the tube elements A_i and A_{i+1}. If the right-hand tube were infinitely long with characteristic impedance Z_{i+1}, a plane wave transmitted and continuing to the right would have magnitude $p_T = (p^+ + p^-)$ and must satisfy

$$\frac{p_T}{U_{i+1}} = Z_{i+1} = \frac{Z_i(p^+ + p^-)}{(p^+ - p^-)}. \tag{6.85}$$

Then, the left-going wave in the left pipe is

$$p^- = \left(\frac{Z_{i+1} - Z_i}{Z_{i+1} + Z_i}\right) p^+ = R_{i+1} p^+$$

and

$$p_T = (p^+ + p^-) = (1 + R_{i+1}) p^+, \tag{6.86}$$

where R_{i+1} is the reflection coefficient at the junction of A_i and A_{i+1}. If the tubes are lossless, their characteristic impedances are real

$$Z_i = \rho c / A_i; \quad Z_{i+1} = \rho c / A_{i+1}$$

and

$$R_{i+1} = \left(\frac{A_i - A_{i+1}}{A_i + A_{i+1}}\right). \tag{6.87}$$

For a plane wave coming originally from the right, instead of the left, the sign of R_{i+1} is changed.

The Eq. (6.86) can therefore be used to represent each junction in a cascade of right-circular elements which approximate the non-uniform tract. The relations for right and left going waves are given in Fig. 6.44b, where the delay τ is the transit time through each section, $\tau = l/c$, and the unilateral amplifier boxes denote multiplication by the indicated parameters. (The $\tau/2$ delays can be lumped into single τ delays, one in the lower branch, one in the upper branch without altering the behavior.)

For any section of the quantized pipe, recursion equations describe the transient values of the (+) and (−) waves. The temporal sampling times correspond to the transit times through the uniform sections. Using i as the spatial index and j as the temporal index, the difference equations are

$$p_{i,j}^+ = -R_i p_{i,j-1}^- + p_{i-1,j-1}^+(1 + R_i)$$

$$p_{i,j}^- = R_{i+1} p_{i,j-1}^+ + p_{i+1,j-1}^-(1 - R_{i+1}) \tag{6.88}$$

$$p_{i,j} = (p_{ij}^+ + p_{ij}^-),$$

or, more conveniently for digital computation,

$$p_{i+1, j}^{+} = R_{i+1}(p_{i, j-1}^{+} - p_{i+1, j-1}^{-}) + p_{i, j-1}^{+}$$

$$p_{i, j}^{-} = R_{i+1}(p_{i, j-1}^{+} - p_{i+1, j-1}^{-}) + p_{i+1, j-1}^{-}. \qquad (6.89)$$

The last pipe element of the line terminates in a load that is the radiation impedance of the mouth. Let A_L be the area of the last pipe element and Z_L the terminating radiation load. At the load terminals (the end of pipe A_L), the right-going and left-going pressure waves satisfy

$$\frac{p_L}{U_L} = Z_L = \frac{A_L(p_L^{+} + p_L^{-})}{\rho c (p_L^{+} - p_L^{-})}.$$

If Z_L is written in terms of a z-transform, the reflected wave p_L^{-} can be obtained in terms of weighted and delayed values of p_L^{+}; that is, a reflection coefficient relation can be set down in which $p_L^{-} = p_L^{+} f(z^{-1})$. The load pressure $(p_L^{+} + p_L^{-})$ produces a mouth volume velocity U_L through Z_L, which, when differentiated, represents the radiated pressure. Formulations such as these have been used in a phoneme-driven vocal-tract synthesizer (KELLY and LOCHBAUM) and in a simulation of articulatory activity (MERMELSTEIN).

A further useful approach for digital representation of the distributed vocal tract follows the bilateral transmission line developed in Chapter III. Once the line composed of elemental T or π sections is set down, transient solutions of pressure and volume velcoity along the line may be obtained from difference equation approximations to the differential equations for the network. Area variations are reflected in network element changes. This approach also permits duplication of absolute acoustic impedances. For this reason it has been used in a vocal-tract synthesizer to study the acoustics of vocal-cord vibration and turbulent sound generation (FLANAGAN and CHERRY; see Section 6.243).

VII. Perception of Speech and Speech-Like Sounds

As a general topic, auditory perception can be divided a number of ways. From the standpoint of communication, one separation might be between classical auditory psychophysics, on the one hand, and the recognition of acoustic signals presented within a linguistic framework, on the other. The former relates principally to the abilities and limitations of the hearing organ as a mechano-neural transducer of all acoustic signals. The latter bears mainly upon the identification and classification of auditory patterns which are significant within the communicative experience of the listener.

Classical auditory psychophysics strives to discover the "resolving power" of the hearing mechanism. Discrimination is usually examined along fundamental dimensions of the stimulus—usually along only one dimension at a time. The measurements are generally conducted under conditions which are most favorable for making the relevant discriminations, that is, differential discriminations or close comparisons. Differential thresholds for dimensions such as intensity and frequency fall into this classification. Intuitively one feels that large neural storage and complex central processing probably are not brought into play in such detections. The measures more likely reflect the capacity of the transducer and the peripheral neural net to preserve details about a given stimulus dimension. The discussion in Chapter IV, for example, touched upon these properties of the peripheral system. The apparent relations between physiological and psychoacoustic response were analyzed for several stimulus cases. The acoustic signals were of the "classical" type in that they were either temporally punctate or spectrally simple, or both.

Speech, on the other hand, is a multidimensional signal that elicits a linguistic association. For it to be an effective communication code, some sort of absolute perceptual categorization must be made of its content. That is, the signal must be broken down into a finite number of discrete message elements. The "size" of these perceptual elements, and the manner in which they are processed to yield the percept, are questions of considerable debate and not little speculation. Our present knowledge brings us nowhere near a good understanding of the process. Theorizing about speech perception—cloaked in all of its linguistic and over-learned functions—abounds with pitfalls. An even larger problem, perhaps, is reconciling physiological, psychophysical and linguistic factors. As in other difficult situations, it is tempting to push back to some still-higher center the final decision-making process that is the real seat of perception.

Although a complete theory of speech perception remains in the future, a good deal can be said about auditory discrimination. Some of the "classical" measurements relate strongly to signal dimensions important to speech—even though the measurements are made outside of linguistic or contextual frames. In addition, a respectable amount of information has been accumulated on the acoustic cues associated with synthetic approximants to simple speech elements—for example, syllables and phonemes.

From the practical point of view, articulation tests and intelligibility measures based upon absolute recognition of sentences, words, syllables, and isolated phonemes can be used to good effect in evaluating transmission facilities. For a given processing of the voice signal, these tests often help to identify factors upon which perception depends (although they serve poorly, if at all, in supplying a description of the perception process itself). Under certain conditions, the so-called articulation index can be used to compute intelligibility scores from physical measurements on the transmission system. Still ancillary to intelligibility testing, some data are available on the influences of linguistic, contextual and grammatical constraints. Contrariwise, measures of the prosodic and quality features of speech are not well established.

The present chapter proposes to circumscribe some of these problems. In particular, the aim is to indicate current level of understanding in the perception of speech and speech-related sounds.

7.1. Differential vs. Absolute Discrimination

Classical psychophysics generally deals with discriminations made in close comparison. Speech perception, on the other hand, seems more likely an absolute classification of an acoustic signal. Can the former provide useful information about the latter, or vice versa?

Man is highly sensitive to differences in the frequency or intensity of sounds presented for comparison. Under certain conditions the threshold for detecting a difference in the frequencies of two successively presented pure tones may be as small as one part in 1000 (ROSENBLITH and STEVENS). The threshold for detecting a difference in intensity may be less than one db (RIESZ). On the basis of comparative judgments, it has been estimated that the normal listener can distinguish about 350000 different tones (STEVENS and DAVIS).

Contrasting with this acute differential sensitivity, a listener is relatively inept at identifying and labelling sounds presented in isolation. When equally-loud pure tones are presented individually for absolute judgment of frequency, listeners are able to accomplish perfect identification among only five different tones (POLLACK). This identification corresponds to an information transfer of about 2.3 bits per stimulus presentation. If, however, the sound stimulus is made multidimensional, for example by quantizing it in frequency, loudness, duration, etc., the correct identifications increase, and the information transferred may be as high as five to seven bits per stimulus presentation (POLLACK and FICKS). This rate is equivalent to correct identification from an ensemble of from 32 to 128 stimuli.

It is clear that absolute and differential discriminations yield substantially different estimates of man's informational capacity. The former suggest that few subdivisions along a given dimension can be identified, whereas the latter indicate that a much larger number may be discriminated. The differential measure, however, reflects the ability to discriminate under the most favorable circumstances for detecting a difference (namely, a close comparison usually along a single dimension). In a sense, it represents an upper bound on the resolving ability of the perceptual mechanism.

So far as absolute judgments are concerned, the differential estimate of discrimination is an optimistic one. The probability is extremely small that stimulus quantizations as small as a difference limen[1] could ever be detected absolutely. Even so, differential measures quantify perception in a "clinical" way, and they place a rough ceiling (albeit over-optimistic) on the ability to detect changes in a signal. In any speech processing system, fidelity criteria based upon differential discriminations would be expected to be very conservative. Lacking more directly applicable measures, however, they can often be useful in estimating the performance and channel capacity requirements of a transmission system (FLANAGAN, 1956 b).

7.2. Differential Discriminations Along Signal Dimensions Related to Speech

The results of Chapter III and IV suggest that significant dimensions for the speech signal might be defined in either the acoustic or articulatory domains. Both domains have perceptual correlates. The analyses in Chapter III, for example, attempted to separate the properties of vocal transmission and excitation. Perceptually-important acoustic dimensions of the system function are those of the mode pattern—that is, the complex frequencies of the poles and zeros of the transmission. Alternatively, the same information is specified by the bandwidths and frequencies of the maxima and minima of the amplitude spectrum and by the values of the phase spectrum. In a similar manner, relevant dimensions of the excitation source for voiced sounds are intensity, fundamental frequency and perhaps spectral zero pattern (or equivalently, glottal wave asymmetry and duty factor). For the unvoiced source, intensity and duration are significant dimensions.

Auditory sensitivity to some of these factors—divorced of any linguistic or contextual frame—has been measured in psychoacoustic experiments. For example, data are available on just-discriminable changes in formant frequency, fundamental frequency, over-all intensity and formant bandwidth. Without going into the details of any specific experiment, the nature of the results can be summarized.

7.21. Limens for Vowel Formant Frequencies

Using synthetic vowel sounds generated by a terminal-analog synthesizer (see Section 6.22, Chapter VI), just-discriminaable changes in

---

[1] The terms difference limen (DL) and just-noticeable difference (JND) are synonomous with differential threshold or just-discriminable change.

the frequencies of the first and second formants have been measured (FLANAGAN, 1955b). The synthesizer was operated as it would be used in a formant-vocoder system. Although the difference limens (DL's) depend to an important extent upon the proximity of the formants, they are found to be on the order of three to five percent of the formant frequency[1].

7.22. Limens for Formant Amplitude

The results of Chapter III and VI show that the relative amplitude of a given formant in the speech signal is a function of several factors, among them formant frequency, vocal damping, transmission zeros and excitation characteristics. One measure of the differential discriminability of formant amplitude has been made with a parallel-connected, terminal-analog synthesizer (FLANAGAN, 1957a). The intensity limen for the second formant of a near-neutral vowel (/æ/) is found to be about 3 db.

A related measurement of the limen for over-all intensity of a synthetic vowel gives a value of about 1.5 db (FLANAGAN, 1955a). Because the first formant is usually the most intense formant in vowel sounds, the over-all figure might be taken as a rough estimate of the first-formant intensity limen.

Another experiment determined the intensity limens for single harmonic components of synthetic vowels (FLANAGAN, 1965). Values found for intensity changes at the first and second formant frequencies support well the values just mentioned. Intensity limens for harmonic components located in spectral "valleys" can be quite large, as much as $+13$ db to $-\infty$ db, i.e., complete absence.

7.23. Limens for Formant Bandwidth

Apparently, no direct measures of the discriminability of changes in formant bandwidth, or damping, have been made on synthetic vowels. However, some related measurements, and their extrapolations, suggest what might be expected.

STEVENS (1952) measured the descriminability of changes in the tuning and damping of a single electrical resonator. The resonator was excited by periodic pulses at a fundamental frequency of 125 cps. The output signal was therefore representative of a one-formant vowel. In

---

[1] This experiment considered changes in the frequency of only one formant at a time. In real speech—and in formant-coding of speech—the formants usually move simultaneously. A relevant and practically-useful extention of the experiment might be the determination of "DL solids" in $F1-F2-F3$ space. Proximity effects of the formants should, in general, give these "solids" ellipsoidal shapes. Similar comments about discrimination of simultaneous changes in signal dimensions apply in several of the following experiments.

general, changes on the order of 20 to 40% in formant bandwidth were just-discriminable.

Also, the results of Chapter III show that the amplitude of a formant peak is inversely related to formant damping. The 1.5 db figure found for the amplitude limen of the first formant corresponds to a bandwidth change of about 20%. Similarly, the 3 db figure for the second formant corresponds to a bandwidth change of about 40%[1].

7.24. Limens for Fundamental Frequency

Following an experimental procedure similar to that used with the formant measurements, a difference limen has been measured for the fundamental excitation frequency of synthetic vowel sounds (FLANAGAN and SASLOW). For synthetic vowels appropriate to a man, the funda-mental-frequency limen is found to be about 0.3 to 0.5 per cent of the fundamental-frequency. From this and the previously-mentioned meas-urements, a hierarchy in frequency acuity emerges. The formant-fre-quency limen is an order of magnitude more acute than the formant-bandwidth limen, and the fundamental-frequency limen is an order of magnitude more acute than the formant-frequency limen.

7.25. Limens for Excitation Intensity

For a given glottal wave shape and vocal transmission, the over-all intensity of a voiced sound is directly proportional to the amplitude of the glottal pulse. As mentioned previously, a measure of the limen for over-all vowel intensity gives a value of about 1.5 db.

Similarly, the over-all intensity of an unvoiced sound is directly related to the amplitude of the unvoiced source. Fricative consonants are relatively broadband, noise-excited, continuant sounds. The dis-criminability of changes in their over-all amplitude might be expected to be somewhat similar to that of wide-band noise. Intensity limens have been measured for the latter (G. A. MILLER, 1947). They are found to be of the order of 0.4 db for sensation levels above 30 db. The mini-mum perceptible intensity change is therefore about 5%. Only a few fricative consonants have relatively flat spectra, but the figure might be used as an order-of-magnitude estimate. Experience with speech synthesis confirms that it is a conservative figure.

7.26. Limens for Glottal Zeros

The differential discriminability of changes in the spectral zero pat-tern of the vocal cord source (see Section 6.24, Chapter VI), or in the

---

[1] Another multidimensional DL of interest might be that for simultaneous changes in formant bandwidth and frequency. In other words, one might determine DL "areas" in the complex-frequency plane for vocal tract poles.

detailed spectrum of the glottal wave, have, to the author's knowledge, been observed only informally (FLANAGAN, 1961 b). The glottal source may contribute significant factors to speech quality and to speaker recognition. Therefore, liminal measures of parameters such as the duty factor and asymmetry of the glottal wave could be valuable in establishing bounds on their importance to speech naturalness.

It is clear that if complex source zeros lie far enough away from the $j\omega$-axis of the frequency plane they have negligible effect on signal quality. One experiment in which only gross features of the source spectrum and waveform were preserved suggests that many temporal and spectral details are unimportant to quality (ROSENBERG) (see Section 6.241 h).

7.27. Discriminability of Maxima and Minima in a Noise Spectrum

The vocal tract transmission for fricative consonants, like other sounds, is characterized by certain poles and zeros. Broadband noise excitation is filtered by this transmission. Some of the poles and zeros (and their related spectral maxima and minima) are perceptually significant. Others are not. One measurement considered the differential discriminability of a single peak or valley in an otherwise flat noise spectrum (MALME). A single pole and zero filtering of a broadband noise was used to produce the spectral variations shown in the insert of Fig. 7.1. The equivalent complex frequencies (half-power bandwidths vs. center frequencies) of the irregularities which were just-detectable from the flat spectrum are also plotted in Fig. 7.1. The db numbers next to the points are the just-perceptible peak heights and notch depths, respectively. These data indicate that, at least in a flat-noise surround, spectral peaks with Q's (i.e., ratios of center frequency to bandwidth) less than about 5, and spectral notches with Q's less than about 8 are not differentially perceptible.

The results suggest, therefore, that many of the small spectral irregularities seen in a fricative consonant such as /f/ are not perceptually significant. In the same vein, certain spectral peaks such as in /s/ or /ʃ/ are of course significantly different from a flat spectrum. Synthesis of fricative consonants has been demonstrated by representing the spectrum in terms of two poles and one zero (HEINZ and STEVENS). Appropriate Q's for the poles are found in the range of about 5 to 13. For the zero, Q's of the order of 2 to 4 appear appropriate. The suggestion is, therefore, that to the extent the results in Fig. 7.1 can be applied, the poles are more significant perceptually than the zero, the latter apparently having importance only in contributing to the gross spectral shape.

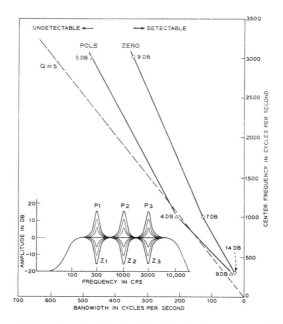

Fig. 7.1. Detectability of irregularities in a broadband noise spectrum. (After MALME)

This appears to be the case, for the zero has been found to be relatively noncritical of frequency position and often can be placed automatically about an octave below the first pole (HEINZ and STEVENS).

A similar discrimination measurement has been made for a noise spectrum with exactly periodic maxima — that is, for a comb filtering of the noise (ATAL and SCHROEDER). The objective was to investigate the preceptual effects of irregularities in the frequency response of rooms. The comb-filtered noise was differentially compared with white noise of equal power, and a limen was obtained for the minimum detectable periodic irregularity. The minimum detectable ratio of maximum-to-minimum spectral amplitude was found to be about one db. This figure is in close agreement with the intensity limen measured for white noise (see Section 7.25).

The results of this same experiment provide information on the weighting function used by the ear in performing its short-time spectral analysis. The weighting function deduced from the measurements is approximately exponential in form, with an initial slope corresponding to a time constant of 9 msec. This latter figure compares favorably with the time constant deduced for loudness measurements on periodic clicks (see Section 4.33, Chapter IV).

7.28. Other Close-Comparison Measures Related to Speech

A number of other psychophysical measurements relate, more or less strongly, to differential perception along speech dimensions. Several of these can be mentioned to illustrate the diverse nature of the data.

One experiment measured the perception of a single, time-varying formant (BRADY, HOUSE, and STEVENS). A continuously-tunable resonant circuit was excited by five equi-spaced pitch pulses. The pulses were produced at a rate of $100 \ sec^{-1}$. During the excitation, the tuning of the resonator was moved between 1000 and 1500 cps, according to the rising and falling trajectories shown in Fig. 7.2. The formant transitions were accomplished in 20 msec. To examine how the varying formant frequency is perceived, listeners were asked to adjust the frequency of a nontime-varying resonance until it sounded as much like the varying one as possible. Typical results of the matches are shown in Fig. 7.3. The test stimuli labelled a, b, c, d, e, and f correspond to those diagramed in Fig. 7.2. The data show a strong tendency to set the steady resonance to a frequency corresponding to the final value of the varying formant, particularly when the formant change occurs near the beginning of the sound. The tendency to match the final frequency appears somewhat stronger for stimuli in which the resonant frequency ascends.

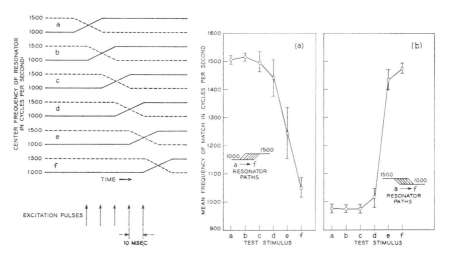

Fig. 7.2. Frequency paths and excitation pattern for a simulated time-varying formant. Rising and falling resonances are used. The epochs of the five excitation pulses are shown. (After BRADY, HOUSE and STEVENS)

Fig. 7.3a and b. Results of matching a nontime-varying resonance to the time-varying resonances shown in Fig. 7.2. Mean values are plotted. The vertical lines indicate the standard deviations of the matches. (After BRADY, HOUSE and STEVENS)

In a different vein, a temporal fine structure is known to exist in the glottal source. The shape and periodicity of the glottal pulse is subject to various perturbations which may be significant to speech quality. In a condition known as diplophonia, for example, alternate glottal pulses may be of different size (S. SMITH). Similarly, successive glottal periods may vary in duration. To quantify this effect, one study analyzed the durations of 7000 pitch periods of real speech (LIEBERMAN). In successive samples of three periods each, the variation in period was greater than ± 0.1 msec in 86% of the cases. In 20% of the cases the duration difference between periods was greater than 0.6 msec, and in 15% it was greater than 1.0 msec. In 38% of the cases the periods were alternately long and short. Adjacent periods were not correlated, but alternate periods were highly correlated.

As one step toward trying to understand the possible perceptual correlates of these factors, a preliminary investigation has examined the effects upon perceived pitch of systematic differences in amplitude and timing of an otherwise periodic pulse train (FLANAGAN, GUTTMAN, and WATSON; GUTTMAN and FLANAGAN, 1962). Among the conditions considered were the pulse wave forms shown in the left-hand column of Fig. 7.4. Starting with exactly periodic trains (of period $T/2$), alternate

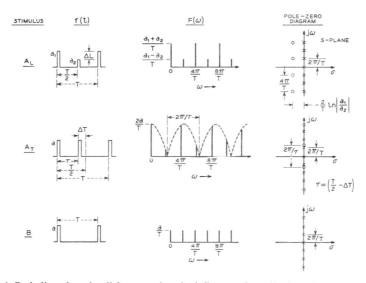

Fig. 7.4. Periodic pulse stimuli for assessing the influence of amplitude and time perturbations upon perceived pitch. The left column shows the time waveforms of the experimental trains; amplitude variation (A_L), time variation (A_T), and the standard matching train (B). The second column shows the corresponding amplitude spectra, and the third column shows the complex-frequency diagram. (After FLANAGAN, GUTTMAN and WATSON; GUTTMAN and FLANAGAN, 1962)

pulses in the train were changed incrementally either in amplitude level (Stimulus A_L) or in time of occurrence (Stimulus A_T). The effect upon pitch was assessed by having listeners adjust the frequency of a uniform, periodic train (Stimulus B) until its pitch matched that of the perturbed train. As either the amplitude difference (ΔL) or the time difference (ΔT) increases, a point is soon reached where the pitch drops by an octave.

The second column of Fig. 7.4 shows the frequency spectra of the amplitude-varied stimulus (A_L), the time-varied stimulus (A_T), and the standard matching stimulus (B). The third column of the figure shows the corresponding pole-zero diagrams for the three periodic trains. Notice that for the A_L signal the relative amplitudes of adjacent spectral lines are dependent only upon the pulse amplitudes a_1 and a_2. For A_T, on the other hand, the spectral amplitudes are conditioned by the fundamental period T and by the cycloidal envelope which, in turn, is determined by the interval τ.

Median matches made by a number of listeners for the ΔL and ΔT conditions are shown in Figs. 7.5a and 7.5b, respectively. In both plots the parameter is the pulse rate of the A stimulus (i.e., twice its fundamental frequency). The results in Fig. 7.5a for ΔL show that, over the frequency range appropriate to the human voice fundamental, an amplitude difference ΔL of about 6 to 8 db, or greater, will produce an octave reduction in the perceived pitch. In the same fashion, the ΔT data in Fig. 7.5b show that in the range of the voice fundamental (i.e., about 100 pps and above) a time shift $2\Delta T/T$ on the order of 0.1 or more, will produce an octave reduction in pitch.

7.29. Differential Discriminations in the Articulatory Domain

The acoustic dimensions considered for the speech and speech-like signals in the preceding discussion have counterparts in the articulatory domain. However, the acoustic and articulatory relations do not generally exist in one-to-one correspondence. For example, a change in a constriction size, or in its location, alters not only one formant frequency, but in general all of them (see Fig. 3.39, Chapter III). It is therefore difficult to interpret, say, limens for formant frequency and amplitude in terms of just-discriminable articulatory changes. One can, nevertheless, make some simple observations about the links between the domains.

The just-discriminable changes in formant frequency were found to be about three to five per cent. For a straight pipe the formants are approximately

$$F_n = \frac{(2n-1)c}{4l}, \qquad n = 1, 2, \dots .$$

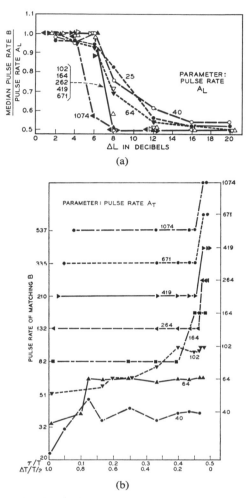

(a)

(b)

Fig. 7.5a and b. Results of matching the pitch of a uniform pulse train (B) to that of:
(a) a periodic train (A_L) whose alternate pulses differ in amplitude by ΔL; and (b) a periodic
train (A_T) whose alternate pulses are shifted in time by ΔT. In both cases the parameter
is the pulse rate of the A stimulus. (After FLANAGAN, GUTTMAN and WATSON; GUTTMAN
and FLANAGAN, 1962)

The sensitivity of the mode frequencies to length changes is

$$\partial F_n/\partial l = -\frac{(2n-1)c}{4l^2}, \quad \text{or} \quad \frac{F_n}{\Delta F_n} = -\frac{l}{\Delta l},$$

so that a given percentage change in the tract length l produces the same
percentage change in the formant frequencies. The DL for tract length

might therefore be expected to be roughly comparable, percentage-wise, to the formant frequency DL. By referring to Fig. 3.39, Chapter III, one can see other, more complex correspondences between formant changes and articulatory changes.

Another simple example is the sensitivity of the mode damping for a straight pipe to changes in the mean glottal area (see Eq. (3.74)). Assume for simplicity that the equivalent glottal impedance is purely resistive and is produced only by kinetic factors, that is,

$$R_g' = \frac{(2\rho P_{so})^{\frac{1}{2}}}{A_0}$$

[using the notation of see Eq. (3.51)]. The pole dampings (i.e., real parts) are given by

$$\sigma_n \cong -\left(\alpha c + \frac{Z_0 c}{l R_g}\right),$$

or

$$\sigma_n \cong -\left[\alpha c + \frac{c Z_0 A_0}{l(2\rho P_{so})^{\frac{1}{2}}}\right]$$

[see Eq. (3.74)]. The sensitivity of the damping with respect to mean glottal area is then

$$\frac{\partial \sigma_n}{\partial A_0} \cong -\frac{c Z_0}{l(2\rho P_{so})^{\frac{1}{2}}},$$

or the change in mode damping is approximately proportional to the change in mean glottal area.

7.3. Absolute Discrimination of Speech and Speech-Like Sounds

Most efforts to establish the acoustic cues for speech-sound recognition have been absolute identification experiments. The test stimuli have generally been synthetic versions of phoneme-length and syllable-length utterances. This approach presumably keeps the stimuli simplified to noncontextual situations where only the physical properties of the specific signal influence the percept. At the same time it may permit association of a linguistic structure, and the perceptual responses are usually interpreted within this frame of reference.

7.31. Absolute Identification of Phonemes

A relatively small number of experiments has dealt solely with isolated phonemes. One study—using a transmission-line vocal tract analog—investigated articulatory configurations appropriate to vowels. It tested a simple three-number articulatory description of vowel production (STEVENS and HOUSE, 1955; HOUSE and STEVENS, 1956). The three-number scheme for describing vowel articulation is illustrated for two configurations in Fig. 7.6. The three parameters used to describe the vocal shape are the radius of the maximum constriction, r_0; the distance from the glottis to the constriction, x_0; and the ratio of mouth area to lip rounding, A/l. The radius of the dashed portion of the tract is described by the function

$$r(x) = [0.025(1.2 - r_0)(x - x_0)^2 + r_0],$$

where the lengths are in centimeters.

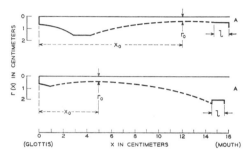

Fig. 7.6. Three-parameter description of vowel articulation. r_0 is the radius of the maximum constriction; x_0 is the distance from the glottis to the maximum constriction; and A/l is the ratio of mouth area to lip rounding. (After STEVENS and HOUSE, 1955)

An electrical transmission line simulated the configurations and synthesized the sounds. Isolated vowels, 500 msec in duration, were judged absolutely by listeners and placed into nine English vowel categories. Pitch was monotonically inflected from 120 to 140 cps. The listener responses in terms of articulatory parameters are illustrated for one value of constriction in Fig. 7.7. The two response contours indicate agreement among 50% and 75% of the responses, respectively. The PETERSON and BARNEY data for natural vowels uttered by men (see Fig. 5.10, Chapter V), when transformed into the same articulatory coordinates, are given in Fig. 7.8. The two plots show that, except for small differences, the three number description does surprisingly well in providing a unique specification of the vowels.

A somewhat similar experiment on synthesis and perception has been carried out for Japanese vowels (NAKATA and SUZUKI). In this experiment, however, the sounds were produced by a terminal-analog synthesizer, and the idea was to find the synthetic formant patterns appropriate to the vowels.

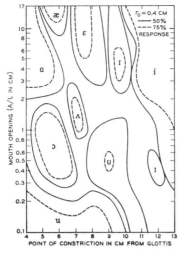

Fig. 7.7. Listener responses to isolated synthetic vowels described by the 3-parameter technique. One value of constriction is shown. Two levels of response corresponding to 50 and 75 % agreement among subjects are plotted. (After HOUSE and STEVENS, 1955)

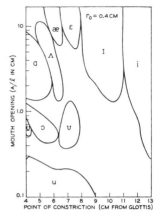

Fig. 7.8. Formant frequency data of PETERSON and BARNEY for 33 men transformed into the 3-parameter description of vowel articulation. (After HOUSE and STEVENS, 1955)

The same transmission-line analog—but with attached nasal tract—has been used to study the perception of nasal consonants (HOUSE). Isolated, 500 msec representations of nasal consonants were synthesized and presented to listeners for absolute judgment. The permissible response categories were the three nasal consonants /m, n, and η/. The articulatory description used for synthesis was similar to that described in the preceding discussion on vowels, but with the additional specification of the velar coupling. Typical confusion matrices of responses (to articulatory configurations which were determined by pre-tests to be representative nasal consonant stimuli) are shown in Table 7.1a.

Table 7.1. *Listener responses to synthetic and natural nasal consonants*

a) Synthetic				b) Natural			
Stimulus	Response %			Stimulus	Response %		
	m	n	η		m	n	η
m	81	11	8	m	96	4	0
n	33	61	6	n	42	56	2
η	20	18	62	η	60	28	12

a) Synthetic: Mean correct response = 68%.
b) Natural: Mean correct response = 55%.

While the responses to the synthetic nasal consonants do not look particularly decisive, they do compare favorably with similar measurements on natural nasal consonants (MALÉCOT). A confusion matrix for the latter are shown in Table 7.1 b. In this case the synthetic nasals are discriminated better than the natural ones! In view of the high functional load that nasals, particularly /n/, carry in connected speech (see Table 1.1, Chapter I), the low discrimination scores suggest that transitions, both from and into adjacent sounds, may be highly important to nasal perception.

7.32. Absolute Identification of Syllables

A substantial amount of research has considered the perception of isolated syllables. The effort has aimed mainly at discovering the acoustic cues important to phoneme recognition. Central to the objective is the determination of the separate contribution each acoustic variable makes to speech perception, as well as an understanding of how the contributions combine in the total percept. Much of the work points up the importance of acoustic environment upon perception; that is, the perception of a given phoneme can be strongly conditioned by its neighbors.

Among the leaders in this work has been the group at the Haskins Laboratories. Many of their experiments have used synthetic syllables generated by the pattern-playback machine. The operation of this synthesizer has been described in Chapter VI, and it is shown in Fig. 6.6. As explained in Section 6.21, the device synthesizes sound from data displayed as a conventional time-frequency-intensity spectrogram.

The nature of the experimentation is exemplified in consonant identification tests on CV syllables. The consonant used is either a voiced or voiceless stop. If it is voiceless (i.e., /p, t, k/), one of the variables that seems to enable listeners to differentiate the sounds is the position along the frequency scale of the brief burst of noise constituting the stop release. To isolate this particular cue and to determine its role in perception, schematized stop-vowel syllables such as shown in Fig. 7.9 c were synthesized (COOPER, DELATTRE, LIBERMAN, BORST and GERST-MAN). The noise burst (the small vertical ellipse in Fig. 7.9 c) was constant in bandwidth and duration, and the vowel was a two-formant vowel that was maintained steady throughout the syllable. Combinations of noise bursts and vowel formants shown in Figs. 7.9 a and b, respectively, produced the test ensemble.

The syllables were presented in isolation to listeners who were asked to judge the initial consonant either as /p, t or k/. The identifications, according to noise-burst location and vowel, are shown in Fig. 7.10. The contours indicate approximately equal response percentages, with the small contours representing the higher percentage response.

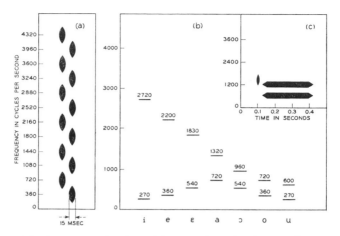

Fig. 7.9 a–c. Stimulus patterns for determining the effect of noise-burst frequency on the perception of voiceless stop consonants: (a) frequency positions of the noise bursts, (b) formant frequencies of the two-formant vowels; (c) one of the synthetic consonant-vowel syllables formed by pairing a noise burst of (a) with a two-formant vowel of (b).
(After Cooper, Delattre, Liberman, Borst and Gerstman)

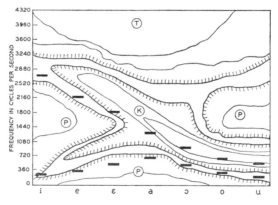

Fig. 7.10. Listener responses to the synthetic consonant-vowel syllables shown in Fig. 7.9.
(After Cooper et al.)

For these particular syllables, the one frequency variable (namely frequency of noise burst) appears adequate to distinguish the three consonants. High frequency bursts are heard as /t/ for all vowels. For /p/ and /k/ the identification depends not only upon frequency of burst but also on its relation to the vowel. Bursts on a level with the second formant, or slightly above, are heard as /k/; otherwise they are heard as /p/. The conclusion is advanced that the perception of these stimuli

—and perhaps their spoken counterparts—requires the CV combination (that is, the syllable) as a minimal acoustic unit. Without information on the following vowel, the consonant percept may be equivocal.

A second cue important in the perception of stop-consonants is the stop-vowel formant transitions. One relevant question is how might this cue and the former one of burst position contribute singly, and how might they combine. To get some indication of the answer, the same voiceless-stop and vowel syllables were generated as before, except the noise burst was eliminated and the consonant cue was produced solely by a transition of the second formant.

The ensemble of transitions tested is shown in Fig. 7.11. The transition numbers, N, ranging from -4 to $+6$, indicate the starting frequencies of the second formant. In terms of actual cps, the starting frequencie

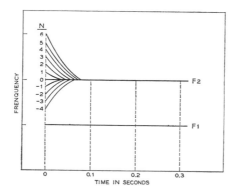

Fig. 7.11. Second-formant trajectories for testing the contribution of formant transitions to the perception of voiceless stop consonants. (After Cooper *et al.*)

are given by $[F2+N(120)]$ cps, where $F2$ is the steady-state second formant frequency of the two-formant vowels shown in Fig. 7.9[1]. The first formant was maintained constant at the values given in Fig. 7.9. The fundamental frequency of the sound was also held constant at 120 cps. The durations of the transitions were 40 msec for ± 1, and 80 msec for $+6$. For transitions in between, the durations varied linearly. The form of the transition curve is unspecified except that an effort was made to approximate the transitions seen in spectrograms of real speech. In the experience of the authors, variations in the duration

---

[1] An exception, apparently, was the negative $F2$ transitions of the vowels /o/ and /u/. This was $\left[F2+N\left(\dfrac{120}{2}\right)\right]$ (see Lieberman, Delattre, Cooper and Gerstman).

of the transition and its curvature do not cause the sound to change from one stop consonant to another.

The median /p, t, k/ responses of 33 listeners, for these transitions coupled with seven different vowels, are shown in Fig. 7.12. The lengths of the plotted bars show the quantile ranges of the responses. The results indicate that the second formant transition effectively cues the /p, t, k/ discrimination.

In extending this line of investigation to other consonants, the same authors found that the second formant cues also apply to the voiced

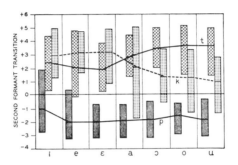

Fig. 7.12. Median responses of 33 listeners to stop consonant and vowel syllables generated by the patterns shown in Fig. 7.11. The bars show the quartile ranges. (After COOPER *et al.*)

cognates /b, d, g/. Distinctions between the voiced and unvoiced cognates are made by the first formant transition and by the voice bar. When vowel plus nasal-consonant syllables are generated in a similar manner, but with the formant transitions at the ends of the vowels and with an added, constant nasal resonance, the second formant transitions that serve to distinguish /p, t, k/ and /b, d, g/ also serve to distinguish /m, n, ʒ/ (LIBERMAN, DELATTRE, COOPER and GERSTMAN).

Returning to the syllables composed of voiceless stop and vowel, several remarks can be made. The two sets of results show the individual contributions of the noise burst in the stop release and the formant transition in the following vowel. The results do not, however, suggest how these cues combine and how they may relate to each other. One might expect that identification would be improved by the combined burst and transition cues, and that they might complement each other; when one is weak, the other might be strong. In some syllables both cues may not be sufficient, and a still different factor, such as third formant transition, may be vital to the discrimination.

The dependence of consonant perception upon the following vowel suggests to the authors that listeners perceive speech in acoustic units of syllable length or perhaps half-syllable length[1]. A one-to-one correspondence between sound and phoneme is not found, and the phoneme may not exist in the speech wave in a free form. Clearly, one should not expect to find absolute acoustic invariants for the individual phoneme.

The experiments of the preceding discussion concerned sounds generated from abstracted spectrograms and by a particular synthesizer. Similar experiments have aimed to determine the perceptual adequacy of other synthesizers and to examine the influence of still different acoustic cues upon recognition. One of these has treated the synthesis of isolated fricatives and fricative-vowel syllables (HEINZ and STEVENS). Fricative consonants were generated by filtering noise with a single pole-zero electrical circuit. The frequency of the zero was always maintained an octave below that of the pole. The object was to determine whether such an idealized spectral representation can elicit fricative responses, and further, to establish the ranges of pole-zero locations associated with the particular responses. (Recall from Chapter III that the mode pattern of fricatives usually involves a number of poles and zeros. Recall, too, that the discussion in Section 7.27 suggests that many of the modes may not be perceptually significant.)

In one test, fricative consonants were generated and tested in isolation. A range of tuning and bandwidth was explored for the pole and zero. Identifications were made from an ensemble of five phonemes; namely, /ʃ, ç, s, θ, and f/. The synthetic sounds were 200 msec in duration. The results show that different resonant bandwidths, ranging in Q from about 5 to 10, produce no significant changes in the fricative responses. Changes in tuning of the resonance, however, produce important differences in response. The effect is illustrated by the percentage response *vs* resonant frequency plotted in Fig. 7.13. The /f/ and /θ/ responses are combined.

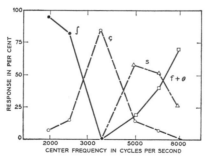

Fig. 7.13. Listener responses in absolute identification of synthetic fricatives produced by a pole-zero filtering of noise. The frequency of the pole is indicated on the abscissa, and the frequency of the zero is approximately one octave lower. (After HEINZ and STEVENS)

---

[1] This point, and other views on it, will be discussed further in Section 7.5.

Using the same synthetic fricatives, consonant-vowel syllables were synthesized with a terminal-analog synthesizer. The vowel used was always /ɑ/, and the syllable synthesized is illustrated by the schematic spectrogram in the upper part of Fig. 7.14. The timing sequence of control functions for the terminal-analog synthesizer is shown by the lower curves in Fig. 7.14. The first two curves show the build-up and decay characteristics of the noise (voiceless) and buzz (voiced) excitation. The third curve shows the timing of the formant transitions. The $F1$ vowel transition always started from 200 cps. The initial $F2$ value was either 900, 1700 or 2400 cps. Fricative resonances of 2500, 3500, 5000, 6500 and 8000 cps were used. Listeners were required to identify the initial consonant as /f, θ, s, or ʃ/.

The consonant judgments – as functions of the fricative resonance frequency and second-formant transition – are plotted in Fig. 7.15. The results for two ratios of consonant-to-vowel intensity are shown,

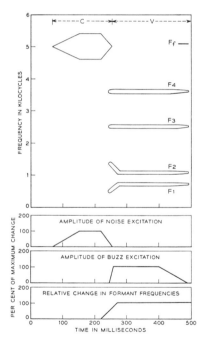

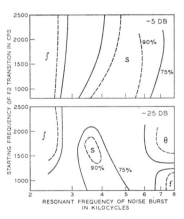

Fig. 7.14. Abstracted spectrogram showing the synthesis of a syllable with fricative consonant and vowel. The single fricative resonance is F_f. The four-formant vowel is an approximation of /ɑ/. The lower three curves represent the temporal variation of the excitation and formant frequencies in the syllable. (After HEINZ and STEVENS)

Fig. 7.15. Absolute identifications of the initial consonant in the synthetic syllable schematized in Fig. 7.14. Two response contours are shown corresponding to 90 and 75 % identification. Two consonant-to-vowel intensities (−5 and −25 db) are shown. (After HEINZ and STEVENS)

namely -5 db and -25 db. Two response contours are also shown. Inside the dashed lines the indicated fricative is responded in more than 90% of the presentations. Inside the solid lines the response is greater than 75%. The two consonant-to-vowel intensities dramatize the importance of relative level in the perception of $/\theta/$ and $/f/$, and to a lesser extent, $/s/$. The responses also suggest that the fricative $/f/$ is distinguished from $/\theta/$ largely on the basis of the $F2$ transition in the vowel. Contrariwise, the formant transition does not have much influence upon the $/s/$ and $/\int/$ discrimination, this being determined more by the frequency of the fricative resonance. Another study, closely related in form and philosophy to the present one, has been carried out for Japanese fricatives (NAKATA, 1960).

In much the same vein, other experiments have studied formant transitions with a transmission-line analog (STEVENS and HOUSE, 1956). The results show that low $F2$ loci (1 000 cps or less) are generally associated with bilabial or labio-dental articulatory configurations. On the other hand, $F2$ loci in the middle frequency range (1 500 to 2 000 cps) are associated with alveolar configurations, and $F2$ loci above 2 000 cps are associated with palatal configurations.

A still different approach to synthesis and perception is exemplified by the generation of connected speech from individual, spectrally-constant synthetic segments (COHEN and 'T HART). The segments are of phoneme length and are time-gated with prescribed build-up, decay and duration. From these results the suggestion is advanced that proper dimensioning of the time parameter makes it possible to neglect a number of details of formant information usually considered to be of paramount importance. It seems reasonably clear, however, that the ear accomplishes a short-time spectral analysis (see Chapter V) and that it appreciates continuous variations both in frequency and intensity. The "time parameter" view implies a trading relation of a sort between spectral information and temporal detail. Such a trade may in fact exist, but the extent to which it can be exploited may be limited. It would appear unlikely that high-quality, high-intelligibility speech could be consistently synthesized without taking account of mode transitions within phoneme-length segments.

7.33. Effects of Learning and Linguistic Association in Absolute Identification of Speech-Like Signals

It was suggested earlier that at least two limitations exist in applying classical psychophysical data to speech recognition. First, the classical measures are generally restricted to differential discriminations. Second, they are usually made along only one dimension of the stimulus. Speech, however, appears to be a multidimensional stimulus. Its perceptual units, whatever they might be—and they probably vary according to the detection task—are presumably perceived absolutely. At least one experiment has attempted to measure the effects of learning and linguistic association in absolute discriminations. The tests treated several dimensions of complex, speech-like sounds (HOUSE, STEVENS, SANDEL and ARNOLD).

Four different groups of stimuli (*A*, *B*, *C* and *D*), varying in their similarity to speech, were used. The stimuli of each group were further divided into subgroups. The signals of each subgroup were coded in a given number of dimensions. Each member of the subgroup was designed to convey three bits of information per presentation. The signals of the *A* group, for example, were produced by filtering random noise with a simple resonant circuit. They could be coded along time, frequency and intensity dimensions. Stimuli in subgroup *A*1 were coded unidimensionally in terms of 8 frequency positions of the noise resonance. The center frequency of the resonance varied from 500 to 5000 cps, and its corresponding bandwidth varied from 300 to 3120 cps. One intensity (namely, a reference intensity) and one duration (300 msec) were used. In contrast, stimuli of subgroup *A*7 were coded in terms of two frequency positions of the noise (820 or 3070 cps), two intensity values (± 8 db *re* *A*1), and two durations (150 or 450 msec). The subgroups *A*2 through *A*6 utilized different combinations of dimensions and quantizations between these extremes.

The *B* stimuli were also rudimentary signals but with slightly more speech-like properties. They had temporal and spectral properties roughly analogous to vowel-consonant syllables. The vowel element was produced by exciting a single resonant circuit with 125 pps pulses. The center frequency of the resonator was 300 cps and its bandwidth was 60 cps. The consonant portion was produced by exciting a simple resonant circuit with white noise. The coded dimensions of the *B* signals were center frequency and bandwidth of the noise portion (center frequencies 500 to 5000 cps, bandwidths 100 to 1000 cps); intensity of noise (± 14 db); and duration of the silent interval (gap) between the vowel and consonant (10 to 180 msec). The total duration was always 350 msec. Like the *A* group, set *B*1 was a one-dimensional coding and had eight frequency values, one intensity and one duration. Set *B*7 was a three-dimensional coding and had two frequencies, two intensities and two gap durations.

The *C* group was constructed to be still more similar to speech. It incorporated many of the characteristics of acceptable synthetic speech samples. Like *B*, the *C* stimuli were vowel-consonant syllables, but the vowel was generated from four resonators whose center frequencies were fixed at 500, 1500, 2500, and 3350 cps. Their bandwidths were approximately those of spoken vowels. The first formant was given a falling transition to the time gap, in analogy to the vowel-to-stop consonant transition. The consonant portion was generated by a single pole-zero filtering of noise, similar to the circuit described in the preceding section for producing fricative consonants (HEINZ and STEVENS). Voiced excitation during the vowel was inflected from 120 to 150 pps. The stimulus dimensions and the varied parameters were similar to those of the B signals. In set $C1$, the consonant resonance varied from 500 to 5000 in eight steps. The vowel duration was 250 msec, the gap 50 msec, and the consonant 100 msec. (Total duration was always 400 msec.) In set $C7$, the consonant dimensions of resonance, intensity and gap were all binary.

The D stimuli were real, monosyllabic speech utterances produced by one speaker. Only a single, three-dimensional subgroup was used. The eight syllables were composed of two vowels, /I/ and /Λ/, and four consonants /f, s, p, t/. Four of the eight syllables were monosyllabic English words, and four were nonsense syllables.

In the tests the stimuli were presented singly in isolation. Listeners were required to associate each with one of eight unlabelled buttons on a response panel. After the subject made his selection, one of eight lights on the panel flashed, indicating the correct button with which to associate the stimulus. The next sound was then presented. There was no speed requirement.

The results show how the median probability of correct identification increases with learning. Identification data from twelve listeners for the unidimensional, frequency-coded stimuli are shown in Fig. 7.16. Each test block involved the randomized presentation of sixteen items from a given (8-component) stimulus ensemble. The responses to the tri-dimensional stimuli are given in Fig. 7.17.

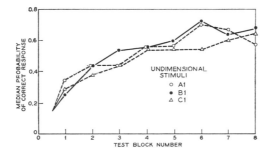

Fig. 7.16. Median probability of correct response for frequency-coded, one-dimensional stimuli. (After HOUSE, STEVENS, SANDEL and ARNOLD)

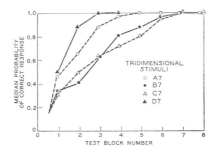

Fig. 7.17. Median probability of correct response for time-frequency-intensity coded three-dimensional stimuli. (After HOUSE, STEVENS, SANDEL and ARNOLD)

The two sets of results show that learning is more rapid for the tri-dimensional stimuli than for the one-dimensional items. Of the tri-dimensional signals, real speech ($D7$) is learned the fastest. The least speech-like artificial signal ($A7$) is learned the next fastest. The results suggest two conclusions. First, performance during learning is better when the stimuli are coded in several physical dimensions than when they lie along a unidimensional continuum. Second, as the physical characteristics of the stimuli are made more similar to speech, there is a deterioration of performance, except for stimuli that are actual speech signals!

The explanation advanced for this latter and somewhat surprising result is that neither the A, B, nor C stimulus ensembles were sufficiently like speech to elicit a linguistic association. Hence, they had to be identified in a manner different from speech. Real speech sounds, however, are categorized with great facility by listeners, and presumably the subjects made use of linguistic categories in discriminating the D stimuli. The A, B, and C signals, lacking linguistic association, were probably identified in terms of what may be more "natural" basic dimensions in perception, namely, loudness, pitch and duration. Discrimination of these fundamental dimensions might be expected to be more clear cut for the A stimuli. The B and C signals apparently do not order well along these dimensions because of the fixed initial vowel segment.

The results are therefore interpreted to argue against the existence of a speech-like continuum. Although the signals may bear more or less resemblance to speech from a physical point of view, the subjective responses exhibit a sharp dichotomy. Either the sounds are associated with linguistic entities or they are not. In the present experiment presumably none of the synthetic sounds were associated with linguistic quantities. Within a linguistic frame, the tendency is to categorize a signal according to dimensions established by the language structure. Perception of the signal as a linguistic unit probably depends strongly upon nonperipheral processes. Small details of the signal, routinely preserved at the periphery of the ear, may not be of primary importance. For nonlinguistic signals, on the other hand, the tendency is to order them along what seem to be natural psychological dimensions. Their discrimination probably requires less central processing than does the perception of speech.

7.34. Influence of Linguistic Association Upon Differential Discriminability

A listener's linguistic learning and experience provide an acute ability to categorize speech signals. In the experiment of the preceding section, listeners presumably resorted to linguistic associations for the $D7$ stimuli. They apparently did not for the other stimuli, either because the signals were not sufficiently speech-like, or because the listener's attention was not drawn to such an association by the instructions given him.

The results therefore raise a further question. Assuming that a linguistic association is made, is its effect reflected in the differential discriminations a listener can make? In other words, can the learning and discriminability acquired in linguistic experience carry over into a more classical differential comparison. At least one experiment suggests that it can (LIBERMAN, HARRIS, HOFFMAN and GRIFFITH). The objective was to demonstrate that the differential discriminability of formant motion in a synthetic speech syllable is more acute when the change traverses a phoneme boundary.

Consonant-vowel syllables were synthesized with the pattern play-back device described in Section 6.21, Chapter VI. Two formants were used and the vowel was always /e/ $(F1=360, F2=2160 \text{ cps})$. The consonants were various two-formant transitions spanning the known approximations to /b, d, and g/. The set of synthetic syllables used is shown in Fig. 7.18. The positive first-formant transition is the same in all the syllables and is a necessary cue to voicing. The second formant

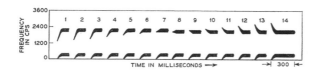

Fig. 7.18. Synthetic two-formant syllables with formant transitions spanning the ranges for the voiced consonants /b, d, g/. The vowel is the same for each syllable and is representative of /e/. (After LIBERMAN, HARRIS, HOFFMAN and GRIFFITH)

transitions range from highly negative to highly positive. The duration is the same for all syllables, namely 300 msec.

Two tests were made. In one, the stimuli were presented singly for absolute judgment of the consonant. The allowed response categories were /b, d, and g/. In the second, an *ABX* presentation was made. Stimuli *A* and *B* were different syllables from Fig. 7.18. They were separated by either one, two or three successive steps shown in Fig. 7.18. Sound *X* was identical to either *A* or *B*. On the basis of any cues they chose to use, listeners judged whether *X* was most like *A* or *B*. The second test therefore gave a measure of relative discriminability at each step on the continuum described by the stimuli in Fig. 7.18.

The absolute identification results of the best subject in the experiment are shown in Fig. 7.19. This same subject's responses in the *ABX* test, when the step size between *A* and *B* is two (that is, the *B* stimulus number is *A* plus two in Fig. 7.18), are given in Fig. 7.20. Comparison of the data shows a clear diminution of differential discriminability of formant transition for the stimuli contained *within* the /b/ and /d/ response ranges. A corresponding drop for the /g/ range apparently is not obtained. The other subjects in the experiment did not give data with maxima and minima so well defined, but the indications are that somewhat similar variations exist.

A rough approximation of differential discriminability can be made on the assumption that listeners can discriminate only so well as they can identify. This assumption tends to predict the relative variations in discriminability, but it underestimates the absolute level of discriminability. The difference may represent a so-called margin of true dis-

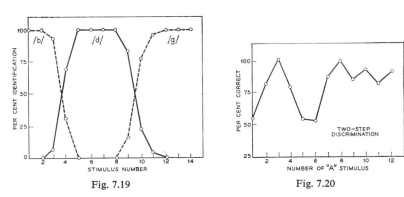

Fig. 7.19   Fig. 7.20

Fig. 7.19. Absolute consonant identifications of one listener for the stimuli of Fig. 7.18. (After LIBERMAN *et al.*)

Fig. 7.20. *ABX* responses of the listener whose absolute responses are shown in Fig. 7.19. The step size between *A* and *B* stimuli was two positions in the stimulus set of Fig. 7.18. (After LIBERMAN *et al.*)

crimination, that is, the ability of listeners to distinguish speech sounds not solely on the basis of phoneme labels, but also more directly by acoustic differences.

The suggestion is advanced that the inflection points in discrimination are not innately built into the human. Different languages have phoneme boundaries in different places. The case for acquired discriminability would of course be strengthened by demonstrating that native speakers of other languages exhibit maxima of differential sensitivity placed along the continuum in accordance with their languages. The crucial factor in the present experiment is the extent to which linguistic associations are elicited by the stimuli[1]. Lacking the ability to categorize, the differential discriminability might be expected to be monotonic along the stimulus continuum.

To inquire into this last point, a similar experiment was conducted on synthetic vowel sounds (LIBERMAN, COOPER, HARRIS, and MACNEILAGE). No increase in discrimination was found at the phoneme boundaries. In addition, the differential discriminability lay considerably above that predicted simply on the basis that listeners can discriminate only so well as they can identify. (In other words, listeners can discriminate many within-phoneme differences.) The conclusion is that the perception of vowels tends to be continuous and is not as categorized as, for example, the stop consonants. A further experiment with two other phonemic distinctions, namely vowel length and tone in Thai, also failed to show sharpening at the phoneme boundary (LIBERMAN, COOPER, HARRIS, and MACNEILAGE).

7.4. Effects of Context and Vocabulary Upon Speech Perception

The precision with which listeners identify speech elements is intimately related to the size of the vocabulary and to the sequential or contextual constraints that exist in the message. The percent correct response is higher the more predictable the message, either by virtue of higher probability of occurrence or owing to the conditional probabilities associated with the linguistic and contextual structure. This influence is apparent in intelligibility scores for various types of spoken material. Fig. 7.21 illustrates the effect in an experiment where speech was masked by varying amounts of noise (MILLER, HEISE, and LICHTEN).

Three different types of test material were used. Articulation tests were made with the same subjects and experimental apparatus. One set of material was the spoken digits zero to nine. Another was complete

---

[1] The question is made more pointed, perhaps, by the results of the previous section where apparently no linguistic association was made with synthetic syllables.

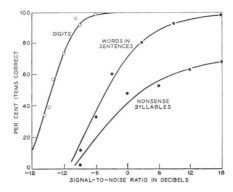

Fig. 7.21. Intelligibility scores for different types of spoken material as a function of signal-to-noise ratio. (After MILLER, HEISE and LICHTEN)

sentences read and scored for the major words. A third was nonsense syllables which were pronounced and recorded using an abbreviated phonetic notation. As Fig. 7.21 shows, the signal-to-noise ratios necessary to produce 50 percent correct response are approximately −14 db for the digits, −4 db for the words in sentences, and +3 db for nonsense syllables. The discriminations among a small number of possibilities are obviously better than among a large number. The sequential constraints present in the sentences apparently result in higher intelligibility scores than for the nonsense material.

The effect of vocabulary size was examined in further detail. The same type of articulation tests were performed on monosyllabic word sets numbering 2, 4, 8, 16, 32, 256, or an unspecified number. For the restricted vocabularies, the listeners were informed of the alternatives. The results of the intelligibility tests are shown in Fig. 7.22. The results show clearly that as vocabulary size increases, the signal-to-noise ratio necessary to maintain a given level of performance also increases.

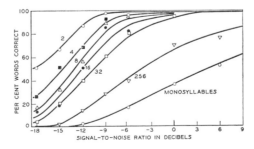

Fig. 7.22. Effects of vocabulary size upon the intelligibility of monosyllabic words. (After MILLER, HEISE and LICHTEN)

Semantic and syntactical constraints also influence the predictability of a speech utterance and hence its intelligibility. The grammatical rules of a given language prescribe allowable sequences of words. Semantic factors impose constraints upon those words which can be associated to form a meaningful unit. Experiments have demonstrated that the intelligibility of words is substantially higher in grammatically-correct, meaningful sentences than when the same words are presented randomly in isolation (MILLER, HEISE, and LICHTEN). The sentence context reduces the number of alternative words among which a listener must decide, and the improvement in intelligibility is due, at least partially, to this reduction.

Reduction in the number of alternatives, however, is not the sole factor. Experiments have compared the intelligibility of words in grammatically-correct, meaningful sentences to the intelligibility in nongrammatical, pseudo-sentences (G. A. MILLER, 1962). The pseudo-sentences were constructed so that the number of word alternatives was exactly the same as for the grammatical sentences. In the grammatical structures a listener apparently accomplishes perception in terms of phrases, or longer elements. He may delay decisions about words, rather than make them about each word as it occurs. The nongrammatical structures, on the other hand, cannot be processed this way. They must be perceived in terms of shorter temporal elements.

A somewhat different emphasis can be placed on context from the standpoint of acoustic environment and reference. Many perceptual evaluations seem to be made by a relative rather than absolute assessment of physical properties. That is, the physical surround establishes a frame of reference for the decoding operation. A simple example might be the pitch inflection of an utterance. The relative change, or pattern of inflection, is probably more significant perceptually than the absolute number of cycles per second.

Such acoustic "referencing" has been demonstrated in synthetic speech. It can be present to the extent that identification of a given monosyllabic word is strongly influenced by the time-frequency-intensity frame within which it is placed (LADEFOGED and BROADBENT). For example, a given synthetic vowel was produced as the central element of the synthetic word /b−t/. This word was used in synthetic sentences having different relative patterns of formant frequencies. Depending upon the acoustic reference established by the formant patterns in the rest of the sentence, the physically same synthetic word was variously identified as *bit*, *bet* or *bat*.

7.5. The Perceptual Units of Speech

The data in the preceding discussions suggest that speech perception is an adaptive process. It is a process in which the detection procedure probably is tailored to fit the signal and the listening task. If the listener is able to impose a linguistic organization upon the sounds, he may use information that is temporally dispersed to arrive at a decision about a given sound element. If such an association is not made, the decision tends to be made more upon the acoustic factors of the moment and in comparison to whatever standard is available.

The suggestion that a listener uses temporally spread information raises the question as to the size of the temporal "chunks" in which speech is perceived. Very probably the size of the perceptual element varies with the discrimination task, and the listener adjusts his processing rate to suit different types of speech information. He may, for example, attend to prosodic information while phonemic information is momentarily predictable. For nonspeech or nonlinguistically associated discriminations, the perceptual processing may be substantially different. In either case, however, the information must funnel through the same sensory transducer. As mentioned earlier, differential discriminations of "classical" psychoacoustic signals probably reflect the fundamental limitations of the transducer and the peripheral processing, whereas linguistically-connected discriminations probably reflect the storage and processing characteristics of the central mechanism.

Speech recognition presumably requires that sound elements be identified in absolute terms. For some sounds, however, distinctiveness is not so much an acoustic, or even articulatory factor, but a consequence of linguistic experience. A distinctiveness, which may be salient in connected speech, may be diminished or altogether lost in isolation. A case in point concerns the nasal consonants. These sounds carry a heavy functional load in connected speech (see Table 1.1, Chapter I), but are poorly identified in isolation (see Table 7.1, Section 7.31).

A number of studies have aimed at determining the units in which perception occurs. For the most part the experiments arrive at disparate results, probably owing to the large differences in perceptual tasks and to the fact that there may be no single answer to the question. Perhaps exemplifying one extreme in perception is the task of speech "shadowing" (CHISTOVICH, 1962). This approach aims to resolve whether, upon hearing the beginning of a speech sound, a listener immediately begins to make some preliminary decisions and corrects them as more information becomes available, or whether he stores long portions of data before interpreting them. The question was examined in two ways. First, the latency was measured for the articulatory movements of a listener who was repeating as rapidly as possible ("shadowing") the speech syllables he heard over earphones. The syllables were either vowel-consonant-vowel or consonant-vowel. Second, the latency was measured for a written transcription of the consonant sounds in the syllables heard.

The results showed that in the vocal shadowing, the consonant latencies were on the order of 100 to 120 msec for the *VCV* syllables, and on the order of 150 to 200 msec for the *CV*'s. In the *VCV* syllables the subject apparently anticipates the *C* before it is completely articulated, perhaps getting a good deal of information from the formant transitions in the initial *V*. He is often wrong initially, but generally corrects himself (on a running basis) by the end of the *C*. Because the subject reacts before he perceives the whole consonant—and even makes responses that are not possible in his language—the interpretation is advanced that the subject makes a number of simple decisions about the articulatory origin of the acoustic event (that is, whether the origin is dental, voiced, voiceless, nasal, etc.). The decisions are corrected as the sound proceeds, and a set of features are finally accumulated to form the phoneme. It is therefore suggested that shadowing is "phoneme creation" from simple decisions about articulatory parameters.

The latencies for the written mode of response were found to be very nearly the same as the latencies to the ends of the *C*'s in shadowing (that is, the interval between ends of the original and the shadowed *C*'s). The conclusion is therefore put forward that consonant writing is closely related to consonant shadowing.

It is difficult to say precisely how perception under these conditions relates to perception of running speech. The results may be strictly interpretable only within the frame of the task. If the task is made different, the measures are likely to indicate a different duration for the "unit". Another experiment perhaps illustrates the opposite extreme in evaluating the unit. It suggests that listeners are not only aware of large parts of an utterance at any moment, but actually may find it difficult to consider speech in terms of small segments, even when asked to make an effort to do so (LADEFOGED).

The spoken word "dot" was superimposed on the recording of a complete sentence. Listeners were asked to note and report the precise moment in the sentence when the superimposed word commenced. The judgments were generally inaccurate, but it was not uncommon for subjects to report that the superimposed item occurred two or three words earlier in the sentence than was actually the case.

This behavior suggests that the mechanisms and times for processing on-going contextual information may be considerably different from those for isolated stimuli, even though the latter are speech sounds. It also suggests that continuous speech produces complex temporal patterns that are preceived as a whole. Items such as syllables, words, phrases, and sometimes even sentences, may therefore have a perceptual unity. In such an event, efforts to explain perception in terms of sequential identification of smaller segments would not be successful. As a consequence, attempts to build machines that recognize speech in terms of brief acoustic units may be of little or no profit.

It was suggested earlier (see Section 7.33) that "natural" auditory dimensions apparently include subjective attributes such as pitch, loudness, and temporal pattern, and that these dimensions appear useful in discriminating nonlinguistically associated sounds. These same dimensions may of course apply to continuous speech signals, but they may be assessed in different ways — perhaps in ways that are related to production. For example, there is some evidence that the loudness of speech is assessed more in terms of the respiratory effort required to produce the necessary subglottal pressure than it is in terms similar to, say, the loudness scale for sine waves (LADEFOGED). If the "motor theory" of speech perception has validity, a listener may evaluate a speech signal in terms of the motor activity that produced it, as well as in terms of other acoustic factors not directly under motor control.

Many theorists in speech perception appeal to a link between production and perception. How tight this link is, is not known. If it is close, perception could conceivably occur in terms of "articulatory" segments rather than acoustic segments. In producing speech, the human has at least three kinds of feedback: auditory, tactile and proprioceptive. Blocking of one or more of these channels apparently causes some of its functions to be assumed — but generally less well — by one of the other channels. Speech attributes such as vowel quality, nasality and pitch seem highly dependent upon auditory feedback, while features such as lip and tongue movements in consonant articulation seem more dependent upon tactile and proprioceptive channels. If perception is linked to these processes, some speech properties might be identified by reference to acoustic factors, and others by reference to articulatory activity.

7.51. Models of Speech Perception

Much progress remains to be made in understanding and in modeling the mechanism of human speech perception. Not least is the problem of quantifying behavior in response to speech signals. Appeal to the mechanism of speech production is sometimes made on the basis that perceptual factors, at some level, must correspond to those necessary to speak the same message. This "motor theory of speech perception" has been the focus of considerable speculation and not little controversy (LIBERMAN *et al.*). If truly invoked by humans — which has not been shown — it has the advantage that motor commands to the vocal mechanism are more amenable to psychological study than are, say, electrical representations of speech signals in the human contex. Further, acoustic and linguistic correlates of the motor commands are more accessable for study.

At least one view (BONDARKO *et al.*) has maintained that the development of a model of human speech perception is the same problem as the development of an automatic speech recognizer, and further, that present knowledge embraces only the most rudimentary aspects of such a model. The proposal for such a model involves the hierarchial structure shown in Fig. 7.23. The model is envisioned as a chain of transformations in which each stage acts as an information filter to

Fig. 7.23. Block diagram model of stages in speech perception.
(After BONDARKO, ZAGORUYKO, KOZHEVNIKOV, MOLCHANOV and CHISTOVICH)

reduce the dimensionality of the signal. For example, the first three blocks transform an acoustic signal into a succession of words where each word is described by a set of lexical and grammatical features and by prosodic characteristics. Syntax and finally semantic analysis complete the transformations necessary for message understanding. The natures of the transformations, if in fact they exist in identifiable and separable forms, are not known. Perceptual experiments do, however, suggest certain characteristics of the first two stages.

The peripheral auditory analysis made by the human cochlea is such that features of the short-time spectrum of the input signal are preserved. This analysis preserves temporal detail relevant to changes in spectral distribution, periodicity (or non-periodicity) and intensity. That this is true can be shown by psychoacoustic experiments on perception of changes in pitch, formants or intensity of speech and speech-like sounds. That this information is reduced in "dimensionality" for later processing is supported by experiments which show that consonant perception is influenced only by the direction and rate of change of formant transitions, and not by absolute values of their "loci" or initial frequencies. Similar perceptions of the direction and rate of change of fundamental frequency, or pitch, influence nasal-non-nasal discriminations in labial consonants (CHISTOVICH).

The reduction of dimensionality performed in the phonetic analysis is likely to be one of feature analysis rather than one of comparison to a stored reference pattern. This view is supported by data on syllable recognition where features such as manner of production may be perceived correctly while, say, place of production is perceived incorrectly. Similarly, prosodic features may be perceived without discrimination of phonetic factors. Experiments on mimicking and shadowing (CHISTOVICH, KOZHEVNIKOV, and ALYAKRINSKII) are consistent with this in that some phonematic features can be recognized and produced even before a listener hears a whole syllable. This type of feature analysis also argues that the input to the phonemic analysis block of Fig. 7.23 may already be organized for parallel, multichannel processing.

Exactly what duration of signal may be subjected to such analysis in not clear, but data on short-term auditory memory provides some insight. In recall experiments with speech (MILLER; NEVEL'SKII) a sequence of three vowels or three tones is recalled as a sequence of decisions regarding the stimuli and not as a sequence of acoustic descriptions (CHISTOVICH, KLAAS, ALEKIN). The phonemic analysis must therefore work with speech segments shorter than average word length. Furthermore, experiments show that a man cannot remember sequences of nonsense syllables longer than 7 to 10 syllables (MILLER; CHISTOVICH, KOZHEVNIKOV, and ALYAKRINSKII). This fact bears on the size of the short-time storage and characterizes the "time window" through which the message is "seen" by the morphological analysis stage.

On the other side it is clear that a listener does not make separate decisions about every phoneme in running speech. The units with which he operates likely correspond to words, or to even longer segments. Information handed from the morphological analysis to the syntactic and semantic analysis can, consequently, be reduced in dimensionality to this extent. Auditory segments need not coincide with phonemes— i.e., each segment need not contain information about one and only one phoneme and the number of segments need not equal the number of phonemes.

Experiments on recall show that a listener remembers phonemes as a set of features (WICKELGREN; GALUNOV). Therefore, the phonemic information at the output of the phonetic analysis block should be represented by abstract, distinctive features. Several different acoustic (or auditory) features may contain information about one and the same distinctive feature.

7.6. Subjective Evaluation of Transmission Systems

7.61. Articulation Tests

A conventional technique for evaluating a communication facility is to determine the intelligibility of the speech it transmits. This is customarily done by counting the number of discrete speech units correctly recognized by a listener. Typically, a speaker reads a list of syllables, words, or sentences to a group of listeners. The percentage of items recorded correctly is taken as the articulation score. By choosing test material representative of the sound statistics of a language, a realistic test can be made of the transmission system. The development of the so-called phonetically-balanced (PB) test words has this objective (EGAN). The techniques for administering and scoring articulation tests have been described in many places, and there is little need to repeat the procedures here (see for example, BERANEK, 1954; HARRIS, ed.; RICHARDSON, ed.).

An articulation score is not an absolute quantity. It is a function of parameters such as test material, personnel, training, and test procedure. It consequently should be treated as a relative measure. Usually the significant information is a difference between scores obtained with the same material, procedures and personnel. Syllable and word items can be scored in terms of the correctness of their written response. Sentences can be scored either in terms of their meaning conveyed, or in terms of key words in the sentence. Contextual constraints usually make the scores for sentences higher than those for isolated words. One relation that has been worked out between word articulation and sentence intelligibility (in terms of meaning conveyed) is shown in Fig. 7.24 (EGAN).

Articulation tests are typically done without speed requirements, and the stimulus presentation rates are favorable for careful consideration of each item. More realistic articulation tests — so far as the informational capacity of a transmission system is concerned — should

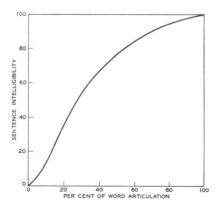

Fig. 7.24. A relation between word articulation score and sentence intelligibility. Sentences are scored for meaning conveyed. (After EGAN)

include time limitations. Some research into the design of such tests has been initiated (D'EUSTACHIO). The philosophy of adding stress to the communication task is that "fragile" systems will fail before more robust systems with perhaps valuable redundancy. Time limitation is but one way stress can be introduced. Additional mental activities, such as required with simultaneous motor or visual tasks, also load the listener. The aim is to control the sensitivity of the test by varying the subjective load (NAKATANI; MONCUR and DIRKS).

7.62. Quality Tests

In the conventional articulation test, a listener is usually required to respond with the written equivalent of the speech he hears. The quality or naturalness of the signal is not specifically evaluated. Methods for quantitatively rating speech quality have not been well established, mainly because the physical correlates of quality are poorly understood. Various rating-scales and rank-order methods have been examined (EGAN). However, generally applicable techniques for uniquely relating speech quality and acoustic factors are not presently available.

One proposal has suggested that speaker recognition is an important and measurable aspect of naturalness (OCHIAI and KATO; OCHIAI, 1958). Results along these lines suggest that spectral distortions of a speech signal affect the accuracy of speaker identification much differently from the way they affect phoneme identification. Another proposal has been to consider voice quality as the "spectral remainder" after inverse filtering a prescribed number of formants out of the signal (FUJIMURA). A large contribution to what remains is then attributed to the source of vocal excitation.

Perhaps one of the most promising tools for assessing speech quality is Multi-dimensional Scaling (SHEPARD; KRUSKAL; CARROLL). In this technique, non-metric data, corresponding to subjective judgments on a signal, are analyzed to reveal preferred rankings, and to show how individual subjects weight (in importance to preference) different attributes of the stimulus.

The technique assumes that observers use a common set of subjective factors (or coordinates) on which to base their judgements. The analysis indicates the number of such factors needed to account for prescribed amounts of variance in the subjective judgments. It does not, however, identify the physical correlates of the factors. This interpretation is a human one, and must rest upon knowledge of the physical properties of the stimuli.

The method is applicable to judgments made in close comparison (say, similarity or difference judgments on stimulus pairs) and to judgments made on an absolute basis (say, absolute assignment of quality ratings). Numerous variations of the method exist. An explanation of all would fill a book itself. The most expedient vehicle to illustrate the nature of the method is a specific example.

In one application, multidimensional scaling was used to assess the acceptability of amplitude-modulated, periodic pulses as an electronic telephone ringing signal (BRICKER and FLANAGAN). Physical variables were pulse repetition frequency (f_0), harmonic content (c), modulation frequency (f_m) and modulation duty-factor (df)[1]. Listeners heard single presentations of each signal condition and assigned an absolute numerical rating chosen from an unbounded range of positive and negative integers. Positive ratings were assigned to signals that were liked and negative to those disliked. The assigned ratings of each subject were converted to standard scores having zero mean and unity standard deviation.

The normalized judgments of n subjects on m different signal conditions produce an $n \times m$ data matrix S. The multidimensional procedure factors this data matrix into an $n \times r$ matrix of subject vectors and an $r \times m$ matrix of stimulus coordinates in r-dimensional space. The product of the subject and stimulus matrices is an $n \times m$ matrix S^* which is, in a least-squares sense, the best approximation of rank r to the original data matrix S. In particular, the r-dimensional projections of the stimuli onto each subject's vector constitute the best approximation to that subject's original data vector. The r-dimensional projections of a subject's vector onto the r orthogonal coordinates indicate the relative weights assigned to the coordinates by that subject.

The goal is to find directions in r-space along which signals are ordered in a physically interpretable manner. These directions are then related to the common perceptual attributes assumed as the basis for judgment. The relation of the subject vectors to these directions indicate the weight (or importance) of the attributes in the individual subjective ratings.

The r-dimensions are ordered according to the size of their characteristic roots, or to the proportion of the variance they account for in the original data. In the present example 40 subjects rated 81 signal conditions, and three dimensions accounted for most of the variance $(r=3)$. The projections of the subject vectors onto the two most important dimensions are shown in Fig. 7.25a.

Each arrowhead is the endpoint of a unit vector in the 3-dimensional unit sphere generated by the program. The vector thus specified may be imagined as a line segment from the end point extending through the origin and an equal distance beyond; the arrow points in the direction of higher rating by that subject. The relative weights given to each

---

[1] The modulation waveform was a half-wave vectified version of $(a + \sin 2\pi f_m t)$. The constant a was used to control duty factor.

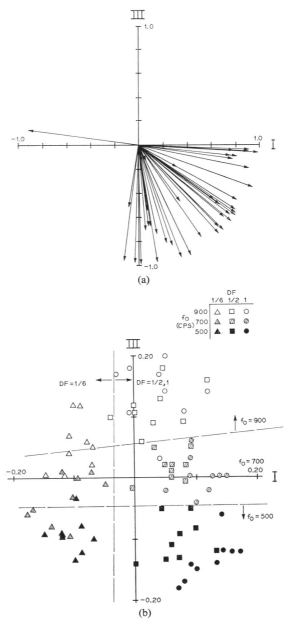

Fig. 7.25 a and b. (a) Subject vectors obtained from a multi-dimensional scaling analysis projected onto the two most important perceptual dimensions I and III. The data are for a tone ringer experiment. (b) Preference judgments on 81 tone-ringer conditions, projected onto the two most important perceptual dimensions I and III. Direction of high preference is indicated by the vectors in Fig. 7.25a. (After BRICKER and FLANAGAN)

of the three dimensions by a given subject, according to the assumptions of the technique, are reflected graphically by the perpendicular projections on the three axes of that subject's endpoint. Specifically, the squares of the projected values sum to 1.0 (by definition of the unit vector) and the subject weights are quantitatively related as the squares of the projected values. Thus, a subject whose endpoint is close to the end of one axis is described by the model as weighting that dimension heavily and the other two negligibly. One subject in Fig. 7.25a is seen to assign weights particularly different from the other 39.

The 81 stimulus coordinates of the preference judgments on the 81 signal conditions are shown projected onto the same factor plane in Fig. 7.25b. Each point represents a single signal condition. On this plane, a distinction is made between those signals differing only in duty factor (df) and fundamental frequency (f_0) (see insert key)[1]. The axes are scaled so that the variances of stimulus values on the two coordinates are equal. Dimension I can be associated with the physical attribute duty factor. Dimension III can be interpreted as fundamental frequency. The signal conditions can be divided according to duty factor and fundamental frequency, as shown by the dashed lines. Considering the direction of subject vectors in Fig. 7.25a, one sees there is a general preference for low duty factor and low fundamental frequency signals.

Multidimensional scaling in its many forms appears particularly promising for quality assessment of speech signals. Synthetic speech is a good case in point. Here the intelligibility may be made high, and the interest is in finding physical factors that relate to (and may be used to improve) naturalness. In other instances, multi-dimensional scaling has been valuable in assessing quality degradations due to non-linear distortions in speech transmission systems.

7.7. Calculating Intelligibility Scores from System Response and Noise Level: The Articulation Index

Articulation tests, properly done to get stable and consistent results, are immensely time consuming. More desirable is the ability to estimate intelligibility from the physical transmission characteristics of the system; for example, from the frequency-amplitude response and the noise level. Under certain restrictive conditions, the well-known articulation index is a technique for making such an estimate (FRENCH and STEINBERG). The concept has been extended and organized into graphical and tabular

---

[1] Each triangle, for example, represents nine different combinations of modulation rate and harmonic content.

operations for rapid, practical application (BERANEK, 1947, 1954; KRYTER).

The articulation index method is limited to particular distortions in systems using conventional "waveform" transmission. These distortions include relatively smooth variations and limitations in the transmission bandwidth, and the masking of the transmitted signal by ongoing, continuous-spectra noises. Under certain conditions, interference caused by temporally interrupted noise, nonlinear amplitude distortion (peak clipping), and masking by reverberation can be accounted for. In general, however, the technique is not applicable to systems whose transmission bands exhibit many sharp peaks and valleys, to periodic line spectra masking noises, to intermodulation distortions and nonlinearities, and to transmission systems generally of the analysis-synthesis type (that is, where the speech information is coded in terms other than the facsimile waveform).

The technique for calculating the articulation index (*AI*) has been described in detail in many other places. The intent here is simply to recall its principles and, in a brief way, to indicate its applicability and utility. Its calculation is illustrated by the graph in Fig. 7.26 (BERANEK, 1954). This plot shows several spectral densities laid off on a special frequency scale. The frequency scale is similar to the mel (pitch) scale. It is experimentally partitioned into twenty bands that contribute equally to intelligibility. The various spectral densities, or rms sound pressure levels per cycle, show: (a) the threshold of audibility

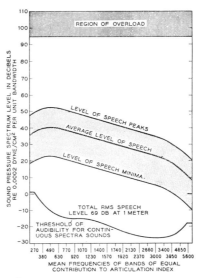

Fig. 7.26. Diagram for calculating the articulation index. (After BERANEK)

for continuous spectra sounds, (b) the peak, average and minimum levels of speech for a man's raised voice at a distance of one meter (see Section 5.17, Chapter V), and (c) an approximate overload spectrum level for the human ear.

In its simplest form, calculation of the articulation index proceeds as follows. The level and shape of the plotted speech spectrum is modified according to the amplification and bandpass characteristics of the transmission system. The spectrum level of any added masking noise is plotted onto the graph. So long as the system response and noise level are such that all of the shaded "speech region" (between minima and maxima) lies above threshold, above the masking noise, and below overload, the intelligibility will be near perfect. In such a case the articulation index is 100%. If any of the speech region is obscured by noise, threshold or overload, the articulation index is diminished by the percentage of the area covered.

Having obtained a number for *AI*, it is necessary to relate it to intelligibility. The relation is an empirical one and is established from articulation tests. As mentioned earlier, articulation tests are subject to considerable variability and their results depend strongly upon testing technique and procedure. Absolute values of scores so derived must be used and interpreted with great discretion. Usually it is more relevant to consider *differences* in intelligibility scores, arrived at by the same technique, than to consider absolute values. Representative empirical relations between intelligibility score and articulation index for a range of test conditions are shown in Fig. 7.27 (KRYTER).

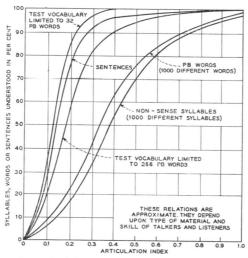

Fig. 7.27. Several experimental relations between articulation index and speech intelligibility (After KRYTER)

7.8. Supplementary Sensory Channels for Speech Perception

Supplementary methods for speech communication are of great importance to persons either totally deafened or with partial auditory impairment. Not only is it difficult for them to hear the speech of others, but they cannot hear their own speech. It consequently is common that they also experience difficulty in speaking.

At least three avenues have been considered at the research level for providing supplementary perceptual channels and machine aids for speech communication. They include visual, tactile, and auditory approaches. The latter is oriented toward making use of whatever hearing ability may remain. Each approach can be illustrated briefly by a specific example. Other interests and efforts exist in the area.

7.81. Visible Speech Translator

One well-known technique for visually displaying speech information is the "Visible Speech" method (POTTER, KOPP, and GREEN). A real time sound spectrograph, called a Visible Speech Translator, produces a running, continuous spectrographic display on a phosphor screen (RIESZ and SCHOTT; DUDLEY and GRUENZ). The format is similar to the conventional sound spectrogram (shown in Section 5.14, Chapter V) except that the pattern is "painted" continuously, either on a rotating cathode ray tube or on a phosphor belt. As the trace advances with time, a given duration of the past speech is retained and displayed by the persistence of the trace.

Some experiments have been made into the ability of viewers to "read" the direct-translator displays (POTTER, KOPP, and GREEN). The results showed that after relatively lengthy training, trainees were able to converse among themselves by talking clearly and at a fairly slow rate. Within the limits of their vocabulary, they learned to carry on conversations with about the same facility as a similarly advanced class in a foreign language. The learning rates observed in the tests correspond roughly to 350 vocabulary words per one hundred hours of training.

Real-time spectrographic displays appear to have more promise for speech teaching, that is, articulatory training, than for speech reading. Some research has applied spectrographic methods in teaching articulation to deaf children (STARK, CULLEN, and CHASE; RISBERG; PICKETT).

Because of the complex apparatus and important training procedures, visible speech techniques still remain in the realm of research. These and related methods—for example, the display of articulatory data and of formant data—are all valid problems for research and may hold potential for supplementary communication. Particularly promising are simple devices which signal rudimentary speech features, such as voicing, friction and stop gap (UPTON). At present, however, much remains to be learned about modes of visual presentation of speech information.

7.82. Tactile Vocoder

The sense of touch offers another possibility for real-time communication. A filter bank analyzer, similar to that used in a vocoder, is one means for supplying cutaneous information about the short-time amplitude spectrum of speech (PICKETT, 1969). The technique is shown in Fig. 7.28. Ten contiguous bandpass filters, spanning the frequency range 100 to 8000 cps, receive the speech signal. Their outputs are rectified and smoothed to obtain values of the short-time spectrum at ten frequency positions. The ten time-varying voltages are used to amplitude-modulate individual sinusoidal carriers of 300 cps[1]. The modulated carriers are then applied to fingertip vibrators (actually bone conduction transducers). The analyzing channel of lowest frequency is led to the small finger of the left hand, and the channel of highest frequency connects to the small finger of the right hand.

After practice with the presentation, some subjects are able to make sound discriminations comparable to, and sometimes better than, that

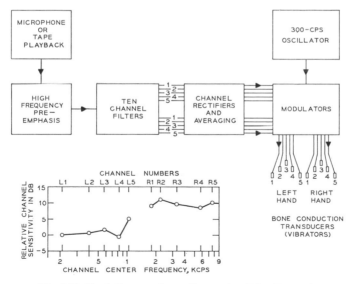

Fig. 7.28. Block diagram of a tactile vocoder. (After PICKETT)

---

[1] This tactile "carrier" is used because the frequency range of the skin's vibratory sensitivity is limited to about 100 to 800 cps.

achieved in lip reading. When the tactile information is used in combination with lip reading, the ability to identify spoken words is considerably increased. For example, in one measurement of discrimination among 12 words, the lip reading response was about 60% correct. When supplemented by the tactile information, the response increased to 85% (PICKETT).

As in the visible speech method, the vocoder apparatus for tactile display is relatively complex. A much simplified tactile device is shown in Fig. 7.29 (KRINGLEBOTN). This device employs only five vibrators

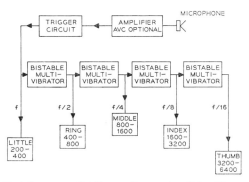

Fig. 7.29. A frequency-dividing tactile vocoder. (After KRINGLEBOTN)

applied to one hand. No filters are used, but stages of frequency division are arranged to divide five frequency ranges of the speech signal so as to vibrate the fingers individually. The vibrations on each finger are felt most strongly in the frequency range 200 to 400 cps. Because of the successive frequency divisions, this sensitivity range corresponds to successively higher frequency ranges in the input signal when distributed over the fingers, going from little finger to thumb. This method probably transmits some frequency information about the speech signal in terms of tactile frequency and other frequency information in terms of tactile location. Training tests with this system have been carried out with deaf children (KRINGLEBOTN).

A number of other efforts in kinesthetic and tactile communication are in progress. Although many of these aim toward machine aids for the blind rather than for the deaf, the presentation of sensory information involves problems common to both areas (BLISS; LINVILL).

7.83. Low Frequency Vocoder

The conventional electronic hearing aid is an amplifying and frequency shaping device. It facilitates the use of whatever residual hearing a deafened person may have. In severe cases, however, the residual hearing is often confined to a very small bandwidth, usually at the low-frequency end of the audible spectrum. For example, a typical audiogram might show 60 to 80 db loss from 30 to 400 cps and 110 db above 500 cps.

One proposal is to make maximal use of such residual hearing. Slowly varying signals that describe the short-time speech spectrum (such as vocoder channel signals) are modulated either onto sinusoidal carriers of very low frequency, or onto distinctive complex signals of relatively small bandwith (PIMONOW). In one implementation, seven spectrum channels extending to 7000 cps are used. The rectified, smoothed outputs amplitude modulate the same number of low-frequency, sinusoidal carriers. The carriers are spaced from 30 to 300 cps. The modulated carriers are summed and presented as an auditory signal. In an alternative arrangement, the modulated signals are non-sinusoidal and include a low-frequency noise band, a periodic pulse train, and a band of actual speech. In one series of experiments, deafened subjects who could not use ordinary hearing aids apparently learned to discriminate well among a limited ensemble of words (PIMONOW).

Various devices for spectrum shifting, transposing or dividing have also been considered (JOHANSSON; GUTTMAN, and NELSON; LEVITT and NELSON). These devices generally aim to recode high-frequency information into a lower-frequency range where residual hearing exists. Like visible speech displays, their value appears to lie more in articulatory training than in speech reception. Like the other sensory aids discussed in this section, frequency scaling devices are still in the research stage. Extended experimentation and technical development will determine their potential as practicable aids to hearing.

VIII. Systems for Analysis-Synthesis Telephony

The discussions in Chapters III and IV considered the basic physics of the mechanisms for speech production and hearing. The topics of Chapters V, VI and VII set forward certain principles relating to the analysis, artificial generation, and perception of speech. The present and final chapter proposes to indicate how the foregoing results, in combination, may be applied to the efficient transmission of speech.

Efficient communication suggests transmission of the minimum information necessary to specify a speech event and to evoke a desired response. Implicit is the notion that the message ensemble contains only the sounds of human speech. No other signals are relevant. The basic problem is to design a system so that it transmits with maximum efficiency only the perceptually significant information of speech.

One approach to the goal is to determine the physical characteristics of speech production, perception and language and to incorporate these characteristics into the transmission system. As such, they represent information that need not be transmitted. Ideally, the characteristics are described by a few independent parameters, and these parameters serve as the information-bearing signals. Transmission systems in which a conscious effort is made to exploit these factors are generally referred to as *analysis-synthesis* systems.

In the ideal analysis-synthesis system, the analysis and synthesis procedures are presumably accurate models of human speech production. To the extent this is true, the resulting signal is coded and synthesized in a distortionless form. Additional economies in transmission can accrue from perceptual and linguistic factors. The pure analysis-synthesis system therefore has the greatest potential for bandsaving, and its analysis and synthesis processings typically require complex operations.

In contrast, other transmission systems aim for modest or little band-savings, with terminal apparatus which is simple and inexpensive. Such systems typically exploit fewer properties of speech, hearing and language than do the pure analysis-synthesis systems. Nevertheless, they are of considerable interest and importance, and their potential applications range from mobile radio and scatter links to various commercial wire circuits. Although emphasis in this chapter is given to analysis-synthesis techniques, systems of the latter category are also brought in for discussion, especially in the context of digital coding and transmission.

The results of Chapter III and VI showed that speech signals can be described in terms of the properties of the signal-producing mechanism, that is, the vocal tract and its excitation. This characterization suggests important possibilities for efficient encoding of speech. In fact, it forms the common basis for a large class of bandwidth-compression systems. The idea is schematized in Fig. 8.1. Three operations are involved. First, the automatic analysis of the signal into quantities that describe the vocal excitation and mode structure; second, the multiplexing and transmission of these parameters; and finally, the reconstruction of the original signal from them.

In a parallel manner, the discussion in Chapter IV suggested that the ear performs a kind of short-time frequency analysis at its periphery. The analysis includes a mechanical filtering, the equivalent of a rectification, and a neural encoding which — apparently at an early stage — involves an integration. In such a process, certain details of the original speech wave are lost and are not perceptually significant. Presumably a transmission system might also discard this information without noticeably influencing the preceived signal. It might thereby effect an economy in requisite channel capacity.

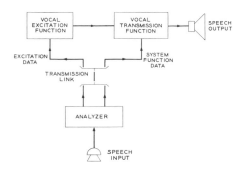

Fig. 8.1. Source-system representation of speech production

In a similar fashion, other aspects of the signal — for example, the sequential constraints on the sounds of a given language, or the natural pauses in connected speech — might be used to advantage. In short, practically all aspects of speech production, hearing and language have relevance to analysis-synthesis telephony. The following sections propose to discuss complete analysis-synthesis systems, and a number of these factors will be put in evidence.

8.1. Channel Vocoders

Analysis-synthesis telephony came of age, so to speak, with DUDLEY's invention of the Vocoder. This was more than three decades ago. In recent years, the name Vocoder (for *Vo*ice *Coder*) has become largely a generic term, commonly applied to analysis-synthesis systems in which the excitation and system functions are treated separately (see Fig. 8.1). The original Vocoder — now referred to as a spectrum channel vocoder — has probably been described in the literature more times than any other single system. Nevertheless, for the sake of completeness, as a convenient point of departure, and because it set forth, at such an early time, an important philosophy in voice transmission, a brief description of the idea will be repeated once more.

Following the coding scheme illustrated in Fig. 8.1, the Vocoder incorporates one important constraint of speech production and one of perception. It recognizes that the vocal excitation can be a broad-spectrum, quasi-harmonic sound (voiced), or a broad-spectrum, random signal (unvoiced). It also recognizes that perception, to a large degree, is dependent upon preservation of the shape of the short-time amplitude spectrum. A block diagram of an early Vocoder is shown in Fig. 8.2 (DUDLEY, 1939b).

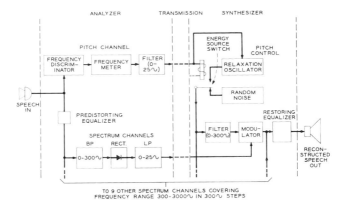

Fig. 8.2. Block diagram of the original spectrum channel vocoder. (After DUDLEY, 1939b)

The excitation information is measured by the top branch of the circuit. A frequency discriminator and meter measure the fundamental component of the quasi-periodic voiced sounds. Values of the fundamental frequency and its temporal variations are represented by a proportional electrical voltage from the meter. This "pitch" signal is smoothed by a 25 cps low-pass filter. Unvoiced sounds normally have insufficient power in the fundamental frequency range to operate the frequency meter. Nonzero outputs of the pitch meter therefore indicate voicing as well as the value of the pitch.

Ten spectrum channels in the lower part of the circuit measure the short-time amplitude spectrum at ten discrete frequencies. Each channel includes a band-pass-filter (300 cps wide originally), a rectifier and a low-pass filter (25 cps). The measured spectrum is therefore precisely that described in Section 5.1, Chapter V. The predistorting equalizer pre-emphasizes the signal to produce nearly equal average powers in the spectrum-analyzing filters. The spectrum-defining channel signals consequently have about the same amplitude ranges and signal-to-noise ratios for transmission. The eleven 25-cps wide signals occupy a total bandwidth of less than 300 cps and must be multiplexed in frequency or time for transmission.

At the receiver, the speech spectrum is reconstructed from the transmitted data. Excitation, either from a pitch-modulated, constant average power pulse-generator, or from a broadband noise generator, is applied to an identical set of band-pass filters. The outputs from the filters are amplitude modulated by the spectrum-defining signals. A short-time spectrum, approximating that measured at the transmitter, is recreated.

With proper design the synthesized speech can be made surprisingly intelligible. An example of speech transmitted by a 15-channel vocoder is shown by the spectrograms in Fig. 8.3. Important features such as formant structure and voiced-unvoiced excitation are relatively well preserved.

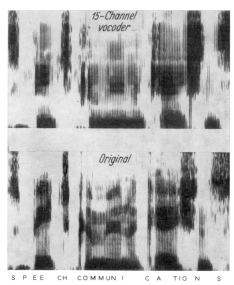

Fig. 8.3. Spectrogram of speech transmitted by a 15-channel vocoder

8.11. Design Variations in Channel Vocoders

Since the original development of the Vocoder many different versions and variations have been constructed. Number and spacing of the analyzing filters along the frequency scale, their bandwidths, degree of overlap, and selectivity are all matters of design variation. Similarly, many different pitch extraction and voiced-unvoiced detection circuits have been examined, as well as the characteristics of the rectifier and low-pass filter. The number of channels used has ranged from as few as eight to as many as 100, and the filter characteristics have ranged from broad, steep, flat-topped responses to narrow, simple-tuned circuits. Space does not permit a detailed discussion of all these investigations. However, typical analog hardware implementations include those of R. L. MILLER, 1953; DAVID, 1956; VILBIG and HAASE, 1956a, b; SLAYMAKER; SHEARME, and HOLMES; COOPER, PETERSON, and FAHRINGER; WERNER and DANIELSSON; YAGGI; YAGGI and MASON; and STEELE and CASSEL, 1963a, b. Digital implementations have been nearly equally

varied, and include the work of GOLDEN; FREUDBERG *et al.*; GOLD; and
GOLD and RADER. In particular, Fast Fourier Transform techniques
have been found advantageous in digital implementations.

Although intelligibility may be high, practical realizations of conventional channel vocoders generally exhibit a perceptible degradation of
speech naturalness and quality. The synthetic speech possesses a machine-
like quality which is characteristic of the device. Several factors seem to be
responsible. One is the coding of excitation data. Voiced-unvoiced discriminations often are made with noticeable errors. Relevant structure in
the pitch signal may not be preserved, and, under certain conditions,
octave errors may be made in the automatic pitch extraction. Voiced
sounds are synthesized from a pulse source whose waveform and phase
spectrum do not reflect certain details and changes of the real vocal
cord wave. The spectral analysis also has a granularity, or lack of resolution, imposed by the number, bandwidth and spacing of the analyzing
filters. A given speech formant, for example, might be synthesized with
too great a bandwidth. Further, the large dynamic range of the amplitude
spectrum may not be covered adequately by practical rectifiers and
amplifiers.

The basic channel vocoder design can be improved in several ways.
The important excitation problems can be obviated to a large extent by
the voice-excitation technique to be discussed in a following section.
Also sophisticated pitch extraction methods, such as the cepstrum method
described in Section 5.3, Chapter V, provide more precise pitch and
voiced-unvoiced data. The spectral representation problems can be
lessened by careful filter design, or by the use of digital techniques
such as the Fast Fourier Transform.

8.12. Multiplexing Channel Vocoders

8.121. Frequency-Space Multiplexing. The customary techniques for
transmitting a multiplicity of simultaneous signals are frequency-space
multiplexing and time-division multiplexing. In the former, the requisite
amount of spectrum bandwidth is allocated to each signal. The individual
signals are modulated onto separate carriers, which are transmitted
simultaneously within the allocated channels and are demodulated at
the receiver. In the latter, the several signals time-share a single transmission path of appropriate bandwidth.

Frequency multiplexing of vocoder signals is attractive from the
standpoint of circuit simplicity and existing analog communication
links. Certain relations can be observed to conserve spectrum space and,
at the same time, provide accurate transmission. Since the vocoder
signals normally contain a dc component, the modulation method must

be chosen to preserve this response. Conventional double-sideband (DSB) amplitude modulation would satisfy the response requirement, but would not be economical of bandwidth. Conventional single-sideband (SSB) modulation with suppressed carrier, although taking only half the bandwidth, would not reliably preserve the low-frequency components of the modulation. Vestigial sideband transmission might suffice. However, a two-phase (or quadrature) modulation method has been advanced as the best solution (HALSEY and SWAFFIELD).

A pair of channel signals DSB modulate separate carriers of the same frequency but differing in phase by $\pi/2$ radians. The two double-sideband signals then occupy the same frequency band. Provided the transmission path has attenuation and phase characteristics symmetrical about the carrier frequency, either signal-complex can be rejected at the receiver by demodulating (multiplying and integrating) with a synchronous quadrature carrier. Frequency and phase synchrony of the carriers at the transmitter and receiver are of course critical.

The quadrature method is generally not satisfactory for transmission of conventional voice signals. Practical stabilities are such that the crosstalk between circuits cannot be kept low enough. For vocoder signals, however, a crosstalk attenuation between spectrum channels of about 25 db seems adequate[1]. This figure is within the practical limits of the quadrature method. The signal-to-crosstalk ratio is the cotangent of the phase error between the modulating and demodulating carriers. Therefore, a crosstalk attenuation of 25 db, or more, requires a phase error of about 3.3 degrees, or less.

8.122. Time-Division Multiplexing. Time-division multiplexing involves the transmission of sample values of the channel signals taken in time sequence. According to the sampling theorem, the rate of sampling must be at least twice the highest frequency contained in the channel signals. The vocoder signals are typically bandlimited to about 20 cps, hence sampling rates on the order of 40 sec^{-1}, or higher, are indicated. Practically, to provide adequate channel separation in the desampling (distributing) operation, a total transmission bandwidth about twice the sum of the input signals, that is, the same as for DSB frequency-multiplex, is required (BENNETT, 1941). Even then, the crosstalk between channels may be only marginally acceptable. For example, in a 12-channel system the signal-to-crosstalk ratio is only on the order of 20 db. Without further coding, therefore, this multiplexing method appears somewhat less attractive from the fidelity standpoint than the quadrature frequency-space multiplex. On the other hand, its simplicity, and the

---

[1] The pitch channel is more sensitive to crosstalk. For it, an attenuation on the order of 40 db is desirable.

possibility for analog smoothing of the spectral shape, make it of interest.

One vocoder developed on the time-multiplex principle is called the Scan Vocoder (VILBIG and HAASE, 1956a, b). It is illustrated in Fig. 8.4. One hundred spectrum channels, using high frequency (130 kc) magneto-striction rods as the filters, produce a short-time spectrum. The filter outputs are scanned at $30\ \text{sec}^{-1}$ and the time-multiplexed spectral

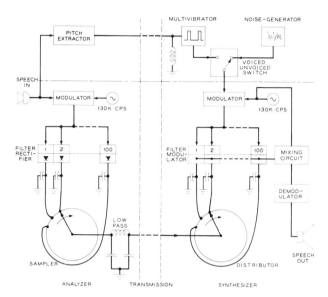

Fig. 8.4. Channel vocoder utilizing time-multiplex transmission.
(After VILBIG and HAASE, 1956)

envelope is smoothed by a 200 cps low-pass filter. The envelope signal is demultiplexed by a synchronously scanning distributor at the receiver. The pitch information is transmitted in a separate channel.

8.123. Digital Transmission of Vocoder Signals. Transmission of signals in the form of binary pulses has a number of advantages. One is the possibility for repeated, exact regeneration of the signal. Noise and distortion do not accumulate as they do in analog amplification. Quality of the digital signal can, within limits, be made independent of transmission distance. Another advantage is the freedom to "scramble" the message in complex ways for secure or private communication. The price paid for these important advantages is additional transmission bandwidth. Time-divison multiplexing, coupled with pulse code modulation (PCM) of the channel signals, is consequently an attractive means for vocoder transmission. The signal value in each sampled channel is represented by a sequence of binary pulses. The ordered and "framed" pulses are transmitted over a relatively broadband channel, synchronously distributed at the receiver, and reconverted from digital to analog form.

Although the digital signal requires comparatively greater bandwidth, the vocoded speech signal makes feasible full digital transmission over about the same bandwidth as normally used for nondigital conventional telephony. An important question is how many binary pulses are sufficient to represent each sample of the channel signals. The answer of course depends upon the quality of received signal that is acceptable. Current technology has used pulse rates from 1200 to 4800 bits/sec in particular applications (YAGGI and MASON). A typical design, for example, uses 18 spectrum channels which are sampled at $40 \sec^{-1}$ and which are normalized in amplitude. The number of binary digits used to specify the sampled values of channels 1 through 14 is three bits; for channels 15 through 18, two bits; for the over-all amplitude level, three bits, and for pitch and voiced-unvoiced indication, seven bits. Therefore, 60 bits are included in one scan or "frame", and 2400 bits/sec is the transmitted data rate. Numerous variations in the design for digital transmission can be found.

8.13. Vocoder Performance

Although voice quality and naturalness normally suffer in transmission by vocoder, the intelligibility of the synthesized speech can be maintained relatively high, often with a vocoder having as few as ten

Table 8.1. *Consonant intelligibility for a vocoder. Percent of initial consonants heard correctly in syllables (logatoms).* (After HALSEY and SWAFFIELD)

b — 90%	l — 97%	r — 100%	w — 100%
f — 74	m — 85	s — 94	sh — 100
h — 100	n — 99	t — 91	th — 43
k — 85	p — 77	v — 96	none — 70

channels. For a high-quality microphone input and a fundamental-component pitch extractor, typical syllable intelligibility scores for a ten-channel (250 to 2950 cps) vocoder are on the order of 83 to 85 per cent (HALSEY and SWAFFIELD). Typical intelligibility scores for initial consonants range over the values shown in Table 8.1.

Weak fricatives such as *th* are not produced well in this system. The 30 per cent error indicated for no initial consonant (i.e., for syllables beginning with vowels) indicates imprecision in the voiced-unvoiced switching. Such syllables were heard as beginning with consonants when in fact they did not. Even so, the consonant intelligibilities are reasonably good.

Comparable performances can also be obtained when the vocoder signals are time-sampled (scanned), quantized and encoded in terms of binary pulses. An early model 10-channel vocoder, arranged for digital transmission, gave typical consonant intelligibility scores shown in Table 8.2. The data rates are exclusive of pitch information. Four different quantizing levels were used (R. L. MILLER and D. K. GANNETT, unpublished; quoted in DAVID, 1956).

Table 8.2. *Vocoder consonant intelligibility as a function of digital data rate.*
(After DAVID, 1956)

	Number of quantizing levels			
	6	5	4	3
Binary pulse rate (bits/sec)	1 300	1 160	1 000	788
Consonant intelligibility (%)	82	79	79	69

More elaborate designs provide somewhat higher intelligibilities. For example, a consonant intelligibility of approximately 90 per cent is typical of a 16-channel vocoder whose channel signals are sampled 30 sec^{-1} and quantized to three bits (i.e., 1440 bits/sec) (DAVID, 1956).

8.2. Reduced Redundancy Channel Vocoders

It is generally recognized that vocoder channel signals are not completely independent, and that possibilities exist for further processing the signals to orthogonalize them. Several investigations have considered methods for further eliminating redundancy.

8.21. "Peak-Picker"

The results of the vocal-tract computations in Chapter III show that the values of the speech spectrum at adjacent frequency positions are closely related. In a vowel sound, for example, the entire vocal transmission spectrum is specified by the formant frequencies. Usually, therefore, the neighboring channel signals in a vocoder are strongly correlated. One transmission system, called a peak-picking vocoder, attempts to eliminate this dependence. It operates by transmitting a few — three to five — channel signals which at any instant represent local maxima of the short-time spectrum.

The circuitry employed is modeled upon that described for the formant-extracting system in Section 5.2, Chapter V. Inhibitory connections prevent two adjacent channels from being selected. The identities of the "picked" maximum channels and their amplitudes are signaled to a conventional 18-channel vocoder synthesizer. A pitch signal is also sent. Thus at any one time only a few channels of the synthesizer are activated. Intelligibility scores as high as 70 per cent are reported for nonsense syllables, and a digital transmission rate of about 1000 bits/sec is estimated to be required (PETERSON and COOPER).

8.22. Linear Transformation of Channel Signals

A related approach attempts to discover the dependence among the channel signals and to eliminate this redundancy in a smaller number of signals (KRAMER and MATHEWS). For n channel signals, a set of m signals, where $m \leq n$, are formed which are a linear combination of the original n. The coefficients of the linear transformation constitute an $(m \cdot n)$ matrix of constants. The transformation matrix is realized practically with an $(m \cdot n)$ array of fixed resistors. Decoding of the m signals to retrieve an approximation to the original n is also accomplished by a linear transformation, namely, the transpose of the $(m \cdot n)$ matrix. The coefficients of the transformation are obtained to minimize the mean square difference between the original n signals and the reconstructed n signals.

The technique was applied to the spectrum signals of a 16-channel vocoder (i.e., $n = 16$). For a reduction to $m = 6$, it was reported that the output was almost completely understandable, although quality was substantially less than that of the 16-channel vocoder. For $m = 10$, the quality was judged to be better than existing, conventional 10-channel vocoders. In the latter condition, the additional saving in channel capacity is estimated to be in the ratio of 3 to 2.

Another related study used a Hadamard matrix transformation to reduce the redundancy among the channel signals of a 16-channel vocoder (CROWTHER and RADER). The Hadamard transformation produces unit-weight linear combinations of the channel signals. It therefore requires no multiplications, but only additions and subtractions. This technique, implemented digitally in a computer, was applied to two different 16-channel vocoders. The results showed that the quality provided by the vocoders when digitized for 4000 bits/sec could be retained in the Hadamard transformation for a data rate as low as 1650 bits/sec. The Hadamard transformation is therefore suggested as a simple, useful means for improving the quality of low bit-rate vocoders (CROWTHER and RADER).

8.23. Pattern-Matching Vocoders

Another variation of the vocoder involves classification of the frequency *vs* amplitude spectral information of the channel signals into a limited number of discrete patterns (SMITH, 1957). In one such study (DUDLEY, 1958), spectral pattern are associated with phonetic units of speech. The sound analysis is carried out according to the pattern recognition scheme described in Section 5.5, Chapter V. At any instant, the best match between the short-time speech spectrum and a set of stored spectral patterns is determined. A code representing the matching pattern is signaled to a vocoder synthesizer, along with conventional pitch and voiced-unvoiced data. New information is signalled only when the phonetic pattern changes. At the receiver, a set of spectral amplitude signals, approximating the signalled pattern, are applied to the modulators of the synthesizer. The pitch signal supplies the appropriate excitation. Filter circuits are included to provide smooth transitions from one sound pattern to the next.

An early version of the device used a ten-channel vocoder and only ten stored patterns. It is illustrated in Fig. 8.5. The stored patterns corresponded to the steady-state spectra of four consonant continuants and six vowels (s, f, r, n, and i, ɪ, ε, ɑ, o, u, respectively). For one speaker (from whose speech the spectral patterns were derived), digits uttered in isolation were recognized by two listeners with scores of 97 and 99 per cent correct, respectively. On common monosyllables, however, the intelligibility fell to around 50 per cent. The addition of six more patterns increased the score by a small amount. The bandwidth required for transmission was only on the order of 50 cps, or around 60 times less

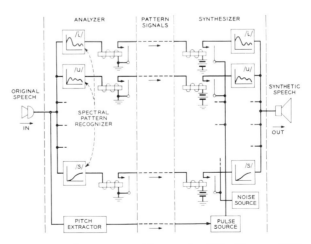

Fig. 8.5. Phonetic pattern-matching vocoder. (After DUDLEY, 1958)

than that for a conventional voice channel! While the intelligibility and quality of the speech processed by the device are clearly inadequate for most applications, the implementation does indicate the possibilities of narrow-band transmission for restricted message ensembles and limited speaker populations.

The obvious question suggested by the rather surprising performance with only ten stored patterns is how many stored spectral patterns would be needed to approach the performance of the conventional vocoder? At least one investigation has aimed to examine the question (SMITH, 1957, 1963). The outputs of the analyzer of a channel vocoder are sampled at $50 \, \text{sec}^{-1}$, normalized in amplitude, and quantized. The digital description of the short-time spectrum is then compared to a large library of digital patterns stored in a rapid-access memory. No requirement is imposed that these spectral patterns correspond to specific phonetic units of speech. Using digital processing techniques, the best fitting pattern is selected and its code transmitted. The objective is to determine the smallest population of patterns necessary to meet given performance criteria. The processing cannot, of course, result in better speech quality than provided by the conventional vocoder. It may, however, afford a useful bandsaving beyond that the of channel vocoder. Digital data rates for the transmission of the spectral patterns and excitation are estimated to be on the order of 400 to 800 bits/sec (SMITH, 1957a, 1963).

8.3. Voice-Excited Vocoders

Despite their high potential for transmitting intelligible speech with bandwidth savings on the order of ten-to-one, or more, vocoders have been applied only in special communication situations. Little or no commercial use has been made, largely because speech quality and naturalness suffer in the processing[1]. The resulting synthetic speech tends to have a "machine accent", and its naturalness is less than that of a conventional voice circuit.

The seat of the difficulty is largely the extraction of excitation information—that is, the pitch measurement and the voiced-unvoiced discrimination. The difficult problem of automatic pitch extraction is well known. The device must faithfully indicate the fundamental of the voice over a frequency range of almost a decade (if male and female voices are to be handled) and over a large range of signal intensity. Practically, the pitch extractor must cope with unfavorable conditions where the speech signal may be produced in noisy and reverberant

---

[1] Other considerations include the cost of terminal equipment compared to the cost of bandwidth.

environments. In addition, the signal may suffer band limitation that eliminates the first several lowest harmonics, requiring that the fundamental frequency be generated from some non-linear operation. These difficulties are compounded by the human ear's ability to detect small imprecisions in pitch data. (See Section 7.24, Chapter VII.)

Some of the many approaches that have been made to the pitch extraction problem have been briefly outlined in Section 5.3, Chapter V. It suffices here to say that solutions are yet to be implemented to bring the quality of the spectrum channel vocoder up to the quality of conventionally-coded voice circuits. The same general remark applies to the voiced-unvoiced discrimination which is also signalled in the pitch channel.

One method for avoiding the difficulties inherent in automatic analysis of excitation data is the voice-excited vocoder (SCHROEDER and DAVID; DAVID, SCHROEDER, LOGAN, and PRESTIGIACOMO). In this device excitation information is transmitted in an unprocessed, subband of the original speech. At the receiving end, this baseband is put through a nonlinear distortion process to spectrally flatten and broaden it. It is then used as the source of excitation for regular vocoder channels covering the frequency range above the baseband. A block diagram of the arrangement is shown in Fig. 8.6.

The flattened excitation band reflects the spectral line structure of the quasi-periodic voiced sounds and the continuous spectral character of the unvoiced sounds. Because it is derived from a real speech band, it inherently preserves the voiced-unvoiced and pitch information. At some sacrifice in bandwidth, the overall quality of the processed signal can be made comparable to conventional voice circuits. A higher quality signal is therefore realized together with a part of the band-saving advantage of the channel vocoder.

In one implementation of the device the baseband is taken as 250 to 940 cps. The frequency range 940 to 3650 cps, above the baseband, is covered by 17 vocoder channels. The first 14 of these channels have

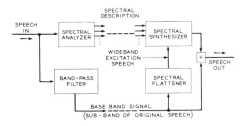

Fig. 8.6. Block diagram of voice-excited vocoder. (After DAVID, SCHROEDER, LOGAN and PRESTIGIACOMO)

analyzing bandwidths of 150 cps, and the upper three are slightly wider. The total transmission band occupancy is 1000 to 1200 cps, yielding a bandwidth compression of about three-to-one. The method of spectral flattening is shown in Fig. 8.7. The transmitted baseband is rectified and applied to the bandpass filters of the vocoder synthesizer. The filter outputs are peak-clipped to remove amplitude fluctuations. They are then applied as inputs to amplitude modulators which are controlled by the vocoder channel signals.

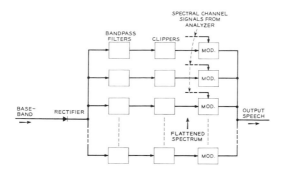

Fig. 8.7. Block diagram of spectral flattener. (After DAVID, SCHROEDER, LOGAN and PRESTIGIACOMO)

Intelligibility and speech quality tests, using speech from a carbon button microphone, were carried out to compare the voice-excited vocoder to telephone handset speech bandlimited to the same frequency range (DAVID, SCHROEDER, LOGAN, and PRESTIGIACOMO). To provide a more sensitive test, and to keep intelligibility substantially below 100%, masking noise was added to provide an 18 db speech-to-noise ratio. Phonetically balanced (PB) words were used in articulation tests (see Section 7.6, Chapter VII). For male speakers, the intelligibility of the voice-excited vocoder was found to be 6.1% less than the carbon-microphone speech of the same bandwidth. For female speakers the intelligibility was 10.1% less than the carbon-microphone speech.

Over-all speech quality of the voice-excited vocoder was assessed, along with that for three other transmission methods, by presenting listeners with sentences in isolation. The subjects were asked to rate each sentence "as good as normal telephone" or "worse than normal telephone". In 72% of the cases, the voice-excited vocoder was rated as good as normal telephone. In the same test, for comparison, a long distance carrier telephone circuit rated 82%, an 1800 cps lowpass circuit rated 36%, and a regular 18-channel vocoder rated 17%. The results show the voiced-excited system to be better than the spectrum channel vocoder and to approach the quality of conventional voice circuits. Its application, as with similar methods, depends upon desired trade-offs between cost of terminal equipment, amount of bandsaving and signal quality.

8.31. Multiplexing and Digitalization

The problems in multiplexing the voice-excited vocoder are essentially similar to those discussed in Section 8.2 for the channel vocoder. The main difference is the unprocessed baseband. For economical transmission in a frequency multiplex system, it should be left unaltered or produced as a single sideband modulation. Transmission of the spectrum-defining channel signals can be the same in both cases.

One design of a voice-excited vocoder uses 500 cps of unprocessed baseband and 13 spectrum channels above the baseband (HOWELL, SCHNEIDER, and STUMP, 1961a, b). The baseband is transmitted by single sideband modulation, and the channel signals are transmitted by vestigial sideband. Another analog implementation uses an unprocessed baseband of 250 to 925 cps and 10 vocoder channels covering the range to approximately 3000 cps (GOLDEN, MACLEAN, and PRESTIGIACOMO). The channel signals are double-sideband amplitude modulated onto 10 carriers spaced by 60 cps in the range 925 to 1630 cps. A bandwidth compression of approximately two-to-one is thereby realized.

Digital simulation and current computer techniques have also been used to design and study a complete voice-excited vocoder (GOLDEN). To realize the digital simulation, the sampled-data equivalents of all filters and all circuits of an analog 10-channel voice-excited vocoder were derived (see, for example, Section 6.26, Chapter VI). Transformation of the continuous system into the sampled-function domain permits its simulation in terms of discrete operations which can be programmed in a digital computer. In the present instance, the entire vocoder was represented inside the computer, and sampled-quantized input speech signals were processed by the program.

The immense advantage that this technique offers for research and design of signal-processing systems cannot be overemphasized. The entire transmission system can be simulated and evaluated before constructing a single piece of hardware. The usual price paid is non-real time operation of the system. The time factor for the present simulation was 172 to 1, or 172 sec of computation to process one second of speech. However, as digital techniques develop and as computers become even faster, this time factor will shrink proportionately.

Another vocoder development has resulted in a time-multiplexed, fully digitalized voice-excited vocoder (YAGGI; YAGGI and MASON).

The device is designed to operate at a data rate of 9600 bits/sec and to use PCM encoding. The system operates with a baseband whose upper cutoff is, optionally, either 800 cps or 950 cps. For the former, 12 vocoder channels cover the range to 4000 cps; for the latter, 11 channels are used. The baseband signal is sampled at the Nyquist rate and quantized to 5 bits. The spectrum channels are sampled at 50 sec^{-1} (64 sec^{-1} for the 950 cps baseband); the lower three are quantized to 3 bits, and the higher ones to 2 bits. Amplitude normalization of the spectrum signals is also used. Comparable choices have been made in alternative digital implementations (GOLD and TIERNEY).

Other coding techniques which, like the voice-excited vocoder, avoid the pitch tracking problem include the phase vocoder, the vobanc and the analytic rooter. These methods are discussed in later sections.

8.4. Correlation Vocoders

The channel vocoder demonstrates that speech intelligibility, to a large extent, is carried in the shape of the short-time amplitude spectrum. Any equivalent specification of the spectral shape would be expected to convey the same information. One equivalent description of the squared amplitude spectrum is the autocorrelation function. The correlation function can be obtained strictly from time-domain operations, and a spectral transformation is not required. Time-domain processing therefore offers simplicities in implementation. The relations linking these quantities have been discussed in detail in Section 5.1, Chapter V. A short-time autocorrelation specification of the speech signal might therefore be expected to be a time-domain equivalent of the channel vocoder.

In Chapter V, a short-time autocorrelation function of the function $f(t)$ was defined for the delay parameter, τ, as

$$\varphi(\tau, t) = \int_{-\infty}^{t} f(\lambda) f(\lambda + \tau) k(t - \lambda) d\lambda, \qquad (8.1)$$

where $k(t) = 0$ for $t < 0$ and is a weighting function or time apperture [usually the impulse response of a physically realizable low-pass filter, see Eq. (5.15)]. Under the special condition $k(t) = 2\alpha e^{-2\alpha t} = h^2(t)$, $\varphi(\tau, t)$ can be related to the measurable short-time power spectrum

$$\Psi(\omega, t) = |F(\omega, t)|^2,$$

where

$$F(\omega, t) = \int_{-\infty}^{t} f(\lambda) h(t - \lambda) e^{-j\omega\lambda} d\lambda. \qquad (8.2)$$

In fact, it was shown that

$$\varphi(\tau, t) = \frac{e^{\alpha |\tau|}}{2\pi} \int_{-\infty}^{\infty} \Psi(\omega, t) e^{j \omega \tau} d\tau; \qquad (8.3)$$

and

$$\Psi(\omega, t) = \int_{-\infty}^{\infty} e^{-\alpha |\tau|} \varphi(\tau, t) e^{-j \omega \tau} d\tau. \qquad (8.4)$$

In this case the measurable short-time power spectrum — which is essentially the quantity dealt with in the channel vocoder (or rather the square root of it) — is the Fourier transform of the product of the weighting $e^{-\alpha|\tau|}$ and the short-time autocorrelation function $\varphi(\tau, t)$. The spectral information might therefore be specified in terms of the correlation. Several transmission methods for utilizing this relation have been examined (HUGGINS, 1954; SCHROEDER, 1959, 1962; KOCK; BIDDULPH).

One method for applying the principle is shown in Fig. 8.8. In the top branch of the circuit, the input speech is submitted to pitch extraction. This information is derived and employed in a manner identical to the channel vocoder. In the lower branch of the circuit, the input signal is put through a spectral equalizer which, in effect, takes the square root of the input signal spectrum. The basis for this operation is that the ultimate processed signal is going to be a correlation function whose Fourier transform is the power spectrum (or, the squared amplitude spectrum) of the input signal. Although spectrum-squared speech is generally quite intelligible, it has an unnatural intensity or stress variation. Since the spectrum squaring is inherent in the process, it is taken into account at the outset.

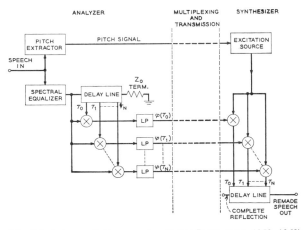

Fig. 8.8. Autocorrelation vocoder. (After SCHROEDER, 1959, 1962)

After spectral square-rooting, the short-time autocorrelation function of the signal is computed for specified delays. This is done by multiplying the appropriate output of a properly terminated delay line with the original input, and low-pass filtering the product (in this case with a 20-cps low-pass filter). The impulse response of the low-pass filter is the $k(t)$ as given in Eq. (8.1). Since the autocorrelation function is bandlimited to the same frequency range as the signal itself, the correlation function is completely specified by sampling at the Nyquist interval (i.e., $1/2\,BW$). For a 3000 cps signal, therefore, a delay interval $\Delta\tau = 0.167$ msec is sufficient. The greatest delay to which the function needs to be specified, practically, is on the order of 3 msec (SCHROEDER, 1962). Thus a total of 18 delay channels — each using about 20 cps bandwidth — are required. The total bandwidth is therefore 360 cps and is about the same as required by the channel vocoder.

At the synthesizer, voiced sounds are produced by generating a periodic waveform in which the individual pitch period is the correlation function described by the values existing on the $n\tau$-channels at that instant. The waveform is generated by letting the pitch pulses of the excitation "sample" the individual τ-channels. The sampling is accomplished by multiplying the excitation and each channel signal. The samples are assembled in the correct order by a delay line, and are low-pass filtered to yield the continuous correlation function. Since the correlation function is even, the synthesized wave is made symmetrical about the τ_0 sample. This can be done practically with the delay line correctly terminated at its output end, but unterminated and completely reflecting at the far end, as shown in Fig. 8.8. Low-pass filtering of the samples emerging from the line recovers the continuous signal.

Because a finite delay is used in the analysis, the measured correlation function is truncated, and discontinuities will generally exist in the synthesized waveform. This leads to a noticeable distortion. The distortion can be reduced by weighting the high-delay correlation values so that they have less influence in the synthesized wave. The discontinuities are thereby smoothed, and the processed speech obtained approaches that from channel vocoders of the same bandwidth compression[1].

8.5. Formant Vocoders

The results of the acoustic analyses in Chapter III suggest that one efficient way to code speech is in terms of the vocal mode pattern. The

---

[1] This truncation distortion in synthesis can be avoided if the correlation data are used to control a recursive filter. See the technique devised for the Maximum Likelihood Vocoder (ITAKURA and SAITO, 1968) in Section 8.8.

results show, for example, that adjacent values of the short-time amplitude spectrum are not independent, but are closely correlated. In fact, specification of the complex poles and zeros is equivalent to specifying the spectrum at all frequencies. The formant vocoder aims to exploit this fact and to code the speech signal in terms of the mode pattern of the vocal tract. Because it does not use multiple control signals to describe strongly correlated points in the speech spectrum, the formant-vocoder hopes to achieve a band-saving in excess of that accomplished by the channel vocoder. The practicability of formant vocoders depends upon how well formant-mode data, or the equivalent, can be automatically derived. In addition, excitation information must be provided as in the channel vocoder.

A number of formant-vocoder systems have been designed and instrumented. Although it is not possible to treat each in detail, this section proposes to indicate typical circuit realizations and the results obtained from them.

Formant-vocoders generally divide into two groups — essentially defined by the synthesis philosophies set forth in Chapter VI. That is, the classification relates to the cascade and parallel connections of the synthesis circuits. The cascade approach strives to reconstruct the signal by simulating, usually termwise, the perceptually significant pole and zero factors of the vocal transmission. The complex frequencies of the poles and zeros, and the excitation data (pitch and voiced-unvoiced) are the coding parameters.

The parallel connection attempts to reconstruct the same signal in a different, but equivalent, way — namely, from information on the frequencies of the formants (poles) and their spectral amplitudes (residues). Ideally, the mode frequencies and their residues are specified in complex form. The complex residues are equivalent to specification of the spectral zeros. The discussion of Section 6.2, Chapter VI, has set down in some detail the relations between the cascade and parallel representations of the speech signal. If the requisite data for either synthesis arrangement can be obtained automatically and with sufficient accuracy, the formant vocoder has the potential for producing intelligible speech of perhaps better quality than that of the channel vocoder. Because it attempts to duplicate the vocal mode structure, it innately has the potential for a better and more natural description of the speech spectrum.

One of the earliest, complete formant-vocoder systems was a parallel arrangement (MUNSON and MONTGOMERY). It is illustrated in Fig. 8.9. At the analyzer, the input speech band is split into four subbands. In each band, the average frequency of axis-crossings,

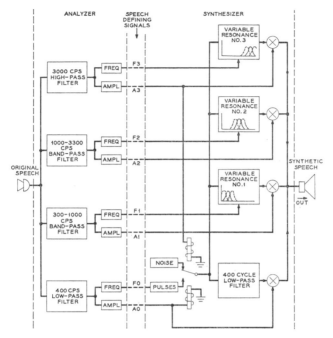

Fig. 8.9. Parallel-connected formant vocoder. (After MUNSON and MONTGOMERY)

F, and the average rectified-smoothed amplitude, A, are measured[1]. Signal voltages proportional to these quantities are developed. These eight parameters, which approximate the amplitudes and frequencies of the formants and of voicing, are transmitted to the synthesizer.

The synthesizer contains excitation circuitry, three variable resonators connected in parallel, and a fourth parallel branch with a fixed low-pass filter. Voiced (pulse) excitation of the parallel branches is signalled by the voicing amplitude, $A0$. The $A0$ control also determines the amplitude of the signal passing the fixed low-pass branch of the circuit. As in the channel vocoder, the frequency of the pulse source is prescribed by $F0$. Unvoiced (noise) excitation of the parallel branches is determined by amplitude $A3$. The amplitudes and frequencies of the three formant branches are continuously controlled and their outputs combined.

Intelligibility scores reported for the system were approximately 100% for vowel articulation and about 70% for consonant articulation.

---

[1] Note in this design the highest two bands normally contain more than a single formant. Their amplitude and frequency measures primarily reflect the most prominent formants in these ranges.

The total bandwidth occupancy of the eight control signals was about 300 cps, or about the same as for the channel vocoder. A number of different versions of parallel-connected formant vocoders have subsequently been constructed (for example, CHANG; CAMPANELLA; AYERS; STEAD and JONES; HOWARD). Two of these will receive further comment in the following section on digitalizing and multiplexing.

An early effort at realizing a cascade system also investigated the effects of severe band-limitation of the control signals (FLANAGAN and HOUSE). One synthesizer configuration considered in the study is shown in Fig. 8.10. The control data employed were pitch $F0$; amplitude of

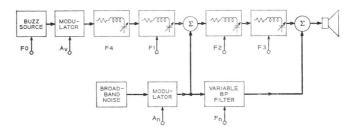

Fig. 8.10. Cascade-connected formant vocoder. (After FLANAGAN and HOUSE)

voicing AV; three formant frequencies $F1$, $F2$, $F3$ (covering the range approximately 100 to 3000 cps); a single, relatively-broad, fricative noise resonance FN (the major resonance in the range 3000 to 7000 cps); and the amplitude of noise excitation AN.

The formant frequency data were obtained from a peak-picking analyzer as described in Section 5.2, Chapter V. The amplitude of voicing was determined from the rectified-smoothed signal in a low-pass band of the original speech, and the amplitude of noise excitation was determined from the rectified-smoothed signal in the 3000 to 7000 cps band. Pitch was measured with a fundamental-extracting circuit, as in the channel vocoder. Each of the seven control signals was band-limited to slightly less than 10 cps by a low-pass filter, so that the total bandwidth occupancy was on the order of 60 cps.

All voiced sounds were produced by the upper resonator string of the circuit, following strictly the cascade approach. The unvoiced sounds were produced by a cascade-parallel connection which introduced zeros, as well as poles, into the transmission. Data on frequencies of zeros, as such, were not transmitted.

Although the band saving was high, detailed articulation testing of the system showed its performance to be relatively poor. In nonsense monosyllables, the vowel articulation was on the order of 82%. For the consonants, the mean score was 27%. Confusion-matrix analysis of listener responses showed that voiced-unvoiced errors were few. Errors in discriminating voiced-stops and nasals, however, were relatively numerous, the synthesizer being congenitally incapable of simulating these sounds. In addition, errors in discriminating affricates and stops were due in large part to temporal imprecision resulting from the severe band-limitation of the control signals.

A more recent, digital computer simulation of an improved version of the synthesizer corrects some of the shortcomings (FLANAGAN, COKER, and BIRD). It provides for an additional pole-zero pair in the voiced branch and a controllable zero in the unvoiced branch (see Fig. 6.38 and Section 6.2, Chapter VI). When combined with a sophisticated digitally-simulated formant analyzer, the performance as a complete real-time formant vocoder is unusually good (COKER). The formant analysis in the computer is accomplished by a detailed matching of the real speech spectrum by a pole-zero model spectrum, similar to the analysis-by-synthesis procedure. (See Section 5.21.) The digital processing provides much greater accuracy than can be obtained with analog equipment. The precision in the formant tracking, and the more detailed accounting for system and excitation characteristics by means of the additional pole-zero pair, contribute significantly to the quality of the synthetic speech.

A further word may be appropriate concerning the relative merits of parallel versus cascade connections, and about the approach which may result in the most efficient and practical set of parameters. The vocal transmission for vowel sounds contains only poles. The residues in these poles are therefore functions only of the pole frequencies. Given the formant frequencies, any formant amplitude specification is redundant because the amplitudes are implied by the frequencies. In this case, the cascade synthesizer provides correct formant amplitudes automatically from formant frequency data alone. For nonvowel sounds the vocal transmission can have zeros, one or two of which may prove to be perceptually significant. To simulate these factors, the cascade synthesizer requires controllable antiresonances. Again, given the proper pole *and* zero frequencies, spectral amplitudes are automatically accounted for.

The parallel synthesizer, on the other hand, requires the significant pole frequencies and, ideally, the complex residues in these poles. The residues, in effect, specify the spectral zeros. The contribution to perception of the residue phases is modest but not negligible (FLANAGAN, 1965). (See Section 6.223.) A relevant question about formant synthesis is then "Which is easier to analyze automatically, the frequencies of spectral zeros or the amplitudes and phases of spectral maxima?" The question is complicated by one other matter—the excitation source.

What are its perceptually important characteristics? Are they easier to include in one model than in the other? At the present stage of study, the ultimate practical choice is not clear.

8.51. Multiplexing and Digitalization of Formant Vocoders

One real-time formant vocoder that has been given extensive tests is the parallel configuration shown in Fig. 8.11 (STEAD and JONES). Besides being tested in the unmultiplexed "back-to-back" connection, this system has also been examined in a fully digitalized version using time-division PCM techniques (STEAD and WESTON). The components of the system have several similarities with devices discussed previously. In one version, the synthesizer is based upon an earlier development (LAWRENCE, 1953). The formant-frequency extractor is based upon the peak-picking technique described in Section 5.2, Chapter V. The over-all implementation and circuit design are unusually refined, and considerable effort is made to insure adequate dynamic range for the extraction of frequency and amplitude data. In the analog form, low-pass filters confine the eight control parameters to approximately 20 cps each, resulting in a total bandwidth occupancy of about 160 cps. Typical intelligibility scores for phonetically-balanced words and for relatively naive listeners are reported to average approximately 70%.

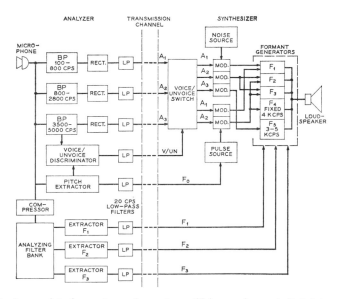

Fig. 8.11. A complete formant-vocoder system utilizing analog and digital transmission techniques. (After STEAD and JONES; STEAD and WESTON)

As mentioned earlier, the advantages of digital transmission are several. Not least is the ability to regenerate the signal repeatedly — essentially free of accumulating distortion. Problems in switching, time sharing and security are also amenable to straightforward solutions with the signal in digital form. One difficulty, however, is that transmission of the digital signal requires more bandwidth than does the analog form. For example, a 3000 cps speech band sampled at the Nyquist rate $(6000 \sec^{-1})$ and quantized to 6 or 7 bits may require — without further coding — a bandwidth on the order of 50000 cps. If, through appropriate coding, the data rate could be brought down to the order of 1000 bits/sec, the digital signal could easily be transmitted over ordinary 3000 cps voice channels. The formant vocoder holds promise for providing such a coding.

In the formant vocoder of Fig. 8.11, the control parameters were band-limited to 20 cps. For digitalizing the control signals, however, a sampling rate of $32 \sec^{-1}$ was found to be a safe working minimum. This rate suggests that the control parameters have little significant energy above about 16 cps. The amplitude quantization found acceptable for digitalizing the control data of this system is shown in Table 8.3.

Table 8.3. *Quantization of formant-vocoder signals.* (After STEAD and WESTON)

Parameter	Number of levels	Bits
$F1$:	16	4
$F2$:	16	4
$F3$:	8	3
$A1$:	8	3
$A2$:	8	3
$A3$:	8	3
V/UN:	2	1
$F0$:	64 [a]	6
		27

[a] Estimated for linear coding of fundamental frequency.

In evaluating the digital transmission, 16 levels were thought too generous for the first formant frequency, but 8 levels were too coarse. For the three amplitude parameters, the 8 levels each were also thought too generous and that additional saving could be effected by coding the functions on a log-amplitude scale[1].

---

[1] These observations have been confirmed, extended and quantified in greater depth by computer-perceptual experiments on the bandlimitation and quantization of formant data in synthesis (ROSENBERG, SCHAFER and RABINER).

It is relevant to compare the practical figures of Table 8.3 with earlier estimates of the precision necessary in quantizing similar parameters (FLANAGAN, 1957b). The earlier estimates were based upon the just-perceptible changes which listeners could detect in the formant parameters of synthetic vowels (see Section 7.2, Chapter VII). The quantizing accuracy estimated to be necessary is given in Table 8.4.

In view of the limitations of the perceptual data on which the estimates are based, the correspondence with the numbers in Table 8.3 is surprisingly close. It suggests that psychoacoustic measures of the type discussed in Chapter VII might be judiciously applied with some confidence to estimate system performance.

Table 8.4. *Estimated precision necessary in quantizing formant-vocoder parameters*

The estimates are based upon just-discriminable changes in the parameters of synthetic vowels. (After FLANAGAN, 1957b)[a].

Parameter	Number of levels	Bits
$F1$:	14	3.8
$F2$:	14	3.8
$F3$:	9	3.2
$A1$:	3	1.6
$A2$:	3	1.6
$A3$:	2	1.0
$F0$:	40	5.3
		20.3

[a] The amplitude parameters are considered to be logarithmic measures.

After sampling and quantizing, the data of Fig. 8.11 are PCM encoded for transmission. At a sampling rate of $32 \sec^{-1}$, the control data, exclusive of pitch, are specified with 672 bits/sec. A 6-bit pitch parameter produces a total rate of 864 bits/sec, a rate which could be transmitted by conventional 3000 cps channels. Although detailed testing has not been carried out, the digitally transmitted signal is reported to differ only slightly in intelligibility and quality from the analog connection. One interesting observation about the system is that the spectrum of the quantizing noise associated with digitalizing the control signals does not lie in the audio band. Rather, the noise corresponds to a sort of quasi-random uncertainty in the synthesis process. Its subjective effects have not been fully explored.

A preliminary study has considered the effects of digital errors in the PCM-encoded parameters of a formant vocoder (CAMPANELLA,

COULTER, and IRONS). The system on which the tests were performed is similar to that shown in Fig. 8.11, except the voiced-unvoiced decision is transmitted by the pitch signal. The total bandwidth occupancy of the control signals is 140 cps. The formant parameters are quantized to 3 bits. Pitch is quantized to 5 bits. A $43.5 \, sec^{-1}$ scan rate in the time multiplexing produces a data rate of 1 000 bits/sec. Under error free conditions, articulation scores of about 80 % on PB words are claimed for this bit rate. A digital error rate of 3 % degrades the articulation score by 15 %. This impairment is found to be equivalent to reducing the signal-to-noise ratio of the analog parameters to 9.5 db.

8.52. Voice-Excited Formant Vocoders

The voice-excitation technique described in Section 8.3 has also been applied to a parallel-connected formant vocoder (FLANAGAN, 1960b). The circuit arrangement is shown in Fig. 8.12. In this implementation, a baseband of about 400 cps (300 to 700 cps) is transmitted in unprocessed form. Three formant vocoder channels cover the frequency range 800 to 3 200, and the amplitude and frequency of three spectral maxima in this range are transmitted. Formant extraction is accomplished according to the maximum-picking technique described in Section 5.2, Chapter V. All control signals are low-passed to 17 cps. The total bandwidth occupancy is therefore slightly more than 500 cps.

At the synthesizer the baseband is spectrally broadened. It is peak-clipped, differentiated, half-wave rectified and used to trigger a one-shot multivibrator. The pulse output of the multivibrator provides the excitation source for the formant channels. Unvoiced sounds create shot noise from the multivibrator. Voiced sounds produce periodic pulse trains which sometimes may have more than one pulse per fundamental

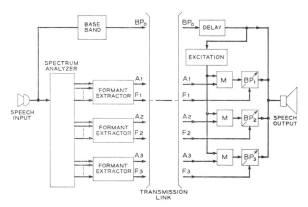

Fig. 8.12. Voice-excited formant vocoder. (After FLANAGAN, 1960b)

period. The technique generally provides an improvement in the quality and naturalness of the formant vocoder transmission. However, because the baseband is such a large percentage of the total bandwidth, it is almost as economical to use conventional vocoder channels above the baseband.

A related voice-excited technique uses the spectral shape of the first formant region to shape the second and third formants (DE JAGER, personal communication, 1961). A baseband about 300 to 800 cps is separated and transmitted in unprocessed form. In two other (formant) bands, 800 to 2000 cps and 2000 to 3200 cps, zero-crossing counters and rectifier-integrator circuits determine signals representing the amplitudes and frequencies of the formants. These four signals are low-passed to 40 cps each, and are sent with the baseband to the receiver.

The synthesizer reconstructs a spectrum in which the baseband (essentially the first formant) is produced in its original position. A second formant is synthesized in a separate parallel branch by heterodyning the baseband to the measured second formant frequency position. A third is generated in a similar fashion. The output speech is obtained by adding the three parallel branches in accordance with the measured amplitudes. The spectral components of the heterodyned bands generally become inharmonic, and the pitch frequency is preserved in them only to the extent of line spacing. Perceptually, the degradation of pitch information is less than might be expected, since the baseband is retained in original form with its correct line structure, and it is an effective masker.

8.6. Orthogonal Function Vocoders

One approach to describing a signal with the fewest independent parameters is to approximate the signal, in some sense, by a series of orthogonal functions. The coefficients of the expansion then become the information-bearing quantities. The orthogonal functions chosen for the representation presumably should capitalize upon some known characteristic of the signal.

The orthogonal function approach has been considered for describing both the speech waveform and the amplitude spectrum. A precise waveform description holds relatively small potential for bandwidth reduction — unless information such as phase is discarded and use is made of voiced-unvoiced and pitch tracking measurements. The spectral description , or its time-domain equivalent, promises more. The relationships between short-time spectral analysis and correlation analysis suggest techniques for efficient description of the speech spectrum.

8.61. Expansion of the Speech Waveform

A general method has been described in the literature for representing signal waveforms by orthogonalized, exponential functions (HUGGINS, 1957; KAUTZ). The method has been applied to the analysis of single pitch periods of voiced sounds (DOLANSKY, 1960). If $f(t)$ is a single pitch period, then the approximation

$$f(t) \simeq \sum_m c_m g_m(t) \tag{8.5}$$

is made, where the $g_m(t)$ are the set of orthogonalized, exponential functions. Their Laplace transforms of odd and even orders are given by

$$G_{2n-1}(s) = \sqrt{2\alpha_n} \frac{s+|s_n|}{(s-s_n)(s-s_n^*)} \prod_{j=1}^{n-1} \frac{(s+s_j)(s+s_j^*)}{(s-s_j)(s-s_j^*)}$$

$$G_{2n}(s) = \sqrt{2\alpha_n} \frac{s-|s_n|}{(s-s_n)(s-s_n^*)} \prod_{j=1}^{n-1} \frac{(s+s_j)(s+s_j^*)}{(s-s_j)(s-s_j^*)} \tag{8.6}$$

where

$$s_n = (-\alpha_n + j\beta_n).$$

The inverse transforms of Eq. (8.6) are

$$g_{2n-1}(t) = \sum_{k=1}^{n} \frac{1}{\beta_k} |\mathcal{K}_{2n-1}(s_k)| e^{-\alpha_k t} \sin[\beta_k t - \vartheta_{2n-1}(s_k)]$$

$$g_{2n}(t) = \sum_{k=1}^{n} \frac{1}{\beta_k} |\mathcal{K}_{2n}(s_k)| e^{-\alpha_k t} \sin[\beta_k t - \vartheta_{2n}(s_k)] \tag{8.7}$$

where

$$\mathcal{K}_m(s_k) = \{G_m(s)[(s+\alpha_k^2) + \beta_k^2]\}_{s=s_k}$$

and

$$\vartheta_m(s_k) = \frac{\operatorname{Re} \mathcal{K}_m(s_k)}{|\mathcal{K}_m(s_k)|}.$$

The first two $g_m(t)$'s, therefore, are simple damped sinusoids which differ in amplitude and phase. The product-series components of $G_m(s)$ are seen to be all-pass functions. An n of 7 (or an m of 14) is considered to be adequate for the speech wave approximation (DOLANSKY). The critical frequencies s_n are fixed and are chosen to span the voice frequency range, typically in intervals of a few hundred cps.[1]

Assuming $f(t)$ is zero for $t<0$, and since

$$\int_0^\infty g_p(t) g_q(t) dt = 1; \quad p=q$$

$$= 0; \quad p \neq q,$$

---

[1] A relevant question might inquire as to the potential of this technique if the s_n could be derived in an adaptive way; that is, if the s_n could be varied to match the signal.

the k-th coefficient of the orthonormal series is given by

$$c_k = \int_0^\infty f(t)\, g_k(t)\, dt. \tag{8.8}$$

One straightforward, but impractical, means for measuring the coefficients is apparent. Suppose the signal $f(t)$ is filtered with a realizable filter whose impulse response is $g_k(t)$, the result is

$$O(t) = \int_0^\infty g_k(\tau)\, f(t-\tau)\, d\tau. \tag{8.9}$$

If, however, the time-reversed signal $f(-t)$ is filtered, the result is

$$O(t) = \int_0^\infty g_k(\tau)\, f(t+\tau)\, d\tau. \tag{8.10}$$

The value $O(0)$, that is, the result at the instant when the time reversed $f(t)$ ends, is the value of c_k. This measurement, performed for all the $g_m(t)$'s, provides the requisite coefficients.

A perhaps more practicable, real-time application of the orthogonal function for speech waveform transmission is shown by the system in Fig. 8.13a (MANLEY and KLEIN). For voiced sounds the input speech is led to a pitch extractor which generates an impulse train at the fundamental frequency. These impulses produce the set of orthogonal functions $g_m(t)$ by exciting realizable networks having the functions as their impulse responses. Approximations to the coefficients of the series (8.5) are obtained by calculating.

$$c_k = \int_0^T g_k(t)\, f(t)\, dt, \tag{8.11}$$

where T is a given pitch period. The calculation is carried out by the multipliers, the reset integrators and the sample-and-hold elements shown in the diagram. The pitch pulses reset the integrators and trigger the sampling circuits to read and store the value of the integral at the end of period T. Before multiplexing and transmission, the pitch pulse-frequency is converted into an analog signal by a frequency meter, and the time-varying coefficients $c_1(t)$, $c_2(t) \ldots c_m(t)$ are further smoothed by low-pass filtering.

At the receiver, in Fig. 8.13b, the signal is reconstructed, pitch period by pitch period, according to Eq. (8.5). A pitch-modulated pulse generator excites an identical set of $g_m(t)$ networks and their outputs are respectively modulated by the $c_m(t)$ coefficients. The sum is an approximation to the original voiced sound.

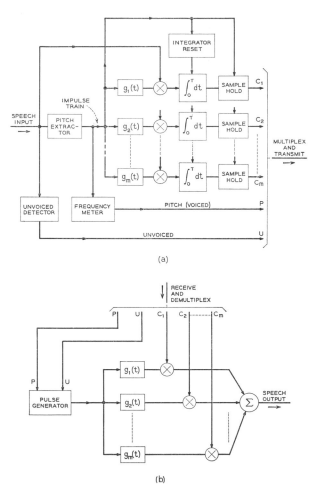

Fig. 8.13 a and b. System for transmitting speech waveforms in terms of orthogonal functions. (After MANLEY and KLEIN.) (a) Analyzer. (b) Synthesizer

The processing of unvoiced, aperiodic sounds is slightly different. Ideally they are treated as if their waveforms constituted one pitch period. The onset of an unvoiced sound is detected and, if the unvoiced sound is relatively brief, as in a stop, only one pitch pulse is generated in the transmitter and in the receiver. The unvoiced indication is signalled to the receiver by the $u(t)$ parameter. If the unvoiced sound is sustained (for example, a fricative), the pulse generators are made to continue generating pulses with periods long enough that the periodicity is not significant perceptually.

8.62. Expansion of the Short-Time Amplitude Spectrum

At least one orthogonal-function description of the short-time amplitude spectrum has been proposed as a bandsaving means for coding
speech (PIROGOV). The approach is particularized to a Fourier series
description where, in effect, a spectrum of the amplitude spectrum is
obtained. The technique is illustrated in Fig. 8.14.

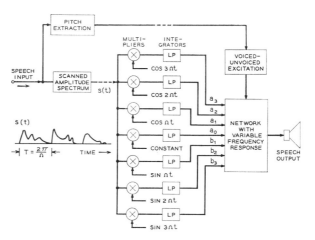

Fig. 8.14. Method for describing and synthesizing the short-time speech spectrum in terms
of Fourier coefficients. (After PIROGOV)

A short-time amplitude spectrum is produced as a time function by
scanning at a frequency $1/T$. The operation can be implemented as
in the formant extractor described in Section 5.2, or in the manner
of the "scan vocoder" discussed in Section 8.1, or even with a single
scanning filter. The frequency $1/T$ would normally range from 25 to
50 cps, depending upon the requirements imposed on the quality of
transmission. As in the "scan vocoder", the spectral description $s(t)$
is transmitted over a restricted bandwidth channel. A bandwidth between
75 and 250 cps is reported to be adequate. Excitation information,
that is, pitch and voiced-unvoiced indications, must also be transmitted.
As in the conventional vocoder, a bandwidth of 25 to 50 cps is expected
to be adequate for these data. Synchronizing information about the scanning must also be made known to the receiver.

At the receiver, a Fourier series description of the amplitude spectrum
is computed, namely,

$$s(t) = \frac{a_0}{2} + \sum_{n=1}^{N} [a_n \cos n\Omega t + b_n \sin n\Omega t], \qquad (8.12)$$

where, as usual, the coefficients are

$$a_n = \frac{2}{T} \int_0^T s(t) \cos n\Omega t \, dt$$

$$b_n = \frac{2}{T} \int_0^T s(t) \sin n\Omega t \, dt,$$

and $\Omega = 2\pi/T$. Practically, the Fourier coefficients are obtained by multiplying $s(t)$ by the outputs of several harmonic oscillators each synchronized to the scanning frequency Ω. An $N=3$ to 5 is claimed to provide an adequate spectral description (PIROGOV).

The coefficients vary relatively slowly with time. They are used to control an electrical network so that its frequency response is approximately the same as the measured spectral envelope of the speech signal. The network is then excited in a manner similar to the conventional vocoder, that is, either by periodic pulses or by noise. The reconstructed speech is the output of the variable network shown in Fig. 8.14.

The operation of the controllable network is based upon the fact that $s(t)$ is actually a spectral amplitude $S(\omega)$, $0 \leq \omega \leq \omega_{max}$. Hence, $\Omega = 2\pi/T = 2\pi/\omega_{max}$, so that Eq. (8.12) can be rewritten as

$$S(\omega) = \frac{a_0}{2} + \sum_{n=1}^{N} a_n \cos \frac{2\pi n \omega}{\omega_{max}} + b_n \sin \frac{2\pi n \omega}{\omega_{max}}. \qquad (8.13)$$

If the excitation amplitude spectrum is $G(\omega)$, then the output of the variable network should be $S(\omega) \cdot G(\omega)$. Assuming the excitation spectrum is flat and of unity amplitude, a given sine component ω_1 in the excitation spectrum should produce an output time function

$$f_1(t) = \frac{a_0}{2} \sin \omega_1 t + \sin \omega_1 t \sum_{n=1}^{N} a_n \cos \frac{2\pi n \omega_1}{\omega_{max}}$$
$$+ \sin \omega_1 t \sum_{n=1}^{N} b_n \sin \frac{2\pi n \omega_1}{\omega_{max}}. \qquad (8.14)$$

Expanding the second and third terms as sums and differences of angles gives

$$2 f_1(t) = a_0 \sin \omega_1 t + \sum_{n=1}^{N} a_n \left[\sin \left(\omega_1 t - \frac{2\pi n \omega_1}{\omega_{max}} \right) \right.$$
$$\left. + \sin \left(\omega_1 t + \frac{2\pi n \omega_1}{\omega_{max}} \right) \right] \qquad (8.15)$$
$$+ \sum_{n=1}^{N} b_n \left[\cos \left(\omega_1 t - \frac{2\pi n \omega_1}{\omega_{max}} \right) - \cos \left(\omega_1 t + \frac{2\pi n \omega_1}{\omega_{max}} \right) \right].$$

The second terms of the arguments, i.e., $\dfrac{2\pi n\,\omega_1}{\omega_{max}}$ correspond to time advances and delays of

$$n\tau = n \cdot \frac{2\pi}{\omega_{max}}.$$

The time function can therefore be constructed by the circuit shown in Fig. 8.15. The cosine terms of Eq. (8.15) are obtained by Hilbert transforming a difference of sine terms (i.e., by incurring a broadband $\pi/2$ phase shift). Although (8.15) is particularized for a given spectral component of excitation, namely ω_1, the process is the same for all other components. It is reported that with a spectral description of $N=4$ or 5, the synthesized speech quality is natural enough to satisfy the requirements of ordinary voice channels.

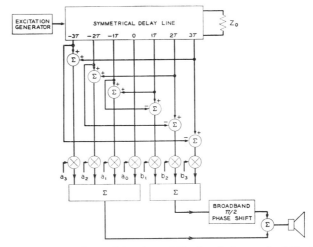

Fig. 8.15. Technique for realizing the variable electrical network of Fig. 8.14

8.63. Expansion of the Short-Time Autocorrelation Function

For an on-going time function $f(t)$, the discussion of Chapter V derived the relation between the short-time autocorrelation function (defined for positive delays)

$$\varphi(\tau, t) = \int_{-\infty}^{t} f(\lambda)f(\lambda - \tau)\,k(t - \lambda)\,d\lambda, \qquad \tau \geqq 0, \qquad (8.16)$$

and the measurable short-time amplitude spectrum

$$F(\omega, t) = \int_{-\infty}^{t} f(\lambda)\,h(t - \lambda)\,e^{-j\omega\lambda}\,d\lambda. \qquad (8.17)$$

For the specific weighting function

$$k(t) = h^2(t) = 2\sigma e^{-2\sigma t},$$

the short-time correlation and spectrum are linked by the weighted Fourier cosine transform

$$|F(\omega, t)|^2 = \int_{-\infty}^{\infty} e^{-\sigma |\tau|} \varphi(\tau, t) \cos \omega \tau \, d\tau$$

$$= \frac{1}{2\pi} |H(\omega)|^2 * \Phi(\omega, t), \tag{8.18}$$

where $H(\omega)$ and $\Phi(\omega, t)$ are the Fourier transforms of $h(t)$ and $\varphi(\tau, t)$, respectively. The transform-pair (8.18) implies that $\varphi(\tau, t)$ is an even function of τ.

The preceding section described a technique for representing the short-time amplitude spectrum $|F(\omega, t)|$ in terms of an orthogonal function expansion. Since the correlation function and power spectrum are uniquely linked, it might be expected that a related orthonormal expansion can be written for the correlation function. This expansion leads to an alternative time-domain representation of the signal. In particular, Laguerre functions have been found a convenient expansion for this description (Y. W. LEE; MANLEY; KULYA).

Suppose the short-time correlation function of $f(t)$ for positive delays is expanded in terms of a realizable function set $\{\xi_i(\tau)\}$, orthonormal on the internal $0 \leq \tau \leq \infty$ and zero for $\tau < 0$. Then

$$\varphi(+\tau, t) = \sum_{i=0}^{\infty} a_i(t) \xi_i(\tau), \qquad \tau \geq 0. \tag{8.19}$$

Because of the orthogonal properties

$$a_i(t) = \int_0^{\infty} \varphi(+\tau, t) \xi_i(\tau) \, d\tau$$

$$= \int_0^{\infty} \xi_i(\tau) \, d\tau \int_{-\infty}^{t} f(\lambda) f(\lambda - \tau) k(t - \tau) \, d\lambda. \tag{8.20}$$

Changing the order of integration and substituting $\gamma = (\lambda - \tau)$ gives

$$a_i(t) = \int_{-\infty}^{t} f(\lambda) k(t - \lambda) \, d\lambda \int_{-\infty}^{\lambda} f(\gamma) \xi_i(\lambda - \gamma) \, d\gamma. \tag{8.21}$$

The coefficients $a_i(t)$ are therefore obtained by first filtering $f(t)$ with a network whose impulse response is $\xi_i(t)$, multiplying the result by $f(t)$ and then filtering the product with a network whose impulse response is $k(t)$. The operations are illustrated in Fig. 8.16.

The $a_i(t)$ coefficients obtained from (8.21) describe $\varphi(\tau, t)$ for positive delays $(\tau \geq 0)$. If, as defined and as discussed in Chapter V, $\varphi(\tau, t)$ is an even function of τ, the correlation for negative delay may be written

$$\varphi(-\tau, t) = \sum_{i=0}^{\infty} a_i(t)\, \xi_i(-\tau), \qquad \tau < 0, \tag{8.22}$$

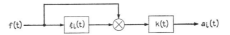

Fig. 8.16. Expansion coefficients for the short-time auto-correlation function

and the correlation function for all τ is

$$\varphi(\tau, t) = \varphi(+\tau, t) + \varphi(-\tau, t)$$
$$= \sum_{i=0}^{\infty} a_i(t)\, [\xi_i(\tau) + \xi_i(-\tau)]. \tag{8.23}$$

The Fourier transform of $\varphi(\tau, t)$ is the power spectrum

$$\Phi(\omega, t) = \sum_{i=0}^{\infty} a_i(t) \int_{-\infty}^{\infty} [\xi_i(\tau) + \xi_i(-\tau)]\, e^{-j\omega\tau}\, d\tau$$
$$= \sum_{i=0}^{\infty} a_i(t)\, \{\Xi_i(\omega) + \Xi_i^*(\omega)\} \tag{8.24}$$

where $\Xi_i(\omega)$ is the Fourier transform of $\xi_i(\tau)$.

The spectrum $\Phi(\omega, t)$ is related to the measurable power spectrum of Eq. (8.18) such that

$$|F(\omega, t)|^2 = \sum_{i=0}^{\infty} a_i(t)\, \{\Xi_i'(\omega) + \Xi_i'^*(\omega)\}, \tag{8.25}$$

where $\Xi_i'(\omega)$ is the Fourier transform of $[e^{-\sigma|\tau|}\, \xi_i(\tau)]$.

Writing $\Xi_i(\omega)$ in terms of its magnitude and phase,

$$\Xi_i(\omega) = \alpha_i(\omega)\, e^{-j\beta_i(\omega)}. \tag{8.26}$$

Then

$$\Phi(\omega, t) = \sum_{i=0}^{\infty} a_i(t)\, \alpha_i(\omega)\, [e^{-j\beta_i(\omega)} + e^{+j\beta_i(\omega)}]$$
$$= 2 \sum_{i=0}^{\infty} a_i(t)\, \alpha_i(\omega)\, \cos \beta_i(\omega). \tag{8.27}$$

Thus the coefficients $a_i(t)$ of an orthonormal expansion of the auto-correlation function [Eq. (8.19)] are also the coefficients of a Fourier series expansion of the power spectrum.

So far, the orthogonal filter functions $\xi_i(t)$ have not been particulariz-ed. They have only been assumed to be physically realizable impulse responses. One simple set of orthonormal filters — and one that leads to a familiar result — is an ideal delay line with radian bandwidth B and with delay taps spaced at the Nyquist interval $1/2B$. The frequency response at the i-th tap is

$$\Xi_i(\omega) = e^{-j\left(\frac{i\omega}{2B}\right)}, \quad 0 \leq \omega \leq B$$

$$= e^{j\left(\frac{i\omega}{2B}\right)}, \quad -B \leq \omega \leq 0 \qquad (8.28)$$

$$= 0, \quad \text{elsewhere}.$$

The impulse response at the i-th tap is therefore

$$\xi_i(t) = \frac{B}{\pi} \frac{\sin\left(Bt - \frac{i}{2}\right)}{\left(Bt - \frac{i}{2}\right)}. \qquad (8.29)$$

As prescribed by Eq. (8.28), the amplitude response is $\alpha_i(\omega) = 1$, and the phase response is

$$\beta_i(\omega) = \left(\frac{i\omega}{2B}\right).$$

The power spectrum expansion of Eq. (8.27) is therefore the Fourier series

$$\Phi(\omega, t) = 2\sum_i a_i(t) \cos\left(\frac{i\omega}{2B}\right). \qquad (8.30)$$

The $a_i(t)$, on the other hand, which are computed according to the operations of Fig. 8.16, are simply values of the short-time autocorrelation function $\varphi(\tau, t)$ for $\tau = (i\omega/2B)$. These coefficients could be supplied directly to the left side of the synthesizer of Fig. 8.15 and used to generate the spectrum $\Phi(\omega, t)$. In this case, one has a correlation-vocoder syn-thesizer as described in Section 8.4.

Ideal broadband delay lines are neither physically wieldy nor particularly easy to construct. It is consequently of interest to consider other orthonormal function sets which might be useful in representing the short-time autocorrelation function or the power spectrum. Preferably, the functions should be realizable with simple lumped-element networks. The choice of Laguerre functions has advantages in this connection (Y. W. LEE).

Such an orthogonal set is

$$\{\xi_i(t)\} = \{l_i(t)\},$$

where the $l_i(t)$ are described by

$$l_i(t) = (2\lambda)^{\frac{1}{2}} e^{-\lambda t} \sum_{n=0}^{i} \frac{(-1)^n (2\lambda t)^{i-n} (i!/n!)}{[(i-n)!]^2}. \tag{8.31}$$

Its frequency transform is

$$
\begin{aligned}
L_i(\omega) &= \frac{(2\lambda)^{\frac{1}{2}}}{2\pi} \cdot \frac{(\lambda - j\omega)^i}{(\lambda + j\omega)^{i+1}} \\
&= (-1)^i \frac{1}{\pi (2\lambda)^{\frac{1}{2}}} \left(\frac{\lambda}{j\omega + \lambda} \right) \left(\frac{j\omega - \lambda}{j\omega + \lambda} \right)^i \tag{8.32} \\
&= A_i [u(\omega)] [v(\omega)]^i.
\end{aligned}
$$

The function (8.32) can be realized by cascading RC circuits of the type shown in Fig. 8.17, together with an amplification A_i.

If (8.32) is put in the form

$$L_i(\omega) = \alpha_i(\omega) e^{-j\beta_i(\omega)}, \tag{8.33}$$

then

$$L_i(\omega) = \frac{(2\lambda)^{\frac{1}{2}}}{2\pi} \cdot \frac{1}{(\omega^2 + \lambda^2)^{\frac{1}{2}}} \cdot e^{j\left[(2i+1)\tan^{-1}\frac{\omega}{\lambda}\right]}. \tag{8.34}$$

Further,

$$[L_i(\omega) + L_i^*(\omega)] = \frac{(2\lambda)^{\frac{1}{2}}}{\pi} \frac{1}{(\omega^2 + \lambda^2)^{\frac{1}{2}}} \cos\left[(2i+1)\tan^{-1}\frac{\omega}{\lambda}\right]. \tag{8.35}$$

The spectrum $\Phi(\omega, t)$ according to (8.24) and (8.27) is

$$
\begin{aligned}
\Phi(\omega, t) &= 2 \sum_{i=0}^{\infty} a_i(t) \alpha_i(\omega) \cos\beta_i(\omega) \\
&= \left(\frac{2}{\pi^2\lambda} \right)^{\frac{1}{2}} \sum_i a_i(t) \frac{\cos\left[(2i+1)\tan^{-1}\frac{\omega}{\lambda}\right]}{\left(1 + \frac{\omega^2}{\lambda^2}\right)^{\frac{1}{2}}}. \tag{8.36}
\end{aligned}
$$

To show how the positive frequency domain is spanned by the Laguerre functions, the first several terms of the final factor in (8.36) are plotted in Fig. 8.18 (MANLEY). The functions are seen to have the desirable feature that they attenuate with increasing frequency, as does the speech spectrum.

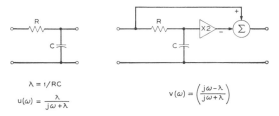

$$\lambda = 1/RC$$

$$u(\omega) = \frac{\lambda}{j\omega + \lambda}$$

$$v(\omega) = \left(\frac{j\omega - \lambda}{j\omega + \lambda}\right)$$

Fig. 8.17. Realization of Laguerre functions by RC networks [see Eq. (8.32)]

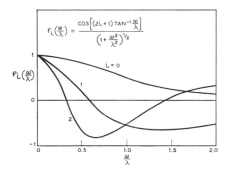

$$f_i\left(\frac{\omega}{\lambda}\right) = \frac{\cos\left[(2i+1)\,\text{TAN}^{-1}\frac{\omega}{\lambda}\right]}{\left(1 + \frac{\omega^2}{\lambda^2}\right)^{\frac12}}$$

Fig. 8.18. Plot of the final factor in Eq. (8.36) showing how the positive frequency range is spanned by the first several Laguerre functions. (After MANLEY)

A transmission system based upon these relations can be constructed. The assumption is that the spectrum-squaring operation, that is, the synthesis of a signal having a spectrum $\Phi(\omega, t)$, is perceptually acceptable. (See Sections 8.1 and 8.4 for other comments on spectrum squaring.) Such a signal is

$$\varphi(\tau, t) = \sum_{i=0}^{\infty} a_i(t)\left[l_i(\tau) + l_i(-\tau)\right],$$

having the spectrum

$$\Phi(\omega, t) = \sum_{i=0}^{\infty} a_i(t)\left[L_i(\omega) + L_i^*(\omega)\right]. \tag{8.37}$$

The correlation $\varphi(\tau, t)$ is an even function of τ and is produced from $l_i(\tau)$, $\tau \geq 0$. But with the circuits of Fig. 8.17, it is not possible to generate $l_i(-\tau)$. However, the ear is relatively insensitive to modest phase differences, and it suffices perceptually to generate a spectrum whose modulus is the same as $\Phi(\omega, t)$. Such a spectrum can be obtained from the odd function $[l_{m-i}(\tau) + l_{m+i+1}(\tau)]$ (KULYA). The corresponding spectrum is then

$$\Phi'(\omega, t) = \sum_{i=0}^{\infty} a_i(t)\left[L_{m-i}(\omega) + L_{m+i+1}(\omega)\right],$$

where, from Eq. (8.34),

$$[L_{m-i}(\omega)+L_{m+i+1}(\omega)]$$
$$=\frac{(2\lambda)^{\frac{1}{2}}}{\pi}\frac{1}{(\omega^2+\lambda^2)^{\frac{1}{2}}}\left[e^{j\,2\,(m+1)\,\tan^{-1}\frac{\omega}{\lambda}}\right]\cos\left[(2\,i+1)\tan^{-1}\frac{\omega}{\lambda}\right].\,(8.38)$$

Except for the phase angle $\left[e^{j\,2(m+1)\,\tan^{-1}\frac{\omega}{\lambda}}\right]$, Eq. (8.38) is identical to Eq. (8.35). The complete transmission system is therefore the circuit shown in Fig. 8.19. In Fig. 8.19a, the Laguerre expansion coefficients are developed according to Eq. (8.37) and after the fashion of Fig. 8.16. A pitch signal $p(t)$ is also extracted. The coefficients and pitch data are multiplexed and transmitted to the synthesizer in Fig. 8.19b. As in the vocoder, the synthesizer excitation is either wide-band noise or pitch-modulated pulses. By resorting to the odd function $[l_{m-1}(\tau)+l_{m+i+1}(\tau)]$, the synthesizer imposes the spectrum $\Phi'(\omega, t)$ upon the broadband excitation. Similar results can be obtained from an orthonormal expansion of the correlation function in terms of Tschebyscheff polynomials (KULYA).

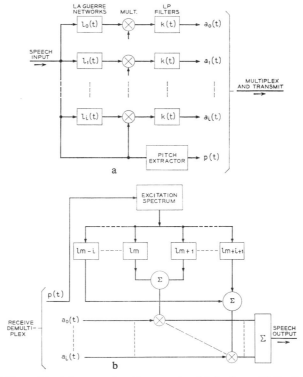

Fig. 8.19a and b. A Laguerre function vocoder. (a) Analyzer. (b) Synthesizer.
(After KULYA)

8.7. Homomorphic Vocoders

In a further approach toward exploiting the source-system distinction in the speech signal, a processing technique called homomorphic filtering has been applied to vocoder design (OPPENHEIM; OPPENHEIM and SCHAFER). The approach is based on the observation that the mouth output pressure is approximately the linear convolution of the vocal excitation signal and the impulse response of the vocal tract. Homomorphic filtering[1] is applied to deconvolve the components and provide for their individual processing and description.

The analyzer and synthesizer operations for a complete homomorphic vocoder are shown in Fig. 8.20. Fig. 8.20a illustrates the analysis. At successive intervals (typically every 20 msec), the input speech signal is multiplied by a data window (a 40 msec Hamming

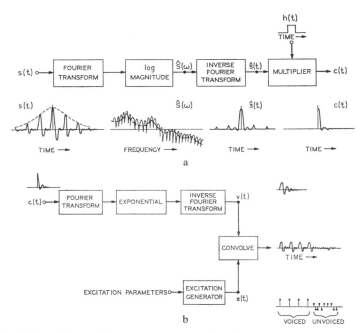

Fig. 8.20a and b. Analysis and synthesis operations for the homomorphic vocoder. (After OPPENHEIM)

---

[1] Homomorphic filtering is a generic term applying to a class of systems in which a signal-complex is transformed into a form where the principles of a linear filtering may be applied (OPPENHEIM). In the case of a speech signal, whose spectrum is approximately the product of the excitation spectrum and the vocal-tract transmission, a log-taking operation produces an additive combination of the source and system components. The cepstrum technique is therefore a special form of homomorphic filtering (see Sections 5.214 and 5.3).

window in this case) and the short-time Fourier transform is computed[1]. For each analysis interval the logarithm of the spectral magnitude is taken to produce the log-spectrum $\hat{S}(\omega)$. A further inverse Fourier transform produces the real, even time function $\hat{s}(t)$ which is defined as the cepstrum (see Sections 5.214 and 5.3). The low-time parts of $\hat{s}(t)$ characterize the slow fluctuations in $\hat{S}(\omega)$ due to the vocal-tract reso-nances, and the high-time parts of $\hat{s}(t)$ characterize the rapid fluctuations in $\hat{S}(\omega)$ due to vocal excitation properties. The high-time part of $\hat{s}(t)$ is used for voiced-unvoiced analysis and for pitch extraction, in accord-ance with the techniques described in Sections 5.214 and 5.3.

The final step in the analysis is to derive an equivalent minimum-phase description of the vocal-tract transmission by truncating and saving the positive low-time part of the cepstrum[2]. This is accomplished by multiplication with the time window $h(t)$. The result is $c(t)$ which together with the excitation information constitute the transmission parameters. The transform of $c(t)$ has a spectral magnitude illustrated by the dashed curve in $\hat{S}(\omega)$.

Synthesis is accomplished from $c(t)$ and the excitation information as shown in Fig. 8.20b. Periodic pulses, generated at the analyzed pitch, are used for synthesis of voiced sounds, and uniformly spaced pulses of random polarity are used for unvoiced sounds. The transmitted $c(t)$ is Fourier transformed, exponentiated (to undo the log-taking of the analysis), and an inverse transform yields a minimum-phase approxi-mation to the vocal-tract impulse response. This impulse response is convolved with the excitation pulses to produce the output signal.

The system of Fig. 8.20 was implemented digitally on a general-purpose computer. Fast Fourier transform techniques and fast con-volution techniques were used for the computations. The spectral analyses consisted of 512-point discrete Fourier transforms corre-sponding to a spectral resolution of approximately 20 cps. Cepstrum computations also consisted of 512-point inverse transforms. Spectra and cepstra were computed at 20-msec intervals along the input speech waveform and $c(t)$ was described by the first 32 points of the cepstrum. Linear interpolation over the 20 msec intervals was used for the excita-tion and impulse response data. Listening tests performed on the system in a back-to-back mode yielded judgments of good quality and natural sound. In a separate experiment the $c(t)$ data were reduced to 26 in number and quantized to six bits each for a transmission rate of 7800 bits/sec. At this bit rate no noticeable degradation was reported (OPPENHEIM).

---

[1] See Section 5.11 for properties of the short-time Fourier transform.

[2] The minimum-phase properties of this function are not obvious. A proof can be found in OPPENHEIM et al.

A further study of the homomorphic vocoder utilized a time-varying data window for analysis and a digital implementation for transmission at 3 700 bits/sec (HAMMETT). At this bit rate, a signal of good quality was reported, with some reduction in naturalness.

Another study has applied predictive coding (see Section 8.13) to the transmission of the homomorphic vocoder signals. Using this technique, transmission of spectral information was digitally implemented for a data rate of 4 000 bits/sec with modest impairment in quality. Listening tests concluded that spectral information digitized to around as 5 000 bits/sec permits a quality indistinguishable from the unquantized system (WEINSTEIN and OPPENHEIM).

8.8. Maximum Likelihood Vocoders

All vocoder devices attempt to represent the short-time spectrum of speech as efficiently as possible. Exact reproduction of the waveform is not necessary. Some devices, such as channel vocoders, depend upon a frequency-domain transformation of the speech information, while others, such as correlation vocoders (Section 8.4) and orthogonal function vocoders (Section 8.6), use strictly a time-domain representation of the signal.

In all vocoder devices, the greatest step toward band conservation derives from observing the source-system distinctions in the production of speech signals (see Fig. 8.1). Vocal excitation information and system function data are treated separately, and decisions about voiced-unvoiced excitation and pitch-period measurement are typically made. Devices which do not make the source-system distinction and which do not perform pitch extraction — such as the voice-excited vocoder and some transmission methods described in later sections of this chapter — derive their bandsaving solely from the ear's acceptance of a signal having a short-time spectrum similar to that of the original speech. Their representation of the signal is commensurately less efficient.

Differences among vocoder devices lie in how they attempt to represent the perceptually-important information in the short-time speech spectrum. The channel vocoder merely samples the spectrum at prescribed frequency intervals and transmits these values. An orthonormal expansion of the amplitude spectrum aims to give adequate definition of the spectrum through a few coefficients of a prescribed set of basis functions. The formant vocoder assumes a pole-zero model for the vocal transmission and aims to locate the first few formant frequencies to effect an efficient description of the whole spectrum. The time-domain approach of the correlation vocoder transmits samples of the correlation function and synthesizes a wave composed of the even, truncated correlation funciton.

The Laguerre vocoder, another time-domain method, uses an ortho-normal expansion of the short-time correlation function and attempts to represent it by a few coefficients.

Another technique, called the Maximum Likelihood Method (ITAKURA and SAITO, 1968), attempts to combine the advantages of time-domain processing and formant representation of the spectrum. The method is also amenable to digital implementation.

An all-pole model of the power spectrum of the speech signal is assumed. Zeros are omitted because of their lesser importance to perception and because their effect can be represented to any accuracy by a suitable number of poles. The synthesizer includes a recursive digital filter, shown in Fig. 8.21, whose transmission function in z-transform notation is

$$T(z) = \frac{1}{1 + H(z)}$$
$$= \left[\frac{1}{1 + a_1 z^{-1} + a_2 z^{-2} + \cdots + a_p z^{-p}} \right], \tag{8.39}$$

where $z^{-1} = e^{-sD}$ is the delay operator, D is the sampling interval and s is the complex frequency (see, for example, Section 6.26).

The complex roots of the denominator polynomial are the complex formants (bandwidths and frequencies) used to approximate the speech signal. The coefficients, a_i, of the denominator polynomial are obtained from time-domain calculations on samples of a short segment of the speech waveform; namely, $s_1, s_2 \ldots s_N$, where $N \gg p$. Under the assumption that the waveform samples s_i are samples of a random gaussian process, a maximum likelihood estimate is obtained for the a_i's. This estimate corresponds to minimization of a function of the logarithmic

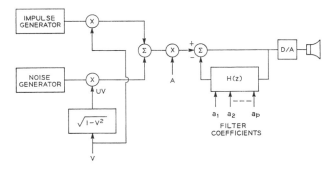

Fig. 8.21. Synthesis method for the maximum likelihood vocoder. Samples of voiced and voiceless excitation are supplied to a recursive digital filter of p-th order. Digital-to-analog (D/A) conversion produces the analog output. (After ITAKURA and SAITO, 1968)

difference between the power spectrum of the filter $|T(z)|^2$ and the short-time power spectrum of the signal samples

$$S(\omega) = \frac{1}{2\pi N} \left| \sum_{n=1}^{N} s_n e^{-jn\omega D} \right|^2 . \tag{8.40}$$

The minimization results in a fit which is more sensitive at the spectral peaks than in the valleys between formants. Perceptually this is an important feature of the method. The fit of the all-pole model to the envelope of the speech spectrum is illustrated in Fig. 8.22.

The maximum likelihood estimate of the filter coefficients is obtained from the short-time correlation function

$$\Phi_i = \frac{1}{N} \sum_{j=1}^{N-i} s_j s_{j+i}, \quad (i=0, 1, \dots, N-1) \tag{8.41}$$

by solving the set of equations

$$\sum_{i=1}^{p} \Phi_{|i-j|} a_i = -\Phi_j, \quad (j=1, 2, \dots, p). \tag{8.42}$$

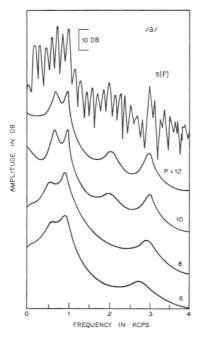

Fig. 8.22. Approximations to the speech spectrum envelope as a function of the number of poles of the recursive digital filter. The top curve, $S(f)$, is the measured short-time spectral density for the vowel /a/ produced by a man at a fundamental frequency 140 cps. The lower curves show the approximations to the spectral envelope for $p=6$, 8, 10 and 12. (After ITAKURA and SAITO, 1970)

The maximum likelihood estimate also produces the amplitude scale factor for matching the speech signal power spectrum, namely

$$A^2 = \sum_{i=-p}^{p} A_i \Phi_i,$$

where

$$A_i = \sum_{j=0}^{p} a_j a_{j+|i|}; \qquad a_0 = 1, \qquad a_k = 0 \, (k > p). \tag{8.43}$$

As shown in Fig. 8.21, excitation of the synthesizer follows vocoder convention and uses a pulse generator and a noise generator of the same average power. Extraction of pitch period T is accomplished by a modified correlation method which has advantages similar to the cepstrum method, but relies strictly upon time domain techniques and does not require transformation to the frequency domain. A voicing amplitude signal, V, is also derived by the pitch extractor. The voiced and voiceless excitations are mixed according to the amplitude of the voicing signal, V. The unvoiced (noise) excitation level is given by $UV = \sqrt{1-V^2}$. The mixing ratio therefore maintains constant average excitation power. Overall control of the mixed excitation, by amplitude signal A, completes the synthesis[1].

Typical parameters for the analysis and synthesis are: sampling rate of input speech, $1/D = 8$ kcps; number of poles, $p = 10$; and number of analyzed samples, $N = 240$ (i.e., 30 msec duration). For transmission purposes, the control parameters are quantized to: 9 bits for each of the 10 a_i's, and 6 bits for each of the three excitation signals. Sampling these quantized parameters at 50 $\sec^{-1}$ yields a 5400 bit/sec encoding of the signal for digital transmission. The technique is demonstrated to be substantially better than digitized channel vocoders (ITAKURA and SAITO, 1968).

Furthermore, the maximum likelihood method has been shown to be valuable for automatic extraction of formant frequencies and formant bandwidths. The complex roots z_i of $[1 + H(z)]$ in (8.39) give the real and imaginary parts of the formant frequencies, i.e., their bandwidths and center frequencies. Given $H(z)$ as defined by the coefficients a_i, a root-finding algorithm is applied to determine the z_i. Formant tracking tests on real speech show that the method with $p = 10$ produces accurate estimates of formant bandwidths and frequencies. An example of automatic formant tracking for a five-vowel sequence is shown in Fig. 8.23 (ITAKURA and SAITO, 1970).

---

[1] Note that while the coefficients a_i are derived from the short-time correlation function Φ_i, the synthesis method utilizes a recursive filter and avoids the "truncation" distortion present in the open-loop synthesis of the correlation vocoder (see Section 8.4).

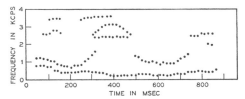

Fig. 8.23. Automatic tracking of formant frequencies determined from the polynomial roots for $p=10$. The utterance is the five-vowel sequence $/a, o, i, u, e/$. (After ITAKURA and SAITO, 1970)

8.9. Linear Prediction Vocoders

Another time-domain vocoder method for speech analysis and synthesis employs the properties of linear prediction (ATAL and HANAUER, 1971). This method also utilizes an all-pole recursive digital filter excited either by a pitch-modulated pulse generator or a noise generator to synthesize the signal. The filter coefficients in this case represent an optimum linear prediction of the signal[1]. The coefficients are determined by minimizing the mean square error between samples of the input signal and signal values estimated from a weighted linear sum of past values of the signal. That is, for every sample of the input signal, s_n, an estimate $\hat{s}_n$ is formed such that

$$\hat{s}_n = \sum_{k=1}^{p} a_k s_{n-k}.$$

The filter coefficients, a_k, are determined by minimizing $\overline{(s_n - \hat{s}_n)^2}$ over an analysis interval that is typically a pitch period, but which may be as small as 3 msec for $p=12$ and a sampling rate of 10 Kcps. The a_k's are given as a solution of the matrix equation

$$\Phi a = \psi, \tag{8.44}$$

where a is a p-dimensional vector whose k-th component is a_k, Φ is a $(p \times p)$ covariance matrix with term φ_{ij} given by

$$\varphi_{ij} = \sum_n s_{n-i} s_{n-j}, \quad \begin{array}{l} (i=1, \dots, p) \\ (j=1, \dots, p) \end{array} \tag{8.45}$$

and ψ is a p-dimensional vector with the j-th component $\psi_j = \varphi_{j0}$, and the sum extends over all speech samples N in a given analysis interval. Since the matrix Φ is symmetric and positive definite, Eq. (8.44) can be solved without matrix inversion. These relations are similar to those obtained from the Maximum Likelihood method [See Eq. (8.42).] except for the difference in the matrix Φ. The two solutions approach each other for the condition $N \gg p$.

---

[1] A general discussion of the theory of optimum linear prediction of signals is given in Section 8.13.

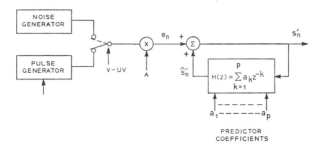

Fig. 8.24. Synthesis from a recursive digital filter employing optimum linear prediction. (After ATAL and HANAUER, 1971)

Synthesis is accomplished as shown in Fig. 8.24. Excitation either by pitch-modulated pulses or by random noise is supplied to a recursive filter formed from the linear predictor. The amplitude level, A, of the excitation is derived from the rms value of the input speech wave. The filter transmission function, is

$$T(z) = \frac{1}{1 - H(z)}, \tag{8.46}$$

where

$$H(z) = \sum_{k=1}^{p} a_k z^{-k},$$

which, except for the sign convention, is the same as the Maximum Likelihood method (Section 8.8). The filter coefficients a_k account both for the filtering of the vocal tract and the spectral properties of the excitation source. If e_n is the n-th sample of the excitation, then the corresponding output sample of the synthesizer is

$$s'_n = e_n + \sum_{k=1}^{p} a_k s'_{n-k},$$

where the primes distinguish the synthesized samples from the original speech samples. The complex roots of $[1 - H(z)]$ in (8.46) therefore include the bandwidths and frequencies of the speech formants. The filter coefficient data can be transmitted directly as the values of the a_k, or in terms of the roots of $[1 - H(z)]$. The latter requires a root-finding calculation. Alternatively, the coefficient data can be transmitted in terms of the correlation functions φ_{ij}. Further, it can be shown that the recursive filter function describes an equivalent hard-walled pipe composed of right-circular sections in cascade. Its area is expected to be similar to that of the real vocal tract. The area data therefore provide an equivalent form for the coefficient information. Because they can insure a stable filter function, the area and correlation functions are attractive for transmission and interpolation of the control data.

In one implementation, extraction of the pitch period, T, is accomplished by calculating the short-time autocorrelation function of the input speech signal after it has been raised to the third power. This exponentiation emphasizes the pitch periods of voiced passages. The voiced-unvoiced decision, $V-UV$, is based on the peak amplitude of the correlation function and on the density of zero crossings in the speech wave. Another implementation uses the error $(s_n - \hat{s}_n)$ and a peak-picking algorithm to determine the pitch period. Good-quality synthesis at a digital bit rate as low as 3600 bps has been reported for $p=12$ (ATAL and HANAUER, 1971).

Because the roots of polynomial $[1-H(z)]$ describe the complex formant frequencies, the linear prediction method is also effective for extracting formant bandwidths and center frequencies. For $p=12$ the accuracy in obtaining formant frequencies is considered to be within perceptual tolerances. An example of formant extraction from a voiced sentence is shown in Fig. 8.25 (ATAL and HANAUER, 1971).

The Linear Prediction Vocoder and the Maximum Likelihood Vocoder implement their analysis-synthesis procedures in much the same way. MARKEL has pointed out that they are fundamentally similar, and that both utilize an analysis technique devised earlier by Prony

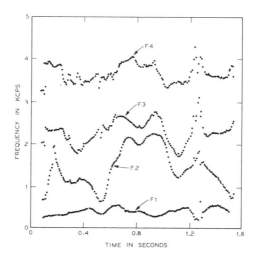

Fig. 8.25. Formant frequencies determined from the recursive filter coefficients. The utterance is the voiced sentence "We were away a year ago" produced by a man at an average fundamental frequency of 120 cps. (After ATAL and HANAUER, 1971)

(MARKEL, 1971). Further, an inverse digital filter, designed along the principles of Eqs. (8.39) and (8.46) and Figs. 8.21 and 8.24, has also been found useful for automatic formant extraction (MARKEL, 1972).

8.10. Articulatory Vocoders

An attractive approach to the general vocoder problem is to code speech in terms of articulatory parameters. Such a description has the advantage of duplicating, on a direct basis, the physiological constraints that exist in the human vocal tract. Nondiscontinuous signals that describe the vocal transmission would then produce all sounds, consonants and vowels.

The idea is to transmit a set of data which describes the tract configuration and its excitation as functions of time. The nature of the analysis — although neither its completeness nor sufficiency — is exemplified by the articulatory-domain spectral matching techniques described in Section 5.4, Chapter V. The synthesizer could be a controllable vocal tract model, such as described in Section 6.2, Chapter VI, or some equivalent device. At the present time no complete vocoder system based upon these principles has been demonstrated. However, the approach appears to be promising and to have much to recommend it. Its success will depend largely upon the precision with which articulatory data can be obtained automatically from the acoustic signal. As the discussion of Chapter V has indicated, computer techniques may provide the requisite sophistication for the analysis.

8.11. Frequency-Dividing Vocoders

A class of vocoder devices aims to avoid the difficult problems of pitch tracking and voiced-unvoiced switching that conventional vocoders use. The intent is to settle for modest savings in bandwidth in order to realize a simpler implementation and a synthetic signal of higher quality. The voice-excited vocoder described in Section 8.3 represents one such effort. The band saving which accrues is due primarily to the ear's criteria for representing the short-time spectrum of the signal.

Frequency division is a well-known process for reducing the bandwidth of signals whose spectral widths are determined primarily by large-index frequency modulation. While speech is not such a signal, subbands of it (for example, formant bands or individual voice harmonics) have similarities to large-index frequency modulation. Frequency division by factors of two or three are possible before intelligibility deteriorates substantially.

Frequency division generally implies possibilities for frequency multiplication. Similarly, spectral division-multiplication processes suggest possibilities for compression and expansion of the signal's time scale. Reproduction of a divided signal at a rate proportionately faster restores the frequency components to their original values, and compresses the time scale by a factor equal to the frequency divisor.

8.111. Vobanc

Various methods — including electrical, mechanical, optical and digital — have been used to accomplish division and multiplication. All cannot be described in detail. Several, however, serve to illustrate the variety of designs and applications.

One frequency-division method for bandwidth conservation is the Vobanc (BOGERT, 1956). Although constructed practically using heterodyne techniques, the principle involved is shown in Fig. 8.26. The speech

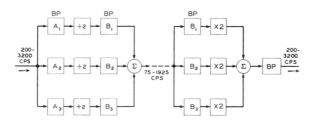

Fig. 8.26. Block diagram of the Vobanc frequency division-multiplication system. (After BOGERT, 1956)

band 200 to 3 200 cps is separated into three contiguous band-pass channels, A_1, A_2, A_3. Each channel is about 1 000 cps wide and normally covers the range of a speech formant. Using a regenerative modulator, the signal in each band is divided by two and limited to one-half the original frequency range by BP filters B_1, B_2, B_3. The added outputs of the filters yield a transmission signal which is confined to about one-half the original bandwidth.

At the receiver, the signal is again filtered into the three bands, B_1, B_2, and B_3. The bands are restored by frequency doubling and are combined to provide the output signal. In consonant articulation tests with 48 listeners and 10 talkers, the Vobanc consonant articulation was approximately 80 per cent. In the same test, an otherwise unprocessed channel, band-limited to 200 to 1 700 cps, scored a consonant intelligibility of about 66 per cent.

Other systems similar in band-division to Vobanc have been investigated (SEKI; MARCOU and DAGUET). One proposal, called Codimex, considers potential division by factors as high as eight (DAGUET), although practical division appears limited to factors of two or three.

8.112. Analytic Rooter

Another technique for frequency division of formant bands of speech is called analytic rooting (SCHROEDER, FLANAGAN and LUNDRY). The processing is done in terms of the analytic signal. This approach avoids characteristic degradations that frequency division methods such as used in the Vobanc introduce.

The analytic signal $\sigma(t)$ of a real, bandlimited signal $s(t)$ is defined as

$$\sigma(t) = s(t) + j\,\hat{s}(t), \tag{8.47}$$

where $\hat{s}(t)$ is the Hilbert transform of $s(t)$. In polar form the analytic signal is

$$\sigma(t) = a(t)\, e^{j\,\Phi(t)}, \tag{8.48}$$

where

$$a(t) = [s^2(t) + \hat{s}^2(t)]^{\frac{1}{2}}$$
$$\Phi(t) = \tan^{-1}[\hat{s}(t)/s(t)].$$

It follows that

$$s(t) = a(t)\cos[\Phi(t)], \quad \text{and} \quad \hat{s}(t) = a(t)\sin[\Phi(t)]. \tag{8.49}$$

A real signal $s_{1/n}(t)$ corresponding to the n-th root of the analytic signal can be defined as

$$\begin{aligned}
s_{1/n}(t) &= \mathrm{Re}\,[\sigma(t)]^{1/n} \\
&= \mathrm{Re}\,[s(t) + j\,\hat{s}(t)]^{1/n} \\
&= [a(t)]^{1/n}\cos[\Phi(t)/n].
\end{aligned} \tag{8.50}$$

The analytic signal rooting therefore implies division of the instantaneous frequency by a factor n, and taking the n-th root of the signal envelope [1]. For the case $n=2$ the relations are particularly tractable for computer simulation.

$$\begin{aligned}
s_{\frac{1}{2}}(t) &= [a(t)]^{\frac{1}{2}}\cos[\tfrac{1}{2}\Phi(t)] \\
&= [a(t)]^{\frac{1}{2}}\,[\tfrac{1}{2}(1+\cos\Phi(t))]^{\frac{1}{2}}.
\end{aligned} \tag{8.51}$$

---

[1] Note that for those cases where perceived pitch is determined by the envelope of the signal waveform, this process leaves the pitch unaltered. This method is therefore attractive for restoring speech distorted by a helium atmosphere, such as breathed by a deep-sea diver.

Since $a(t)\cos\Phi(t)=s(t)$, one may write (8.51) as

$$s_{\frac{1}{2}}(t)=(\tfrac{1}{2})^{\frac{1}{2}}[a(t)+s(t)]^{\frac{1}{2}}. \tag{8.52}$$

Similarly, it can be shown that the Hilbert transform $\hat{s}_{\frac{1}{2}}(t)$ of $s_{\frac{1}{2}}(t)$ is

$$\hat{s}_{\frac{1}{2}}(t)=(\tfrac{1}{2})^{\frac{1}{2}}[a(t)-s(t)]^{\frac{1}{2}}. \tag{8.53}$$

Eq. (8.53) also follows from (8.52) by the observation that multiplication of $s(t)$ by -1 is equivalent to a phase shift of π and that, according to (8.51), this corresponds to a phase shift of $\pi/2$ in $s_{\frac{1}{2}}(t)$, i.e., a Hilbert transformation.

Eq. (8.52) is a simple relation which is easy to simulate on a computer and amenable to straight-forward instrumentation — except for one difficulty: the sign of the square root and therefore of $s_{\frac{1}{2}}(t)$, according to (8.52), is indeterminate.

The proper sign can be recovered by changing the sign of the square root in (8.52) every time the phase $\Phi(t)$ of the original signal $s(t)$ goes through 2π (or an integer multiple of 2π). According to (8.49) this is the case when $\hat{s}(t)=0$, while $s(t)<0$.

A remaining phase ambiguity of π in $s_{\frac{1}{2}}(t)$ is unavoidable and is a direct consequence of the 2π phase ambiguity in the original signal $s(t)$. This phase ambiguity has no practical consequence.

The inverse operation of analytic-signal rooting is given by

$$s_n(t)=\mathrm{Re}\,[s(t)+j\,\hat{s}(t)]^n. \tag{8.54}$$

By writing

$$s_n(t)=[a(t)]^n\cos[n\,\Phi(t)], \tag{8.55}$$

and by comparing (8.55) with (8.50), the inverse relationship is evident.

For $n=2$, (8.54) yields

$$s_2(t)=\mathrm{Re}\,[s^2(t)+2j\,s(t)\,\hat{s}(t)-\hat{s}^2(t)], \tag{8.56}$$

or

$$s_2(t)=s^2(t)-\hat{s}^2(t).$$

If process (8.56) is applied to $s_{\frac{1}{2}}(t)$, the original signal $s(t)$ is recovered. This can be verified by substituting $s_{\frac{1}{2}}(t)$ and $\hat{s}_{\frac{1}{2}}(t)$ from (8.52) and (8.53) into (8.56):

$$s_2(t)=\tfrac{1}{2}\{[a(t)+s(t)]-[a(t)-s(t)]\},$$

or

$$s_2(t)=s(t). \tag{8.57}$$

The Hilbert transform of the original signal can be recovered by multiplying $s_{\frac{1}{2}}(t)$ and $\hat{s}_{\frac{1}{2}}(t)$:

$$2s_{\frac{1}{2}}(t) \cdot \hat{s}_{\frac{1}{2}}(t) = \{[a(t)+s(t)][a(t)-s(t)]\}^{\frac{1}{2}}$$
$$= \{a^2(t)-s^2(t)\}^{\frac{1}{2}} \tag{8.58}$$
$$= \hat{s}(t).$$

For a signal whose bandwidth is narrow compared to its center frequency, the original signal can be approximately recovered by squaring $s_{\frac{1}{2}}(t)$ and subsequent bandpass filtering. From (8.52),

$$2s_{\frac{1}{2}}^2(t) = a(t)+s(t). \tag{8.59}$$

If the spectrum of $a(t)$ does not overlap that of $s(t)$, which is approximately true for narrowband signals, then $s(t)$ can be recovered by bandpass filtering.

A complete transmission system based upon the foregoing principles has been simulated on a digital computer. In the simulation, the speech spectrum is first divided into four contiguous passbands, each nominally containing no more than one formant. Each bandpass signal is then analytically rooted, band-limited, and recovered in accordance with the previous explanation.

To accomplish square rooting of the signal, and a band reduction of 2-to-1, a typical channel in the flow diagram for the simulation program is shown in Fig. 8.27. The bandpass filter BPF1 separates a spectral segment which nominally contains no more than one formant. The Hilbert transform of this signal is formed by a transversal filter HT1. Since the Hilbert transform filter ideally has a response which is neither time-limited nor band-limited, an approximation is made to the transform which is valid over the frequency range of interest and which is truncated in time.

In a parallel path, the bandpass signal $s(t)$ is delayed by an amount DEL1 equal to one-half the duration of the impulse response of the Hilbert filter. It, too, is squared and $(s^2 + \hat{s}^2)$ is formed by ADD1. The square root of this result yields $a(t)$ in accordance with (8.48), and the addition of the delayed $s(t)$ in ADD2 gives $[a(t)+s(t)]$. Multiplication by $\frac{1}{2}$ and the subsequent square rooting form $s_{\frac{1}{2}}(t)$, according to (8.52).

Selection of the sign of $s_{\frac{1}{2}}(t)$ is accomplished by the following logical decisions in SWITCH. The algebraic sign of $s_{\frac{1}{2}}(t)$ is changed whenever $\hat{s}(t)$ goes through zero while $s(t)<0$. The signal $s_{\frac{1}{2}}(t)$, so signed, is then applied to $BPF\frac{1}{2}$, having cutoff frequencies, and hence bandwidth, equal to one-half the values for BPF1.

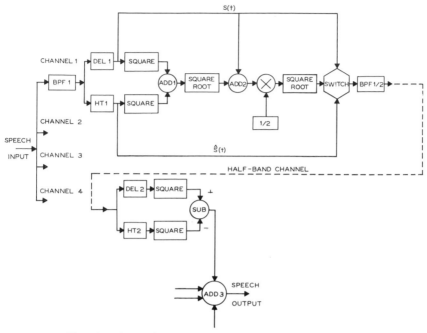

Fig. 8.27. Diagram for computer simulation of the analytic rooter.
(After SCHROEDER, FLANAGAN and LUNDRY)

Analytic squaring of this band-limited version of $s_{\frac{1}{2}}(t)$ is accomplished in accordance with (8.56). The Hilbert transform is produced by HT2, which is similar to HT1 except that the duration of the impulse response of the former is twice that of the latter. Subtracting $\hat{s}^2(t)$ from $s^2(t)$ recovers an approximation to the original bandpassed signal $s(t)$.

The programmed operations in all four channels are identical except that the bandpass filters, Hilbert transform filters, and delays are chosen in accordance with the desired passband characteristics. In the computer implementation, eighth-order Butterworth filters with cutoff frequencies listed in Table 8.5 are used for the bandpass filters.

Table 8.5. *Eighth-order Butterworth filter cutoff frequencies in cps*

	BPF1	BPF $\frac{1}{2}$	Formants nominally in passband
Channel 1	238–714	119–357	$F1$
Channel 2	714–1428	357–714	$F1$ or $F2$
Channel 3	1428–2142	714–1071	$F2$ or $F3$
Channel 4	2142–2856	1071–1428	$F3$

The Hilbert filters are realized from a band-limited and time-limited approximation to the Hilbert transform. Ideally, the impulse response (inverse) of the Hilbert transform is $h(t) = 1/\pi t$, and the magnitude of the transform is unity at all frequencies. Truncating the spectrum of the transform at frequency ω_c produces an impulse response $\bar{h}(t) = (\cos \omega_c t - 1)/\pi t$, which although band-limited is not time-limited. The function $\bar{h}(t)$ is asymmetric and its even Nyquist samples are identically zero. Odd Nyquist samples have the value $2/\pi n T$, where n is the sample number and T is the Nyquist interval. The response $\bar{h}(t)$ can be truncated (limited) in time at a sufficiently long duration so that over the frequency range of interest the transform remains acceptable.

For programming ease, the transform is realized by an asymmetric transversal filter whose even (Nyquist) coefficients are zero and whose odd coefficients are $2/\pi n T$, weighted with a Hamming window of duration τ. Specifically,

$$\tilde{h}(nT) = \frac{2}{\pi n T} \left\{ 0.54 - 0.46 \cos \left(\frac{2\pi(nT + \tau/2)}{\tau} \right) \right\}, \qquad (8.60)$$

where $n = 1, 2, 3, \ldots, \tau/2T$ represents values for one-half the coefficients of the asymmetrical filter. The simulation is for a 10-kHz bandwidth (ω_c) and $T = 0.5 \times 10^{-4}$ second. The values of the Hamming window used for each of the four bands are given in Table 8.6.

Table 8.6. *Impulse response durations for the Hilbert filters*

	τ in ms	
	HT1	HT2
Channel 1	5.0	10.0
Channel 2	2.5	5.0
Channel 3	1.3	2.5
Channel 4	0.9	1.7

A typical result from the system, with the BPF$\frac{1}{2}$ filters included in the transmission path, is shown by the spectrograms in Fig. 8.28. The upper spectrogram shows an input sentence to the system. The lower spectrogram shows the signal recovered from the half-bandwidth transmission. As the spectrograms show, original formant structure and pitch information is preserved relatively well in the recovered signal. The result is a transmission of respectable quality over a channel bandwidth equal to one-half that of the original signal.

At least one practical hardware implementation of the analytic-rooter, using solid-state circuitry, has been constructed and tested (SASS and MACKIE).

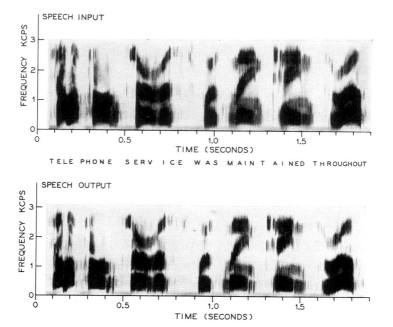

Fig. 8.28. Sound spectrograms of speech analyzed and synthesized by the analytic rooter. The transmission bandwidth is one-half the original signal bandwidth. (After SCHROEDER, FLANAGAN and LUNDRY)

8.113. Harmonic Compressor

Another complete division-multiplication transmission system, designed with a sufficient number of filters to operate on individual voice harmonics, has been investigated by digital simulation (SCHROEDER, LOGAN and PRESTIGIACOMO). The method, called the "harmonic compressor", uses 50 contiguous bandpass filters, each 60 cps wide, covering the range 240 to 3 240 cps. The circuit is shown in Fig. 8.29. It is designed to achieve a bandwidth reduction of two-to-one. On the transmitter side, the signals from the bandpass filters are divided by two and combined for transmission over one-half the original bandwidth. At the receiver the components are again separated by filtering and restored by multiplication by two. All filters and operations are simulated in a large digital computer. From informal listening tests, the quality and intelligibility of the transmitted speech are judged to fall between that of a voice-excited vocoder with a 700 cps baseband and an unprocessed signal of the same bandwidth. A time speed up by a factor of two can also be applied to the transmitted signal to restore it to the original frequency range.

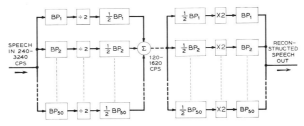

Fig. 8.29. Block diagram of "harmonic compressor".
(After SCHROEDER, LOGAN and PRESTIGIACOMO)

A related investigation in which attention is focused upon the individual harmonic components of the signal has considered optical methods, mechanical string-filter methods, and ultrasonic storage devices for frequency division-multiplication (VILBIG, 1950, 1952; VILBIG and HAASE, 1956 a, b). A part of this same effort produced an electrical "speech stretcher" (GOULD). The idea is to expand the time scale of speech by the arrangement shown in Fig. 8.30. The speech signal is filtered by 32 contiguous BP-filters covering the range 75 to about 7000 cps. The filter bandwidths are approximately 100 cps wide up to 1000 cps, and increase logarithmically to 7000 cps. Full-wave rectification doubles the frequency components of each band. Band-pass filtering at twice the original bandwidth eliminates much of the harmonic distortion. Recording the combined signal and playing back at one-half speed restores the components to their original frequency positions. The time scale of the signal, however, is expanded by two.

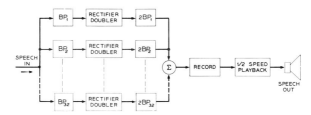

Fig. 8.30. A "speech stretcher" using frequency multiplication to permit expansion of the time scale. (After GOULD)

8.114. Phase Vocoder

A final frequency division-multiplication method makes use of the short-time phase derivative spectrum of the signal to accomplish the band saving. The method permits non-integer divisions as well as integer values. It can be applied either to single voice harmonics or to wider subbands which can include single formants. It also permits a flexible means for time compressing or expanding the speech signal. The method is called Phase Vocoder (FLANAGAN and GOLDEN).

If a speech signal $f(t)$ is passed through a parallel bank of contiguous band-pass filters and then recombined, the signal is not substantially degraded. The operation is illustrated in Fig. 8.31, where $BP_1 \ldots BP_N$ represent the contiguous filters. The filters are assumed to have relatively

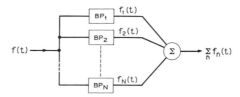

Fig. 8.31. Filtering of a speech signal by contiguous band-pass filters

flat amplitude and linear phase characteristics in their pass bands. The output of the n-th filter is $f_n(t)$, and the original signal is approximated as

$$f(t) \cong \sum_{n=1}^{N} f_n(t). \tag{8.61}$$

Let the impulse response of the n-th filter be

$$g_n(t) = h(t) \cos \omega_n t, \tag{8.62}$$

where the envelope function $h(t)$ is normally the impulse response of a physically-realizable low-pass filter. Then the output of the n-th filter is the convolution of $f(t)$ with $g_n(t)$,

$$\begin{aligned} f_n(t) &= \int_{-\infty}^{t} f(\lambda) h(t-\lambda) \cos\left[\omega_n(t-\lambda)\right] d\lambda \\ &= \operatorname{Re}\left[\exp(j\omega_n t) \int_{-\infty}^{t} f(\lambda) h(t-\lambda) \exp(-j\omega_n \lambda) d\lambda\right]. \end{aligned} \tag{8.63}$$

The latter integral is a short-time Fourier transform of the input signal $f(t)$, evaluated at radian frequency ω_n. It is the Fourier transform of that part of $f(t)$ which is "viewed" through the sliding time aperture $h(t)$. If we denote the complex value of this transform as $F(\omega_n, t)$, its magnitude is the short-time amplitude spectrum $|F(\omega_n, t)|$, and its angle is the short-time phase spectrum $\varphi(\omega_n, t)$. Then

$$f_n(t) = \operatorname{Re}\left[\exp(j\omega_n t) F(\omega_n, t)\right]$$

or

$$f_n(t) = |F(\omega_n, t)| \cos[\omega_n t + \varphi(\omega_n, t)]. \qquad (8.64)$$

Each $f_n(t)$ may, therefore, be described as the simultaneous amplitude and phase modulation of a carrier $(\cos \omega_n t)$ by the short-time amplitude and phase spectra of $f(t)$, both evaluated at frequency ω_n.

Experience with channel vocoders shows that the magnitude functions $|F(\omega_n, t)|$ may be band-limited to around 20 to 30 Hz without substantial loss of perceptually-significant detail. The phase functions $\varphi(\omega_n, t)$, however, are generally not bounded; hence they are unsuitable as transmission parameters. Their time derivatives $\dot\varphi(\omega_n, t)$, on the other hand, are more well-behaved, and may be band-limited and used to advantage in transmission. To within an additive constant, the phase functions can be recovered from the integrated (accumulated) values of the derivatives. One practical approximation to $f_n(t)$ is, therefore,

$$\tilde{f}_n(t) = |F(\omega_n, t)| \cos[\omega_n t + \tilde\varphi(\omega_n, t)], \qquad (8.65)$$

where

$$\tilde\varphi(\omega_n, t) = \int_0^t \dot\varphi(\omega_n, t)\, dt.$$

The expectation is that loss of the additive phase constant will not be unduly deleterious.

Reconstruction of the original signal is accomplished by summing the outputs of n oscillators modulated in phase and amplitude. The oscillators are set to the nominal frequencies ω_n, and they are simultaneously phase and amplitude modulated from band-limited versions of $\dot\varphi(\omega_n, t)$ and $|F(\omega_n, t)|$. The synthesis operations are diagrammed in Fig. 8.32.

These analysis-synthesis operations may be viewed in an intuitively appealing way. The conventional channel vocoder separates vocal excitation and spectral envelope functions. The spectral envelope functions of the conventional vocoder are the same as those described

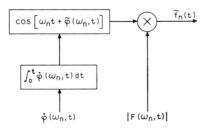

Fig. 8.32. Speech synthesis from short-time amplitude and phase-deviative spectra.
(After FLANAGAN and GOLDEN)

here by $|F(\omega_n, t)|$. The excitation information, however, is contained in a signal which specifies voice pitch and voiced-unvoiced (buzz-hiss) excitation. In the phase vocoder, when the number of channels is reasonably large, information about excitation is conveyed primarily by the $\dot{\varphi}(\omega_n, t)$ signals. At the other extreme, with a small number of broad analyzing channels, the amplitude signals contain more information about the excitation, while the $\dot{\varphi}$ phase signals tend to contain more information about the spectral shape. Qualitatively, therefore, the number of channels determines the relative amounts of excitation and spectral information carried by the amplitude and phase signals. If good quality and natural transmission are requisites, the indications are that the $\dot{\varphi}(\omega_n, t)$ signals require about the same channel capacity as the spectrum-envelope information. This impression seems not unreasonable in view of experience with voice quality in vocoders.

   A complete phase vocoder analyzer and synthesizer has been simulated on a digital computer. In the analyzer, the amplitude and phase spectra are computed by forming the real and imaginary parts of the complex spectrum

$$F(\omega_n, t) = a(\omega_n, t) - j b(\omega_n, t),$$

where

$$a(\omega_n, t) = \int_{-\infty}^{t} f(\lambda) h(t-\lambda) \cos \omega_n \lambda \, d\lambda$$

and

$$b(\omega_n, t) = \int_{-\infty}^{t} f(\lambda) h(t-\lambda) \sin \omega_n \lambda \, d\lambda. \qquad (8.66)$$

Then,

$$|F(\omega_n, t)| = (a^2 + b^2)^{\frac{1}{2}}$$

and

$$\dot{\varphi}(\omega_n, t) = \left(\frac{\dot{a} b - \dot{b} a}{a^2 + b^2} \right).$$

The computer, of course, deals with sampled-data equivalents of these quantities. Transforming the real and imaginary parts of (8.66) into discrete form for programming yields

$$a(\omega_n, mT) = T \sum_{l=0}^{m} f(lT) [\cos \omega_n lT] h(mT - lT)$$

$$b(\omega_n, mT) = T \sum_{l=0}^{m} f(lT) [\sin \omega_n lT] h(mT - lT), \qquad (8.67)$$

where T is the sampling interval. In the simulation, $T = 10^{-4}$ sec. From these equations, the difference values are computed as

$$\Delta a = a[\omega_n, (m+1)T] - a[\omega_n, mT]$$

and

$$\Delta b = b[\omega_n, (m+1)T] - b[\omega_n, mT]. \qquad (8.68)$$

The magnitude function and phase derivative, in discrete form, are computed (8.67) and (8.68) as

$$|F[\omega_n, mT]| = (a^2 + b^2)^{\frac{1}{2}}$$

$$\frac{\Delta \varphi}{T}[\omega_n, mT] = \frac{1}{T} \frac{(b\Delta a - a\Delta b)}{a^2 + b^2}. \qquad (8.69)$$

Fig. 8.33 shows a block diagram of a single analyzer channel as realized in the program. This block of coding is required for each channel.

In the simulation, a sixth-order Bessel filter is used for the $h(lT)$ window. The simulation uses 30 channels ($N = 30$) and $\omega_n = 2\pi n(100)$ rad/sec. The equivalent passbands of the analyzing filters overlap at their 6 dB down points, and a total spectrum range of 50 to 3050 cps is analyzed.

Programmed low-pass filtering is applied to the amplitude and phase difference signals as defined by Fig. 8.33. Simulation of the whole system is completed by the synthesis operations for each channel performed

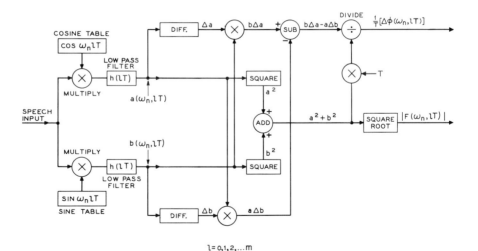

$l = 0, 1, 2, \ldots m$

Fig. 8.33. Programmed analysis operations for the phase vocoder.
(After FLANAGAN and GOLDEN)

according to

$$f_n(mT) = |F(\omega_n, mT)| \cos\left[\omega_n mT + T \sum_{l=0}^{m} \frac{\Delta\varphi(\omega_n, lT)}{T}\right]. \quad (8.70)$$

Adding the outputs of the n individual channels, according to (8.61), produces the synthesized speech signal.

As part of the simulation, identical (programmed) low-pass filters were applied to the $|F(\omega_n, lT)|$ and $(1/T)[\Delta\varphi(\omega_n, lT)]$ signals delivered by the coding block shown in Fig. 8.33. These low-pass filters are similar to the $h(lT)$ filters except they are fourth-order Bessel designs. The cut-off frequency is 25 cps, and the response is -7.6 dB down at this frequency. This filtering is applied to the amplitude and phase signals of all 30 channels. The total bandwidth occupancy of the system is therefore 1 500 cps, or a band reduction of 2:1.

After band-limitation, the phase and amplitude signals are used to synthesize an output according to (8.70). The result of processing a complete sentence through the programmed system is shown by the sound spectrograms in Fig. 8.34[1]. Since the signal band covered by the analysis and synthesis is 50 to 3050 cps, the phase-vocoded result

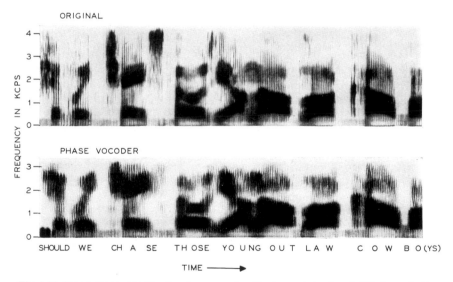

Fig. 8.34. Speech transmitted by the phase vocoder. The transmission bandwidth is one-half the original signal bandwidth. Male speaker: "Should we chase those young outlaw cowboys." (After FLANAGAN and GOLDEN)

---

[1] The input speech signal is band limited to 4000 cps. It is sampled at 10000 cps and quantized to 12 bits. It is called into the program from a digital recording prepared previously.

is seen to cut off at 3050 cps. In this example, the system is connected in a "back-to-back" configuration, and the band-limited channel signals are not multiplexed.

Comparison of original and synthesized spectrograms reveals that formant details are well preserved and pitch and voiced-unvoiced features are retained to perceptually significant accuracy. The quality of the resulting signal considerably surpasses that usually associated with conventional channel vocoders.

A frequency-divided signal may be synthesized by division of the $[\omega_n t + \int \dot{\varphi}_n dt]$ quantities by some number q. This frequency-divided synthetic signal may be essentially restored to its original spectral position by a time speed-up of q. Such a speed-up can be accomplished by recording at one speed and replaying q-times faster. The result is that the time scale is compressed and the message, although spectrally correct, lasts $1/q$-th as long as the original. An example of a 2:1 frequency division and time speed-up is shown by the sound spectrograms in Fig. 8.35.

Time-scale expansion of the synthesized signal is likewise possible by the frequency multiplication $q[\omega_n t + \int \dot{\varphi}_n dt]$; that is, by recording the frequency-multiplied synthetic signal and then replaying it at a speed q-times slower. An example of time-expanded speech is shown by the spectrograms in Fig. 8.36.

An attractive feature of the phase vocoder is that the operations for expansion and compression of the time and frequency scales can be realized by simple scaling of the phase-derivative spectrum. Since the frequency division and multiplication factors can be non-integers, and can be varied with time, the phase vocoder provides an attractive tool for studying non-uniform alterations of the time scale (HANAUER and SCHROEDER).

A number of multiplexing methods may be used for transmission. Conventional space-frequency and time-division methods are obvious techniques. A "self multiplexing" method is also possible in which, say, a two-to-one frequency-divided synthetic signal is transmitted over an analog channel of $\frac{1}{2}$ the original signal bandwidth. Re-analysis, frequency expansion and synthesis at the receiver recovers the signal[1]. Further, at least one digital implementation of the phase vocoder has been made. The phase and amplitude functions were sampled, quantized and framed for digital transmission at digital rates of 9600 bits/sec and 7200 bits/sec.

---

[1] The greatest number q by which the ω_n and $\dot{\varphi}_n$'s may be divided is determined by how distinct the side-bands about each ω_n/q remain, and by how well each $\dot{\varphi}_n/q$ and $|F_n|$ may be retrieved from them. Practically, the greatest number appears to be about 2 or 3 if transmission of acceptable quality is to be realized.

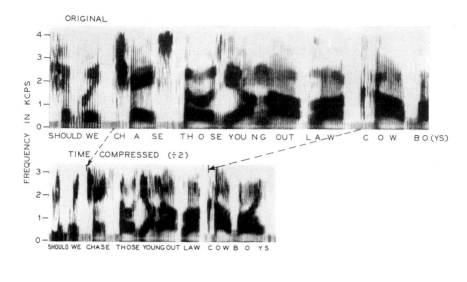

Fig. 8.35. Phase vocoder time compression by a factor of 2. Male speaker

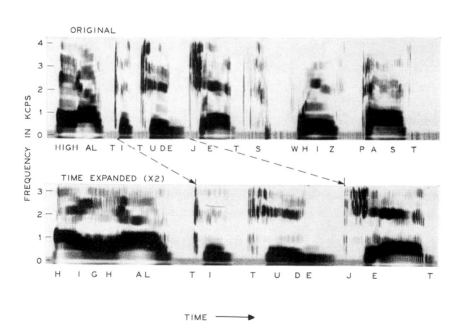

Fig. 8.36. Phase vocoder time expansion by a factor of 2. Female speaker

These transmission rates were compared in listening tests to the same signal coded as log-PCM. The results showed the digital phase vocoder to provide a signal quality comparable to log-PCM at bit rates two to three times higher (CARLSON).

8.12. Time-Assignment Transmission of Speech

In two-way conversation, one party is normally silent and listening on the average of one-half the time. In addition, natural speech has many pauses and silent intervals. A given talker, therefore, transmits a signal only on the order of 35 to 40 per cent of the total time. In long-distance communication, where amplification of the signal is necessary, the two-way communication channels are normally four-wire circuits — or two unilateral transmission paths. Each party has a transmit circuit and a receive circuit. Because of the relative inactivity of each talker, a single one-way channel is not used on the order of 60 to 65 per cent of the time. When a large group of such connections are accessible from single transmit and receive locations, the statistical properties of the conversation ensemble make a significant amount of time and bandwidth available for signal transmission. A method for practicably utilizing this capacity is called Time Assignment Speech Interpolation, or "TASI" (O'NEIL; BULLINGTON and FRASER).

The TASI system has available a group of unilateral transmit and receive circuits — typically the line-pairs in an undersea cable. The system is to serve a greater number of talkers than the number of uni-lateral circuits. The incoming transmit circuit of each talker is equipped with a fast-acting speech detector, or voice switch. When the detector indicates the presence of speech on its line, an automatic electronic switch connects the line to an available transmit path of the TASI group. Incoming signals for transmission are assigned transmit circuits until all have been filled. When the number of signals to be transmitted exceeds the number of transmit paths, the TASI switch searches the connections to find one that has fallen silent, disconnects it, and assigns that path to a channel which has a signal to transmit.

During pauses and silent intervals, a given talker loses his priority on the transmit link. He is reassigned a channel — often a different one — when he again becomes active. The TASI switch must consequently keep track of who is talking to whom, and it must identify the recipient of each signal presented for transmission. This message "addressing" information can be transmitted in the form of a very short identification signal, either before each talk spurt or over an auxiliary channel that serves the entire system.

A limit obviously exists to the number of incoming signals that can be transmitted by a given group of transmit paths before some "freeze-out" or loss of speech signals occurs. Among other things, this limit is a function of the size of the cable group, the circuit signal-to-noise ratio, and the sensitivity of the speech detectors. Several TASI systems have been put into practical operation on undersea cables. On a 36-channel cable, for example, the effective transmission bandwidth is on the order of two to three times that of the physical circuit.

As mentioned at the beginning of the section, natural pauses of phonemic, syllabic or longer durations occur in a single "one-way" speech signal. These pauses or gaps suggest that the TASI principle might be applied to a single speech channel to realize a band-saving. An experimental circuit, called a "one-man TASI", has considered this point (FLANAGAN, SCHROEDER and BIRD). The system has been tested by simulation in a digital computer. Its principle of operation is illustrated by the schematic sound spectrogram in Fig. 8.37.

As shown in Fig. 8.37, suppose that a speech band of BW cps is to be transmitted, but that a channel width of only BW/2 is available. The natural pauses and gaps in one BW/2 of the signal might be used to transmit information about the other BW/2 band of the signal. If the BW/2 bands are called high band (HB) and low band (LB), four signal possibilities exist. The processing strategies employed in the four situations are illustrated by corresponding letters on Fig. 8.37, and are:

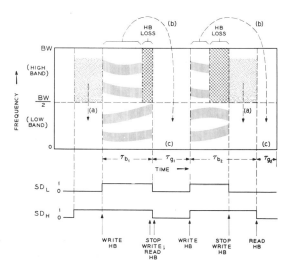

Fig. 8.37. Schematic sound spectrogram illustrating the principle of the "one-man TASI".
(After FLANAGAN, SCHROEDER and BIRD)

a) When only HB signal (and no LB signal) is present, the HB is detected, heterodyned down to the LB range, and transmitted immediately over the BW/2 channel.

b) When HB and LB are detected simulataneously, the LB is transmitted immediately, while the HB is heterodyned down and read into a storage for transmission later. (See τ_b intervals in Fig. 8.37).

c) When neither HB nor LB signal is detected, a gap exists. (See τ_g intervals in Fig. 8.37.) During this interval, as much of the previously-stored HB is transmitted as there is time for. Generally some trailing edge of the HB will be lost. One set of speech-burst statistics gives average burst durations of about 130 msec followed by average silent intervals of 100 msec (BOLT and MACDONALD). On the basis of these statistics, about 3/13 of the HB signal would be expected to be lost. None of the LB signal is lost.

d) When LB only is present, it is transmitted immediately in the conventional manner.

Two speech detectors, one for each band, are required. In the present study, they were full-wave rectifiers with 15-msec smoothing time constants. Their outputs operated threshold devices with prescribed hysteresis characteristics. The binary output signals from the detectors, shown as SD_L and SD_H in Fig. 8.37, must also be transmitted over a narrow-band channel so that the speech may be properly reassembled at the receiver. Because of the storage on the transmitter side, a fixed transmission delay is incurred before the reassembled signal is available.

The reassembly operations are evident in the block diagram of the complete system in Fig. 8.38. Two delay elements are used at the receiver. One is a fixed, maximum transmission delay τ_m in the LB channel. Its value is equal to or greater than the duration of the longest speech burst to be stored. The other is a variable delay whose value is the difference between τ_m and the last speech-burst duration τ_b. The various switch conditions—corresponding to the SD_L and SD_H signal outputs—are shown in the table.

In testing the system by simulation in a digital computer, the effective size of the HB store was taken as 500 msec. In the unlikely instance of a speech-burst duration longer than 500 msec, the high-band information was discarded, rather than reassembled in the wrong place. Typical operation of the system, as simulated in the computer, is shown by the spectrograms of Fig. 8.39. The utterance is "High altitude jets whiz past screaming". In comparing what the complete system provides over and above a single BW/2 channel, one sees that a substantial amount of the high band is transmitted. All high frequencies from unvoiced bursts are present, and a large percentage of the voiced HB is preserved.

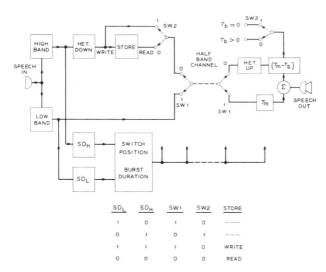

Fig. 8.38. Block diagram of "one-man TASI" system for 2:1 band-width reduction.
(After FLANAGAN, SCHROEDER and BIRD)

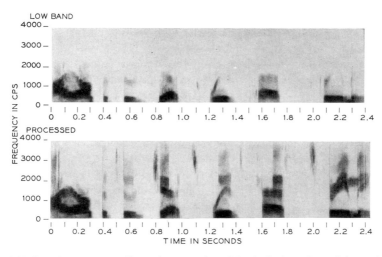

Fig. 8.39. Sound spectrograms illustrating operation of the single channel speech interpolator

The price of the improvement is the complexity of the storage and switching and the 500-msec transmission delay.

Alternatively, the silent gaps in the speech signal may be used to interleave another signal, such as digital data read on demand from a buffer store. In one computer simulation of this technique (SCHROEDER

and HANAUER), the speech envelope was used as a control to switch
between speech and data. It was found possible to make available as
much as 55% of the speech-signal time for interleaving the alternate
information.

8.13. Predictive Coding of Speech

For many classes of information signals, including speech, the value
of the signal at a given instant is correlated with its values at other
instants, and hence represents redundant information. One theory of
data compression in digital systems is therefore based upon forming
an error signal, e_i, between the samples of an input sequence, s_i, and
linear estimates of those samples, $\hat{s}_i$,

$$e_i = (s_i - \hat{s}_i).$$

Generally, the estimate $\hat{s}_i$ of sample s_i is formed as a weighted linear
combination of samples from some portion of the input sample sequence.

The weighting coefficients used for the estimate are computed from
statistics of the sample sequence in a manner which is optimum in some
sense. If the input sample sequence is not stationary, the weighting
coefficients must be updated periodically.

In order to transmit a block of M samples to the receiver, it is
necessary that the error samples and the weighting coefficients be transmitted to the receiver. Suppose the desired accuracy of the input sample
sequence requires "r" bits per sample. By straightforward quantization,
it would take $(M \cdot r)$ bits to transmit the block of M samples. However,
if the sample sequence is processed through a data compression system,
the number of bits needed to transmit the block is hopefully less. Usually
the error signal is transmitted at the same rate as the input sample
sequence, but the weighting coefficients are transmitted typically at a
rate $1/M$ times the input sequence. Suppose the error signal is quantized
to q bits and the N weighting coefficients are coded to w bits per coefficient. The number of bits needed the specify the M samples to the receiver
is then $(Mq + Nw)$. In order to obtain a saving, it is required that

$$M q + N w < M \cdot r$$

or

$$q + \frac{N}{M} w < r.$$

If the sample sequence is highly correlated, the power in the error
signal will be significantly less than the power in the input sample
sequence. Hence, fewer bits will be required to describe the error samples

than the input samples. If $M \gg N$, then the term $\dfrac{N}{M} w$ becomes negligible and the objective can be achieved.

One such method of data compression is linear prediction (ELIAS). Linear prediction has been found to provide significant improvements in picture transmission, speech transmission, and the transmission of telemetry data. A linear predictor forms its estimates of the input samples from past samples in the input sequence. Another method of data compression is linear interpolation. An interpolator forms its estimates of the input samples from both past and future samples in the input sequence.

Linear interpolation has the potential for reducing the power in the error signal beyond that for an equal-order prediction. However, interpolation requires more computation and complex implementation. Also, it looses some of its advantages when the error signal is quantized inside a feedback loop (HASKEW). The present discussion will therefore focus on prediction.

A linear N-th-order predictor estimates the magnitude of the present input sample, s_i, by a linear combination, $\hat{s}_i$, of N weighted past samples.

$$\hat{s}_i = \sum_{j=1}^{N} a_j s_{i-j}, \tag{8.71}$$

where a_j is the weighting coefficient applied to the past sample s_{i-j}.

When the statistics of the input signal are nonstationary (changing as a function of time), the weighting coefficients must be updated periodically. Only the weighting coefficients computed for intervals near the present sample yield accurate estimates of the sample magnitude. In this case, weighting coefficients are updated, for example, every M input samples, where M is usually much larger than the order of the predictor, N.

The output of the predictor, the error e_i, is formed by subtracting the estimated value of the present sample from the actual value of the present sample.

$$e_i = s_i - \sum_{j=1}^{N} a_j s_{i-j}. \tag{8.72}$$

The input signal is now described by the output of the predictor (the error signal) and the weighting coefficients. In z-transform notation

$$e(z) = [1 - P(z)] s(z),$$

where

$$P(z) = \sum_{j=1}^{N} a_j z^{-j}. \tag{8.73}$$

These relations are shown schematically in Fig. 8.40. Recovery of original input signal is obtained from the inverse relation

$$s(z) = e(z)[1 - P(z)]^{-1}, \qquad (8.74)$$

and is given by the operations of Fig. 8.41. Typically, however, the transmitted signals, i.e., the e_i and a_i, are quantized, and the receiver has access only to corrupted versions of them.

The criterion by which the a_i are typically determined is a minimization of the power of the error signal (that is, minimization of the square difference between $\hat{s}_i$ and s_i). For M samples the error power is

$$\varepsilon^2 = \frac{1}{M} \sum_{j=1}^{M} e_j^2 = \frac{1}{M} \sum_{j=1}^{M} (s_j - \hat{s}_j)^2. \qquad (8.75)$$

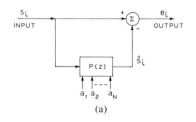

(a)

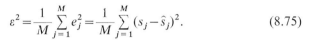

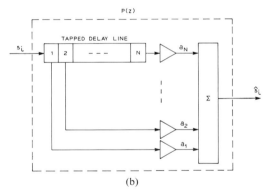

(b)

Fig. 8.40 a and b. Block diagram of linear prediction

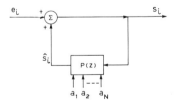

Fig. 8.41. Linear prediction receiver

Substitution for the estimate $\hat{s}_i$ gives

$$\varepsilon^2 = \frac{1}{M} \sum_{j=1}^{M} \left[s_j - \sum_{k=1}^{N} a_k s_{j-k} \right]^2$$

or

$$\varepsilon^2 = \frac{1}{M} \sum_{j=1}^{M} s_j^2 - \frac{2}{M} \sum_{j=1}^{M} \sum_{k=1}^{N} a_k s_j s_{j-k}$$
$$+ \frac{1}{M} \sum_{j=1}^{M} \left[\sum_{k=1}^{N} a_k s_{j-k} \right] \left[\sum_{l=1}^{N} a_l s_{j-l} \right]. \tag{8.76}$$

Interchanging summations and rearranging terms,

$$\varepsilon^2 = \frac{1}{M} \sum_{j=1}^{M} s_j^2 - 2 \sum_{k=1}^{N} a_k \left[\frac{1}{M} \sum_{j=1}^{M} s_j s_{j-k} \right]$$
$$+ \sum_{k=1}^{N} \sum_{l=1}^{N} a_k a_l \left[\frac{1}{M} \sum_{j=1}^{M} s_{j-k} s_{j-l} \right]. \tag{8.78}$$

Define the signal power σ^2 and its covariance function r_{ki} as

$$\sigma^2 = \frac{1}{M} \sum_{j=1}^{M} s_j^2,$$

and

$$r_{kl} = \frac{1}{M\sigma^2} \sum_{j=1}^{M} s_{j-l} s_{j-k}. \tag{8.79}$$

The error power then becomes

$$\varepsilon^2 = \sigma^2 \left[1 - 2 \sum_{k=1}^{N} a_k r_{0k} + \sum_{k=1}^{N} \sum_{l=1}^{N} a_k a_l r_{kl} \right]. \tag{8.80}$$

This result can be simplified by matrix notation. Define the column matrix containing the weighting coefficients as

$$A = \begin{bmatrix} a_1 \\ a_2 \\ \vdots \\ a_N \end{bmatrix}. \tag{8.81}$$

Define the column matrix containing the elements r_{0k} as

$$G = \begin{bmatrix} r_{01} \\ r_{02} \\ \vdots \\ r_{0N} \end{bmatrix}. \tag{8.82}$$

Define the $(N \times N)$ matrix containing the elements r_{kl} as

$$R = \begin{bmatrix} r_{11} & r_{12} & \cdots & r_{1N} \\ r_{21} & r_{22} & \cdots & r_{2N} \\ \vdots & \vdots & & \vdots \\ \vdots & \vdots & & \\ r_{N1} & r_{N2} & \cdots & r_{NN} \end{bmatrix}. \tag{8.83}$$

Note from the equation for r_{kl} that

$$r_{kl} = r_{lk};$$

hence, R is a symmetric matrix. The error power can then be written as

$$\varepsilon^2 = \sigma^2 [1 - 2A^T G + A^T R A]. \tag{8.84}$$

To optimize the predictor, the column matrix, A, must be selected such that ε^2 is a minimum. This is accomplished by taking the derivative of ε^2 with respect to A and equating the result to zero.

$$\frac{\partial \varepsilon^2}{\partial A} \bigg|_{A = A_{opt}} = 0,$$

$$\frac{\partial \varepsilon^2}{\partial A} = 2G + 2RA = 0.$$

Solving the latter equation for A yields

$$A = R^{-1} G. \tag{8.85}$$

The minimum mean-square value of the error signal for the interval of M samples, ε^2, is found by substituting the optimum, A, given by Eq. (8.85) in Eq. (8.84) for ε^2 and simplifying. The result is

$$\{\varepsilon^2\}_{min} = \sigma^2 (1 - G^T R^{-1} G), \tag{8.86}$$

where σ^2 is the mean-square value of the input sequence over the interval of M samples.

For practical digital transmission the error samples and the predictor coefficients are quantized to the fewest possible levels. The receiver of the prediction system uses these data to reconstruct estimates of the sample sequence of the original signal. If care is not exercised, quantizing noise may accumulate in the sample sequence.

This difficulty can be simply illustrated. Consider the "open-loop" quantization of the error signal shown in Fig. 8.42. Let tildas represent quantized versions of the signals. The quantizing noise present in the reconstructed received signal is therefore

$$(s_i - \tilde{s}_i) = (e_i - \tilde{e}_i) + (\hat{s}_i - \tilde{\hat{s}}_i),$$

Fig. 8.42. Open-loop quantization of a predictor error signal

where

$$\hat{\tilde{s}}_i = \sum_{j=1}^{N} a_j \tilde{s}_{i-j}. \tag{8.87}$$

The quantizing noise in the received signal is not merely the same as the quantizing noise of the error signal, but also includes the quantizing error in the estimate. Since $\hat{\tilde{s}}_i$ is formed from a sum over N past samples the quantizing noise may accumulate.

One encoder arrangement commonly used to avoid this problem is a form generally identified as differential pulse code modulation (DPCM). This system uses feedback around the quantizer to prevent accumulation of quantizing noise. The encoder forms estimates of the input samples from a sample sequence reconstructed after the quantizer.

8.131. Predictive Quantizing; Differential Pulse Code Modulation

Predictive quantizing, or feedback around the quantizer, is a method used in a wide class of digital encoders for reducing the redundancy of a signal. The idea is to form an estimate of the sample of the input signal, and quantize the difference between the signal and its estimate. For accurate estimates, the variance of the difference, or error signal, is less than that of the input and fewer bits are required to transmit the error. Estimators typically include linear prediction networks (both adaptive and nonadaptive) and single or multiple integrators. Differential pulse code modulation (DPCM) and delta modulation (DM) are special cases of predictive quantizing, the latter using merely a 1-bit quantizer for the error signal.

Estimation or prediction of the signal requires knowledge of input signal statistics. In a nonadaptive predictor these data are built into a fixed feedback network. In adaptive prediction, the network is changed as the input signal changes its characteristics.

Digital transmission can be made relatively free of channel errors in well-designed systems. The controlling impairment is consequently noise introduced by the quantization process.

Fig. 8.43 shows a predictive quantizing system (R. A. McDONALD). Input signal samples are s_i; the local (transmitter) estimate of the signal is $\hat{s}_i$; the error signal is e_i, which when quantized is $\tilde{e}_i$. The locally

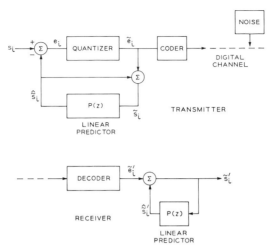

Fig. 8.43. Predictive quantizing system. (After R. A. McDonald)

reconstructed signal is $\tilde{s}_i = (\tilde{e}_i + \hat{\tilde{s}}_i)$. For transmission, $\tilde{e}_i$ is coded into a prescribed digital formant and transmitted. Any digital errors in transmission cause a corrupted version of the error signal, $\tilde{e}'_i$, to be received. Detection produces the reconstructed signal $\tilde{s}'_i$.

   This type of differential quantizing has the important feature that the quantization noise in the reconstructed signal is the same as that in the error signal — that is, quantization noise does not accumulate in the reconstructed signal. Quantization noise samples are

$$q_i = (e_i - \tilde{e}_i)$$
$$= (s_i - \hat{\tilde{s}}_i - \tilde{e}_i) \qquad (8.88)$$
$$= (s_i - \tilde{s}_i).$$

The quantization noise in the transmitted error signal is therefore identical to the quantization noise in the reconstructed signal.

   A logical measure of the effectiveness of the predictor in reducing signal redundancy is the amount by which the power of the error signal is reduced below that of the input signal. This ratio is

$$\xi^2 \equiv \frac{E[s_i^2]}{E[e_i^2]} \qquad (8.89)$$

where $E[x]$ denotes the expected value of x. To assess this figure one needs to know explicitly the predictor characteristics. Linear prediction represents a well known class of feedback networks. For linear prediction

the signal estimate is formed from a linear combination of past values
of the reconstructed input signal. That is,

$$\hat{\tilde{s}}_i = \sum_{j=1}^{N} a_j \tilde{s}_{i-j}{}^1$$

$$= \sum_{j=1}^{N} a_j [s_{i-j} - (e_{i-j} - \tilde{e}_{i-j})] \tag{8.90}$$

$$= \sum_{j=1}^{N} a_j s_{i-j} - \sum_{j=1}^{N} a_j q_{i-j}$$

for an N-th order predictor. The variance of the error signal is

$$E[e_i^2] = E[(s_i - \hat{\tilde{s}}_i)^2]. \tag{8.91}$$

If the correlation between error samples is vanishingly small (i.e., if the
power spectrum of the error is uniform) and if the correlation between
input and error samples is negligible, then

$$E[e_i^2] \cong E\left[\left(s_i - \sum_{j=1}^{N} a_j s_{i-j}\right)^2\right] + E[q_i^2] \sum_{j=1}^{N} a_j^2. \tag{8.92}$$

For a given signal, therefore, maximizing ξ^2 is equivalent to minimizing $E[e_i^2]$. Differentiation of $E[e_i^2]$ with respect to a_j and setting
the resulting equations to zero gives

$$\rho_1 = (1 + 1/R) a_1 + a_2 \rho_1 + a_3 \rho_2 + \cdots + a_N \rho_{N-1}$$

$$\rho_2 = a_1 \rho_1 + (1 + 1/R) a_2 + a_3 \rho_1 + \cdots + a_N \rho_{N-2}$$

$$\vdots \tag{8.93}$$

$$\rho_N = a_1 \rho_{N-1} + a_2 \rho_{N-2} + a_3 \rho_{N-3} + \cdots + (1 + 1/R) a_N,$$

where $R = E[s_i^2]/E[q_i^2]$ is the signal-to-quantizing noise ratio, and $\rho_j = E[s_i s_{i-j}]/E[s_i^2]$ is the signal autocovariance. The minimum of $E[e_i^2]$
can be written (R. A. McDonald)

$$E[e_i^2]|_{\min} = E[s_i^2]\left[1 - \sum_{j=1}^{N} a_j \left(\frac{\rho_j}{(1 + 1/R)}\right)\right],$$

so that

$$\xi^2|_{\max} = \left[1 - \sum_{j=1}^{N} a_j \rho_j/(1 + 1/R)\right]^{-1}. \tag{8.94}$$

The quantization noise power $E[q_i^2]$ depends upon properties of the
quantizer. For example, for a linear quantizer of L steps, of step size

---

[1] The absence of an a_0 term implies delay around the loop.

Δ_l and step probability P_l, the quantizing noise power can be shown to be (CARLSON)

$$E[q_i^2] = \sum_{l=1}^{L} P_l \frac{\Delta_l^2}{12}. \tag{8.95}$$

For relatively fine quantizing, the quantizer noise is negligible compared to other terms in $E[e_i^2]$.

Historically, a commonly-used feedback network in DPCM systems is a simple integrator or accumulator. For this case $N=1$ and

$$a_1 = 1,$$

$$a_j = 0, \quad j \neq 1$$

and

$$\hat{\hat{s}}_i = \sum_{j=1}^{\infty} \tilde{e}_{i-j}$$

$$e_i = s_i - (\hat{\hat{s}}_{i-1} + \tilde{e}_{i-1}). \tag{8.96}$$

The error power from (8.92) is

$$E[e_i^2] = E[s_i^2][2(1-\rho_1)] + E[q_{i-1}^2]. \tag{8.97}$$

Neglecting the quantizing noise,

$$\xi^2 \cong \frac{1}{2(1-\rho_1)}. \tag{8.98}$$

The optimum $N=1$ predictor (in the least error power sense) is however

$$a_1 = \frac{\rho_1}{(1+1/R)},$$

for which

$$\xi^2 = \frac{1}{(1-\rho_1^2)}. \tag{8.99}$$

The optimum predictor therefore shows a slight advantage (for the case $N=1$) over the simple ideal integrator (R. A. McDONALD).

Computer studies on speech show that DPCM with a fixed linear predictor network optimized according to the preceding discussion gives approximately $\xi^2 = 10$ dB. Over 9 dB of this improvement is achieved by an $N=2$ optimum predictor. Compared to a straight PCM encoding, this means that 1 to 2 bits per sample may be saved in the encoding.

Predictive coding and quantizing has been applied in several forms to the digital transmission of speech. Optimum nonadaptive linear predictors for speech have been studied to reduce the bit rate for transmission below that of conventional PCM (R. A. McDONALD; HASKEW;

FUJISAKI). Adaptive predictive coding has also been used in which the predictor is designed to represent the pitch of voiced sounds and the shape of the signal spectrum (ATAL and SCHROEDER; J. M. KELLY *et al.*). Predictive quantizing can be implemented with adaptive quantization as well as with adaptive prediction.

8.132. Adaptive Predictive Coding

Adaptive predictive coding has been used to reduce signal redundancy in two stages: first by a predictor that removes the quasi-periodic nature of the signal, and second by a predictor that removes formant information from the spectral envelope (ATAL and SCHROEDER). The first predictor is simply a gain and delay adjustment, and the second is a linear combination of past values of the first predictor output. The equivalent operations are shown in Fig. 8.44, where

$$P_1(z) = \alpha z^{-k}$$

$$P_2(z) = \sum_{j=1}^{N} a_j z^{-j} \tag{8.100}$$

$$P(z) = \{P_1(z) + P_2(z)[1 - P_1(z)]\} \,.$$

This predictor is used in the DPCM encoder form with a two-level (1 bit) quantizer for the error signal, as shown in Fig. 8.45. The quantizer level is variable and is adjusted for minimum quantization noise power in the error signal. The quantizer representation level Q is set to the average absolute value of the error samples being quantized, i.e.,

$$Q = \frac{1}{N} \sum_{j=1}^{N} |e_j| \,. \tag{8.101}$$

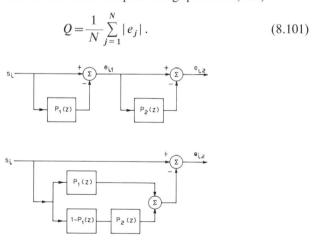

Fig. 8.44. Two stage predictor for adaptive predictive coding.
(After ATAL and SCHROEDER)

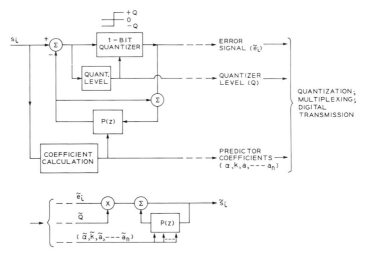

Fig. 8.45. Adaptive predictive coding system. (After ATAL and SCHROEDER)

The coefficients for predictor $P_2(z)$ are calculated as described previously. Those for $P_1(z)$, i.e., α and k, are obtained by minimizing the error power from the first predictor

$$\varepsilon_1^2 = \sum_{j=1}^{N} (s_j - \alpha s_{j-k})^2. \qquad (8.102)$$

The minimum is given by

$$\alpha = \sum_{j=1}^{N} (s_j s_{j-k}) \bigg/ \sum_{j=1}^{N} s_{j-k}^2 \bigg|_{k=\text{optimum}}, \qquad (8.103)$$

where the optimum k maximizes the normalized correlation

$$\rho = \sum_{j} s_j s_{j-k} \bigg/ \bigg\{ \sum_{j} s_j^2 \sum_{j} s_{i-k}^2 \bigg\}^{\frac{1}{2}}. \qquad (8.104)$$

The optimum k is found by a search of computed and tabulated values of ρ.

One implementation of the predictive system has been made for digital transmission at 9 600 bps and at 7 200 bps (J. M. KELLY *et al.*). The system was optimized in extensive computer-simulation studies. It used the following parameters and quantization to achieve digital transmission at 9 600 bps: signal bandwidth = 2950 cps; sampling rate = 6 kcps; prediction optimization interval = 10 msec ($N=60$ samples); $P_1(z)$ predictor quantization: $\alpha = 3$ bits, $k = 7$ bits (determined by maximum delay of 20 msec, or 120 samples at 6 kcps, for the computation of ρ); quantizer level = 4 bits; four $P_2(z)$ coefficients at 5 bits each; error signal $= 60$ bits/frame (i.e. 60 samples at 6 kcps); parameter normalization $= 2$ bits (to normalize the $P_2(z)$ coefficients to a range of ± 1 for quantizing accuracy). The transmission coding therefore included a total of 96 bits/frame and a frame rate of 100 sec^{-1}, for a total bit rate of 9600 bps. By sampling at a slower frame rate, and using fewer predictor coefficients [for $P_2(z)$] and fewer bits for the error signal, the total bit rate could be reduced to 7200 bps.

In subjective tests it was found that the 9600 bps predictive coding is equivalent in quality to 4.5 bit log PCM, corresponding to a signal-to-quantizing noise ratio of 16.9 dB. At 7200 bps, the predictive coder was found equivalent in quality to 4.1 bit log PCM, with a corresponding signal-to-quantizing ratio of 14.7 dB. Sensitivity to digital errors in the transmission channel was also studied. Resulting error rates and associated qualities were found to be: 10^{-3} and lower, satisfactory; 10^{-2}, marginal performance; 10^{-1}, unacceptable (J. M. KELLY et al.).

8.14. Delta Modulation

Considerable interest attaches to realizing the advantages of digital transmission in economical ways. Multi-bit quantizers, such as used in PCM, are relatively expensive. In telephone communication they normally are not dedicated to individual customers, but typically are shared in time-division multiplex. This requires individual analog transmission to a central point where the digitizing occurs.

In many instances it is desirable to digitize the signal immediately at the source (for example, in some rural telephone systems). Inexpensive digital encoders which can be dedicated to individual customers are therefore required. Delta modulation is one solution.

Delta modulation (DM) may be considered perhaps the simplest form of DPCM. Quantization of the error signal is to one-bit only (i.e., a simple comparator), and a single or double integrator is typically used as the predictor network, as shown in Fig. 8.46a. The transmitted binary samples, $\tilde{e}_i$, are either $+1$ or -1 and represent the sign of the error, $e(t)$. The integrator can be implemented many ways, including a simple analog storage capacitor. A digital implementation, using the terminology employed in the earlier discussion of predictive quantizing, is shown in Fig. 8.46b. The box T is a one-sample delay and $a_1 = 1$ for an ideal integrator. A sample-and-hold converts the discrete samples to a continuous function.

The local estimate provided by the integrator, $\hat{\tilde{s}}(t)$, is the staircase function shown in Fig. 8.47. The step size of the staircase function is determined by the amplifier constant, k. The step-size is typically chosen

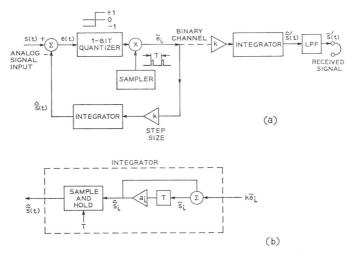

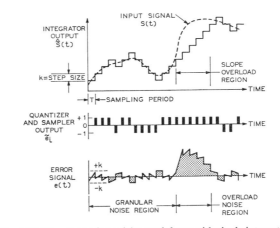

Fig. 8.46 a and b. Delta modulator with single integration

Fig. 8.47. Waveforms for a delta modulator with single integration

small compared to the input signal magnitude. Two types of distortion can occur in the estimate—granular distortion and slope overload. The former is determined by the step size of the quantization (that is, by the amplifier k). The latter is caused by the inability of the encoder to follow the signal when its slope magnitude exceeds the ratio of step size to sampling period,

$$|\dot{s}| > k/T. \tag{8.105}$$

These two types of distortion are indicated in Fig. 8.47.

Granular distortion can be made small by using a small step size. Slope overload can be reduced by using a large step size or by running the sampler (clock) faster. The latter of course increases the transmitted bit rate. In typical designs, for a prescribed bit rate, the step size is selected to effect a compromise "mix" between quantizing distortion and slope overload. Perceptually, more overload noise power is tolerable than granular noise power (JAYANT and ROSENBERG). During granular distortion the samples of the error signal tend to be uncorrelated and the error signal power spectrum tends to be uniform.

For high-quality speech transmission, say with signal-to-noise ratio of the order of 40 dB, the resulting bit rate for simple DM is relatively high, typically greater than 200 Kbps. Tolerable channel error rates are typically 10^{-4}. The signal-to-quantizing noise present in the received signal is strongly dependent upon the final low-pass filter. If simple low-pass filters are used for desampling, the transmission bit rate must be pushed into the Mbps range to achieve high quality. Such high bit rates cannot be supported in many transmission facilities. Consequently, there is strong interest in techniques for reducing the bit rate of DM while at the same time retaining most of its advantages in circuit simplicity. Adaptive delta modulation (ADM) is one such solution.

In ADM the quantizer step size is varied according to a prescribed logic. The logic is chosen to minimize quantizing and slope distortion when the sampler is run at a relatively slow rate[1]. The additional control is typically effected by a step size multiplier incorporated in the feedback loop, as shown in Fig 8.48. As in simple DM, the feedback network may be a single or double integration. The step control logic may be discrete or continuous (JAYANT, GREEFKES, DE JAGER, ABATE), and it may act with a short time constant (i.e., sample-by-sample)

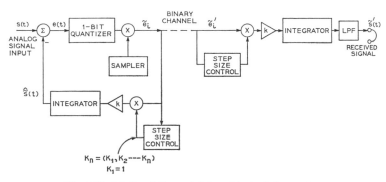

Fig. 8.48. Adative delta modulator with single integration

---

[1] Adaptation is normally not applied to the feedback network, but this is an attractive possibility for further improvement in the encoding.

or with a time constant of syllabic duration (GREEFKES, TOMASAWA). Normally the step size is controlled by information contained in the transmitted bit stream, but it may be controlled by some feature of the input signal; for example, the slope magnitude averaged over several msec (DE JAGER). In this case, the control feature must be transmitted explicitly along with the binary error signal.

The receiver duplicates the feedback (predictor) branch of the transmitter, including an identical step size control element. In the absence of errors in the transmission channel, the receiver duplicates the transmitter's estimate of the input signal. Desampling by a low-pass filter to the original signal bandwidth completes the detection.

The manner in which discrete adaptation is implemented is illustrated in Fig. 8.49. As long as the slope of the input signal is small enough that the signal can be followed with the minimum step size, k, the multiplier is set to $K_n = K_1 = 1$. When the input signal slope becomes too great, the step size multiplier is increased to permit more accurate following and to minimize slope overload. In the logic illustrated, an increase in step size is made whenever three successive samples of $\tilde{e}_i$ have the same polarity. At the point of greatest input signal slope, a step multiplication by K_3 is attained. Further increases can be accomplished in successive samples, if needed, until a maximum multiplication of K_N is achieved. Any situation where the current channel bit and the past two bits are not the same results in a reduction in step size. Reductions can likewise be accomplished successively until the minimum value $K_n = K_1 = 1$ is again attained.

Exponential adaptation logics have been found valuable for speech encoding (JAYANT). In this case, the multiplier is typically $K_n = P^{n-1}$,

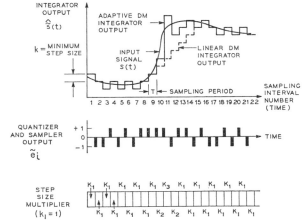

Fig. 8.49. Waveform for an adaptive delta modulator with discrete control of the step size

$n=1, ..., N$. A typical value of P is in the order of 1.5 to 2.0. As few as eight ($N=8$) discrete multiplier values are found adequate in some applications of exponential ADM.

Because of the ability to "shift gears" automatically, ADM can be designed to yield signal quality comparable to 7-bit log PCM at bit rates commensurate with PCM; typically, 56 Kbps for a 4 KC signal band. At lower bit rates, ADM can surpass PCM in signal-to-noise (S/N) performance. This relation results because S/N for ADM varies roughly as the cube of the sampling rate. For PCM the growth in S/N is 6 dB/bit of quantizing. At low bit rates, ADM wins out. However, the range of normally useful quality is restricted to rates greater than 20 Kbps. A S/N comparison is shown for ADM and PCM in Fig. 8.50.

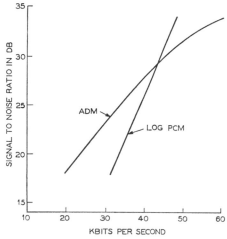

Fig. 8.50. Signal-to-noise ratios as a function of bit rate. Performance is shown for exponentially adaptive delta modulation (ADM) and logarithmic PCM. (After JAYANT)

Because delta modulators can be implemented very economically in digital circuitry, they constitute an attractive means for initial analog-to-digital conversion of signals. However, other formats of digital encoding are frequently used in digital communication systems. Techniques for direct digital conversion from one signal format to another, with no intervening analog detection, are therefore of great interest. Present work in digital communication includes direct digital transformation between simple DM, ADM, linear PCM, log PCM, and DPCM (FLANAGAN and SHIPLEY; GOODMAN; GOODMAN and FLANAGAN). These and related studies aim to establish coding relations which make the transmission system and switching network "transparent" to the signal, regardless of its digital form.

References

ABATE, J. E.: Linear and adaptive delta modulation. Proc. IEEE **55**, 298–308 (1967).

AHLFORS, L. V.: Complex analysis. New York: McGraw-Hill Book Co. 1953.

ALLEN, J.: Speech synthesis from unrestricted text. IEEE Int. Conv. Digest. New York, March 1971.

ATAL, B. S., HANAUER, S. L.: Low-bit-rate speech transmission by linear prediction of speech signals. J. Acoust. Soc. Am. **49**, 133 (A) (1971).

— — Speech analysis and synthesis by linear prediction of the speech wave. J. Acoust. Soc. Am. **50**, 637–655 (1971).

— SCHROEDER, M. R.: Predictive coding of speech signals. Proc. Int. Congr. Acoust. C-5-4, Tokyo, Japan, August 1968.

AYERS, E. W.: Speech synthesizers using formant principles. British Post Office Res. Station. Report 20315, August 1959.

BARNEY, H. L., DUNN, H. K.: Speech analysis; Speech synthesis; Chapters 12 and 13. In: Manual of phonetics (L. KAISER, ed.). Amsterdam: North-Holland Publ. Co. 1957.

BAUMANN, R. H., LICKLIDER, J. C. R., HOWLAND, B.: Electronic word recognizer. J. Acoust. Soc. Am. **26**, 137 (A) (1954).

BAYSTON, T. E., CAMPANELLA, S. J.: Development of a continuous analysis speech compression system. Final Engineering Rpt., Project No. 6 (7-4313)-43004, Melpar, Inc., July 1957.

— — Continuous analysis speech landwidth compression system. J. Acoust. Soc. Am. **29**, 1255 (A) (1957).

BÉKÉSY, G. V.: Über die Schwingungen der Schneckentrennwand beim Präparat und Ohrenmodell. Akust. Z. **7**, 173–186 (1942).

— Über die Resonanzkurve und die Abklingzeit der verschiedenen Stellen der Schneckentrennwand. Akust. Z. **8**, 66–76 (1943).

— Shearing microphonics produced by vibrations near the inner and outer hairs cells. J. Acoust. Soc. Am. **25**, 786–790 (1953).

— Experiments in hearing. New York: McGraw-Hill Book Co. 1960.

— ROSENBLITH, W. A.: Chapter 27. In: Handbook of experimental psychology, (S. S. STEVENS, ed.). New York: John Wiley & Sons 1951.

BELL, A. G.: Prehistoric telephone days. Natl. Geographic Mag. **41**, 223–242 (1922).

BELL, C. G., FUJISAKI, H., HEINZ, J. M., STEVENS, K. N., HOUSE, A. S.: Reduction of speech spectral by analysis-by-synthesis techniques. J. Acoust. Soc. Am. **33**, 1725–1736 (1961).

BENNETT, W. R.: Time-division multiplex systems. Bell System Tech. J. **20**, 199–221 (1941).

— The correlatograph. Bell System Tech. J. **32**, 1173–1185 (1953).

BERANEK, L. L.: The design of speech communication systems. Proc. I.R.E. **35**, 880–890 (1947).

— Acoustics. New York: McGraw-Hill Book Co. 1954.

BERG, J. W. VAN DEN: Transmission of the vocal cavities. J. Acoust. Soc. Am. **27**, 161–168 (1955).

— An electrical analogue of the trachea, lungs and tissues. Acta Physiol. Pharmacol. Neerl. **9**, 361–385 (1960).

— ZANTEMA, J. T., DOORNENBAL, P., Jr.: On the air resistance and the Bernoulli effect of the human larynx. J. Acoust. Soc. Am. **29**, 626–631 (1957).

BERGEIJK, W. A. VAN: Studies with artificial neurons. II. Analog of the external spiral innervation of the cochlea. Kybernetik **1**, 102–107 (1961).

BIDDULPH, R.: Short-term autocorrelation analysis and correlatograms of spoken digits. J. Acoust. Soc. Am. **26**, 539–544 (1954).

BJÖRK, L.: Velopharyngeal function in connected speech. Suppl. **202**, Acta radiol. (1961).

BLACKMAN, R. B., TUKEY, T. W.: The measurement of power spectra. New York: Dover Publications, 1959.

BLISS, J. C.: Kinesthetic-tractile communications. IRE Trans. Inform. Theory IT-8, 92–99 (1962).

BLOCH, B., TRAGER, G. L.: Outline of linguistic analysis. Linguistic Society of America. Baltimore: Waverly Press 1942.

BOGERT, B. P.: Determination of the effects of dissipitation in the cochlear partition by means of a network representing the basilar membrane. J. Acoust. Soc. Am. **23**, 151–154 (1951).

— The vobanc—a two-to-one spech bandwidth reduction system. J. Acoust. Soc. Am. **28**, 399–404 (1956).

— HEALY, M. J. R., TUKEY, J. W.: The frequency analysis of time-series for echoes. Proc. Symp. Time Series Analysis, (M. ROSENBLATT, ed.), chap. 15, 209–243, 1963.

— KOCK, W. E.: Narrowband transmission of speech. U.S. Patent 2, 890, 285, June 1959.

BOGNER, R. E., FLANAGAN, J. L.: Frequency multiplication of speech signals. IEEE Trans. Audio and Electroacoust. **AU-17**, 202–208 (1969).

BOLT, R. H., *et al.*: Speaker identification by speech spectrograms: A scientists' view of its reliability for legal purposes. J. Acoust. Soc. Am. **47**, 597–612 (1970).

— MACDONALD, A. D.: Theory of speech masking by reverberation. J. Acoust. Soc. Am. **21**, 577–580 (1949).

BONDARKO, L. U., ZAGORUYKO, N. G., KOZEVNIKOV, V. A., MOLCHANOV, A. P., CHISTOVICH, L. A.: A model of human speech perception. Acad. Sci., U.S.S.R., Sibirsk, Nauka, 1968.

BONDARKO, L. V., VERBITDKAYA, L. A., ZINDER, L. R., PAVLOVA, L. P.: Distinguishable sound units of Russian Speech. Sb. Mekhanizmy Recheobrazovaniya I Vospriyativa Slozhnykh Zvukov (1966).

BORST, J. M.: The use of spectrograms for speech analysis and synthesis. J. Audio Eng. Soc. **4**, 14–23 (1956).

— COOPER, F. S.: Speech research devices based on a channel vocoder. J. Acoust Soc. Am. **29**, 777 (A) (1957).

BRADY, P. T., HOUSE, A. S., STEVENS, K. N.: Perception of sounds characterized by a rapidly changing resonant frequency. J. Acoust. Soc. Am. **33**, 1357–1362 (1961).

BRICKER, P. D., FLANAGAN, J. L.: Subjective assessment of computer-simulated telephone calling signals. IEEE Trans. Audio and Electroacoust. **AU-18**, 19–25 (1970).

BROWMAN, C. P., COKER, C. H., MCMAHON, L. E., UMEDA, N.: Automatic system for synthesis-by-rule. J. Acoust. Soc. Am. **49**, 118 (A) (1971).

— — UMEDA, N.: Toward rules for natural prosodic features in American English. J. Acoust. Soc. Am. **47**, 94 (A) (1969).

BROWN, J. M., BROLIN, S. J.: Companded delta modulation for telephony. IEEE NEREM Rec. 1966.

BULLINGTON, K., FRASER, J. M.: Engineering aspects of TASI. Bell System Tech. J. **38**, 353–364 (1959).

BURON, R. H.: Generation of a 1000 word vocabulary for a pulse excited vocoder operating as an audio response unit. Proc. Conf. on Speech Communication and Processing, A.F. Cambridge Res. Laboratories and IEEE Audio and Electroacoust. Group. Cambridge, Mass., November 1967.

CAMPANELLA, S. J., COULTER, D. C., IRONS, R.: Influence of transmission error on formant coded compressed speech signals. Proc. Stockholm Speech Comm. Seminar, R.I.T., Stockholm, Sweden, September 1962.

CARLSON, A. B.: Communication systems. New York: McGraw-Hill Book Co. 1968.

CARLSON, J. P.: Digitalized phase vocoder. Proc. Conf. on Speech Communication and Processing, A.F. Cambridge Res. Labs. and IEEE Audio and Electroacoust. Group, Cambridge, Mass., November 1967.

CARROLL, J. D.: Individual differences and multidimensional scaling. In: R. N. SHEPARD, A. K. ROMNEY, and S. NERLOVE (Eds.), Multidimensional scaling: Theory and applications in the behavioral sciences, 1971, in press.

CHANG, S.-H.: Two schemes of speech compression system. J. Acoust. Soc. Am. **28**, 565–572 (1956).

— PIHL, G., ESSIGMANN, M. W.: Representations of speech sounds and some of their statistical properties. Proc. I.R.E. **39**, 147–153 (1951).

CHAPMAN, W. D.: Techniques for computer voice response. IEEE Int. Conv. Digest, New York, March 1971.

CHERRY, C.: On human communication. New York: John Wiley & Sons 1957.

CHIBA, T., KAJIYAMA, M.: The vowel, its nature and structure. Tokyo: Tokyo-Kaiseikan Pub. Co. 1941.

CHISTOVICH, L. A.: On the discrimination of complex audio signals, report I. Problemy Fiziol. Akust. **3**, 18–26 (1955).

— Temporal characteristics of hearing. Doctoral Dissertation, Pavlov Institute of Physiology, Leningrad, 1958, Publ. by Academy of Sciences of the U.S.S.R. (Abstract).

— Temporal course of speech sound perception. Proc. IV Int. Congr. Acoust., Copenhagen, Denmark, August 1962.

— Direction of transition as a perceptual parameter of time-varying stimuli. Proc. Int. Congr. Acoust. B-3-7, Tokyo, Japan, August 1968.

— Change in the fundamental voice frequency as a distinctive feature of consonants. Akust. Zh. 1968.

— KLAAS, A. YU., ALEKIN, R. O.: The importance of imitation in the recognition of sound sequences. Vopr. Psikhol. **5**, 173–182 (1961).

— KOZHEVNIKOV, V. A., ALYAKRINSKII, V. V.: Speech, articulation and perception. Acad. Sci., U.S.S.R., Nauka, 1965.

COHEN, A., 'THART, J.: Speech synthesis of steady-state segments. Proc. Stockholm Speech Comm. Seminar, R.I.T. Stockholm, Sweden, September 1962.

COKER, C. H.: Computer-simulated analyzer for a formant vocoder. J. Acoust. Soc Am. **35**, 1911 (A) (1963).

— Real-time formant vocoder, using a filter bank, a general, purpose digital computer, and an analog synthesizer. J. Acoust. Soc. Am. **38**, 940 (A) (1965).

— Synthesis by rule from articulatory parameters. Proc. Conf. on Speech Communication and Processing, A.F. Cambridge Res. Labs, and IEEE Audio and Electroacoust. Group, Cambridge, Mass., November 1967.

— Speech synthesis with a parametric articulatory model. Proc. Kyoto Speech Symposium, Kyoto, Japan, A-4-1–A-4-6 (1968).

— An experiment in computer communications through a data loop. Bell System Tech. J. April 1972.

— CUMMISKEY, P.: On-line computer control of a formant synthesizer. J. Acoust. Soc. Am. **38**, 940 (A) (1965).

— UMEDA, N.: Acoustical properties of word boundaries. J. Acoust. Soc. Am. **47**, 94 (A) (1969).

— — On vowel duration and pitch prominence. J. Acoust. Soc. Am. **47**, 94 (A) (1969).

— — Text-to-speech conversion. IEEE Int. Conv. Digest, New York, 216–217, March 1970.

COKER, C. H., UMEDA, N., BROWMAN, C. P.: Automatic synthesis from text. IEEE Int. Conv. Digest, New York, March 1971.

COLTON, F. B.: Miracle men of the telephone. Natl. Geographic Mag. **41**, 273–316 (1947).

COOLEY, J. W., TUKEY, J. W.: An algorithm for the machine calculation of complex Fourier series. Math. Comp. **19**, 297–301 (1965).

COOPER, F. S.: Spectrum analysis. J. Acoust. Soc. Am. **22**, 761–762 (1950).

— DELATTRE, P. C., LIBERMAN, A. M., BORST, J. M., GERSTMAN, L. J.: Some experiments on the perception of synthetic speech sounds. J. Acoust. Soc. Am. **24**, 597–606 (1952).

— GAITENBY, J. H., MATTINGLY, I. G., UMEDA, N.: Reading aids for the blind: A special case of machine-to-man communication. IEEE Trans. Audio and Electroacoust. **AU-17**, 266–270 (1969).

— LIBERMAN, A. M., BORST, J. M.: The inter-conversion of audible and visible patterns as a basis for research in the perception of speech. Proc. Nat. Acad. Sci. U.S. **37**, 318–325 (1951).

— PETERSON, E., FAHRINGER, G. S.: Some sources of characteristic vocoder quality. J. Acoust. Soc. Am. **29**, 183 (A) (1957).

— RAND, T. C., MUSIC, R. S., MATTINGLY, I. G.: Voice for the laboratory computer. IEEE Int. Conv. Digest, New York, March 1971.

CROWTHER, W. R., RADER, C. M.: Efficient coding of vocoder channel signals using linear transformation. Proc. IEEE **54**, 1594–1595 (1966).

DAGUET, J.: "Codimex" speech compression system. Proc. Stockholm Speech Comm. Seminar, R.I.T. Stockholm, Sweden, September 1962.

DAS, S. K., MOHN, W. S.: Pattern recognition in speaker verification. Proc. Fall Joint Computer Conference, 721–732 (1969).

DAVID, E. E., Jr.: Naturalness and distortion in speech-processing devices. J. Acoust. Soc. Am. **28**, 586–589 (1956).

— Computer-catalyzed speech research. Proc. IV Int. Congr. Acoust., Copenhagen, Denmark, August 1962.

— McDONALD, H. S.: Note on pitch synchronous processing of speech. J. Acoust. Soc. Am. **28**, 1261–1266 (1956a).

— — Techniques for Coding speech signals for transmission over a reduced capacity digital channel. J. Acoust. Soc. Am. **28**, 767 (A) (1956b).

— SCHROEDER, M. R., LOGAN, B. F., PRESTIGIACOMO, A. J.: New applications of voice-excitation to vocoders. Proc. Stockholm Speech Comm. Seminar, R.I.T., Stockholm, Sweden, September 1962.

DAVIS, H.: Chapter 28. In: Handbook of experimental psychology (S. S. STEVENS, ed.). New York: John Wiley & Sons 1951.

— Chapter 4. In: Handbook of noise control (C. M. HARRIS, ed.). New York: McGraw-Hill Book Co. 1957.

— A mechano-electrical theory of cochlear action. Ann. Otol. Rhinol. Laryngol. **67**, 789–801 (1958).

— A model for transducer action in the cochlea. Cold Spring Harbor Symp. Quant. Biol. **30**, 181–190 (1965).

DAVIS, K. H., BIDDULPH, R., BALASHEK, S.: Automatic recognition of spoken digits. J. Acoust. Soc. Am. **24**, 637—642 (1952).

DENES, P. B., MATHEWS, M. V.: Spoken digit recognition using time-frequency pattern matching. J. Acoust. Soc. Am. **32**, 1450–1455 (1960).

DENNIS, J. B.: Computer control of an analog vocal tract. Proc. Stockholm Speech Comm. Seminar, R.I.T., Stockholm, Sweden, September 1962.

D'EUSTACHIO, D., D'EUSTACHIO, I.: Articulation testing in moderate sized rooms. J. Acoust. Soc. Am. **32**, 1525 (A) (1960).

DEWEY, G.: Relative frequency of English speech sounds. Cambridge, Massachusetts: Harvard University Press 1923.

DIXON, N. R., MAXEY, H. D.: Terminal analog synthesis of continuous speech using the diphone method of segment assembly. IEEE Trans. Audio and Electroacoust. **AU-16**, 40–50 (1968).

DODDINGTON, G. R.: A method of speaker verification. J. Acoust. Soc. Am. **49**, 139 (A) (1971).

DOLANSKY, L. O.: An instantaneous pitch-period indicator. J. Acoust. Soc. Am. **27**, 67–72 (1955).

— Choice of base signals in speech signal analysis. IRE Trans. Audio **8**, 221–229 (1960).

DREYFUS-GRAF, J.: Phonetograph und Schallwellen-Quantelung. Proc. Stockholm Speech Comm. Seminar, R.I.T., Stockholm, Sweden, September 1962.

DUDGEON, D. E.: Two-mass model of the vocal cords. J. Acoust. Soc. Am. **48**, 118 (A) (1970).

DUDLEY, H.: Remaking speech. J. Acoust. Soc. Am. **11**, 169–177 (1939a).

— The vocoder. Bell Lab. Record **17**, 122–126 (1939b).

— Phonetic pattern recognition vocoder for narrow-band speech transmission. J. Acoust. Soc. Am. **30**, 733–739 (1958).

— BALASHEK, S.: Automatic recognition of phonetic patterns in speech. J. Acoust. Soc. Am. **30**, 721–732 (1958).

— GRUENZ, O., Jr.: Visible speech translators with external phosphors. J. Acoust. Soc. Am. **18**, 62–73 (1946).

— RIESZ, R. R., WATKINS, S. A.: A synthetic speaker. J. Franklin Inst. **227**, 739–764 (1939).

— TARNÓCZY, T. H.: The speaking machine of Wolfgang von Kempelen. J. Acoust. Soc. Am. **22**, 151–166 (1950).

DUNN, H. K.: The calculation of vowel resonances, and an electrical vocal tract. J. Acoust. Soc. Am. **22**, 740–753 (1950).

— Methods of measuring vowel formant bandwidths. J. Acoust. Soc. Am. **33**, 1737–1746 (1961).

— BARNEY, H. L.: Artificial speech in phonetics and communications. J. Speech Hear. Res. **1**, 23–39 (1958).

— FLANAGAN, J. L., GESTRIN, P. J.: Complex zeros of a triangular approximation to the glottal wave. J. Acoust. Soc. Am. **34**, 1977 (A) (1962).

— WHITE, S. D.: Statistical measurements on conversational speech. J. Acoust. Soc. Am. **11**, 278–288 (1940).

EGAN, J.: Articulation testing methods, II. OSRD Report No. 3802 November 1944 (U.S. Dept. of Commerce Report PB 22848).

ELIAS, P.: Predictive coding. IRE Trans. Information Theory **IT-1**, 16–33 (1955).

ESTES, S. E., KERBY, H. R., MAXEY, H. D., WALKER, R. M.: Speech synthesis from stored data. I.B.M. J. Res. Develop. **8**, 2–12 (1964). Also, J. Acoust. Soc. Am. **34**, 2003 (A) (1962).

FAIRBANKS, G.: Voice and articulation drillbook, second ed. New York: Harper & Brothers 1940.

— EVERITT, W. L., JAEGER, R. P.: Method for time or frequency compression-expansion of speech. IRE Trans. Audio **AU-2**, 7–12 (1954).

FANO, R. M.: Short-time autocorrelation functions and power spectra. J. Acoust. Soc. Am. **22**, 546–550 (1950).

FANT, G.: On the predictability of formant levels and spectrum envelopes from formant frequencies. In: For Roman Jakobson. 's-Gravenhage: Mouton & Co. 1956.
— Modern instruments and methods for acoustic studies of speech. Acta Polytech. Scand. Ph. 1, 1–81 (1958).
— Acoustic analysis and synthesis of speech with applications to Swedish. Ericsson Technics 15, 3–108 (1959a).
— The acoustics of speech. Proc. III Int. Congr. Acoust., Stuttgart, Germany 1959b.
— Acoustic theory of speech production. 's-Gravenhage: Mouton & Co. 1960.
— STEVENS, K. N.: Systems for speech compression. Fortschr. Hochfrequenztechn. 5, 229–262 (1960).
FARNSWORTH, D. W.: High-speed motion pictures of the human vocal cords. Bell Lab. Record. 18, 203–208 (1940).
FISCHER, F. A.: Versuche zur rationellen Übertragung gesprochener Information. Jahrbuch des elektrischen Fernmeldewesens 1956–1957, S. 103–112. Verlag für Wissenschaft.
FLANAGAN, J. L.: Difference limen for the intensity of a vowel sound. J. Acoust. Soc. Am. 27, 1223–1225 (1955a).
— A difference limen for vowel formant frequency. J. Acoust. Soc. Am. 27, 613–617 (1955b).
— Automatic extraction of formant frequencies from continuous speech. J. Acoust. Soc. Am. 28, 110–118 (1956a).
— Bandwidth and channel capacity necessary to transmit the formant information of speech. J. Acoust. Soc. Am. 28, 592–596 (1956b).
— Band width and channel capacity necessary to transmit the formant information of speech. J. Acoust. Soc. Am. 28, 592–596 (1956).
— Estimates of the maximum precision necessary in quantizing certain 'Dimensions' of vowel sounds. J. Acoust. Soc. Am. 29, 533–534 (1957).
— Difference limen for formant amplitude. J. Speech Hear. Dis. 22, 205–212 (1957a).
— Estimates of the maximum precision necessary in quantizing certain "Dimensions" of vowel sounds. J. Acoust. Soc. Am. 29, 533–534 (1957b).
— Note on the design of "Terminal-Analog" speech synthesizers. J. Acoust. Soc. Am. 29, 306–310 (1957c).
— Some properties of the glottal sound source. J. Speech Hear. Res. 1, 99–116 (1958).
— Analog measurements of sound radiation from the mouth. J. Acoust. Soc. Am. 32, 1613–1620 (1960a).
— Resonance-vocoder and baseband complement. IRE Trans. Audio AU-8, 95–102 (1960b).
— Audibility of periodic pulses and a model for the threshold. J. Acoust. Soc. Am. 33, 1540–1549 (1961a).
— Some influences of the glottal wave upon vowel quality. Proc. 4th Int. Congr. Phonetic Sciences, Helsinki, Finland, September 1961b.
— Models for approximating basilar membrane displacement-part II. Bell System Tech. J. 41, 959–1009 (1962a).
— Computer simulation of basilar membrane displacement. Proc. IV Int. Congr. Acoust., Copenhagen, Denmark, August 1962b.
— Recent studies in speech research at Bell Telephone Laboratories (II). Proc. 5th Int. Congr. on Acoust., Liege, Belgium, September 1965.
— Use of an interactive laboratory computer to study an acoustic.oscillator model of the vocal cords. IEEE Trans. Audio and Electroacoust. AU-17, 2–6 (1969).
— Focal points in speech communication research. Proc. VIIth Int. Cong. Acoust., Budapest, Hungary, August 1971. Also IEEE Trans. Com. Tech. COM-19, 1006–1015 (December 1971).

FLANAGAN, J. L., BIRD, C. M.: Minimum phase responses for the basilar membrane. J. Acoust. Soc. Am. **34**, 114–118 (1962).
— CHERRY, L.: Excitation of vocal tract synthesizers. J. Acoust. Soc. Am. **45**, 764–769 (1969).
— COKER, C. H., RABINER, L. R., SCHAFER, R. W., UMEDA, N.: Synthetic voices for computers. IEEE Spectrum **7**, No. 10, 22–45 (1970).
— — BIRD, C. M.: Computer simulation of a formant-vocoder synthesizer. J. Acoust. Soc. Am. **35**, 2003 (A) (1962).
— DAVID, E. E., Jr., WATSON, B. J.: Physiological correlates of binaural lateralization. Proc. IV Int. Congr. Acoust., Copenhagen, Denmark, August 1962.
— GOLDEN, R. M.: Phase vocoder. Bell System Tech. J. **45**, 1493–1509 (1966).
— GUTTMAN, N.: On the pitch of periodic pulses. J. Acoust. Soc. Am. **32**, 1308–1328 (1960).
— — WATSON, B. J.: Pitch of periodic pulses with nonuniform amplitudes J. Acoust. Soc. Am. **34**, 738 (A) (1962).
— HOUSE, A. S.: Development and testing of a formant-coding speech compression system. J. Acoust. Soc. Am. **28**, 1099–1106 (1956).
— LANDGRAF, L.: Self-oscillating source for vocal-tract synthesizers. IEEE Trans. Audio and Electroacoust. **AU-16**, 57–64 (1968).
— SASLOW, M. G.: Pitch discrimination for synthetic vowels. J. Acoust. Soc. Am. **30**, 435–442 (1958).
— SCHROEDER, M. R., BIRD, C. M.: Single channel speech interpolator for 2:1 bandwidth reduction. J. Acoust. Soc. Am. **34**, 2003 (A) (1962).
— SHIPLEY, K.: Digital conversion of adaptive delta modulation to linear delta modulation. J. Acoust. Soc. Am. **50**, 107 (A) (1971).
— et al.: Research on speaker verification. National Acad. Sci. — National Res. Council Report. Contract No. N00014-67-A-0244-0021, March 1971.
FLETCHER, W. W.: A study of internal laryngeal activity in relation to vocal intensity. Ph.D. Thesis, Nordwestern Univ. Evanston, Ill. 1950.
FORGIE, J. W., FORGIE, C. D.: Automatic method of plosive identification. J. Acoust. Soc. Am. **34**, 1979 (A) (1962).
— — DICKEY, E. P.: A recognition program for English fricative consonants. J. Acoust. Soc. Am. **33**, 1676 (A) (1961).
— HUGHES, G. W.: A real-time input system for a digital computer. J. Acoust. Soc. Am. **30**, 668 (A) (1958).
FRANKE, E. K.: Mechanical impedance measurements of the human body surface. AF Tech. Rpt. No. 6469, April 1951, U.S. Air Force, Wright Air Development Center, Wright-Patterson Air Force Base, Dayton, Ohio.
FRENCH, N. R., STEINBERG, J. C.: Factors governing the intelligibilty of speech sounds. J. Acoust. Soc. Am. **19**, 90–119 (1947).
FREUDBERG, R., DE LELLIS, J., HOWARD, C., SCHAFFER, H.: An all-digital pitch excited vocoder technique using the FFT algorithm. Proc. 1967 Conf. on Speech Communication and Processing, Air Force Cambridge Research Labs. and IEEE Audio and Electroacoustics Group, November 1967.
FRICK, F. C.: Degarble. J. Acoust. Soc. Am. **34**, 717 (A) (1962).
FRY, D. B., DENES, P.: The solution of some fundamental problems in mechanical speech recognition. Language and Speech **1**, 35–58 (1958).
FUJIMURA, O.: The Nagoya group of research on speech communication. Phonetica **7**, 160–162 (1961).
— Analysis of nasal consonants. J. Acoust. Soc. Am. **34**, 1865–1875 (1962a).
— Formant-antiformant structure of nasal murmurs. Proc. Stockholm Speech Comm. Seminar, Stockholm, Sweden, September 1962b.

FUJIMURA, O., ISHIDA, H., KIRITANI, S.: Computer controlled dynamic cineradiography. Annual Bulletin (Research Inst. of Logopedics and Phoniatrics), Univ. of Tokyo, No. 2, 6–10 (1968).
— LINDQUIST, J.: Sweep-tone measurements of the vocal tract characteristics. J. Acoust. Soc. Am. **49**, 541–558 (1971).
FUJISAKI, H.: Automatic extraction of fundamental period of speech by autocorrelation analysis and peak detection. J. Acoust. Soc. Am. **32**, 1518 (A) (1960).
— ISHIDA, H.: Simulation and evaluation of predictive coding systems for speech transmission. Research on Information Processing, Annual Rept. 2, Div. of Elec. Eng., Univ. of Tokyo, June 1970.
— KAWASHIMA, T.: The roles of pitch and higher formants in the perception of vowels. Proc. Conf. on Speech Communication and Processing, A.F. Cambridge Res. Labs. and IEEE Audio and Electroacoust. Group, Cambridge, Mass., November 1967.
— YOSHIMUNE, K.: Analysis, normalization and recognition of sustained Japanese vowels. Research on Information Processing, Annual Rept. 2, Div. of Elec. Eng., Univ. of Tokyo, June 1970.
GABOR, D.: Lactures on communication theory. Technical Report No. 238, Research Laboratory of Electronics, Mass. Inst. of Tech., Cambridge, Mass., April 1952.
GALAMBOS, R.: Neural mechanisms in audition. Laryngoscope **68**, 388–401 (1958).
GALUNOV, V. I.: Some features of speech perception. Akust. Zh. **12**, 422–427 (1966).
GILL, J. S.: Automatic extraction of the excitation function of speech with particular reference to the use of correlation methods. Proc. III Int. Congr. Acoust., Stuttgart, Germany, September 1959.
GOLD, B.: Computer program for pitch extraction. J. Acoust. Soc. Am. **34**, 916–921 (1962).
— BIALLY, T.: Voice response with monotone synthetic speech. IEEE Int. Conv. Digest, New York, New Jersey, March 1971.
— JORDAN, K. L., Jr.: A note on digital filter synthesis. Proc. IEEE **56**, No. 10 (1968).
— LEBOW, I., McHUGH, P., RADER, C.: The FDP, a fast programmable signal processor. IEEE Trans. Computers **C-20**, No. 1 (1971).
— RADER, C.: Systems for compressing the bandwidth of speech. IEEE Trans. Audio and Electroacoust. **AU-15**, No. 3 (1967).
— RADER, C. M.: Digital processing of signals. New York: McGraw-Hill Book Co. 1969.
— TIERNEY, J.: Digitalized voice-excited vocoder for telephone quality inputs using bandpass sampling of the baseband signal. J. Acoust. Soc. Am. **37**, 753–754 (1965).
GOLDEN, R. M.: Digital computer simulation of a sampled-datavoice-excited vocoder. J. Acoust. Soc. Am. **35**, 1358–1366 (1963).
— MACLEAN, D. J., PRESTIGIACOMO, A. J.: A frequency multiplex system for a ten spectrum channel voice-excited vocoder. J. Acoust. Soc. Am. **36**, 1022 (A) (1964).
— KAISER, . F.: Design of wideband sampled-data filters. Bell System Tech. J. (pt. II) **53**, 1533–1546 (1964).
GOODMAN, D. J.: The application of delta modulation to analog-to-PCM encoding. Bell System Tech. J. **48**, No. 2, 321–343 (1969).
— FLANAGAN, J. L.: Direct digital conversion between linear delta modulation and adaptive delta modulation. Proc. IEEE Int. Comm. Conf., Montreal, Canada, June 1971.
GOPINATH, B., SONDHI, M. M.: Determination of the shape of the human vocal tract from acoustical measurements. Bell System Tech. J. **49**, No. 6, 1195–1214 (1970).
GOULD, G. T.: Design of a speech stretcher, FM-TV. J. Rad. Comm. **11**, 30–36 (1951).
GREEFKES, J. A., JAGER, F. DE: Continuous delta modulation. Philips Res. Rept. **23**, 233–246 (1968).

GRUENZ, O., Jr., SCHOTT, L. O.: Extraction and portrayal of pitch of speech sounds. J. Acoust. Soc. Am. **21**, 487–495 (1949).

GRÜTZMACHER, M., LOTTERMOSER, W.: Über ein Verfahren zur trägheitsfreien Aufzeichnung von Melodiekurven. Akust. Z. **2**, 242–248 (1937).

GUILD, S. R., CROWE, S. J., BUNCH, C. C., POLVOGT, L. M.: Correlations of differences in the density of innervation of the organ of Corti with differences in the acuity of hearing. Acta Oto-Laryngol. **15**, 269–308 (1931).

GUINAN, J. J., Jr., PEAKE, W. T.: Middle-ear characteristics of anesthetized cats. J. Acoust. Soc. Am. **41**, 1237–1261 (1967).

GUTTMAN, N., FLANAGAN, J. L.: Pitch of nonuniformly spaced pulses in periodic trains. J. Acoust. Soc. Am. **34**, 1994 (A) (1962).

— — Pitch of high-pass filtered periodic pulses. J. Acoust. Soc. Am. **36**, 757–765 (1964).

— NELSON, J. R.: An instrument that creates some artificial speech spectra for the severely hard of hearing. Am. Ann. Deaf. **113**, 295–302 (1968).

HAGGARD, M. P., MATTINGLY, I. P.: A simple program for synthesizing British English. Proc. Conf. on Speech Communication and Processing, A.F. Cambridge Res. Labs. and IEEE Audio and Electroacoust. Group, Cambridge, Mass., November 1967.

HALL, J. L.: Maximum-likelihood sequential procedure for estimation of psychometric functions. J. Acoust. Soc. Am. **44**, 370 (A) (1968).

HALLE, M.: Book Review C. F. HOCKETT, Manual of phonology. J. Acoust. Soc. Am. **28**, 509–510 (1956).

— The sound pattern of Russian. The Hague: Mouton & Co. 1959.

HALSEY, R. J., SWAFFIELD, J.: Analysis-synthesis telephony, with special reference to the vocoder. Inst. Elec. Engrs. (London) **95**, 391–411, pt. III, (1948).

HAMMETT, J. C., Jr.: An adaptive spectrum analysis vocoder. Ph.D. Thesis, Dept. Elec. Eng., Georgia Inst. Tech., Atlanta, Ga. (1971).

HANAUER, S. L., SCHROEDER, M. R.: Non-linear time compression and time normalization of speech. J. Acoust. Soc. Am. **40**, 1243 (A) (1966).

HARLOW, A. F.: Old wires and new waves. New York: Appleton-Century, Co. 1936.

HARRIS, C. M., ed.: Handbook of noise control. New York: McGraw-Hill Book Co. 1957.

HARRIS, K. S., GAY, T.: Some stress effects on electro-myographic measures of Consonant articulation. Proc. Speech Symposium, Kyoto, Japan, August 1968.

— HUNTINGTON, D. A., SHOLES, G. N.: Coarticulation of some disyllabic utterances measured by electromyographic techniques. J. Acoust. Soc. Am. **39**, 1219 (A) (1966).

HASKEW, J. R.: A comparison between linear prediction and linear interpolation. MS Thesis, Electrical Engineering Dept., Brooklyn Polytechnic Institute: New York, New York, June (1969).

HECKER, M. H. L.: Studies of nasal consonants with an articulatory Spech synthesizer. J. Acoust. Soc. Am. **34**, 179–188 (1962).

HEINZ, J. M.: Model studies of the production of fricative consonants. Quart. Progr. Rept. Research Laboratory of Electronics, Mass. Inst. of Tech., Cambridge, Mass., July 15, 1958.

— An analysis of speech spectra in terms of a model of articulation. Proc. IV Int. Congr. Acoust. Copenhagen, Denmark, August 1962a. Also, Proc. Stockholm Speech Comm. Seminar, R.I.T. Stockholm, Sweden, September 1962.

— Reduction of speech spectra to descriptions in terms of vocal tract area functions. ScD. Thesis, Mass. Inst. of Tech., August 1962b.

HEINZ, J. M., STEVENS, K. N.: On the properties of voiceless fricative consonants. J. Acoust. Soc. Am. **33**, 589–596 (1961).

HELMHOLTZ, H. L. F. V.: On the sensations of tone. New York: Dover Publ. Inc. 1954; Translation of the Fourth German Edition of 1877 by A. J. ELLIS.

HENKE, W.: Preliminaries to speech synthesis based upon an articulatory model. Proc. Conf. on Speech Communication and Processing, A.F. Cambridge Res. Labs. and IEEE Audio and Electroacoust. Group, Cambridge, Mass., November 1967.

HILDEBRAND, F. B.: Advanced calculus for engineers. New York: Prentice-Hall Inc. 1948.

— Methods of applied mathematics. New York: Prentice-Hall, Inc. 1952.

HIRAMATSU, K., KOTOH, K.: A spoken digit recognition system using error correcting procedure. Proc. Int. Congr. Acoust. B-4-3, Tokyo, Japan, August 1968.

HIXON, T. J., KLATT, D. H., MEAD, J.: Influence of forced transglottal pressure changes on Vocal fundamental frequency. J. Acoust. Soc. Am. **49**, 105 (A) (1971).

HOLMES, J. N.: A method of tracking formants which remains effective in the frequency regions common to two formants. Rept. JU 8-2. Joint Speech Res. Unit, British Post Office, Eastcote, England, December 1958.

— Research on speech synthesis. Rept. JU 11-4, Joint Speech Res. Unit, British Post Office, Eastcote, England, July 1961.

— An Investigation of the volume velocity waveform at the Larynx during speech by means of an inverse filter, Proc. IV Int. Congr. Acoust., Copenhagen, Denmark, August 1962. Also, Proc, Stockholm Speech. Comm. Seminar, R.I.T. Stockholm, Sweden, September 1962.

— KELLY, L. C.: Apparatus for segmenting the formant frequency regions of a speech signal. Research Report No. 20566. British Post Office Research Station, Dollis Hill, London, January 1960.

— MATTINGLY, I. G., SHEARME, J. N.: Speech synthesis by rule. Language and Speech **7**, 127–143 (1964).

HOUDE, R. A.: A study of tongue body motion during selected speech sounds. Ph.D. Thesis, Univ. of Michigan, 1967.

HOUSE, A. S.: Analog studies of nasal consonants. J. Speech Hear. Disorders **22**, 190–204 (1957).

— PAUL, A. P., STEVENS, K. N., ARNOLD, J. B.: Acoustical description of syllabic nuclei: Data derived by automatic analysis procedures. Proc. Stockholm Speech Comm. Seminar, R.I.T., Stockholm, Sweden, September 1962.

— STEVENS, K. N.: Auditory testing of a simplified description of vowel articulation. J. Acoust. Soc. Am. **27**, 882–887 (1955).

— — Analog studies of the nasalization of vowels. J. Speech Hear. Disorders **21**, 218–232 (1956).

— — Estimation of formant bandwidths from measurements of transient response of the vocal tract. J. Speech Hear. Res. **1**, 309–315 (1958).

— — PAUL, A. P.: Acoustical description of syllabic nuclei: An interpretation in terms of a dynamic model of articulation. Proc. Stockholm Speech Comm. Seminar, R.I.T., Stockholm, Sweden, September 1962.

— — SANDEL, T. T., ARNOLD, J. B.: On the learning of speechlike vocabularies. J. Verbal Learn. and Verbal Behavior **1**, 133–143 (1962).

HOWARD, C. R.: Speech analysis-synthesis schemes using continuous parameters. J. Acoust. Soc. Am. **28**, 1091–1098 (1956).

HOWELL, A. S., SCHNEIDER, G. O. K., STUMP, T. M.: A military semi-vocoder for analog telephone transmission. J. Acoust. Soc. Am. **33**, 1663 (A) (1961).

HOWELL, A. S., SCHNEIDER, G. O. K., STUMP, T. M.: Analog multiplexing of a telephone semi-vocoder. J. Acoust. Soc. Am. **33**, 1663 (A) (1961).

HUGGINS, W. H.: A phase principle for complex-frequency analysis. J. Acoust. Soc. Am. **24**, 582–589 (1952).

— A note on autocorrelation analysis of speech sounds. J. Acoust. Soc. Am. **26**, 790–792 (1954).

— Representation and analysis of signals, part I; the use of orthogonalized exponentials. Johns Hopkins University, Report No. AF 19 (604)-1941, ASTIA No. AD 133741, September 1957.

HUGHES, G. W.: The recognition of speech by machine. Res. Lab. Elect. Tech. Rept. 395, Mass. Inst. Tech., Cambridge, Mass., May 1961.

— HALLE, M.: Spectral properties of fricative consonants. J. Acoust. Soc. Am. **28**, 303–310 (1956).

ICHIKAWA, A., NAKATA, K.: Speech synthesis by rule. Proc. Int. Congr. Acoust. B-5-6, Tokyo, Japan, August 1968.

INGÅRD, U.: On the theory and design of acoustic resonators. J. Acoustic. Soc. Am. **25**, 1037–1061 (1953).

INOMATA, S.: A new method of pitch extraction using a digital computer. J. Acoust. Soc. Japan **16** (4), 283–285 (1960).

ISHIZAKA, K., FLANAGAN, J. L.: Acoustic properties of a two-mass model of the vocal cords. J. Acoust. Soc. Am. **51**, 91 (A) (1972).

— MATSUDAIRA, M.: What makes the vocal cords vibrate. Proc. Int. Congr. Acoust. B-1-3, Tokyo, Japan, August 1968.

ITAKURA, F., SAITO, S.: An analysis-synthesis telephony based on maximum likelihood method. Proc. Int. Congr. Acoust. C-5-5, Tokyo, Japan, August 1968.

— — A statistical method for estimation of speech spectral density and formant frequencies. Electronics and Communications in Japan **53A**, 36–43 (1970).

JAGER, F. DE: Deltamodulation, A method of PCM transmission using the 1-unit code. Philips Res. Rept. **7**, 442–466 (1952).

— GREEFKES, J. A.: "Frena," a system of speech transmission at high noise levels. Philips Tech. Rev. **19**, 73–108 (1957).

JAYANT, N. S.: Adaptive delta modulation with a one-bit memory. Bell System Tech. J. **49**, 321–342 (1970).

— ROSENBERG, A. E.: The preference of slope overload to granularity in the delta modulation of speech. J. Acoust. Soc. Am. **49**, 133 (A) (1971).

JOHNSTONE, B. M., BOYLE, A. J. F.: Basilar membrane vibration examined with the Mössbauer technique. Science **158**, 389–390 (1967).

JUDSON, L. S., WEAVER, A. T.: Voice science. New York: F. S. Crofts & Co. 1942.

KADOKAWA, Y., SUZUKI, J.: A simple calculation of the vocal tract configuration from three formant frequencies. Proc. Int. Congr. Acoust. B-2-5, Tokyo, Japan, August 1968.

KATO, Y., OCHIAI, K., ARASEKI, T.: A terminal analog speech synthesizer in a small computer. IEEE Int. Conv. Digest. New York, March 1971.

KATSUKI, Y.: Neural mechanism of hearing in cats and insects. Pages 53–75. In: Electrical activity of single cells. Tkyo: Igakushoin, Hongo, Tokyo, 1960.

KAUTZ, W. H.: Transient synthesis in the time domain. IRE Trans. Circuit Theory **CT-1**, 29–39 (1954).

KELLY, J. L., Jr., GERSTMAN, L. J.: An artificial talker driven from a phonetic input. J. Acoust. Soc. Am. **33**, 835 (A) (1961).

— — An artificial talker driven from a phonetic input. J. Acoust. Soc. Am. **33**, 835 (A) (1961).

KELLY, J. L., Jr., LOCHBAUM, C.: Speech synthesis. Proc. Stockholm Speech Comm. Seminar, R. I.T., Stockholm, Sweden, September 1962.

— — VYSSOTSKY, V. A.: A block diagram compiler. Bell System Tech. J. **40**, 669–676 (1961).

KELLY, J. M., MILLER, R. L.: Recent improvements in 4800 BPS voice-excited vocoders. Proc. Conf. on Speech Communication and Processing, A.F. Cambridge Res. Labs. and IEEE Group on Audio and Electroacoust., Cambridge, Mass., November 1967.

— et al.: Final report on predictive coding of speech signals, contract No. DAAB03-69-C-0338, Bell Laboratories, June 1970.

KEMPELEN, W. v.: Le mechanisme de la parole, suivi de la Description d'une machine parlante. Vienna: J. V. Degen 1791.

KERSTA, L. G.: Amplitude cross-section representation with the sound spectrograph. J. Acoust. Soc. Am. **20**, 796–801 (1948).

— Voiceprint identification. Nature **196**, 1253–1257 (1962a).

— Voiceprint-identification infallibility. J. Acoust. Soc. Am. **34**, 1978 (A) (1962b).

KHARKEVICH, A. A.: On the possibilities of spectrum compression. Elektrosvyaz **12**, No. 8, 3–8 (1958). Also, Telecommunications No. 11, 1121–1128 (1958).

KIANG, N. Y. S., PEAKE, W. T.: Components of electrical responses recorded from the cochlea. Ann. Otol. Rhinol. Laryngol. **69**, 448–458 (1960).

— WATENABE, T., THOMAS, E., CLARK, L.: Dischange patterns of single fibers in the cat's auditory nerve. Cambridge: M.I.T. Press, Research Monograph No. 35; 1965.

KIRITANI, S., FUJIMURA, O., ISHIDA, H.: Computer controlled radiography for observation of articulatory movement. Proc. Int. Congr. Acoust. 21-C-13 Budapest, Hungary, August 1971.

KOCK, W. E.: Speech bandwidth compression. Bell Lab. Record **34**, 81–85 (1956).

— Speech communication systems. Proc. I.R.E. **50**, 769–776 (1962).

— MILLER, R. L.: Dynamic spectrograms of speech. J. Acoust. Soc. Am. **24**, 783–784 (1952).

KOENIG, R.: Quelque experiences d'acoustique. Paris 1882.

KOENIG, W., DUNN, H. K., LACEY, L. Y.: The sound spectrograph. J. Acoust. Soc. Am. **18**, 19–49 (1946).

KRAFT, L. G.: Correlation function analysis. J. Acoust. Soc. Am. **22**, 762–764 (1950).

KRAMER, H. P., MATHEWS, M. V.: A linear coding for transmitting a set of correlated signals. IRE Trans. Inform. Theory **IT-2**, 41–46 (1956).

KRATZENSTEIN, C. G.: Sur la raissance de la formation des Voyelles. J. phys. **21**, 358–380 (1782). Also, Tentamen Coronatum de Voce, Acta Acad. Petrog. 1780.

KRINGLEBOTN, M.: Experiments with some vibrotactile and visual aids for the deaf. Proc. Conf. on Speech-Analyzing Aids for the Deaf, Amer. Ann. Deaf **113**, 311–317 (1968).

KROPFL, W.: An experimental data block switching system. Bell System Tech. J. April 1972.

KRUSKAL, J.: Nonmetric multidimensional scaling. Psychometrika **29**, 115–129 (1964).

KRYTER, K. D.: Methods for the calculation and use of the articulation index. J. Acoust. Soc. Am. **34**, 1689–1697 (1962).

KULYA, V. I.: Application of Laguerre Functions to parametric coding of speech signals. Elektrosvyaz, No. 7, 33–39 (1962). Also, Telecommunications and Radio Engineering, part I. Telecommunications No. 7, 34–41 (1962).

— Analysis of a Chebyshev-type vocoder. Telecomm. and Radio Engng., Part 1, No. 3, 23–32, March 1963.

KUREMATSU, A., INOUE, S.: Speech recognition with time-normalized frequency pattern. Proc. Int. Congr. Acoust. B-4-5, Tokyo, Japan, August 1968.

LADEFOGED, P.: The perception of speech. Proc. Symp. on Mechanization of Thought Processes, National Physical Laboratory Teddington, England Nov. 24–27, 1958.

— BROADBENT, D. E.: Information conveyed by vowels. J. Acoust. Soc. Am. **29**, 98–104 (1957).

— FROMKIN, V. A.: Experiments on competence and performance. Proc. Conf. on Speech Communication and Processing, A.F. Cambridge Res. Labs. and IEEE Audio and Electroacoust. Group, Cambridge, Mass., November 1967.

LAWRENCE, W.: The synthesis of speech from signals which have a low information rate. Pages 460–469. In: Communication theory (W. JACKSON, ed.). London: Butterworths Sci. Publ. 1953.

— Formant tracking by self-adjusting inverse filtering. Proc. Stockholm Speech Comm. Seminar, R.I.T., Srockholm, Sweden, September 1962.

LEE, F. F.: Reading machine: From text to speech. IEEE Trans. Audio and Electroacoust. **AU-17**, 275–282 (1969).

LEE, Y. W.: Statistical theory of communication. New York: John Wiley & Sons 1960.

LEVITT, H., NELSON, J. R.: Experimental communication aids for the deaf. IEEE Trans. Audio and Electroacoust. **AU-18**, 2–6 (1970).

LIBERMAN, A. M., INGEMANN, F., LISKER, L., DELATTRE, P., COOPER, F. S.: Minimal rules for synthesizing speech. J. Acoust. Soc. Am. **31**, 1490–1499 (1959).

— COOPER, F. S., HARRIS, K. S., MACNEILAGE, P. F.: A motor theory of speech perception. Proc. Stockholm Speech Comm. Seminar, R.I.T., Stockholm, Sweden, September 1962.

— DE LATTRE, P. C., COOPER, F. S., GERSTMAN, L.: The role of consonant-vowel transitions in the stop and nasal consonants. Psychol. Monographs **68**, No. 379 (1954).

— HARRIS, K. S., HOFFMAN, H. S., GRIFFITH, B. C.: The discrimination of speech sounds within and across phoneme boundaries. J. Expt. Psychol. **54**, 358–368 (1957).

LICKLIDER, J. C. R.: The intelligibility of amplitude-dichotomized, time-quantized speech waves. J. Acoust. Soc. Am. **22**, 820–823 (1950).

— On the process of speech perception. J. Acoust. Soc. Am. **24**, 590–594 (1952).

— POLLACK, I.: Effects of differentiation, integration, and infinite peak clipping upon the intelligibility of speech. J. Acoust. Soc. Am. **20**, 42–51 (1948).

— STEVENS, K. N., HAYES, J. R. M.: Studies in speech, hearing and communication. Final Report, Contract W 19122 ac–14, September 30, 1954, Acoustics Lab. Mass Inst. of Tech., Cambridge, Mass.

LIEBERMAN, P.: Perturbations in vocal pitch. J. Acoust. Soc. Am. **33**, 597–603 (1961).

LINDBLOM, B.: On vowel reduction. Rept. 29, Speech Transmission Laboratory, Royal Inst. Tech., Stockholm, Sweden, May 1963.

LINDGREN, N.: Automatic speech recognition. IEEE Spectrum, part (I), **2**, 114–136, March (1965); part (II), **2**, 45–59, April (1965); part (III), **2**, 104–116, May (1965).

LINVILL, J.: Development progress on a microelectronic tactile facsimile reading aid for the blind. IEEE Trans. Audio and Electroacoust. **AU-17**, 271–274 (1969).

LUMMIS, R. C.: Real time technique for speaker verification by computer. J. Acoust. Soc. Am. **50**, 106 (A) (1971).

MALÉCOT, A.: Acoustic cues for nasal consonants. Language **32**, 274–284 (1956).

MALME, C. I.: Detectability of small irregularities in a broadband noise spectrum. Quarterly Rept., Res. Lab. Elec., Mass. Inst. of Tech., Cambridge, Mass. January 1959.

MANLEY, H. J.: Fourier coefficients of speech power spectra as measured by Auto-correlation Analysis. J. Acoust. Soc. Am. **34**, 1143–1145 (1962).

— KLEIN, D. B.: Analysis-synthesis of continuous speech in terms of orthogonalized exponentially damped sinusoids. J. Acoust. Soc. Am. **34**, 724 (A) (1962). Also, J. Acoust. Soc. Am. **35**, 464–474 (1963).

MARCOU, P., DAGUET, J.: New methods of speech transmission. Proc. of 3rd Symp. on Info. Theory, London 1955. Pages 231–244. In: Information theory (ed. C. CHERRY). Butterworths Sci. Publ., London: 1956. Also, Ann. Telecommun. **11**, 118–126 (1956).

MARKEL, J. D.: The Prony method and its application to speech analysis. J. Acoust. Soc. Am. **49**, 105 (A) (1971).

— Digital inverse filtering— a new tool for formant trajectory estimation. IEEE Trans. Audio and Electroacoust. **AU-20**, June 1972.

MARTIN, T. B., NELSON, A. L., ZADELL, A. J.: Speech recognition by feature abstraction techniques. Wright-Patterson AFB, Avionics Labs., Rept. AL-TDR, 64–176 (1964).

MATHEWS, M. V.: External coding for speech transmission. IRE Trans. Inform. Theory **IT-5**, 129–136 (1959).

— MILLER, J. E., DAVID, E. E., Jr.: An accurate estimate of the glottal-waveshape. J. Acoust. Soc. Am. **33**, 843 (A) (1961a).

— — — Pitch synchronous analysis of voiced sounds. J. Acoust. Soc. Am. **33**, 179–186 (1961b).

— WALKER, P.: Program to compute vocal-tract poles and zeros. J. Acoust. Soc. Am. **34**, 1977 (A) (1962).

MATSUI, E.: Computer-simulated vocal organs. Proc. Int. Congr. Acoust. B-5-1, Tokyo, Japan, August 1968.

MATTINGLY, I. G.: Synthesis by rule of prosodic features. Language and Speech **9**, 1–13 (1966).

McDONALD, R. A.: Signal-to-noise and idle channel performance of differential pulse code modulation sytems— particular application to voice signals. Bell System Tech. J. **45**, 1123–1151 (1966).

MEEKER, W. F., NELSON, A. L., SCOTT, P. B.: Experiments in Automatic speech recognition. J. Acoust. Soc. Am. **34**, 1996 (A) (1962).

MERMELSTEIN, P.: Determination of the vocal-tract shape from measured formant frequencies. J. Acoust. Soc. Am. **41**, 1283–1294 (1967).

— Computer simulation of articulatory activity in speech production. Proc. Int. Joint Conf. on Artificial Intelligence, Washington, D.C. 1969.

MEYER-EPPLER, W.: Die Reliefdarstellung von Zeit-Frequenz-Spektren durch photographische Differentiation. Akust. Bcih. No. 1, AB-1-3 (1951).

— Zum Erzeugungsmechanismus der Geräuschlaute. Z. Phonetik **7**, 196–212 (1953).

— Grundlagen und Anwendungen der Informationstheorie. Berlin-Göttingen-Heidelberg: Springer 1959.

— UNGEHEUER, G.: Die Vokalartikulation als Eigenwertproblem. Z. Phonetik **10**, 245–257 (1957).

MILLER, D. C.: Science of musical sounds. New York: Macmillan Co. 1916.

MILLER, G. A.: The magical number seven, plus or minus two: Some limits in our capacity for processing information. Psychol. Rev. **63**, 81–97 (1956).

— Sensitivity to changes in the intensity of white noise and its relation to masking and loudness. J. Acoust. Soc. Am. **19**, 609–619 (1947).

— Decision units in the perception of speech. I.R.E. Trans. Inform. Theory **IT-8**, 81–83 (1962).

— HEISE, G. A., LICHTEN, W.: The intelligibility of speech as a function of the context of the test materials. J. Exptl. Psychol. **41**, 329–335 (1951).

MILLER, R. L.: Improvements in the vocoder. J. Acoust. Soc. Am. **25**, 832 (A) (1953).
— Nature of the vocal cord wave. J. Acoust. Soc. Am. **31**, 667–677 (1959).
MØLLER, A. R.: Network model of the middle ear. J. Acoust. Soc. Am. **33**, 168–176 (1961).
— On the transmission characteristic of the middle ear. Proc. IV Int. Congr. Acoust., Copenhagen, Denmark, August 1962.
MONCUR, J. P., DIRKS, D.: Binaural and monaural speech intelligibility in reverberation. J. Speech Hear. Res. **10**, 186–195 (1967).
MORSE, P. M.: Vibration and sound. New York: McGraw-Hill Book Co. 1948.
MUNSON, W. A., MONTGOMERY, H. C.: A speech analyzer and synthesizer. J. Acoust. Soc. Am. **22**, 678 (A) (1950).
NAKATA, K.: Synthesis of nasal consonants by a terminal-analog synthesizer. J. Radio Res. Lab. (Tokyo) **6**, 243–254 (1959).
— Synthesis and perception of Japanese fricative sounds. J. Radio Res. Lab. (Tokyo) **7**, 319–333 (1960).
— SUZUKI, J.: Synthesis and perception of Japanese vowels and vowel-like sounds. J. Radio Res. Lab. (Tokyo) **6**, 617–634 (1959).
NAKATANI, L. H.: Measuring the ease of comprehending speech. Proc. 7th Int. Congr. Acoust., Budapest, Hungary, 1971.
— McDERMOTT, B.: Effect of pitch and formant manipulation on speech quality. J. Acoust. Soc. Am. **50**, 145 (A) (1971).
NETTER, F.: Anatomical drawings of the ear. In: Clinical Symposia **14**, 39–73 (1962).
NEVEL'SKII, P. B.: Comparative study of the volume of the short-term and long-term memory. Proc. 18th Inter. Psychol. Congr. Symp. 21–26 (1966).
NOLL, A. M.: Short-time spectrum and "cepstrum" techniques for vocal pitch detection. J. Acoust. Soc. Am. **36**, 296–302 (1964).
— Cepstrum pitch determination. J. Acoust. Soc. Am. **41**, 293–309 (1967).
OCHIAI, Y.: Fondamentales des qualités phonémique et vocalique des paroles par rapport au timbre, obtenues en employant des voyelles japonais vocalisées par des sinets japonais. Mem. Fac. Eng., Nagoya Univ. **10**, 197–201 (1958).
— Phoneme and voice identification studies using Japanese vowels. Language and Speech **2**, 132–136 (1959).
— KATO, H.: Sur la netteté et la naturalité de la voix humaine reflechies du point de vue de la qualité de transmission. Mem. Fac. Eng., Nagoya Univ. **1**, 105–115 (1949).
ÖHMAN, S. E. G.: A model of word and sentence intonation. Proc. Int. Congr. Acoust. B-5-4, Tokyo, Japan, August 1968.
OETINGER, R., HAUSER, H.: An electrical network for the investigation of the mechanical vibrations of the inner ear. Acustica **11** (3), 161–177 (1961).
OIZUMI, J., KUBO, E.: Synthesis of speech. J. Acoust. Soc. Japan **10**, 155–158 (1954).
OLIVE, J. P.: Automatic formant tracking by a Newton-Raphson technique. J. Acoust. Soc. Am. **50**, 661–670 (1971).
OLSON, H. F.: Speech machine considerations. Proc. Stockholm Speech Comm. Seminar, R.I.T., Stockholm, Sweden, September 1962.
— BELAR, H.: Phonetic typewriter, III. J. Acoust. Soc. Am. **33**, 1610–1615 (1961).
O'NEAL, J. B., Jr.: Predictive quantizing systems (differential pulse code modulation) for the transmission of television signals. Bell System. Tech. J. **45**, 689–721 (1966).
O'NEIL, E. F.: TASI Bell Lab. Record **37**, 83–87 (1959).
OPPENHEIM, A. V.: Speech analysis-synthesis system based on homomorphic filtering. J. Acount. Soc. Am. **45**, 459–462 (1969).
— SCHAFER, R. W.: Homomorphic analysis of speech. IEEE Trans. Audio and Electroacoust. AU-16, 221–226 (1968).

OPPENHEIM, A.V., SCHAFER, R.W., STOCKHAM, T. G.: Nonlinear filtering of multiplied and convolved signals. Proc. IEEE **56**, 1264–1291 (1968).

— et al.: Papers on digital signal processing. Cambridge, Massachusetts: M.I.T. Press 1969.

PAGET, Sir RICHARD: Human speech. London and New York: Harcourt 1930.

PAPOULIS, A.: Probability, random variables, and stochastic processes. New York: McGraw-Hill Book Co. 1965.

PEAKE, W. T., GOLDSTEIN, M. H., Jr., KIANG, N.Y.-S.: Responses of the auditory nerve to repetitive acoustic stimuli. J. Acoust. Soc. Am. **34**, 562–570 (1962).

— KIANG, N. Y.-S., GOLDSTEIN, M. H., Jr.: Rate functions for auditory nerve responses to bursts of noise. J. Acoust. Soc. Am. **34**, 571–575 (1962).

PERKELL, J. S.: Cineradiographic studies of speech: Implications of certain articulatory movements. Proc. 5th Int. Congr. Acoust., Liège, Belgium, September 1965.

PETERSON, E.: Frequency detection and speech formants. J. Acoust. Soc. Am. **23**, 668–674 (1951).

— COOPER, F. S.: Peakpicker: a bandwidth compression device. J. Acoust. Soc. Am. **29**, 777 (A) (1957).

PETERSON, G. E., BARNEY, H. L.: Control methods used in a study of the vowels. J. Acoust. Soc. Am. **24**, 175–184 (1952).

— LEHISTE, I.: Duration of syllable nuclei in English. J. Acoust. Soc. Am. **32**, 693–703 (1960).

— WANG, W. S.-Y., SIVERSTON, E.: Segmentation techniques in speech synthesis. J. Acoust. Soc. Am., **30**, 739–742 (1958).

PETERSON, L. C., BOGERT, B. P.: A dynamical theory of the cochlea. J. Acoust. Soc. Am. **22**, 369–381 (1950).

PICKETT, J. M.: Tactual vocoder as an aid for the deaf. Proc. Stockholm Speech Comm. Seminar, R.I.T., Stockholm, Sweden, September 1962.

— Some applications of speech analysis to communication aids for the deaf. IEEE Trans. Audio and Electroacoust. **AU-17**, 283–289 (1969).

PIERCE, J. R.: Network for block switching for data. Bell Syst. Tech. J. April 1972.

— Whither speech recognition. J. Acoust. Soc. Am. **46**, 1049–1051 (L) (1969).

— DAVID, E. E., Jr.: Man's world of sound. Garden City, New York: Doubleday & Co., Inc. 1958.

— KARLIN, J. E.: Information rate of a human channel. Proc. I.R.E. **45**, 368 (1957).

PIMONOW, L.: Coded speech and its application in aids for the deaf. Proc. Stockholm Speech Comm. Seminar, R.I.T., Stockholm, Sweden, September 1962.

PIROGOV, A. A.: A harmonic system for compressing speech-spectra. Elektrosviaz No. 3, 8–17 (1959). Also, Telecommunications No. 3, 229–242 (1959).

POLLACK, I.: The information of elementary auditory displays. J. Acoust. Soc. Am. **24**, 745–749 (1952).

— FICKS, L.: Information of elementary multidimensional auditory displays. J. Acoust. Soc. Am. **26**, 155–158 (1954).

POTTER, R. K., KOPP, G. A., GREEN, H. C.: Visible speech. New York: D. van Nostrand Co. 1947.

— STEINBERG, J. C.: Toward the specification of speech. J. Acoust. Soc. Am. **22**, 807–820 (1950).

PRESTIGIACOMO, A. J.: Plastic tape sound spectrograph. J. Speech Hear. Disorders **22**, 321–327 (1957).

— Amplitude contour display of sound spectrograms. J. Acoust. Soc. Am. **34**, 1684–1688 (1962).

PRUZANSKY, S.: Pattern-matching procedure for automatic talker recognition. J. Acoust. Soc. Am. **35**, 354–358 (1963).

Purves, B., Blackett, K., Strong, W.: Speech synthesis with a vocal tract synthesizer. J. Acoust. Soc. Am. **47**, 93 (A) (1970).

Rabiner, L. R.: Digital-formant synthesizer for speech synthesis studies. J. Acoust. Soc. Am. **43**, 822–828 (1968).

— Speech synthesis by rule: An acoustic domain approach. Bell System Tech. J. **47**, 17–37 (1968).

— Gold, B., McGonegal, C. A.: An approach to the approximation problem for non-recursive digital filters. IEEE Trans. Audio and Electroacoust. **AU-18**, 83–106 (1970).

— Jackson, L. B., Schafer, R. W., Coker, C. H.: Digital hardware for speech synthesis. Proc. 7th Int. Congr. Acoust., Budapest, Hungary, August 1971. Also published in IEEE Trans. Com. Tech. **COM-19**, 1016–1020 (December 1971).

— Schafer, R. W., Flanagan, J. L.: Computer voice response using low bit-rate synthetic speech. IEEE Int. Conv. Digest, New York, March 1971.

— — — Speech synthesis by concatenation of formant-coded words. Bell System Tech. J. **50**, May-June (1971).

— — Rader, C. M.: The chirp z-transform algorithm and its application. Bell System Tech. J. **48**, 1249–1292 (1969).

Ragazzini, J. R., Franklin, G. F.: Sampled-data control systems. New York: McGraw-Gill 1958.

Ranke, O. F.: Das Massenverhältnis zwischen Membran und Flüssigkeit im Innenohr. Akust. Z. **7**, 1–11 (1942).

Reddy, D. R.: Computer recognition of connected speech. J. Acoust. Soc. Am. **42**, 329–347 (1967).

— Consonantal clusters and connected speech recognition. Proc. Int. Congr. Acoust. C-5-15, Tokyo, Japan, August 1968.

— Segment-synchronization problem in speech recognition. J. Acoust. Soc. Am. **46**, 89 (A) (1969).

Rhode, W. S.: Observations of the vibration of the basilar membrane in squirrel monkeys using the Mössbauer technique. J. Acoust. Soc. Am. **49**, 1218–1231 (1971).

— Geisler, C. D.: Measurement of the amplitude and phase of vibration of the basilar membrane using the Mössbauer effect. J. Acoust. Soc. Am. **47**, 60 (A) (1970).

Rhodes, F. L.: Beginnings of telephony. New York: Harper Bros. 1929.

Richardson, E. G., ed.: Technical aspects of sound. Amsterdam: Elsevier Publ. Co. 1953.

Riesz, R. R.: Differential intensity sensitivity of the ear for pure tones. Phys. Rev. **31**, 867–875 (1928).

— Schott, L.: Visible speech cathode-ray translator. J. Acoust. Soc. Am. **18**, 50–61 (1946).

Risberg, A.: The use of the transposer for the management of the deaf child. Intern. Audiology **5**, 362–372 (1966).

— Visual aids for speech correction. Proc. Conf. on Speech-Analyzing Aids for the Deaf, Amer. Ann. Deaf **113**, 178–194 (1968).

— A new coding amplifier system for the severly hard of hearing. Proc. 3rd Inter. Congr. on Acoust., Stuttgart, Germany, 1959.

Ritsma, R.: Frequencies dominant in the perception of the pitch of complex sounds. J. Acoust. Soc. Am., **42**, 191–198 (1967).

Rose, J. E., Galambos, R., Hughes, J. R.: Microelectrode studies of the cochlear nuclei of the cat. Bull. Johns Hopkins Hosp. **104**, 211–251 (1959).

Rosen, G.: Dynamic analog speech synthesizer. J. Acoust. Soc. Am. **30**, 201–209 (1958).

ROSENBERG, A. E.: A computer-controlled system for the subjective evaluation of Speech samples. IEEE Trans. Audio and Electroacoust. **AU-17**, 216–221 (1969).

— Effect of masking on the pitch of periodic pulses. J. Acoust. Soc. Am. **38**, 747–758 (1965).

— Effect of pitch averaging on the quality of natural vowels. J. Acoust. Soc. Am. **44**, 1592–1595 (1968).

— Listener performance in a speaker verification task. J. Acoust. Soc. Am. **50**, 106 (A) (1971 a).

— Effect of glottal pulse shape on the quality of natural vowels. J. Acoust. Soc. Am. **49**, 583–590 (1971 b).

— SCHAFER, R. W., RABINER, L. R.: An investigation of the effects of smoothing and quantization of the parameters of formant-coded speech. J. Acoust. Soc. Am. **49**, 123 (A) (1971).

ROSENBLITH, W. A., STEVENS, K. N.: On the DL for frequency. J. Acoust. Soc. Am. **25**, 980–985 (1953).

RUIZ, P. M.: A digital simulation of the time-varying vocal tract. J. Acoust. Soc. Am. **49**, 123 (A) (1971).

RUSSEL, G. O.: The vowel. Columbus: Ohio State Univ. Press 1928.

— Speech and voice. New York: Macmillan Co. 1931.

SAPOZHKOV, M. A.: The speech signal in cybernetics and communication. Moscow: Svyaz'izdat 1963.

— Promising applications of formant vocoders. Telecommunications **23**, 30–34, No. 10 (1969).

SASS, E. J., MACKIE, G. B.: Analog voice compression study. Final Report, Contract No. DCA 100-69-C-0037, Radio Corp. America, May 1970.

SAWASHIMA, M.: Observation of the glottal movements. Proc. Speech Symp., paper C-2-1, Kyoto, Japan, August 1968.

— HIROSE, H., KIRITANI, S., FUJIMURA, O.: Articulatory movements of the larynx. Proc. Int. Congr. Acoust., B-1-1, Tokyo, Japan, August 1968.

SCHAFER, R. W., RABINER, L. R.: Design of digital filter banks for speech analysis. Proc. 5th Annual princeton Conf. on Information Sciences and Systems. Princeton, New Jersey, March 1971.

— — System for automatic formant analysis of voiced speech. J. Acoust. Soc. Am. **47**, pt. 2, 634–648 (1970).

SCHOTT, L. O.: A playback for visible speech. Bell Lab. Record **26**, 333–339 (1948).

SCHROEDER, M. R.: On the separation and measurement of formant frequencies. J. Acoust. Soc. Am. **28**, 159 (A) (1956).

— Recent progress in speech coding at Bell Telephone Laboratories. Proc. III. Int. Congr. Acoust. Stuttgart, Germany 1959.

— Correlation techniques for speech bandwidth compression. J. Audio Eng. Soc. **10**, 163–166 (1962).

— Description of the geometry of the human vocal tract by acoustic measurements. J. Acoust. Soc. Am. **41**, 1002–1010 (1967).

— ATAL, B. S.: Generalized short-time power spectra and autocorrelation function. J. Acoust. Soc. Am. **34**, 1679–1683 (1962).

— DAVID, E. E., Jr.: A vocoder for transmitting 10 kc/s speech over a 3.5 kc/s channel. Acustica **10**, 35–43 (1960).

— HANAUER, S.: Interpolation of data with continuous speech signals. Bell Syst. Tech. J. **46**, 1931–1933 (1967).

— LOGAN, B. F., PRESTIGIACOMO, A. J.: New methods for speech analysis-synthesis and bandwidth compression. Proc. Stockholm Speech Comm. Seminar, R.I.T., Stockholm, Sweden, September 1962.

SCHROEDER, M. R.: Vocoders: Analysis and synthesis of speech. Proc. IEEE **54**, 720–734 (1966).

— FLANAGAN, J. L., LUNDRY, E. A.: Bandwidth compression of speech by analytic signal rooting. Proc. IEEE **55**, 396–401 (1967).

SEKI, H.: A new method of speech transmission by frequency division and multiplication. J. Acoust. Soc. Japan **14**, 138–142 (1958).

SHANNON, C. E.: Prediction and entropy of printed English. Bell System Tech. J. **30**, 50–64 (1951).

— WEAVER, W.: The mathematical theory of communication. Urbana: University of Illinois 1949.

SHEARME, J. N.: A simple maximum selecting circuit. Electronic Eng. **31**, 353–354 (1959).

— Analysis of the performance of an automatic formant measuring system. Proc. Stockholm Speech Comm. Seminar, R.I.T., Stockholm, Sweden, September 1962.

— HOLMES, J. N.: An experiment concerning the recognition of voices. Language and Speech **2**, 123–131 (1959).

— SMITH, G. F., KELLY, L. C.: A formant tracking system for speech measurements. Joint Speech Research Unit Rept. JU 7-2 British post office, Eastcote, England.

SHEPARD, R.: The analysis of proximities: Multidimensional scaling with an unknown distance function (I and II). Psychometrika **27**, 125–140, 219–246 (1962).

— Metric structures in ordinal data. J. Math. Psychol. **3**, 287–315 (1966).

SIMON, PELA: Films radiologiques des articulations et les aspects genetiques des sons du langage. ORBIS **10**, 1 (1961).

SIVIAN, L. J.: Speech power and its measurement. Bell System Tech. J. **8**, 646–661 (1929).

SLAYMAKER, F. H.: Bandwidth compression by means of vocoders. IRE Trans. Audio **AU-8**, 20–26 (1960).

— HOUDE, R. A.: Speech compression by analysis-synthesis. J. Audio Eng. Soc. **10**, 144–148 (1962).

SMITH, C. P.: A phoneme detector. J. Acoust. Soc. Am. **23**, 446–451 (1951).

— Speech data reduction. Air Force Cambridge Research Center Report TR-57-111, Astia No. AD 117290, Bedford, Mass., May 1957.

— Voice-communications method using pattern matching for data compression. J. Acoust. Soc. Am. **35**, 805 (A) (1963).

SMITH, S.: Diphlophonie und Luft-Schall-Explosionen. Arch. Ohren-, Nasen- u. Kehlkopfheilk. ver. Z. Hals-, Nasen- u. Ohrenheilk. **173**, 504–508 (1958).

SONDHI, M. M.: New methods of pitch extraction. Proc. Conf. on Speech Communication and Processing, A.F. Cambridge Res. Labs. and IEEE Audio and Electroacoust. Group, Cambridge, Mass., November 1967.

— GOPINATH, B.: Determination of the shape of a lossy vocal tract. Proc. 7th Int. Congr. Acoust., Budapest, Hungary, August 1971.

STARK, R. E., CULLEN, J. K., CHASE, R.: Preliminary work with the new Bell telephone visible speech translator. Proc. Conf. on Speech-Analyzing Aids for the Deaf, Amer. Ann. Deaf, **113**, 205–214 (1968).

STEAD, L. G., JONES, E. T.: The S.R.D.E. speech bandwidth compression project. Report 1133, Signals Research and Development Establishment, Christchurch, England. March 1961.

— WESTON, R. C.: Sampling and quantizing the parameters of a formant tracking vocoder system. Proc. Stockholm Speech Comm. Seminar, R.I.T., Stockholm, Sweden, September 1962.

STEELE, R. W., CASSEL, L. E.: Effect of transmission errors on the intelligibility of vocoded speech. IEEE Trans. Comm. Sys. **11**, 118–123 (1963).

— — Dynamic encoding as applied to a channel vocoder. J. Acoust. Soc. Am. **35**, 789 (A) (1963).

STEVENS, K. N.: Autocorrelation analysis of speech sounds. J. Acoust. Soc. Am. **22**, 769–771 (1950).
— The perception of sounds shaped by resonant circuits. ScD. Thesis, Mass. Inst. Tech., Cambridge, Mass., 1952.
— Stop consonants. Quart. Rept., Acoustics Laboratory, Mass. Inst. Tech., Cambridge, Mass., December 1956.
— Toward a model for speech recognition. J. Acoust. Soc. Am. **32**, 47–55 (1960).
— BASTIDE, R. P., SMITH, C. P.: Electrical synthesizer of continuous speech. J. Acoust. Soc. Am. **27**, 207 (A) (1955).
— HOUSE, A. S.: Development of a quantitative description of vowel articulation. J. Acoust. Soc. Am. **27**, 484–493 (1955).
— — Studies of formant transitions using a vocal tract analog. J. Acoust. Soc. Am. **28**, 578–585 (1956).
— — Perturbation of vowel articulations by consonantal context. J. Speech Hear. Res. **6**, 111–128 (1968).
— KASOWSKI, S., FANT, C. G. M.: An electrical analog of the vocal tract. J. Acoust. Soc. Am. **25**, 734–742 (1953).
STEVENS, S. S., DAVIS, H.: Hearing. New York: John Wiley & Sons 1938.
STEWART, J. Q.: An electrical analogue of the vocal organs. Nature **110**, 311–312 (1922).
STUMPF, C.: Die Sprachlaute. Berlin: Springer 1926.
SUBRAHMANYAM, D. L., PETERSON, G. E.: Time-frequency scanning in narrowband speech transmission. IRE Trans. Audio **AU-7**, 148–160 (1959).
SUGIMOTO, T., HASHIMOTO, S.: The voice fundamental pitch and formant tracking computer program by short-term autocorrelation function. Proc. Stockholm Speech Comm. Seminar. R.I.T., Stockholm, Sweden, September 1962.
SUZUKI, J., KADOKAWA, Y., NAKATA, K.: Formant frequency extration by the method of moment calculations. J. Acoust. Soc. Am. **35**, 1345–1353 (1963).
— NAKATA, K.: Recognition of Japanese vowels. J. Radio Res. Lab. (Tokyo) **8**, 193–212 (1961).
TASAKI, I., DAVIS, H., ELDREDGE, D. H.: Exploration of cochlear potentials in guinea pig with a microelectrode. J. Acoust. Soc. Am. **26**, 765–773 (1954).
TEAS, D. C., ELDREDGE, D. H., DAVIS, H.: Cochlear responses to acoustic transients. J. Acoust. Soc. Am. **34**, 1438–1459 (1962).
TERANISHI, R., UMEDA, N.: Use of pronouncing dictionary in speech synthesis experiments. Proc. Int. Congr. Acoust. B-5-2, Tokyo, Japan, August 1968.
TITCHMARSH, E. C.: The theory of functions. London: Oxford University Press 1932.
TOMOZAWA, A., KANEKO, H.: Companded delta modulation for telephone transmission. IEEE Trans. Comm. Tech. **COM-16**, 149–157 (1968).
TOSI, O. Speaker identification through acoustic spectography. Proc. XIV Int. Congr. Logopedics and Phoniatrics, Paris, September 1968.
— OYER, H., PEDREY, C., LASHBROOK, B., NICOL, J.: An experiment on voice identification by visual inspection of spectrograms. J. Acoust. Soc. Am. **49**, 138 (A) (1971).
TRUBY, H. M.: Acoustic-cineradiographic analysis considerations, Suppl. 182, Acta Radiol. (1959).
TUNTURI, A. R.: Analysis of cortical auditory responses with the probability pulse. Am. J. Physiol. **181**, 630–638 (1955).
UNGEHEUER, G.: Elemente einer akustischen Theorie der Vokalarticulation. Berlin-Göttingen-Heidelberg: Springer 1962.
UPTON, H.: Wearable eyeglass speech-reading aid. Proc. Conf. on Speech-Analyzing Aids for the Deaf, Amer. Ann. Deaf **113**, 222–229 (1968).

VELICHKO, V. M., ZAGORUYKO, N. G.: Automatic recognition of 200 words. Int. J. Man-Machine Studies 2, 223–234 (1970).

VILBIG, F.: An apparatus for speech compression and expansion and for replaying visible speech records. J. Acoust. Soc. Am. 22, 754–761 (1950).

— Frequency band multiplication or division and time expansion or compression by means of a string filter. J. Acoust. Soc. Am. 24, 33–39 (1952).

— HAASE, K.: Some systems for speech-band compression. J. Acoust. Soc. Am. 28, 573–577 (1956a).

— — Über einige Systeme für Sprachbandkompression. Nachr.-techn. Fachber. 3, 81–92 (1956b).

WAGNER, K. W.: Ein neues elektrisches Sprechgerät zur Nachbildung der menschlichen Vokale. Preuß. Akad. Wiss. Berlin Abh. 2, 44 p. (1936).

WATHEN-DUNN, W., LIPKE, D. W.: On the power gained by clipping speech in the audio band. J. Acoust. Soc. Am. 30, 36–40 (1958).

WATSON, T. A.: How bell invented the telephone. Trans. Am. Inst. Elec. Engrs. 34, 1011–1021 (1915).

WEBER, S.: Modern communication methods. Electronics 32, 94–108 (1959).

WEBSTER, A. G.: Acoustical impedance and the theory of horns. Proc. Nat. Acad. Sci. U.S. 5, 275–282 (1919).

WEBSTER, J. C.: Information in simple multidimensional speech messages. J. Acoust. Soc. Am. 33, 940–944 (1961).

WEGEL, R. L.: Theory of vibration of the larynx. Bell System Tech. J. 9, 207–227 (1930).

WEINSTEIN, C. J.: Short-time Fourier analysis and its inverse. MS Thesis, Dept. of Electrical Engineering, M.I.T., Cambridge, Mass. (1966).

— OPPENHEIM, A. V.: Predictive coding in a homomorphic vocoder. IEEE Trans. Aud. Electroacoust. AU-19, 243–248 (1971).

WERNER, P. A., DANIELSSON, K.: 17 kanals vocoder i laboratorientforande F0A3, Laboratory for National Defense rapport A345, Stockholm 1958.

WHEATSTONE, Sir CHARLES: The scientific papers of Sir Charles Wheatstone. London: Taylor & Francis 1879.

WICKELGREN, W. A.: Distinctive features and errors in short term memory for English consonants. J. Acoust. Soc. Am. 38, 388 (1966)

— Distinctive features and errors in short term memory for English vowels. J. Acoust. Soc. Am. 38, 583–588 (1965).

WIENER, F. M., ROSS, D. A.: The pressure distribution in the auditory canal in a progressive sound field. J. Acoust. Soc. Am. 18, 401–408 (1946).

WIENER, N.: The extrapolation and smoothing of stationary time series with engineering applications. New York: John Wiley & Sons 1949.

YAGGI, L. A., Jr.: Full-duplex digital vocoder. Texas Inst. Inc., Dallas, Report SP 14-A62, June 1962.

— MASON, A. E., Jr.: Polymodal vocoder; a new approach to versatile and reliable voice communications. J. Acoust. Soc. Am. 35, 806 (A) (1963).

YOUNG, M. A., CAMPBELL, R. A.: Effects of context on talker identification. J. Acoust. Soc. Am. 42, 1250–1254 (1967).

ZWISLOCKI, J.: Theorie der Schneckenmechanik. Diss. Eidg. Tech. Hochschule, Zürich, 1948 (Buchdruckerei Gassman Solothurn).

— Some impedance measurements on normal and pathological ears. J. Acoust. Soc. Am. 29, 1312–1317 (1957).

— Electrical model of the middle ear. J. Acoust. Soc. Am. 31, 841 (A) (1959).

Author Index

Page numbers in *italics* refer to the References

Subject Index

Kommunikation und Kybernetik
in Einzeldarstellungen

Herausgegeben von H. Wolter und W. D. Keidel